THE NEW GUIDE TO

CRISIS
&
TRAUMA
COUNSELING

DR. H. NORMAN WRIGHT

Regal

From Gospel Light
Ventura, California, U.S.A.

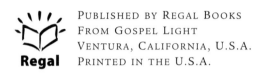

PUBLISHED BY REGAL BOOKS
FROM GOSPEL LIGHT
VENTURA, CALIFORNIA, U.S.A.
Regal PRINTED IN THE U.S.A.

Regal Books is a ministry of Gospel Light, a Christian publisher dedicated to serving the local church. We believe God's vision for Gospel Light is to provide church leaders with biblical, user-friendly materials that will help them evangelize, disciple and minister to children, youth and families.

It is our prayer that this Regal book will help you discover biblical truth for your own life and help you meet the needs of others. May God richly bless you.

For a free catalog of resources from Regal Books/Gospel Light, please call your Christian supplier or contact us at 1-800-4-GOSPEL *or* www.regalbooks.com.

Cover and interior design by Robert Williams
Edited by Amy Simpson

Library of Congress Cataloging-in-Publication Data
Wright, H. Norman.
    The new guide to crisis and trauma counseling / H. Norman Wright.
        p. cm.
Includes bibliographical references (p.   ) and index.
    ISBN 0-8307-3241-1
    1. Pastoral counseling. 2. Crisis intervention (Mental health services) 3. Psychic trauma—Treatment. I. Title.
    BV4012.2.W7536 2003
    253.5—dc21   2003004687

        9   10   11   12   13   14   15   /   13   12   11   10

Rights for publishing this book in other languages are contracted by Gospel Light Worldwide, the international nonprofit ministry of Gospel Light. Gospel Light Worldwide also provides publishing and technical assistance to international publishers dedicated to producing Sunday School and Vacation Bible School curricula and books in the languages of the world. For additional information, visit www.gospellightworldwide.org; write to Gospel Light Worldwide, P.O. Box 3875, Ventura, CA 93006; or send an e-mail to info@gospellightworldwide.org.

CONTENTS

CRISES—THEY'RE ALL AROUND US

In the early 1960s, I served on the staff of a church as a youth pastor and minister of education. Fresh out of seminary, I wasn't sure if I knew what to do. One of my first crisis experiences revolved around the discovery that I would be serving more with the youth than with education. However, I made the adjustment and began to enjoy the ministry, and in time, I saw some results. With 300 junior high, high school and college students in my program, it was a busy time.

Each summer we took a group of high school students on an outreach or study outing. One year we took 25 high school students to the High Sierras in Southern California for several days. We camped in tents, hiked, fished, interacted and studied. Nearby was a formidable, massive rock formation—Crystal Crag—over 1,000 feet high. The sheer wall was a challenge to even the most skilled climber.

One morning two of the high school boys (one, a recent graduate who was waiting to go into the navy) decided on their own to climb the face of this cliff. They left before anyone was awake and did not inform anyone of their plans. They probably knew that we would have told them that the area was off-limits, since they were inexperienced and had no climbing gear. They walked the two miles to the base of the rock formation, made their way up the shale slide at the base of the rock and proceeded to climb.

It's still unclear how they were able to scale the rock face given the lack of equipment and expertise, but they climbed for several hundred feet before Phil lost his handhold and plunged over 400 feet to his death. Every bone in his body was broken. His companion hung there watching in horror as his friend fell to his death, but then he continued to climb until he was off of the sheer wall and went for help. Hours later someone came to our camp and told us. There was a feeling of shock—disbelief—as we thought, *This isn't true.* A few minutes later, I watched a pack train walk by with Phil's body encased in a body bag, hanging over the back of a horse. I watched until they were out of sight and then went to find a phone and call our senior pastor. It became his task to inform Phil's parents.

Did I know what to do at this time? Not really. Did I know what to say? No. Did I feel equipped to handle this event? Not at all. I had no preparation for anything like this. I think I felt like those in ministry in New York City following the 9/11 twin-towers disaster. Most of them said, "I don't know what to say or do. I don't feel equipped." Neither did I. It was my first encounter with a combination crisis and traumatic event.

What would *you* have said or done? Would *you* have known how to respond?

I'll never forget that day. We all sat in small groups, talking in hushed voices, feeling numb and stunned. We fixed dinner, and then, strangely enough, the group began to joke, cut up and laugh for the next hour. Other adults around us were bothered by their response. However, I realized later that this was their way of taking a break from the heaviness of the crisis. It was a normal response, because adolescents tend to move in and out of their grief.

It was a long bus ride home. What was even longer was the walk from my car to the front of Phil's home to talk with his parents. I went there to share with them the details of the day and to minister to them. Yet when I left, I went away with the feeling that everyone who had talked with them had experienced: Rather than ministering to them, I felt they had ministered to me!

This experience prompted me to begin a lifelong journey of learning as much as I could to help others during their times of need. And it wasn't until just recently that it dawned on me that the experience on that day was the first traumatic debriefing I had ever conducted, even though I didn't know what I was doing.

A Time to Learn

About a year later, on a Sunday evening, our church had a minister from another church as a guest speaker. His presentation had a dramatic effect upon every person in attendance. When it came time for the message, he stood up, walked to the pulpit and without reading a note or opening a Bible, proceeded to recite from memory eight passages of Scripture as a basis for his message.

The minister then said to the congregation, "Tonight I would like to share with you what to say and what not to say, what to do and what not to do, at the time of bereavement." He paused, and I saw from my vantage point on the platform that every person in the congregation searched for a piece of paper on which to record the principles the speaker was about to discuss. I, too, looked for some paper. (I still have my notes from that message.) He gave all of us the help and guidance we needed, because we had not known what to say or do when someone had lost a loved one. (This is why people sometimes avoid a bereaved person or family.)

The practicality of that night is etched in my memory, and I have thought so often, *What would happen if pastors equipped their people for life's crises such as this one? We would have helping and caring congregations. We could do a much better job in reaching out to those in need. And what would happen if ministers were given the training they needed during their educational experience?*

Feel Out the Journey

The journey through life is a series of losses, crises and, in some cases, traumas—some are predictable and expected, but others are total surprises. Some crises are developmental; some are situational. You, as a minister, counselor or lay counselor, probably have experienced many crises in your own life, so you know how it feels. Being alive means that we constantly have to resolve problems. Every new situation we encounter provides us the opportunity to develop new ways of using our resources

> **Every new situation we encounter provides us the opportunity to develop new ways of using our resources in order to gain control.**

in order to gain control. Sometimes we have to try over and over again because our first efforts do not work. However, by being persistent, we discover ways to overcome these problems. And when a similar problem confronts us in the future, we find the problem easier to resolve because of what we learned in the past.

One day, however, we will encounter a change or problem that seems beyond our capacity to cope. When a problem is overwhelming, or when our support system—within ourselves or from others—doesn't work, we are thrown off balance. This is called a *crisis*. Losses, crises and traumas are part of life. They should be anticipated and expected to occur. They are inevitable. It used to be that traumatic events weren't as common, but that has changed. And if anyone is ever called upon more than others to help during a time of crisis, it is the minister.

Prepare for the Crises

Helping those in crisis can be a very important phase of one's ministry. Two tasks of the Church's ministry are to equip all members to better handle their own crises and to equip them to help other people in crisis. The principles of understanding losses and crises and helping others during these times can be taught in sermons and classes. Usually, the reason people hesitate to become involved in the lives of others is that they feel inadequate—they don't know what to do or say. Even as a trained minister, you may have struggled with those same feelings and perhaps have even hesitated to get involved in some crisis situation. This is a normal response.

All of us in ministry or professional counseling have felt the pangs of inadequacy at one time or another. And we will most likely continue to feel this way for the rest of our lives. There is always more to learn, and our skills can always stand refining.

CRISIS SITUATIONS

I will share with you some of my counseling experiences over the years. They are no different from what you will encounter as you minister in your church or in a counseling office. As you read them, take the time to visualize the situation and the people involved as if you were the one they came to for help. Consider two important questions: How would you feel? What would you do or say? Too many people bypass the first question and focus only upon resolving the problem. However, our feelings affect what we do. Read the following examples and for each example consider this question: Would you describe this situation as a crisis or a trauma? Each one involves a loss or maybe several losses. Can you identify them?

Situation 1

A woman from your congregation comes into the church office without an appointment and asks to see you. She is visibly shaken, and you ask her to come in and sit down. She says, "The police just left our house. They came to the door this morning and asked to see my husband. They told my husband and me that he had been accused by three of the neighborhood children of sexually molesting them. He says that he did not, but the neighbors filed the complaint. What are we going to do? He wouldn't talk to me about it, and he left. I don't know where he went. What should I do?"

How would you feel, and what would you do?

Situation 2 ℃

You've been called to the hospital by the members of a man's family. You don't know much about the situation, and when you walk in, you are met by the man's wife and his doctor. The doctor says the man is terminally ill and is in such an emotionally upset state that they have not told him of his condition. The man is calling for a minister to talk to, but the doctor advises you to be careful what you say about his condition. You enter the room and immediately the man says to you, "I want to ask you something. Am I going to die? Do you know? Can you tell me? Am I going to die?"

How would you feel, and what would you do?

Situation 3 ⊤

When I was teaching and conducting debriefings in New York a month after 9/11, a woman born in the Philippines made an appointment to talk. She took the subway for hours the day after the conference to find some help. In a workshop, she heard my illustration on how unresolved grief from the past often comes back when there's a current loss. When the question, What is the loss in your life that you've never fully grieved over? was asked, she began to understand what she was experiencing. When she was six years old, the Japanese army invaded the Philippines. She described unimaginable atrocities as well as the planes bombing her area. She and others fled to the mountains, hid and lived in caves. People were killed and tortured all around her. As she talked, she described instances of the past connecting to the present. For example, many of her friends had their fingernails torn out by their captors. Therefore, she was very sensitive when her nails were touched in a certain way, so whenever she had a manicure and her nails were touched in that fashion, she would jerk her hands away. Even though this had not happened to her, she was still impacted.

When she saw the plane flying into the second tower on 9/11, it reactivated all the images of planes bombing her homeland. These images were diminishing, yet she wanted to be free from these memories completely.

How would you feel, and what would you say or do to help her?

Situation 4 (

A man walks into your church office, and you recognize him as one of the leading elders of your church. He's crying. With a pained expression on his face, he cries out, "She left me! I came home today and she was gone! Why? Where is she? Why did she leave? I didn't know there was any problem in our marriage. But she left. She said she didn't love me anymore, and she is moving in with another man! Why? Why? Why?"

How would you feel, and what would you say or do?

Situation 5

A woman in her 30s came in to talk to me—trauma was written all over her face. This was her story: "I was on the eightieth floor sitting at my desk by the window when I heard a loud whistling noise. I looked over at my boss just as he grabbed his head with both hands and cried out, 'Oh my God! Oh my God!' I looked around and saw a wing of the plane right outside my window. I thought it was going to hit me. I saw the nose of the plane bury itself in the other tower with the wings outside, and then the rest of the plane disappeared inside the structure. Then I heard a huge explosion and saw burning debris everywhere. I turned, yelled for everyone to run and motioned to them to get away. We all ran. I could see and hear the debris hitting the windows. I thought the panes of glass were going to break and we'd be killed. I ran to the nearest exit, and it must have been God directing me, since I chose the only stairway that was continuous to the ground floor. All of the other stairs in that building went to a floor where you had to go to another door to connect to the stairs that took you to a lower level. If I'd chosen one of those, I'd be dead. A number of others must have made that choice, since they didn't make it.

"We were around the thirty-sixth floor when I knew I was going to die. We heard an announcement that everything was all right and we should return to our floors. I wanted to, since my purse and keys were at my desk. My friend said no, so we debated this for a minute. But then the building swayed in one direction and then another. Huge cracks appeared in the walls. The second plane had struck our building. I was frozen with fear. I couldn't move. My whole body shook. I couldn't even move one foot. My friend told me, 'You have to move. Your husband and three children need you.' He made me pick up one foot at a time and move down the stairs. Now it was hard to see and breathe because of the smoke. I remembered our company had spent $50 for a breathing apparatus for each person after the bombing of the World Trade Center in the early '90s. These hung on the back of our chairs, but we didn't have time to put them on.

"We finally made it to the ground floor and rushed through the streets. Then the building collapsed. I've been a total mess ever since. At first it was the nightmares. Sounds make me jump. I'm a social person, and my family wants to be around me; however, much of the time I want to be by myself. Even when I come to church, I stay in the back. I've gone back to work because I want to be with the people I know, at least those who are left. Many never made it out. The other day I saw a cloud of smoke drifting by and I ran. I fell apart, sobbing in another room. I just can't hold it together. My eight-year-old son draws pictures of the towers with planes flying toward them, but there's an invisible force field all around them that causes the planes to go up and over them.

"My children don't want me to talk about it anymore. They want me to be normal. So do I."

How would you feel? What could you have said to this woman? How would you have prayed for her?

Situation 6

You're sitting in your office at church and the phone rings. You answer, and a man on the other end of the line states that he wants to talk with you. He will not give his name or any information that will identify him. He says he has recently been divorced from his wife. He explains that he is a Christian and wants to do the Lord's will. His wife is living with another man and has the children with her. He begins to talk with you about what the Bible says about suicide. He states that the only thing keeping him from taking his life is that he feels he will go to hell if he does it. However, he also feels that it would be better to be out of this life. He doesn't want his children to be with his wife, who is "wicked," and he doesn't want them to go through what he has gone through in this life. He also states indirectly that it would be nice to have them with him wherever he goes.

How would you feel, and what would you say?

Situation 7

A woman makes an appointment to see you. You realize that this is the person you heard about from another church member. She recently lost her 15-year-old son in a tragic accident. He fell off the back of a pickup truck and landed on his head on the pavement. For eight days, he lingered in a coma at the hospital. The rest of the family would come and go, but she was there all the time, fasting and praying for her son's recovery. On the seventh day, he began to respond; but suddenly, after their hopes had been raised, he died. As she sits in your office, she looks at you and asks, "Where was God during this time? Why did He punish me in this way? He took my son after He gave me hope that he would recover. I will never recover! I will live a living death until I can go be with my son."

How would you feel, and what would you do or say?

Situation 8

My wife and I had just arrived home from vacation, and the phone rang. It was our house painter. He said, "I remembered that your son died. My daughter just lost two of her little boys. Can you help her?" We agreed, so my wife and I made an appointment. This young mother came in and, as best as she could, told us the story. Her husband had been depressed and even suicidal for some time. He was under the care of both a psychiatrist and a psychologist. He had been treated for attention deficit hyperactivity disorder (ADHD) with medications, but it was discovered later that he was actually bipolar. He had become increasingly depressed a few days earlier. He said that he wanted to take the boys down to the beach and asked his wife to go with him. She said she preferred to stay home with their five-month-old baby. He took his five- and six-year-old sons to the beach, took out a handgun, killed them and attempted to kill himself, which he bungled. Hours later the police came to her home; but it was a media person who broke the news to her by holding a microphone in her face, asking, "How does it feel to know that your husband killed your children?"

How would you feel, and what would you do or say?

This was possibly one of the most difficult and painful cases for us to handle. Often after a session, my wife and I would both cry for that woman's pain and some of our own, which had been activated once again. We spent over two years working with her. The entire community came to her support. The 31 mothers of the preschool where her sons attended provided dinner each night for her and her son for the next year. This was an example of what it means to minister in the name of Jesus. *yes*

A TIME TO MINISTER

These situations may be similar to events that you have experienced in your life. The commonality of our life experiences and the frequency of these events reminds all of us of how our experiences may be used to minister to others. *yes*

> Praise be to the God and Father of our Lord Jesus Christ, the Father of compassion and the God of all comfort, who comforts us in all our troubles . . . with the comfort we ourselves have received from God (2 Cor. 1:3-4).

There is no limit to the number of losses and crises that occur in life. And some of them are inexplicable traumas that affect an entire family: the loss of a job; the loss of a friend or supporting person; the loss of a

> **There is no limit to the number of losses and crises that occur in life—some of them are inexplicable traumas that affect an entire family.**

position of status and respect; an incapacitating illness, operation or accident; the death of a parent, friend, spouse or child; the news that you are terminally ill; the discovery that a child is on drugs or is a homosexual;

the discovery of a handicap in yourself or another family member; an abortion or unwanted pregnancy; experiencing a miscarriage or premature birth; a hurricane, earthquake or tornado; a suicide attempt; separation or divorce; a child-custody battle; being drafted or discharged; the discovery that your child is a member of a cult; enduring a lawsuit; putting parents into a home for the aged; living with a spouse who is experiencing a midlife crisis; living with a chronically depressed person; the discovery that you or a spouse has Alzheimer's disease or Huntington's chorea; experiencing a heart attack and a bypass operation with ensuing loss of memory for your newly married spouse. The list never ends.

None of the situations I mentioned are fictitious. They're all real. And you and I may be called to minister to real people in such situations.

This book is for pastors, counselors and lay counselors in the church setting, as well as for professional counselors. It will provide biblical principles; general instruction in loss, crisis and trauma counseling as well as detailed advice for dealing with specific kinds of crisis situations. Finally, we will conclude with a matter almost as important as knowing how to counsel, and that is knowing when to refer a person to someone with more expertise than yourself.

CHAPTER 1

CRISIS COUNSELING FROM A BIBLICAL PERSPECTIVE

In any type of Christian counseling, knowledge of the biblical approach is essential. One way to develop a biblical approach is to study the life of Jesus and His relationships with others. The way He ministered to others is a model for all of us who seek to help others.

As we look at the characteristics of Jesus' approach in counseling, we must remember that techniques alone are not effective. Jesus' relationships with the people to whom He ministered were the foundation of His approach.

An individual, couple or family coming for counseling needs to know that you care about them. You demonstrate this by your warmth, understanding, acceptance and belief in their ability to change and mature.

Jesus' Exemplary Model

One important observation we can make about Jesus' approach to counseling is that His work with people was a process. He did not see them for just a few minutes during an appointment and then forget about them. He spent time helping them work through life's difficulties in an in-depth manner. He saw people's potential and hopes, despite their problems. Let's delve into what made Jesus the wonderful counselor.

Jesus Was Compassionate

A basic characteristic of Jesus' approach was His compassion for others. We see His compassion expressed in the New Testament:

I feel compassion for the multitude because they have remained with Me now three days, and have nothing to eat (Mark 8:2, *NASB*).

And when He went ashore, He saw a great multitude, and He felt compassion for them because they were like sheep without a shepherd; and He began to teach them many things (Mark 6:34, *NASB*).

His main concern was to alleviate suffering and meet the needs of the people.

Jesus Accepted People

When Jesus first met people, He accepted them as they were. In other words, He believed in them and in what they would become. The characteristic of acceptance is seen throughout the New Testament. When Jesus met the woman at the well, He accepted her as she was without condemning her (see John 4:1-26). He also accepted the woman caught in adultery (see John 8:1-11) and Zacchaeus, the dishonest tax collector (see Luke 19:1-10).

Jesus Gave People Worth

People were Jesus' top priority. He established this priority and gave them worth by putting their needs before the rules and regulations the religious leaders had constructed. He involved Himself in the lives of people who were considered the worst of sinners, and He met them where they had needs. In so doing, He helped elevate their sense of self-worth. This is an important step in crisis counseling.

One of the ways Jesus gave worth to people was to show them their value in God's eyes, by comparing God's care for other creatures with God's care for them:

> Are not two sparrows sold for a cent? And yet not one of them will fall to the ground apart from your Father (Matt. 10:29, *NASB*).

At the heart of many people's problems is a low self-concept or a feeling of lack of worth. Helping a person discover his or her personal worth because of who God is and what He has done for him or her helps to stabilize the person.

Jesus Met People's Needs

Another characteristic of Jesus' ministry was His ability to see the needs of people and to speak directly to them, regardless of what they might have brought to His attention. We see discernment in the example of Nicodemus's coming to Jesus during the night. Whatever might have been Nicodemus's reason for wanting to talk with Jesus at that time, Jesus discerned his real problem and confronted him with the need to be born again (see John 3:1-21).

In meeting the immediate needs of people, Jesus did not use the same approach with everyone. Gary Collins explains this well in his book *How to Be a People Helper:*

> Jesus not only dealt with people in different ways, but He also related to individuals at different levels of depth or closeness. John was the disciple whom Jesus loved, perhaps the Master's nearest friend, while Peter, James, and John together appear to have comprised an inner circle with whom the Lord had a special relationship. Although they were not as close as the inner three, the other apostles were Christ's companions, a band of twelve

men who had been handpicked to carry on the work after Christ's departure. In Luke 10 we read of a group of seventy men to whom Jesus gave special training. Following the resurrection He appeared to a larger group of five hundred people, and then there were crowds, sometimes numbering in the thousands, many of whom may have seen Christ only once and from a distance.[1]

Essentially, each person who comes to you during a loss, a crisis or a trauma has a desperate need.

Jesus Used the Right Words

Sometimes Jesus spoke directly, even harshly. Other times He was soft-spoken. Sometimes He conveyed His feelings nonverbally:

And after looking around at them with anger, grieved at their hardness of heart, He said to the man, "Stretch out your hand." And he stretched it out, and his hand was restored (Mark 3:5, NASB).

Jesus always based His choice of words and inflection of voice on the situation at hand.

Jesus Emphasized Right Behavior

Jesus said to the woman caught in adultery, "Go, and sin no more" (John 8:11, KJV). Jesus' desire was that those who were seeking Him would turn from their wrong ways. Jesus compared the lives of two builders with two different foundations by saying that "Everyone who comes to Me, and hears My words, and acts upon them" will build a house with a deep foundation laid "upon the rock" (Luke 6:47-48, NASB). His emphasis was on living on the foundation of the rock—a righteous life—not the sand—a sinful life.

Jesus Encouraged People to Accept Responsibility

In John 5, Jesus responded to the man at the pool of Bethesda by asking, "Do you want to get well?" (v. 6). By asking this question, Jesus sought to have the man accept responsibility for remaining sick or being made well. In another instance, He asked a blind man, "What do you want me to do for you?" (Mark 10:51).

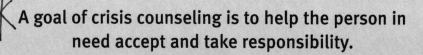

A goal of crisis counseling is to help the person in need accept and take responsibility.

In crisis counseling, the person, couple or family must see that they need to make a choice to remain the same or to change and grow; and they must make that choice before much progress will be seen. A goal of crisis counseling, as you will see, is to help the person in need accept and take responsibility.

Jesus Provided Hope

To many people, Jesus gave hope:

And they were even more astonished and said to Him, "Then who can be saved?" Looking upon them, Jesus said, "With men it is impossible, but not with God; for all things are possible with God" (Mark 10:26-27, *NASB*).

Jesus was the light to a very dark world. He boldly declared that only with God's help could people reach their full potential.

Jesus Encouraged People

How important is encouragement in crisis counseling? Should it be used sparingly in any phase of the crisis sequence? Encouragement provides the counselee with hope and a desire to change. He or she needs to know you believe in them.

Jesus regularly and inclusively encouraged people around Him:

Come to Me, all who are weary and heavy-laden, and I will give you rest. Take My yoke upon you, and learn from Me, for I am gentle and humble in heart; and you shall find rest for your souls. For My yoke is easy, and My load is light (Matt. 11:28-30, *NASB*).

Jesus Emphasized Peace of Mind

Peace I leave with you; My peace I give to you; not as the world gives, do I give to you. Let not your heart be troubled, nor let it be fearful (John 14:27, *NASB*).

If there is one thing a person in crisis usually does not have, it is peace of mind. Jesus offered that hope. Our task is to help others discover it.

Jesus Helped Reshape, or Refashion, People's Thinking

Jesus helped people redirect their attention from the unimportant things of life to the important (see Luke 5:22-25; 12:22-27). He taught that focusing on treasures in heaven instead of on earthly treasures would lead to a joy-filled heart (see Matt. 6:19-21).

Jesus Was a Teacher

Teaching is a definite part of counseling, and we see over and over again how Jesus taught. Often He used direct statements in His teaching. At other times He used questions:

And it came about when He went into the house of one of the leaders of the Pharisees on the Sabbath to eat bread, that they were watching Him closely. And there, in front of Him was a certain man suffering from dropsy. And Jesus answered and spoke to the lawyers and Pharisees, saying, "Is it lawful to heal on the Sabbath, or not?" But they kept silent. And He took hold of him, and healed him, and sent him away. And He said to them, "Which one of you shall have a son or an ox fall into a well, and will not immediately pull him out on a Sabbath day?" And they could make no reply to this (Luke 14:1-6, *NASB*; see also Luke 6:39-42).

How would you summarize your teaching style? Do you try to use various approaches, or do you stick with one well-oiled approach?

Jesus Spoke with Authority

Another characteristic of Jesus' approach was that He spoke with authority. He was not hesitant, backward or bashful; He was authoritative:

> For He was teaching them as one having authority, and not as their scribes (Matt. 7:29, NASB).

Jesus was very conscious of His authority. Those who know Christ and are called to a ministry of helping via counseling have the authority of God's Word behind them.

There is a distinction, however, between using the authority of the Scriptures and being authoritarian. Some counselors pull out a scriptural passage and apply it to any problem without hearing the full extent of the difficulty and without knowing whether Scripture is necessary at that particular time. Some counselors who are unwilling or fail to examine the problems in their own lives, but who nevertheless attempt to counsel and use scriptural authority, might misapply Scripture or distort it because of their own difficulties.

How might your authority as a minister be used properly or misused in counseling a person in crisis?

Jesus Admonished and Confronted

Notice how Jesus, when necessary, admonished and confronted people:

> And He said to them, "Why are you timid, you men of little faith?" Then He arose, and rebuked the winds and the sea; and it became perfectly calm (Matt. 8:26, NASB).

> And if your brother sins, go and reprove him in private; if he listens to you, you have won your brother (Matt. 18:15, NASB).

Another example of how Jesus admonished and confronted is in John 8:3-9 *(NASB)*:

And the scribes and the Pharisees brought a woman caught in adultery, and having set her in the midst, they said to Him, "Teacher, this woman has been caught in adultery, in the very act. Now in the Law Moses commanded us to stone such women; what then do You say?" And they were saying this, testing Him, in order that they might have grounds for accusing Him. But Jesus stooped down, and with His finger wrote on the ground. But when they persisted in asking Him, He straightened up, and said to them, "He who is without sin among you, let him be the first to throw a stone at her." And again He stooped down, and wrote on the ground. And when they heard it, they began to go out one by one, beginning with the older ones, and He was left alone, and the woman, where she was, in the midst.

Sometimes it is necessary to confront the counselee directly about his or her problem. *V and difficult*

JESUS' HOLY LIFE

Jesus' ministry was one of helping people achieve fullness of life and assisting them in developing their ability to deal with the problems, conflicts and burdens of life. Perhaps what's really important for the counselor—whether professional or layman—is to consider why Jesus was so effective in His ministry. As we look at His personal life, the answer is evident.

Jesus Was Obedient to God

Foremost in Jesus' personal life was His obedience to God. The relationship between Him and His Father was centered on His obedience to God—the mainstay of His life. Two verses from the book of John emphasize this point:

For I did not speak of my own accord, but the Father who sent me commanded me what to say and how to say it (John 12:49).

I have brought you glory on earth by completing the work you gave me to do (John 17:4).

Jesus Was Faithful

Another reason Jesus' ministry was effective was that He lived a life of faith and, therefore, was able to put things in proper perspective, seeing

> Jesus' ministry was effective because He lived a life of faith and, therefore, was able to put things in proper perspective, seeing through God's eyes.

through God's eyes. The example of the death of the synagogue official's daughter and Jesus' response to the statement of her death showed His faith:

Don't be afraid; just believe (Mark 5:36).

Jesus uttered these words to the ears of a parent who had just lost a child. Yet Jesus had extreme faith that the child could and would be alive.

Jesus Was a Prayer Warrior

Another reason for Jesus' effectiveness was the power of His prayer life. His example indicates that prayer is a very important element in one's ministry:

But the news about Him was spreading even farther, and great multitudes were gathering to hear Him and to be healed of their sicknesses. But He Himself would often slip away to the wilderness and pray (Luke 5:15-16, *NASB*).

And it was at this time that He went off to the mountain to pray, and He spent the whole night in prayer to God. And when day came, He called His disciples to Him; and chose twelve of them, whom He also named as apostles (Luke 6:12-13, *NASB*).

Some counselors find it helpful to pray either at the beginning or at the end of their counseling sessions. Others might not pray during the session, but prayer is still an important part of their counseling ministry. Some counselors pray specifically for each counselee every day and let the counselee know they are doing this. Some have also asked their counselees to pray for them that God would give them wisdom and insight as they minister.

One pastor says that when he is completely stymied in a counseling session and does not know what to do next, it is his practice to admit this fact openly to the counselee. He states that he would like to pause for a moment and ask God to reveal to him what should be done next, what should be said and the direction he should take. This pastor said that on many occasions, as soon as he finished praying, what needed to be done or said next was very clear to him.

Jesus Was Personally Involved

Jesus was personally involved in His ministry—with the disciples and with others. He was not aloof; rather, He was personal, sensitive and caring.

Jesus Had the Power of the Holy Spirit

The power of the Holy Spirit enabled Jesus to be effective. Some have called this power an anointing of the Spirit. We see how His ministry began when Jesus received the power of the Holy Spirit:

Now it came about when all the people were baptized, that Jesus also was baptized, and while He was praying, heaven was opened, and the Holy Spirit descended upon Him in bodily form like a dove, and a voice came out of heaven, "Thou art My beloved Son, in Thee I am well-pleased" (Luke 3:21-22, *NASB*).

The next chapter of Luke indicates that Jesus was full of the Holy Spirit and was led by the Spirit, and the Spirit of the Lord was upon Him. One of the reasons the power of the Lord was with Jesus was so that He could heal:

> And it came about one day that He was teaching; and there were some Pharisees and teachers of the law sitting there, who had come from every village of Galilee and Judea and from Jerusalem; and the power of the Lord was present for Him to perform healing (Luke 5:17).

William Crane, in his book *Where God Comes In: The Divine Plus in Counseling,* talks about the ministry of the Holy Spirit in the lives of the counselor and counselee:

> The Holy Spirit has access to all the materials that other psychotherapists know and use. In addition, He has direct access to the inner thoughts and feelings of the counselor. When the counselor becomes counselee in the presence of the Wonderful Counselor and sincerely seeks the honest reproval, correction and training in righteousness, which the Holy Spirit promises, then he may find it. Many have.[2]

We all need to remember whom we are representing.

FINAL THOUGHTS

In a small European village was a town square that held a special statue. This statue of Jesus was the pride and joy of this small town. But World War II arrived, and soon the bombs began falling on the town. One day the statue was hit and blown to pieces. The residents collected all the shattered pieces and slowly did what they could to re-create it. When they finished their reconstruction, the only pieces missing were the hands of Jesus, so they placed a plaque at the base of the statue with the words, "Now we are the only hands that Jesus has."

Isn't this our calling to those around us? We are His hands.

CHAPTER 2

APPLICATIONS OF BIBLICAL PRINCIPLES

(PART 1)

In spite of many years of training and experience, ministers and coun-selors—on many occasions every week—still wonder what they should do or say in a counseling session. I've been counseling now for over 40 years, and there are still times when I'm not sure which direction to go. These occasions force us to go to the Lord and ask, "Lord, what should I do now? What does this person need?" If we begin to help people out of our own strength, we'll make mistakes. Therefore, we need to *rely on the power and wisdom of God.*

In Proverbs, we're instructed to "lean on, trust in, and be confident in the Lord with all your heart and mind and do not rely on your own insight or understanding. In all your ways know, recognize, and acknowledge Him, and He will direct and make straight and plain your paths" (3:5-6, *AMP*). A similar thought is expressed in Proverbs 15:28 (*AMP*):

The mind of the [uncompromisingly] righteous studies how to answer, but the mouth of the wicked pours out evil things.

LISTENING IS VITAL TO YOUR COUNSELING PRACTICE

One problem we all suffer from—probably more than any other—is not knowing when to listen and when to keep quiet. Many ministers and lay counselors want to talk and offer advice or exhort from the Scriptures. However, if you're talking more than 25 percent of the time, you're probably talking too much. There is a time for advising and exhorting, but how will one know what to say unless he has first listened? *Listening* is a crucial part of counseling.

As we look into the Scriptures, we see God as our model for listening (see Pss. 34:15-18; 116:1-2; Jer. 33:3). The Scriptures have a lot to say about the importance of listening. James 1:19 says that each of us is to be "a ready listener" (*AMP*). Proverbs 15:31 states: "If you listen to correction to improve your life, you will live among the wise" (*NCV;* see also Prov. 18:13,15; 21:28).

Listening means that you're trying to understand the feelings of *the other* and that you're doing so for his or her sake.

Do You Know What Listening Really Is All About?

Listening means you're not thinking about what you're going to say when the other person stops talking. You are not busy formulating your response. You're concentrating on what is being said.

Listening means that you're completely accepting of what is being said, without judging what the other is saying or how he or she is saying it. If you don't like the person's tone of voice or you can't condone what he or she is doing and, therefore, you react on the spot, you may miss the meaning. Perhaps it hasn't been said in the best way, but just listen, because that someone is most likely hurting. Additionally, he or she probably is not going to be himself or herself. Acceptance doesn't mean that you agree with the content of what the person says, but it means that you acknowledge and understand that what the person is saying is something he or she is feeling. This goes a long way in helping others.

Listening also means being able to repeat what the person said and express what you think he or she is feeling while speaking to you.

Have You Considered What's Involved in Healthy Communication?

Every message a person shares has three parts: (1) the actual content, (2) the tone of voice and (3) the nonverbal communication. It's possible to use the same word, statement or question and express many different messages simply by changing the tone of voice or body movement. Nonverbal communication includes facial expression, body posture and gestures or actions.

> Your counselee needs to sense that you're in sync with him or her. I learned to reflect upon what I saw on another's face and in his or her posture, walk and pace. Then I shared with the counselee what I saw.

It's been suggested that successful communication consists of 7 percent content, 38 percent tone of voice and 55 percent nonverbal communication. We're usually aware of the content of what we're saying but not nearly as aware of our tone of voice. We have the capability of giving one sentence a dozen different meanings just by changing our tone.

Because of my retarded son, Matthew, who didn't have a vocabulary, I learned to listen with my eyes. I learned to read the messages in his nonverbal signals. This, in turn, translated to my skill in listening to what my counselees could not put into words. I learned to listen to the messages behind the message—the hurt, the ache, the frustration, the loss of hope, the fear of rejection, the feeling of betrayal, the joy, the delight and the promise of change.

I also learned to reflect upon what I saw on another's face and in his or her posture, walk and pace. Then I shared with the counselee what

I saw. This provided him or her an opportunity to explain further what he or she was thinking and feeling. The counselee knew I was tuned in to him or her. Your counselee needs to sense that you're in sync with him or her. Listen with your eyes to what he or she can't put into words.

LEARNING HOW TO LISTEN IS A NECESSITY

It is important for you, as a minister or lay counselor, to be aware of some personal factors that influence the way that you listen and interpret what you hear. Here are seven factors that determine how well a person listens.

Age

People in different age groups tend to hear and react to things differently. Different age groups or generations hold differing values, which inevitably lead to a greater possibility for dissension and clashes. In other words, your grandparents hold values and beliefs different from those held by you or your children.

Sex

Men and women have been trained by the socialization process to hear and respond differently. Lack of understanding of gender differences in listening and conversing creates problems. A woman will use more verbal responses to *encourage* the talker. They're more likely than men to use listening signals like "mm-hmmm" and "yeah" just to indicate that they are listening.

A man will usually use these responses only when he's *agreeing* with what a woman is saying. You can see what the outcome could be! A man interprets a woman's listening responses as a sign that she agrees with him. But later on, he discovers she wasn't agreeing with him at all. He didn't realize that she was simply indicating her interest in what he was saying and in keeping the interchange going by her mm-hmmms and yeahs. A woman, on the other hand, may feel ignored and disappointed because a man doesn't make the same listening responses as she does. She interprets his quietness as not listening. This happens all the time in the workplace.

In addition, a man is more likely than a woman to make comments throughout the conversation, but a woman may feel bothered by these comments and interpret them as an interruption. This is why many women complain, "Men always interrupt" or "They never listen to women." When counseling someone who is of the opposite gender, be aware of these differences.

Education

A psychologist well trained in a Ph.D. program that specializes in the psychodynamic orientation will likely hear something differently than the pastor who graduated from an evangelical seminary.

Past Experiences

The variety of experiences and relative degree of pain and difficulty a counselor has lived through will affect his or her level of understanding and capacity for empathetic responses.

Perception of Failed Expectations and Goals

Helpers who tend to be either optimistic or pessimistic about their own future will usually hold the same attitude toward their counselees' expectations and goals.

Personal Feelings About the Counselee

Research shows that counselors are attentive, open and positively responsive to counselees they like, whereas they tend to be less attentive, closed and negatively responsive to counselees whom they dislike. If you are threatened by the counselee or are afraid of being dominated by the person, you'll listen differently from a counselor who is not.

It may be easier for you to listen to an angry person than to a sarcastic person. Some tones or phrases may be enjoyable to listen to; others may be annoying. The repetitive phrases a person uses (and may be unaware of) could bother you (expect repetition when anyone is upset or devastated). Excessive gestures, such as talking with the hands or waving the arms, could be overly distracting.

Current Emotional and Physical Feelings

If you feel depressed, have a headache or have had very little sleep the night before, you'll tend to hear more negative statements from the counselee, while the happy, energetic counselor may hear more positive statements.[1]

Listening is a skill that can be learned. Are you aware that people can listen to human speech at three times the speed normally spoken without any significant loss of comprehension? Try listening to people who speak at different rates and determine which ones you tend to respond to best.

HEARING IS DIFFERENT FROM LISTENING

There's a difference between hearing and listening. Hearing is the gaining of information for oneself, while listening is caring for and being empathetic toward others. In listening, we are trying to understand the feelings of the other person; we are listening for his or her sake. Listening is determined by what is going on inside the other person—what my attentiveness is doing for him or her. But hearing is determined by what goes on inside of me—what effect the conversation has on me.

In listening, we interpret and try to understand what we have heard. Paul Wilczak says:

It is the "heart," however, that is our total emotional response, that integrates these various perceptions into full, personal contact, and this is what is needed today. We can listen with our heads. We can comprehend the thought content of a person's messages and systematically analyze what is communicated. This is cognitive empathy and can be readily learned. But cognitive empathy has severe limitations.

It misses the dimension of meaning that goes beyond what is explicitly said. It overlooks the feelings and experiences usually conveyed without words. These other messages come from the heart, the center of a person's experience.[2]

Listening is one of the most loving gifts you can give to another person, whether it be counselee, friend or family member. Remember:

Something happens when we listen
not just with our ears
but with our eyes.
Something happens when we wait out
a griever's words.
Something happens when we express our care
in calming ways.
Something happens
when we keep our promises
even when less than convenient.
Something happens when we pay attention
to the questions of the griever
rather than offer a cheap answer.
Something happens when hearts touch.
Something happens when we remember
Jesus' promise
"Where two or three are gathered . . .
there I will be, too."
Something happens when a caregiver
becomes a grief sharer.[3]

KNOWING WHEN TO SPEAK AND WHEN TO KEEP QUIET IS CRUCIAL

Ecclesiastes 3:7 emphasizes the next principle of biblical counseling—*knowing when to speak and when to be quiet.* Proverbs 10:19 (*AMP*) further emphasizes this: "In a multitude of words transgression is not lacking, but he who restrains his lips is prudent." *The Living Bible*'s version is very graphic: "Don't talk so much. You keep putting your foot in your mouth. Be sensible and turn off the flow!"

If you understand others' problems, you'll most likely choose your words well:

He who has knowledge spares his words, and a man of understanding has a cool spirit. Even a fool when he holds his peace is considered wise; when he closes his lips he is esteemed a man of understanding (Prov. 17:27-28, *AMP*).

Proverbs 29:20 (*NCV*) is another passage applicable to this principle: "Do you see people who speak too quickly? There is more hope for a foolish person than for them." Being hasty means blurting out what you are thinking without considering the effect it will have upon others. When you are ministering to a person who says something that shocks you, don't feel you have to respond immediately. Take a few seconds to think, and ask God to give you the words. Then formulate what you want to say.

Ask for More Information

If you don't know what to say, then ask for more information, using words such as "Tell me some more about it" or "Give me some more background." This gives you time to think. You don't have to say something right away. There may be times when you say to a person, "I need a few seconds to go through what you said and decide how to respond at this time." This takes the pressure off of you and also off of the counselee.

Show Genuine Interest and Love

You can listen to the person and you can rely upon the power of God for knowing how to counsel, but little will be accomplished without being sincerely interested in the other and loving him or her. Sometimes a counselor or minister will give an off-the-cuff, superficial answer that doesn't meet the counselee's need and doesn't deal with the problem. All of us must ask ourselves, *How do I really feel about this person who is coming to me? Am I genuinely concerned?*

Say the Right Words at the Right Time

The right answer, the correct answer, is the word spoken at the right moment:

A man has joy in making an apt answer, and a word spoken at the right moment—how good it is! (Prov. 15:23, *AMP*).

Keep Confidences
Keeping confidences builds trust. It is a trait of a trustworthy person. "He who goes about as a talebearer reveals secrets, but he who is trustworthy and faithful in spirit keeps the matter hidden" (Prov. 11:13, *AMP*). Nothing that is told to you in a counseling situation should ever escape your lips:

 He who guards his mouth and his tongue keeps himself from troubles (Prov. 21:23, *AMP*).[4]

Say the Right Words in the Right Manner
When a person is in crisis or traumatized, our words, tone of voice and suggestions have a far greater impact than at other times in life. Even offhand comments can have an effect. Whatever you and I say can have one of two effects: (1) our words can heal, or (2) they can harm. What you say to a traumatized person can calm and lower their blood pressure, or it can increase their anxiety. When you don't know what to say, *don't!* It's better to say nothing than to fill the air with words.[5]

> **When a person is in crisis or traumatized, our words, tone of voice and suggestions have a far greater impact than at other times in life.**

Proverbs 25:20 (*NCV*) says: "Singing songs to someone who is sad is like taking away his coat on a cold day or pouring vinegar on soda." Being jovial around a person who is deeply hurting is not appropriate. Comments like "Oh, you really don't feel that way, come on; let me tell you this story I heard" can cause the person to hurt even more. On some occasions, casual or off-the-subject conversation can help lift a person, but it is usually not appropriate for the person who is hurting deeply. Whatever you say needs to be supportive and helpful, since most of those you help will be contending with other people who make statements that hurt rather than console, hinder rather than comfort and prolong the pain rather than relieve it:

> If an enemy were insulting me, I could endure it; if a foe were raising himself against me, I could hide from him. But it is you, a man like myself, my companion, my close friend with whom I once enjoyed sweet fellowship as we walked with the throng at the house of God (Ps. 55:12-14).

> Even my close friend, whom I trusted, he who shared my bread, has lifted up his heel against me (Ps. 41:9).

These people are secondary "wounders." They give unwanted and bad advice, as well as improperly applied Scripture. They're all around, even at church, and your counselee won't be the first to experience this. Remember Job?

> [Job] had four well-meaning but insufferable friends who came over to cheer him up and try to explain [his suffering]. They said that anybody with enough sense to come in out of the rain knew that God was just. They said that anybody old enough to spell his own name knew that since God was just, he made bad things happen to bad people and good things happen to good people. They said that such being the case, you didn't need a Harvard diploma to figure out that since bad things had happened to Job, then *ipso facto* he must have done something bad himself. But Job hadn't, and he said so, and that's not all he said either. "Worthless physicians are you all," he said. "Oh that you would keep silent, and it would be your wisdom" (Job 13:4-5). They were a bunch of theological quacks, in other words, and the smartest thing they could do was shut up. But they were too busy explaining things to listen.[6]

Perhaps these wounders would learn not to make insensitive statements if someone spoke up and said, "That's not true and it's not helpful. If you want to be helpful I would appreciate it if you would . . . " Sometimes we excuse what these people say as well-meaning—which is questionable. Sometimes they're just reflecting their own anxieties, fears or lack of having dealt with issues in their own lives. Remember, what these people say is not advice coming from experts! It's beneficial if you help them anticipate hearing statements they'd rather not hear. It will be difficult for them to respond to these people the way they would like to because of the grief or trauma state.

Teach and Give Advice Sparingly

Sometimes you will need to give directions, advice and help on impending decisions or problems that need to be resolved. Sometimes you'll give guidance on handling conflicts. Teaching should not be overdone and must be used only when there is receptivity. A principle to follow is this: Use the teaching technique when, and only when, a person needs new information that would be difficult for a person to acquire on his or her own. Find out if they already have this information or have access to it. Invite the counselee to describe what he or she knows. Be sure the person is ready to hear what you have to say.

Giving advice is a form of teaching, but it's often overused and not especially effective. Often we leave our role as counselor when we give advice and become more of a friend or parent who is trying to help the counselee. Given in the proper manner, advice is a part of counseling. When you give suggestions in counseling, try to draw them from the person or give them as options: "What if you did . . . ?" "Have you considered . . . ?" "What possibilities have you come up with?"

Don't say, "This is exactly what you need to do." If you do, you're assuming responsibility for the solution. If your suggestion doesn't work, he or she may come back and say, "You really gave me stupid advice. It didn't work. It's your fault." Instead, give the person several tentative suggestions, which is safer for you and which also will help the person think through the alternatives. Most people have the ability to resolve their problems, but they just need encouragement to do so.

Again, you need to believe in their capabilities.

However, what if the counselee wants advice? Then ask yourself, *What's the reason for this request?* It may be that the counselee is looking for the reassurance that you care, or the person may want you to live his or her anxiety. Perhaps the counselee is looking to you as the great miracle worker, or maybe he or she just wants the hope that there's a solution. Whatever the case may be, it is important to think through each situation carefully.

It could be that other responses besides handing out advice would be more beneficial.

Teaching is an effective tool if it helps the counselee become more independent and move toward maturity. Teaching can be most helpful during the adjustment phase of the crisis, which is described in chapter 8.

QUESTIONING IS A POPULAR AND EFFECTIVE TECHNIQUE WHEN USED PROPERLY

One of the most frequently used techniques in counseling is questioning. We have seen how Jesus used questions. In my work with interns and ministers, I have asked them to tape their counseling sessions and then tabulate the number of questions asked compared with the number of statements made. Many found that they responded to the counselees' responses with questions. With this approach, many counselees eventually were able to predict the questions that would come from the minister, which led them to perceive the ministers as nothing more than interrogators. Some said, "I go in to see the pastor; he asks me a question; I answer; and then I wait for the next question to be asked."

Questioning is a greatly overused technique, especially by those just starting to counsel. Why? Because it might make you feel comfortable as it helps you gather information. In addition, you are not as involved nor do you have to work as hard as you do with other responses. It is safe and easy to use. To correct excessive questioning, I usually ask the interns or ministers to go back through their taped interviews, write down each question asked and then rewrite it into a statement rather than a question.

By doing this, they learn a greater variety of ways to respond and will become more conscious of their responses.

Know Why You're Asking a Question

What's the purpose? Was the question necessary? Using this technique can indicate that you assume that you know better what to discuss than does the counselee.

When you ask questions, use open-ended ones that give the person the greatest amount of latitude and freedom to respond. Asking questions calling for a yes or no response won't be helpful for either of you. Be careful that your questions don't convey—through tone or nonverbal messages of inflection—any sense of judgment or suspicion. Asking questions can be helpful through the various stages of counseling and the phases of a crisis, but if the person is already giving information, the need for questions should drop. They're not as necessary during the last phase of a crisis.

Probe to Further Discussion if Necessary

When you think that the person would benefit from further discussion about the situation or issue, it may be beneficial to do a little probing. But this should be done in a low-key, unobtrusive manner, and the counselee needs to carry the responsibility for what's discussed.

Help Your Counselees

Galatians 6:2 (*AMP*) teaches the principle of edifying and helping by bearing one another's burdens:

> Bear (endure, carry) one another's burdens and troublesome moral faults, and in this way fulfill and observe perfectly the law of Christ (the Messiah) and complete what is lacking [in your obedience to it].

Romans 14:19 (*AMP*) reads:

> So let us then definitely aim for and eagerly pursue what makes for harmony and for mutual upbuilding (edification and development) of one another.

The word "edify," which is part of helping, means to hold up or to promote growth in Christian wisdom, grace, virtue and holiness.[7] Our counseling should include edification.

Helping means assisting a person to do something for his or her betterment. We have to ask ourselves, *Is what I am accomplishing with this person going to help him recover, grow in the Christian life and become strong?* A person might come to you and say, "I want you to help me," but what the person really means is that he or she wants you to agree with his or her point of view. If it's a marital dispute, the person will probably want you to take sides. This is where you get into difficulty: taking sides.

Another way of helping others is to encourage them:

Anxiety in a man's heart weighs it down, but an encouraging word makes it glad (Prov. 12:25, *AMP*).

Therefore encourage (admonish, exhort) one another and edify (strengthen and build up) one another, just as you are doing (1 Thess. 5:11, *AMP*).

Encouraging, along with listening, is one of the most important techniques in helping a person in crisis (see 1 Thess. 5:14). Encouraging means urging forward, stimulating a person to do what he or she should

> **Encouraging, along with listening, is one of the most important techniques in helping a person in crisis.**

be doing. It is saying to the person, "I believe in you as an individual. I believe you have the ability and the potential to follow through in doing this." Encouraging a person helps him or her to believe in his or her own personal worth, which is one of the goals of counseling.

Reassuring Your Counselees Will Pave the Way for Growth

Because counseling can be painful as well as helpful for a counselee, reassurance through all the various stages of counseling is important. I don't mean statements such as, "It will be okay" or "Everything is going to turn out for the best." We don't know the outcome, and as people in ministry, we must be careful when and how we offer assurances from the Word of God. The counselees need to be honest with their feelings and to make sure they are being heard by you in order for them to be receptive to the support and comfort of God's Word.

Eight types of reassurance that can be given to a person in crisis are as follows:

1. The counselee might be reassured by knowing that his or her problem is really quite common.
2. Reassurance can be given by saying that the problem has a known cause and that something can be done about it.
3. Reassurance can be given that though the symptoms are annoying, they are not dangerous. Your goal is to normalize what they're experiencing.
4. Counselees can often be reassured that specific treatment methods are available.
5. Reassurances can be given that a resolution of the problem is possible.
6. The counselee may need reassurance that he or she is not going insane.
7. Reassurance may be needed that relapses might occur but that their appearance does not imply the condition is worsening.
8. When appropriate, counselees should be reassured that their problems are not the result of sinful action.[8]

As you counsel people in crisis, remember that to help them become more self-sufficient, you need to wean them gradually from your insights, help and counsel. Your task is to work yourself out of a job and to rejoice with the person when that occurs.

CHAPTER 3

APPLICATIONS
OF BIBLICAL
PRINCIPLES

(PART 2)

Empathy is one of the most important commodities for effective counseling. But unfortunately, the word "empathy," as with other words, means different things to different people. What does "empathy" mean in the counseling relationship? The word comes from the German word *einfuhlung*, which means "to feel unto" or "to feel with." It's as though we're in the driver's seat with the other person, feeling and sensing with him or her. It's viewing the situation through the person's eyes, feeling as he or she feels. The author of Hebrews said:

> Remember those in prison as if you were their fellow prisoners, and those who are mistreated as if you yourselves were suffering (13:3).

Galatians 6:2 and Romans 12:15 admonish us to bear one another's burdens, to rejoice with those who rejoice and to weep with those who weep. To do that is to have empathy.

Empathy also involves discrimination—being able to get inside the other person, looking at the world through the person's perspective and getting a feeling for what his or her world is like. It involves the ability to discriminate as well as the ability to communicate this understanding to the other person in such a manner that the person realizes that we have picked up both his or her feelings and behavior. It's being able to see another person's joy, to understand what underlies that joy and to communicate that understanding to the person.[1]

Empathy is an understanding *with* the counselee rather than a diagnostic understanding *of* the client. It bonds you with the other person.

Empathy requires the ability to go beyond factual knowledge and become involved in the counselee's world of feelings. But it also involves doing this without personally going through what the other person does. You cannot experience the identical emotions of a person—that would be overinvolvement. Empathetic responding focuses exclusively on the feelings expressed by the other person. Sympathetic responding focuses on the expression of your care and compassion in order to comfort the other individual:

Sympathy in the counselor-client relationship is sometimes like two people who do not know how to swim trying to save each other. Instead of saving each other, they will likely drown. Instead of understanding the client's feelings and experience, the counselor might overwhelm him or her with sympathy. The counselor's own feelings—his own outrage, for example—might get triggered by the client's story, which could be counterproductive.

We do not want to imply that sympathy in counseling is bad or wrong. Sympathy has its place and can be an important part of the counseling relationship. In the book of Romans, Paul wrote that it is important for us to sympathize, to "rejoice with those who rejoice; mourn with those who mourn" (12:15). Sympathy is connecting and caring with the heart. "Loving with the head" is to analyze, which can be too objective and aloof. Empathy is the ability to love with both the heart and the head.[2]

EMPATHETIC SITUATION

Test your ability to empathize with people in the following hypothetical situation.

A counselee comes to you upset over the possibility of losing her job. "I have really been trying hard at work to please my supervisor," she says, "but I just can't seem to make him happy. He's cross and blunt when I make a mistake. Just yesterday I made a mistake on a letter. He gave me this hard look and said he would like to have someone who uses better grammar and style than he does."

Which of the following responses would you use?

Minister: He sounds very unreasonable. Why don't you tell him you're doing your best and no one is perfect?

This is an *advice-giving* type of response and shows no awareness of the person's feelings. The counselee might feel misunderstood and may not be willing to divulge too many of her feelings.

Minister: It sounds as though you have a hard person to work for.

This is an *indirect reference to* her *feelings,* and it actually focuses mainly on the supervisor.

Minister: I sense that you're feeling overwhelmed and lost concerning how to please your supervisor and that you wonder if the situation isn't hopeless. Could it be that you're afraid your job might be threatened and that you may be wondering, *What do I do now?*

This type of response seems to *reflect the counselee's feelings* of distress and possible hopelessness in her situation. The last phrase includes an *action* statement, which may help her explore some possible alternatives.

EMPATHETIC RESPONSES

For you to be seen as a person who cares and is sensitive and empathetic, you need to use language that conveys this feeling. What you need is a repertoire of appropriate introductory phrases. What you don't need is a repertoire of phrases that you say over and over again, which border on redundancy.

> **For you to be seen as a person who cares and is sensitive and empathetic, you need to use language that conveys this feeling.**

Below is a list of possible empathetic response leads. If you'll read this list out loud once a day for a month, you'll be amazed at how these phrases *will* just come to mind as you counsel others. I've had students, as well as ministers and counselors, doing this for years. When you fill your reservoir with information, it will be there when you need it.

Empathetic Response Leads

"Kind of feeling . . . "
"Sort of feeling . . . "
"As I get it, you felt that . . . "
"I'm picking up that you . . . "
"Sort of a feeling that . . . "
"If I'm hearing you correctly . . . "
"To me it's almost like you are saying, I . . . "
"Sort of hear you saying that maybe you . . . "

"Kind of made (makes) you feel . . . "

"The thing you feel most right now is sort of like . . . "

"So, you feel . . . "

"What I hear you saying is . . . "

"So, as you see it . . . "

"As I get it, you're saying . . . "

"What I guess I'm hearing is . . . "

"I'm not sure I'm with you, but . . . "

"I somehow sense that maybe you feel . . . "

"You feel . . . "

"I really hear you saying that . . . "

"I wonder if you're expressing a concern that . . . "

"It sounds as if you're indicating you . . . "

"I wonder if you're saying . . . "

"You place a high value on . . . "

"It seems to you . . . "

"Like right now . . . "

"You often feel . . . "

"You feel, perhaps . . . "

"You appear to be feeling . . . "

"It appears to you . . . "

"As I hear it, you . . . "

"So, from where you sit . . . "

"Your feeling is now that . . . "

"I read you as . . . "

"Sometimes you . . . "

"You must have felt . . . "

"I sense that you're feeling . . . "

"Very much feeling . . . "

"Your message seems to be, I . . . "

"You appear . . . "

"Listening to you, it seems as if . . . "

"I gather . . . "

"So your world is a place where you . . . "

"You communicate (convey) a sense of . . . "[3]

Empathetic statements respond to the counselee's surface feelings and also focus on those deeper feelings the person may not be expressing or may not be fully aware of at the time. Often, when a person is expressing his or her anger, he or she is also feeling hurt. You can respond to both of these feelings. These phrases are sometimes called additive empathetic responses, because they attempt to help the counselee put deeper feelings into words. However, they do require the counselor to make an inference, and they are not stated as definite fact but in a very *tentative* manner. This allows the counselee to accept or reject the possibility of the statement. It allows him to say that part of your response was accurate and part inaccurate. The following are some additive empathetic response leads.

Additive Empathetic Response Leads

"It sounds as if . . . "
"I'm wondering if you're saying . . . "
"Perhaps . . . "
"Maybe . . . "
"Is it possible that . . . "
"Would this fit . . . "
"Do you suppose . . . "

EMOTIONAL CONTAGION

Before you become significantly involved in counseling others, there's a problem you need to be aware of since none of us are really immune to it. It has different names, such as compassion fatigue, helper shutdown or helper burnout. It can happen to doctors, nurses, counselors, rescue workers or anyone involved in helping others. It seems to be a case of emotional contagion: You end up catching the disorder of the person or people you are helping. You become emotionally drained by caring too much. It's stress from wanting to help another person. After you reach out to minister to them, they may leave feeling better, but now you're absorbed in their problems, both in your emotions as well as in your thoughts.

There are several reasons why this could happen. If you're helping a number of hurting individuals, it could be an overload. The desire to help others is good, but you need to realize that not everyone will be helped and that there are some who aren't willing to take steps to change. Or you might fear that you may end up with what we call mission failure, or "I didn't help them enough." The fact is, you won't, because the only one bringing the changes is the Lord. We need to relinquish others to His care. Your value in helping others is to be there for them and to follow helpful guidelines, but don't evaluate your effectiveness on how well they respond.

As a counselor, I've learned that sometimes you don't see the results of your own efforts as people move on. If you're too empathetic and feel that the counselee is feeling too much, you will begin to carry their burden around.

If you have unresolved trauma in your own life, be prepared to have it activated if you work with those who have experienced similar trauma. What you hear will hit too close to home.

What will especially impact you is helping children who have experienced trauma. This gets to even the most experienced professional helper.

What can you do? Make sure you maintain a balance in your life. You need to have times just for tending to and nurturing yourself through the Word, healthy friendships, exercise, recreation, devotional books, laughter and care from others.

THE LANGUAGE OF OTHERS

For empathy and rapport to occur, there is one principle above all the others that needs to be implemented. Speak your counselee's language. One of my own personal goals in counseling during the first session is to discover the person's style of communication and communicate back to him or her in the same way. The principle is this: If I speak the counselee's language, real listening and change can occur. I try to discover whether the person is more visually oriented, auditorily oriented or kinesthetically (feeling) oriented. I listen to the tone of voice, volume and the phrases he or she uses. I study the nonverbal communication. Some people are loud, expressive and gesture a lot. Others are somewhat quiet, reserved and very proper, and they choose their words carefully. I join their style of communication, which builds rapport, trust and, eventually, a willingness on their part to listen to me.

This means the counselor will need to become very aware of his or her own style of communication. You will need to be flexible in order to use another style, and you will need to expand your vocabulary in order to make these shifts.

Establish Rapport

To establish rapport in the first session of counseling, you will need to meet people where they are. You must be perceptive to know if your communication is being accepted or rejected by the counselee. You can do this by reading the person's verbal and nonverbal language and his or her responses to you. If you are communicating effectively, you won't have to make many adjustments. If not, you need the flexibility to change and do something different. If you would like the other person to change, you must change your own responses first. The counselee will usually change in response to the change he or she perceives in you. By becoming more flexible, you will have more influence and impact upon others.

Build Your Ability to Respond

Here is another principle to consider: *In relationships, the person with the widest range of responses will have the greatest amount of influence and control.* Too many who counsel not only disregard this important fact but expect their counselees to adapt to their styles of thinking and talking; the result is that they eventually end up missing each other completely.

What happens if you tend to be loud, definite and expressive, and the person you're working with is quiet, reserved and rather shy? Or the other way around? What happens in counseling if you are an expander and give an abundance of detail whenever you say anything and your counselee is very much a bottom-line condenser? Or the other way around? What happens if you're a right-brain-oriented person—emotionally expressive—

and your counselee is very much a cognitive left-brain-oriented individual? Or the other way around?

What happens if you are a very linear thinker who goes from A to B to C to D, but the counselee is very tangential and changes direction in the middle of a sentence, only to return after a few sentences to finish it and, then again, maybe not? Can you track with the person and adapt? And what if it's the other way around?

> **In relationships, the person with the widest range of responses will have the greatest amount of influence and control.**

What if your personality preference is extroversion, in which you talk out loud in order to think (you don't necessarily mean what you say), you have a bit of difficulty listening, and you are energized by being with people, while your counselee's personality preference is introversion? Do you understand the difference? Introverts need to think awhile before they speak (on the average, they take about seven seconds to respond to a question); they don't like to be put on the spot or to be the center of attention; and they are drained by being around people too much. Extroverts tend to ask an introvert a question, and if they don't hear a response in a second or two, they either ask it again (which interrupts the introvert's thinking process) or answer it themselves. Can you see how this creates a problem? A wise extrovert working with an introvert might say, "Here's something I'd like you to think about for a minute. I'm interested in hearing your response." Then this extrovert patiently waits for a response. This is far more productive.[4]

The key factor is to adapt to your counselee. Let him or her set the style and pace. It will take longer and be more difficult for you to discover a person's unique pattern and style when he or she comes to see you in a state of severe loss, crisis or trauma; but in time, it is not only possible but also necessary.

THE ART OF CONFRONTATION

Confrontation Defined

The word "confrontation" is used frequently in discussions of counseling techniques. Too many in the Church have equated counseling with confrontation. That's why we need an extensive discussion of its limited use in the counseling process. Its use is especially limited when loss, crisis or trauma has been experienced.

What is confrontation? When should it be used? A counseling confrontation has been defined as an act by which a counselor points out to the counselee a discrepancy between his or her own perspective and the counselee's manner of viewing reality. Confrontation is really a part of everyday life, and it can be used effectively when we are involved in helping another person. Confrontation is not an attack on another person "for his own good." Such a negative and punitive attack would be detrimental to the counselee. As William Crane puts it:

> A judging confrontation, unprepared for, may end any relationship which would make counseling possible. The person already feels guilty and ashamed, and to be judged and condemned rather than understood and accepted is nothing less than absolute rejection. A person laden with guilt already feels cut off and rejected by all that stands for rightness and justice; he surely does not need to be condemned by the one to whom he goes seeking help.[5]

Actually, confrontation at its best is an extension of advanced, accurate *empathy*. It's a response to a counselee based on a deep understanding of his or her feelings, experiences and behavior. Such a response involves some unmasking of distortion, the client's understanding himself or herself and a challenge to action.[6]

William Crane says, "Only when empathy is established is the climate ready for confrontation; until then it is neither wise nor helpful."[7] The relationship between confrontation and empathy is very important, yet many counselors fail to see it. Let's explore some helpful pointers.

Confrontations have also been called *acts of grace*. Confrontation is defined as "a responsible unmasking of the discrepancies, distortions, games and smoke screens the counselee uses to hide both from self-understanding and from constructive behavioral changes."[8]

Confrontation involves *challenging* the undeveloped, underdeveloped, unused and misused potential *skills and resources* of the counselee with a view to examine and understand those resources in order to put them to use in action programs.

> **Our purpose in confronting people is to help them make better decisions for themselves, become more accepting of themselves and become more productive and less destructive in their lives.**

Our purpose in confronting people is to help them make better decisions for themselves, become more accepting of themselves and become more productive and less destructive in their lives. There are times when professionals and nonprofessionals alike hesitate to confront because it involves a commitment. There's also the possibility that you could be wrong or the person might misunderstand and feel rejected. We also need to be careful that the confrontation doesn't work against what we're trying to accomplish in the counselee's life, even though it is given with proper intentions.

Appropriateness of Confrontation

Earlier it was mentioned that empathy must be a part of the relationship. The quality of the relationship between counselor and counselee is very important. Generally speaking, the stronger the relationship, the more powerful and intense the confrontation can be. A confrontation must come about because the counselor cares about the counselee. If we do not care about the counselee and his or her improvement, confrontation can be harmful.

Another factor involved in confrontation is the ability of the counselee to understand and see what you are saying. Is he or she able to accept the confrontation? Can he or she follow through with what you're suggesting?

At the appropriate time, confrontations can be made in a tentative manner with statements such as, "I wonder if . . . "; and questions such as, "Could he be . . . ?" "Is it possible . . . ?"; "Does this make sense to you . . . ?" and "How do you react to this perception . . . ?"

None of us enjoys being confronted. And a number of those you're attempting to help won't appreciate it either. Some may turn it around and counterchallenge you by

- neutralizing or discrediting you,
- attempting to persuade you to change your view of things,
- devaluing or dismissing the importance of the issue,
- building support elsewhere for the issues being challenged, or
- appeasing or agreeing with you at the time (and then doing nothing about it later).

How do you overcome this? You build a trusting relationship, so the person is prepared to hear, consider and accept the confrontation.[9]

ELEMENTS FOR CULTIVATING TRUST

Adaptability

When you work with people, you can't use the same approach every time. You must be sensitive to their needs. The need for adaptability is stated in 1 Thessalonians 5:14 (*AMP*):

We earnestly beseech you, brethren, admonish (warn and seriously advise) those who are out of line [the loafers, the disorderly, and the unruly]; encourage the timid and fainthearted, help and give your support to the weak souls, [and] be very patient with everybody [always keeping your temper].

It's especially important to remember that each individual will need to be approached differently when you are confronting a wrong behavior. In John 5:6, Jesus asked the man at the pool, "Do you want to get well?" In essence, Jesus wanted to know if the man was really wanting and willing to change. When I work with people, I ask those questions in one way or another. The way you package what you say makes all the difference. When your care and concern are seen through your words, tones and body language, acceptance of your message occurs. In John 8:11 (*AMP*), Jesus responded to the woman caught in adultery by saying, "Go on your way and from now on sin no more."

Honesty and Acceptance

Important principles to follow in all of our counseling practices are honesty and acceptance. Proverbs 28:23 (*TLB*) states, "In the end, people appreciate frankness more than flattery." Proverbs 27:5 (*TLB*) says, "Open rebuke is better than hidden love!" Galatians 6:1 (*NKJV*) says, "Brethren, if a man is overtaken in any trespass, you who are spiritual restore such a one in a spirit of gentleness, considering yourself lest you also be tempted." And John 8:7 (*NKJV*) says, "So when they continued asking Him, He raised Himself up and said to them, 'He who is without sin among you, let him throw a stone at her first.'"

DESTRUCTIVE ELEMENTS IN COUNSELING

Even when we attempt to follow the principles of effective counseling, there's always the possibility that our counseling could affect a person in an adverse manner. This happens when destructive elements enter into the counseling process. We'll identify a number of these in the hope of preventing them from taking place.

Passivity

Passivity on the part of a minister or counselor can be very frustrating to the counselee. Listening and responding with nonverbal encouragement is important, but if there is little or no verbal activity, the counselor's responses will be questioned. The counselor may seem ambiguous. If a counselee is insecure or dependent, he or she may interpret a passive response as lack of care, criticism or even rejection. It's true that your verbal activity will vary from counselee to counselee—this is a judgment you will need to make. The timing of when you are silent as well as when you speak is important but can be determined by sensitive listening on your part.

Counselor Dominance

Counselor dominance is a contrast to passivity. Unfortunately, it occurs all too frequently among those in ministry. Why? Perhaps some ministers are frustrated would-be counselors, and this is their opportunity to show the person what they can do. It could be out of their own insecurity that they feel a need to dominate. Or they may simply want power, and this is a place where it can be obtained.

A dominating counselor or minister doesn't enter into the counselee's world of experience and thinking. Instead, he or she jumps in with advice and erroneous conclusions and makes dogmatic pronouncements or interpretations. Because the counselor responds from an external frame of reference and not within the life of the counselee, the counselor is prone to act as if he or she were all-knowing and infallible. The question then is, Whose needs are being met by this counseling? Certainly not the counselee's. Rather, the needs of the person doing the counseling are being met at the counselee's expense. And this is *not* our calling.

How can we tell if we're becoming dominant? Symptoms include frequent interruptions, impatience, changes of subject, attempts at persuading the person and lectures. Some dependent people may welcome this approach, but it doesn't help them in the growth process.

Self-Disclosure

Another ineffective approach is inappropriate self-disclosure. Talking too much about yourself and your own struggles, feelings, family, successes or failures causes the counselee to wonder how your ego trip relates to his or her problem. Again, the counselee's needs are not being met. There are occasions when describing your own experiences can benefit the counselee, but do it sparingly.

Interrogation

The improper use of questions falls into the category of interrogation, or grilling. We need to do more than use questions to gain access to the counselee's feelings or to gain information. Making statements, encouraging and listening will bring you the information and feelings. The counselee's level of comfort built from your responses will assist him or her in being open with you. Don't overload the early stages of counseling with questions. Let the hurt person talk or just sit quietly and think.

Inappropriate Patterns of Response

Inappropriate patterns of response create a distance between the minister and the counselee. Because they keep the counselee at a distance, genuine caring, trust and openness cannot develop. These patterns protect the counselor from his or her own discomfort, fears or anxieties that are associated with deep involvement in the client's life.

One way to promote distance is to prohibit the counselee from crying in one way or another. By doing this, the counselee begins to feel that crying is a sign of weakness. The counselee needs the beneficial release that tears provide. Denying their expression can be harmful.

Limiting discussion to safe topics only—topics that do not involve emotions or self-disclosure—also creates distance. By doing this, the minister avoids the risk of becoming involved in highly personal, painful or emotionally laden topics. Weather, sports, news and so on all serve as a buffer but accomplish nothing.

False Reassurance

False reassurance is dangerous to the counselee, too. Giving reassurance prematurely or without justification helps the minister avoid exploring significant feelings of the counselee that could include anger, despair, depression, anxiety or hopelessness, or subjects that may be uncomfortable, such as abuse or incest. When there's a genuine basis for reassurance, then it becomes appropriate. Too much usage, however, promotes dependency and raises the question of whether the minister knows what he or she is talking about. Sometimes it can eliminate anxiety and conflict that need to remain awhile so that the person is motivated to continue to seek counsel.

Emotional Detachment

Emotional detachment creates some of the same problems as passivity but is manifested by taking the role of a technical expert who is aloof. Intellectualizing is a form of detachment that again keeps the minister from real involvement. Theorizing about issues may be interesting, but is it productive? Debating or lecturing on theology may be interesting, but is a counseling setting the proper place? If the counselee has the tendency to use intellectualization as a defense, be careful not to respond in the same way.

Judgment

Moralizing, admonishing or passing judgment may actually be expected by some who seek out a minister. In fact, they may have a need for this. But responding in this manner does not bring about genuine change on the part of the counselee. Many counselees are fully aware of the way they are living, and it is best to take the time for them to make their own value judgments. For people in crisis, such responses do not help them move through the crisis phases but may keep them stuck at a specific point.

Inappropriate Confrontation

Inappropriate confrontations must be mentioned even though we have already said much about confrontation. Ministers who use confrontation excessively are betraying a belief that the problem must be fixed as soon as possible.

Pressure Tactics

Pressure tactics also create distance. Pressuring counselees to accelerate their progress by prodding, assigning too much outside work, browbeating, predicting negative consequences if they don't respond and questioning the sincerity of their motivation all fall into this category. These tactics usually ignore the feelings of the person and are perceived as punishment.

FINAL THOUGHT

We need to realize that for some, change will be very slow. They need our encouragement and our faith to move them along. Some counselees lack faith and hope; therefore, they need our sense of faith and hope in the Lord—and in the future—to carry them until their own faith and hope build and they can rely upon their own inner strength. These are just a few of the unproductive patterns that can occur. Becoming familiar with them will help us help others.

CHAPTER 4

HELPING OTHERS
RECOVER FROM
THEIR LOSSES IN LIFE

(PART 1)

When we think of loss, we think of loss through death of people we love.
But loss is a far more encompassing theme in our life. For we lose not only through death,
but also by leaving and being left, by changing and letting go and moving on. And our
losses include not only our separations and departures from those we love but our . . .
losses of romantic dreams, impossible expectations, illusions of freedom and power,
illusions of safety—and the loss of our own younger self.

JUDITH VIORST, *NECESSARY LOSSES*

We have overlooked a word in our life—"loss." Trauma and crisis receive
the attention, but at the heart of trauma and crisis is loss. In order to
understand and appreciate fully the significance of crisis and trauma, we
need to understand the multitude and complexity of loss. Over the years,

I've experienced numerous losses, but it's been my counselees who have taught me about the significance and impact of loss upon a person's life.

I remember in particular a man who had been clinically depressed for 12 years. He could barely function except at his business that he owned. In the process of counseling, we discovered that he had experienced five rejections over the past 20 years, which he had never grieved over. During the year of counseling, I sent him to a physician for help with medication to break the cycle of depression. He also connected with a lay counselor at a new church he was attending. One day when he came in he said, "Norm, you know I've been attending this new church called The Vineyard. On Sunday night, I leave my family at home and go to the evening service by myself. Do you know why I do that?"

I said, "No."

He continued, "During that service they spend 30 to 40 minutes in praise and worship. What I am doing during that time is grieving and weeping over those five rejections—those losses I've never grieved over." After three months, this man's depression of 12 years lifted. Why? Simply because he grieved and put those losses to rest.

We finished counseling, and three months later Christmas came and went. A couple of weeks later, his wife stopped by the office to pick up some books. I asked the typical question, "How was your Christmas?"

She answered, "It was wonderful."

"What did you receive?"

Her reply said it all, "My husband."

This experience taught me to ask everyone I work with, "What is the loss in your life that you've never grieved over?" Over the years, that question has prompted 80 percent of those asked to discover a loss and break the link between it and their present life. How? By completing their grief work.

Several years ago, a woman at a crisis counseling seminar shared an experience with me. She and her husband had moved to a new city three years before. Prior to that time, they had lived in the same town for 15 years. They were deeply involved in their church and had a large number of friends. Their children had been raised there, and they had celebrated each Christmas with the same close family friends.

When they moved, they left all that behind. The woman's husband started his new job immediately. However, because of the nature of her profession, she had to start over again and rebuild from scratch. For the first two years, she experienced a significant amount of depression and couldn't figure out why. Finally, she went for counseling, and as she focused on her family of origin, the reason became apparent. As a child, up to the age of five, she had bonded more with her grandmother than with her mother. They were very close, but then her grandmother died suddenly. Within weeks, her family moved from town to the country, where the nearest neighbor was a mile away. As she and her therapist talked and the connection became clear, she then was able to grieve as she never had over her grandmother and that childhood move. In time, her depression lifted.

WHAT EXACTLY IS LOSS?

Loss. It's a simple four-letter word that is one of everyone's companions throughout life. One writer who specializes in illusions of control said:

> Loss is part of the human condition and an unavailable fixture of life. The inevitability of major loss, however, does not mean that many of us are well prepared to handle this type of stress. Significant losses in life are likely to engender overwhelming negative emotions, disruption in everyday life, and long-term problems in resolving the loss.[1]

No one talks about loss very often. Like a silent conspiracy, we seem to have an unspoken agreement with others not to talk about our losses. Yet with each and every loss comes the potential for change, growth, new insights, understanding and refinement—all positive descriptions and words of hope. However, they are often in the future, and we fail to see that far ahead when we're in the midst of our grief.

Loss Does Not Mean Loser

Nobody likes to lose. When a loss occurs, it means something is wrong. But isn't life supposed to be filled with winners? Look at the headlines on the sports page. The accolades are given to winners not losers. Losing hurts. It carries sharpened points that jab into our nerves and cause pain. A small loss or a large one—it doesn't matter—it hurts. And it hurts even more because we have not been taught to expect or know how to

> **We want to be winners. We want success. We want to be in control of our lives, so we build a wall around us with a sign saying, "Losses—No Trespassing!"**

handle the losses of life. We want to be winners. We want success. We want to be in control of our lives, so we build a wall around us with a sign saying, "Losses—No Trespassing!" And then, if they occur, we feel violated.

Those around us don't particularly want to hear about our losses either. One therapist put her finger on the problem:

> As a culture, we seem to have an intolerance for suffering; we tend to want those who have experienced a loss of any kind to get on with their lives as quickly as possible. Often, by minimizing the impact of significant losses, pathologizing those whose reactions are intense, and applauding those who seem relatively unaffected by tragic events, we encourage the inhibition of our own grief.[2]

The concept that loss means something is wrong carries over into almost every area of life. The following thoughts reflect this concept:

- *She must not have been a good wife for him to leave her.*
- *They failed as parents. Otherwise that child would have stayed in the church and wouldn't have become involved with that crowd.*
- *He lost his job. I wonder what he did wrong.*
- *If they had been living the Christian life, this wouldn't have happened.*

Have you ever had such thoughts about another person? Or about your-self? Do you ever think of counselees in this way? It's an expression of blame.

This attitude has been with us for a long time. The disciples expressed similar thoughts to Jesus about a blind man:

And as He passed by, He saw a man blind from birth. And His disciples asked Him, saying, "Rabbi, who sinned, this man or his parents, that he should be born blind?" Jesus answered, "It was neither that this man sinned, nor his parents; but it was in order that the works of God might be displayed in him" (John 9:1-3, *NASB*).

Loss Requires Identification

When the person you're counseling walks through the door, do you find yourself wondering what losses this person has experienced? Begin to do this and you'll find a new doorway of discovering many of the causes for their present difficulties. For instance, you have experienced many losses in your life already. Some of them you are not even aware of, or you may not have realized that what you experienced was actual-ly a loss. Some are over in 24 hours. Others last for years. How you respond to them and what you do to them or let them do to you will affect the rest of your life. You can't avoid loss or shrug it off. Many try. Loss is not the enemy; not facing its existence is. Unfortunately, many of us have become more proficient in developing denial rather than fac-ing and accepting the losses of life. You'll discover this in the lives of those you counsel. One significant loss can generate a crisis or, depend-ing upon the circumstances, a trauma. A series of small losses can gen-erate a crisis.

Even if you attempt to ignore the loss, the emotional experience of it is implanted in your heart and mind—no eraser will remove it. Whenever there is any kind of attachment, a loss cannot be avoided when the tie is broken. Life is full of relationships with people, things and dreams that break up, and then new attachments occur. As each change takes place, you must experience the grief that accompanies it. It's important that you consider the losses in your own life prior to helping others. Who knows when another loss will activate your own?

Losses Are Not Easily Replaceable

The amount or intensity of loss that you feel is closely tied to the replaceability of whatever you lost. When you break a favorite piece of sporting equipment or your car is stolen, your upset nature and grief will subside in several days or weeks. But a child's or spouse's dying has a different impact. You may decide to have another child or marry again, but you can never replace the original.[3] As you work with counselees, look for any signs of the person trying to replace an original.

HOW DO YOU DISCUSS LOSS?

There are numerous ways for you to engage a counselee in a discussion about his or her losses. You can use a direct question such as, "What was a major loss you can remember experiencing during your teenage years? Describe what it was and how old you were." Or you can ask, "What is the worst loss you have ever experienced?"

Construct a Time Line

A helpful approach to discovering losses is constructing a Loss History Time Line (see Jim's example in figure 1). Ask counselees to draw a horizontal line. On the left-hand side, have them indicate their first conscious memory. In Jim's case, it was the birth of his brother when he was three. As they proceed, have them identify each loss they can remember experiencing, and then have them write down a brief description of the loss, the date of the loss and the intensity of the loss, which is indicated by the length of the vertical line. As you can see in figure 1, the death of Jim's mother and his divorce are the two most intense losses. The dotted or shaded area is an indication that the impact of the loss isn't over—the grief is still present.

Figure 1

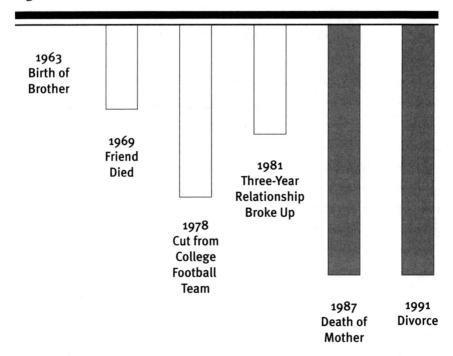

Source: John W. James and Frank Cherry, *The Grief Recovery Handbook* (New York: Harper and Row, 1988), pp. 71-82

In completing such a time line, the counselee will engage in a process that helps him or her identify not only the losses but also the grief work that still needs to be completed. I've seen some time lines that are filled with one loss after another—they seem to go on forever. Many counselees have been amazed to discover that the losses they thought were over were still alive and well. This helped them find resolution. There may be occasions when it's helpful to balance out the losses with the blessings the person has experienced. Using the same time line, the individual can list each blessing and its date with a vertical line. Use the length of the line to indicate the intensity of the blessing.

WHAT DO YOU KNOW ABOUT LOSS?

Life is a blending of loss and gain, loss and acquisition. In creation, loss is the ingredient of growth.

When you were a child, your baby teeth came in after bouts of pain and crying. Then one day, some teeth began to loosen and wiggle, and they soon fell out or were pulled. They were lost to make room for the permanent teeth. Sometimes, these too are lost and replaced by false teeth. On the contrary, high school graduation produces a loss of status, friends and familiarity, but who notices that? Most of us looked forward to it, because it meant going on with our lives. When we're young, some of our losses are celebrated as much as they are mourned. Most of these early losses are developmental and quite necessary. We can accept them fairly easily. However, often we focus on the gain without remembering that there is usually some loss attached to it. Change involves some form of loss of the way things were at one time.

What comes to mind when you think of loss? Usually it's the death of someone you care about. Loss occurs not just through someone's dying but by leaving or being left, by staying in one place or by moving on. How many losses will people experience in their lives by death? Ten? Perhaps 20? Yet other losses can be counted in the hundreds throughout our lives. Loss is an unavoidable fixture of life.

Losses Often Go Unrecognized

Many events occur that contain losses that go unrecognized and are never addressed. Any event that destroys a person's understanding of the meaning of life is felt as a loss. Our beliefs and expectations come under attack. The question, "How could they have done such a thing?" expresses this confusion.

> **Any event that destroys a person's understanding of the meaning of life is felt as a loss.**

Think of all the immigrants who come to our country. These immigrants experience a major cultural loss. Gone are the normal and familiar cues that give their lives meaning, such as road signs, money, language, familiar faces, role patterns, food and relationships.

Missionaries who move to a new field to minister face major adjustments and losses. Then every four years they return to their homeland and encounter new losses as they confront the rapid changes of their own economy, values and lifestyles. What about all the losses that occur when a minister leaves one church for another? The congregation experiences loss, as does the moving family. But there's no memorial service. Life just goes on.

Economic losses abound today. Companies fail or downsize. Corporations deceive investors and wipe out pensions. We may not even realize that an increase at the gas pumps or inflation is a loss to each of us.

There are other more subtle losses that affect us. We may be aware of pain from an experience, but we don't identify it as a loss. For example, a minor failure or socially putting your foot in your mouth can create embarrassment, shame and disappointment. The Asian expression "loss of face" recognizes the "lost" characteristic of these experiences.

While there are obvious losses—losing loved ones through death or divorce, your car's being stolen, your house's being vandalized or burglarized—there are many more not-so-obvious losses—changing jobs, receiving a bad grade in school, obtaining a less-than-hoped-for raise, moving, becoming ill, becoming a new teacher midsemester, changing from an office with windows to one without, not finding success or achievement, a son's or daughter's going off to school, or losing an ideal, a dream or a lifelong goal. Unfortunately, because some losses are not easy to recognize, we usually do not identify them as losses. Therefore, we don't spend time and energy dealing with them.

WHAT ARE SOME DIFFERENT TYPES OF LOSS?

Many of the losses in life are related to aging. As we grow older, the dreams and beliefs of childhood begin to crumble and change.

All childhood and adolescent romances are filled with losses—some daily, even hourly! Moving from school to school, failing a grade, being placed in an accelerated class and leaving friends behind or having your friends move to an accelerated class and your staying behind, dropping out, leaving home for college or just moving out. Even if the change was planned, an element of loss is involved.

Notice the pattern as you look at the Family Life Cycle chart in figure 2. At first, we enter a pattern of accumulation and assume that this continues throughout life. However, even during this time you experience some losses.

Figure 2

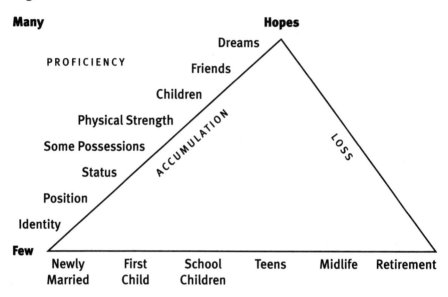

Unspeakable Losses

This pattern of accumulation may be a time when *unspeakable losses* occur. These are the losses that occur but aren't talked about. Pregnancy loss is a big one. Were you aware that every year 890,000 of the 6.5 million pregnancies in the United States end in some form of miscarriage or stillbirth and another 1.5 million end in abortion?[4] In the space of one short year, almost 2.5 million people are affected by pregnancy losses of one kind or another.

Miscarriage, abortion and the inability to have a child are losses that are both devastating as well as shrouded by silence. The silence could be because these losses are such private incidents, or perhaps the incident creates shame or a desire to forget, coupled with self-blame.[5] In any case, these are losses where there is no stream of supporters to walk the affected through the grief. Let's explore some more unspeakable losses.

When you hit the job market, losses multiply as rejections occur. Someone else gets the raise or promotion, the deal, the settlement award; businesses fail; the economy falters; you get stuck in a going-nowhere job.

Then we hit the physical losses—a major one involves the gain of pounds and inches! We lose our youth, beauty, smooth skin, muscle tone, shape, hair, vision, hearing, sexual ability or interest—the list goes on.

In the middle years, the losses take on a different flavor. Now they seem to be more frequent, permanent and, in many cases, negative. Who rejoices over losing their hair and teeth or graduating to bifocals or tri-focals? We don't usually call these growth experiences. It seems that losses now build on other losses.[6]

Frequent Losses

Consider also the frequency of losses. We don't usually lose many of our friends to death early in life. Yet in our later years, it occurs more frequently. The longer we live, the more losses of friends and relatives we experience.

We are builders. The middle years (ages 35-55) are spent building. Family, career, status, a home, emotional attachments, memories and so on. That's the first half of life. The second half is a time when what has been built gradually diminishes and dissolves—and it's hard to let go.

The single most common form of bereavement in this country is the loss of a parent. Often, if the parent is middle-aged or elderly, the death is somehow less of a loss than others. The author of *Losses in Later Life* describes the problem:

The loss of parents is a difficult loss for many adults because its grief is largely ignored and under-valued in our society. The grief that adults feel when their parent(s) die is a secret grief. It is the hidden pain that millions of adults carry around with them year after year.[7]

Gradual Losses

The loss of children (when they move out and establish their own families) can be complicated. For some it involves the loss of identity as a parent, the loss of influence over the children, the loss of dreams or feelings of success if the children didn't turn out as expected and the loss of marriage if the children were the glue.

The loss of children is a gradual loss. They begin to exclude you from their lives, they don't have as much time for you or interest in being with you, and they don't take your advice as much. There will also be a loss of your generational values and beliefs since they are developing a new generational standard.

Accumulated Losses

When you are younger, you may have one physical problem, which is corrected. But when you get older, these accumulate. Muscles don't work as well or recover as fast. You're slower in your response time; you have new glasses, and one day you notice that people are talking in softer tones. You may have to adjust the television volume higher!

We seem to handle losses best when they are infrequent. Yet after midlife, we move into a time zone of accumulated losses. It's difficult to handle the next one when we are still recovering from the present one. Our coping skills may be overtaxed, and if our coping skills were never highly developed, these losses are going to hit us quite hard.

Final Losses

The other difficulty with losses is their finality. If you lose a job at age 27, you simply look for another. But what if you lose your job of 30 years at age 57? What do you do now, especially if this is all you know how to do and there isn't as much demand for your skills anymore?

Losing a spouse when you're older is limiting as well. If you divorce or your partner dies when you are young, it is much easier to find another mate than if you are older. And if you are a woman, it is even more difficult.

Most women who are over 50 and lose their husbands do not remarry.[8]

When the word "loss" is mentioned, death and divorce often come to mind. But what about the impact of a diagnosis? "The doctor said it was cancer or ALS or Parkinson's." Or what about a disability? Where is the ritual in our culture to commemorate the grief of a lifelong disability? Rather, it is a state of chronic grief. In time, we no longer distinguish between the person and the condition. The person is referred to as the condition: "He is CP" or "He is MS."[9] And the date of the diagnosis is an anniversary that brings sorrow.

Identity Losses

Identity losses for men and women may occur periodically throughout their lifetimes. These are difficult for many because of the intangibility of the issues. However, they are real and they have the potential for destruction or tremendous growth.

Threatened Losses

One of the hardest losses of life are threatened losses. Unfortunately, the possibility of their occurring is very present, and there is little that you can do about it—your sense of control is destroyed. For example, you've worked for 19 years at the same company. At 20 years, all of your benefits will be secure. But then you are informed that due to the sluggish economy and lost contracts, 40 percent of the firm's employees will be terminated at the end of the month and that the length of employment is no criteria for being retained. Will you be one of the 40 percent?

There are many other threatened losses in life such as the following:

- awaiting the outcome of a biopsy from the medical clinic
- a spouse's saying, "I'm thinking of divorcing you"
- a business investment's possibly not coming through
- being sued by an angry employee or customer
- being in a foreign country and the government threatens to retain everyone as hostages
- a friend's telling you that they suspect your son has been using drugs

All of the above are potential losses—they could occur. There is little you can do about them, and you feel the loss before it occurs—you feel helpless.

WHAT ARE SOME COMMON WAYS TO GROUP, OR IDENTIFY, LOSSES?

The losses we experience in life can be grouped, or identified, in numerous ways. There are seven major types of loss that can impact any of those we counsel, as well as ourselves.

Material Loss

Material loss occurs when someone has an important attachment to a physical object or familiar surroundings. Most people have material attachments, yet they might not want to admit it if they appear to be materialistic. This material attachment usually is the first loss for children—or at least the first one they're aware of. It could be a broken toy, or that the dog ate their ice-cream cone. In addition, if the loss is replaceable, it could mask grief. The following are some questions to ask:

- What is the most significant material loss you've ever experienced?
- What is the most recent material loss you've experienced?

Relationship Loss

A relationship loss is the ending of opportunities to relate to another person, which involves talking with them, sharing experiences, touching, negotiating, conflicting and being in the emotional and physical presence of another human being. This loss can come from a move, a divorce, a death or just growing up. The following are some questions to ask:

- What is the most significant relationship loss you've ever experienced?
- What is the most recent relationship loss you've experienced?

Intrapsychic Loss

An intrapsychic loss is the way your counselees view themselves when they undergo a change. They lose an emotionally important image of themselves, as well as the possibilities of what might have been. It could involve changing personal plans or giving up a longtime dream. Or there could be an expectation lost. When someone loses courage, faith or hope, it fits here. Often, some of these losses have never been shared with others, so the loss that occurs is also a secret. The following are some questions to ask:

- Has the way in which you view yourself changed recently?
- Could it be that a dream you had or some plans you made have gone by the wayside?

Functional Loss

We're all aware of functional losses such as losing muscular or neurological functions of our bodies. These come with age but also throughout our lives. Memory losses among the elderly can be devastating. Some of these losses occur all at once, whereas some, such as the diminishing ability to hear, are progressive over the years. In addition, these losses reflect another highly significant loss—the loss of autonomy. Gradually, the "I can manage" capability diminishes. While you can replace material losses, you can't replace functional losses. You learn to adapt or adjust if possible; yet some losses, such as losing a breast, a limb or an eye, may be quite overwhelming. The following is a question to ask:

- What physical changes have occurred in your life in the past five years that may have been significant losses for you?

Role Loss

Role loss impacts all of us. It's the loss of a social role or of an accustomed place in some social network. The significance of its impact depends on how much of a person's identity was tied in to the role. Being promoted or demoted, losing a spouse (i.e., you're no longer married), changing your career, no longer being a student and retiring all fit here. When a person experiences this, he or she wonders, *How do I behave at a function now?* One author said, "If that role disappears, we are literally without a part to play, and may indeed not know 'the lines.'"[10]

The following are some questions to ask:

- In what way have any of your roles in life changed?
- How did this change your life and the way you view yourself?

Systemic Loss

There is also a type of loss called systemic loss. It's a bit different than a role loss in that it usually occurs when a person leaves a group, which upsets the balance of the system. It could be a jovial coworker who leaves a hole in the system because his or her cheerfulness and humor are no longer there. It could be a child's leaving home. This is what one father said:

Driving home from dropping off my daughter at college for her first semester, I experienced a great feeling of loss that she had now left our family circle, and our *family life would never be the same.* This was the first instance of one of our children reaching college age, and though intellectually I was prepared for this I found that emotionally I wasn't.[11]

The following is a question to ask:

- Has any significant person left your life or group recently?

Ambiguous Loss

A very difficult and often unrecognized loss is an ambiguous loss. There are two basic kinds of ambiguous loss. In the first type, people are perceived by family members as physically absent but psychologically present, because it's unclear whether they are dead or alive. Missing soldiers and kidnapped children illustrate this type of loss in its worst form. Many who lost loved ones in the 9/11 twin-towers attack continue to search for and yearn for the body or any personal object of the missing person. When nothing is available, there is no closure.

In the second type of ambiguous loss, a person is perceived as physically present but psychologically absent. This condition is illustrated in the extreme by people with Alzheimer's disease, addictions and other chronic mental illnesses.

Of all the losses experienced in personal relationships, ambiguous loss is the most devastating, because it remains unclear and indeterminate.

Perceiving loved ones as present when they are physically gone or perceiving them as gone when they are physically present can make a person feel helpless. It makes them more prone to depression, anxiety and relationship conflicts. It leads to complicated grief. It's not easy for stepchildren to handle a biological parent's being excluded or for a spouse to constantly deal with his or her brain-injured spouse who now functions like a five-year-old. How does ambiguous loss do this?

First, because the loss is confusing, people are baffled and immobilized. They don't know how to make sense of the situation. They can't problem solve because they do not yet know whether the problem (the loss) is final or temporary.

Second, the uncertainty prevents people from adjusting to the ambiguity of their loss. They reorganize the roles and rules of their relationship with the loved one so that the couple or family relationship freezes in place. This is often referred to as a frozen-grief response. This happened with servicemen and their families during their deployment to Afghanistan following the 9/11 terrorist attacks. The uncertainty existed because the servicemen and their families weren't sure where they were going or when they would return.

Third, people are denied the rituals that ordinarily support a clear loss, such as a funeral after a death in the family.[12]

The following is a question to ask:

• Is there any kind of loss that you've experienced that doesn't make sense or you can't seem to get any closure over?

Disenfranchised Grief

Recently a new category of grief has been defined. It's called disenfranchised grief. It is a grief that people experience when they incur a loss that is not or cannot be openly acknowledged, publicly mourned or socially supported.[13]

There are three types of disenfranchised grief. The first type is when the relationship is not recognized. Examples include nonkin relationships such as lovers, friends, neighbors, foster parents, colleagues, in-laws, stepparents and stepchildren, caregivers, counselors, coworkers and roommates. It also includes relationships that are not socially sanctioned, including extramarital affairs, cohabitation and homosexual relationships. There is a certain belief that we should only mourn the loss of a family member, but often the nonkin relationships are stronger. Friendship can be one of the deepest types of relationship, as well as one of the most fragile. There is little place in our society for grief over friends and, thus, limited support.

> **Sudden loss or sudden death usually leaves the survivor with a sense of unreality that may last a long time.**

The second type is when the loss is not recognized as a loss because society does not define it as significant. Kenneth Doka cites examples, which include abortion, pet loss and psychological death (resulting from a coma).

The third type is when the griever is not recognized. A person may be socially defined as not able to grieve. Dr. Doka offers examples such as the very young, the elderly, the mentally disturbed and the mentally retarded.[14]

The unidentified and unrecognized losses go on and on: the loss of passion in a relationship; the losses incurred by multiracial couples; the losses incurred when you're a caregiver, as well as when you no longer have that role; the losses incurred when you can't lose weight or when you are homeless and so on.[15]

How Do You Weigh the Impact of a Loss?

Keep in mind that how and when a loss occurs have an impact upon those you counsel. A loss that is anticipated or gradual has a different effect than a sudden or unexpected loss.

Unexpected Loss

Sudden loss or sudden death usually leaves the survivor with a sense of unreality that may last a long time. The following is a question to ask:

- Did you end up with a feeling that this isn't real or that maybe it's a bad dream and you'll wake up?

Sudden loss or death fosters a stronger-than-normal sense of guilt expressed in "if only" statements. The following is a question to ask:

- Could it be there are some "if only" questions running through your mind?

> **Whenever a loss occurs, it's important to see it in the context of life experiences so that there's an understanding of the full impact of what has happened.**

In sudden loss or death, the need to blame someone else for what happened is extremely strong. The following is a question to ask:

- Often when something like this occurs, we look for someone or something to blame. Has this occurred yet?

Sudden loss or death often involves medical and legal authorities. The following is a question to ask:

• Do you need any assistance dealing with the medical or legal community?

Sudden loss or death often elicits a sense of helplessness on the part of the survivor. The following is a question to ask:

• I'm wondering if you've experienced any feelings of helplessness or the desire for someone to come in and take charge?

Sudden loss or death leaves the survivor with many regrets and a sense of unfinished business. The following is a question to ask:

• Often when something like this happens, there are regrets or a feeling that something is left unfinished. Has that happened to you?

In the event of sudden loss or death, there is the need to understand why it happened. Along with this is the need to ascribe not only the cause but also the blame. Sometimes God is the only available target, and it is not uncommon to hear someone say, "I hate God." The following is a question to ask:

• What are the why questions that you've experienced so far?

Remember, all of these questions are for the purpose of normalizing what they're experiencing and assisting them to face it head-on.

HOW CAN WE NOT FEAR LOSS?

Many losses can be anticipated and even planned for to ease their impact. But the majority of losses your counselee experiences are difficult to grieve over. Why? Because they're usually not accepted as losses.

Everyone lives with fear to some extent; some more than others. The fear of loss is deeply ingrained within all of us. Every loss we experience from early infancy on becomes part of this pool of fear within us.

Sometimes people wear items or amulets around their necks as protection against misfortune, which is another way of saying "loss."

Our society is afraid of misfortune. Some people even tend to avoid those who've experienced loss, for fear that it might be contagious. Ironically, though, we all have and will experience loss.

Whenever a loss occurs, it's important to see it in the context of life experiences so that there's an understanding of the full impact of what has happened. Identifying all of the accompanying losses, as well as the impact of the current loss on a counselee's thinking, will help him or her learn to better handle future losses. Remember that past losses have an effect on current losses and attachments and that all of these facts affect the counselee's fear of future losses and his or her ability to make future attachments.

ADDITIONAL QUESTIONS TO ASK

During the experience of loss, there are hidden questions that fester underground but that at some point need to be addressed. You may want to ask the following questions:

- Do you ever wonder if you'll recover from this loss? or Will you survive?
- Do you wonder if it's all right to continue with your life without whatever or whomever has been lost to you?
- Do you wonder if you can be happy and fulfilled, knowing that what you've lost is really gone and that your life will now be different?

The principles and procedures of helping individuals grieve their losses will be covered in chapters 5 and 6.

RECOMMENDED RESOURCES

Resources for Those Who Help Others

Boss, Pauline. *Ambiguous Loss.* Cambridge, MA: Harvard University Press, 1999.

Doka, Kenneth, ed. *Disenfranchised Grief: Recognizing Hidden Sorrow.* Lanham, MD: Lexington Books, 1989.

Harvey, John H., ed. *Perspectives on Loss: A Sourcebook.* New York: Bruner/ Mazel, 1998.

CHAPTER 5

HELPING OTHERS RECOVER FROM THEIR LOSSES IN LIFE

(PART 2)

We live in a society and culture that has chosen to ignore and avoid two major issues of life—loss and grief. Because of this, many of those you counsel will need to be guided through the process of grief as well as educated about grief. It will be easier with some than with others. It is also important to remember that when attempting to help another person recover, you need to become as knowledgeable as possible about the grief process.

When anyone enters into grief, they enter into the valley of shadows. There is nothing heroic or noble about grief. It is painful. It is work. It is a lingering process. But it is necessary for all kinds of losses. It has been labeled as everything from intense mental anguish to acute sorrow to deep remorse.

Genesis 6:6 says, "He was grieved in His heart" (*NKJV*). Who is this talking about? God Himself experienced grief; He knows what it is like.

GRIEF IS EMOTION FILLED

There are a multitude of emotions involved in the grief process—emotions that seem out of control and often appear in conflict with one another. With each loss come bitterness, emptiness, apathy, love, anger, guilt, sadness, fear, self-pity and helplessness.

A young wife made the following comment when she found out that the baby she and her husband had been planning to adopt was going to be kept by the mother: "I feel as though something has been ripped right out of the inside of me. It hurts so bad. I feel hollow inside." That is grief.

A divorced father said, "For the past 13 years, when my son has come home for the weekend and I have to take him back to his mother, I grieve all over again. The pain comes back with all its intensity. It still cuts like a knife." That, too, is grief.

> **Grief appears differently at different times, and it flits in and out of a person's life.**

Grief encompasses a number of changes. It appears differently at different times, and it flits in and out of a person's life. It is a natural, normal, predictable and expected reaction. It is not an abnormal response. In fact, just the opposite is true. The absence of grief is abnormal. Grief is a person's own personal experience. A loss doesn't have to be accepted or validated by others for someone to experience or express grief.[1]

Grief has been defined as intense emotional suffering. It's a sense of acute sorrow or deep sadness. The word "grief" is actually derived from a Latin verb meaning "to burden." Many feel as though they are carrying such a heavy weight, or burden, that it's all they can do to put one foot in front of the other. Grief is not an illness, but it may feel like one. A person's body reflects the grief—tightness in the chest or throat, heart palpitations, dry mouth, shortness of breath or hollowness in the pit of the stomach. Sleep is disrupted, as are eating patterns.[2]

GRIEF DOES NOT HAVE A COOKIE-CUTTER SOLUTION

Mourning is the expression of grief. The word "mourning" is derived from a Latin verb, which means "be anxious." Mourning is a process of remembering and thinking about what was lost, and this can make a person feel anxious or uncomfortable.

Since mourning is a process, it is appropriate to view it in terms of stages, and indeed, many people writing on the subject of grief have listed 9 to 12 stages of grief. One of the difficulties in using the stage approach is that people do not pass through them sequentially.

Some talk about phases; but as with stages, there are overlaps between the various phases, which are seldom distinct. Others talk about tasks, which are much more consistent with the concept of grief work. The term "tasks" implies that the mourner needs to take action and do something:

> Certainly, grief has distinct components. But bereavement is probably the most complex, intense, and prolonged human emotion. An exact science it isn't. Helen Fitzgerald, author of the wonderfully comprehensive *The Mourning Handbook*, calls grief "unlike other life experiences." It's a jungle in there. Everything inside you is savage and snarled. Screeching emotions and venomous attitudes. No trail in sight. And just when you thought tomorrow was the way out, everything gets overgrown again overnight.[3]

Not everyone will fit the stage, or phase, theory of grieving. Harold Ivan Smith said:

The identification of stages as the "normal" grief pattern infringes on an individual's freedom to grieve uniquely and thoroughly.[4]

There will be times when those you help will hear someone say, "If you're a Christian, you don't need to grieve. After all, Christians are to be different." How is this reconciled with the following:

And taking with Him Peter and the two sons of Zebedee, He began to show grief and distress of mind and was deeply depressed. Then He said to them, My soul is very sad and deeply grieved, so that I am almost dying of sorrow. Stay here and keep awake and keep watch with Me (Matt. 26:37-38, *AMP*)?

Unfortunately, anyone who makes such an uncaring statement has not searched the Scriptures. Note the fact that the Bible is a book filled with grief. You may want to share this chart with those you counsel (see figure 3).

Figure 3

BIBLICAL INSIGHTS FOR UNDERSTANDING GRIEF

The Bible dignifies grief by presenting it as a God-given, therapeutic response to loss.

GOD GRIEVES
The Father grieves over evil in Noah's day (see Gen. 6:6).
The Son grieves over the death of Lazarus (see John 11:35-38).
The Spirit grieves over believers' sin (see Eph. 4:30).

GOD RESPONDS TO OUR GRIEF
Recording our tears (see Ps. 56:8)
Sympathizing with our weakness (see Heb. 4:15-16)
Eventually ending our grief (see Isa. 65:19; Rev. 21:4)

Continued on next page

Figure 3—*Continued*

GRIEF MEASURES THE MEANING OF OUR ATTACHMENTS
Our attachment to friends (see John 11:36)
Our attachment to family (see Gen. 50:1)

GRIEF POTENTIALLY INTERRUPTS LIFE'S ROUTINES
Leaving mourner with little appetite (see 2 Sam. 12:17)
Causing mourner to wish for death (see 2 Sam. 18:33)
Multiplying mourner's illness and death (see 1 Sam. 4:18-22)

GRIEF POTENTIALLY PERSISTS OVER AN EXTENDED PERIOD OF TIME
For seven days (see Gen. 50:10)
For thirty days (see Num. 20:29)
For seventy days (see Gen. 50:3)

GRIEF IS POTENTIALLY EXPRESSED IN A VARIETY OF WAYS
Before a loss (see Matt. 26:37-38)
By shock, numbness or denial (see Mark 8:31-32)
In anger (see Job 10:9)
Through bargaining (see Isa. 38:1-22)
   with depression (see 2 Sam. 12:16-18)
   with acceptance (see Phil. 1:12,21-24; 4:11-13)

GRIEF IS POTENTIALLY FACILITATED BY VARIOUS EXPRESSIONS
Songs (see 2 Sam. 1:17-27)
Poetry (see Lam. 1—5)

GRIEF HAS A PURPOSE

Why grief? Why do we have to go through this experience? What is the purpose? Grief responses basically express three things:

1. Feelings about a loss

2. Protest at a loss as well as a desire to change what happened
   and have it not be true
3. Effects of the devastating impact of a loss[5]

You may want to ask the person you're counseling what he or she believes about grief and what its purpose is. If he or she is unaware, share these reasons with them.

First, the purpose of grieving over loss is to go beyond one's reactions in order to face the loss and to work on adapting to it. This is what one writer said about grief:

A friend used to say that grief is a shadow on the moon that darkens the night into almost unbearable blackness. The shadow must pass slowly across the moon's face before the light is restored and the night softened by lingering memories.[6]

Dr. Gerald May, M.D., said, "Grief is neither a problem to be solved nor a problem to be overcome. It is a sacred expression of love . . . a sacred sorrow."

The way out of grief is through it, which means facing it.

Second, the stages of grief that people pass through are normal and can be immediate or postponed, but the underlying principle is that *people should be encouraged to do their grief work.*

Some people delay their grief work, which results in depression. Instead of feeling sad, they appear apathetic and numb. Unfortunately, some churches teach that we must *always* think positively, be in control and take charge of our lives. Such teaching does not help the bereaved.

Thus, denying grief is an unfortunate response. The person is often not encouraged or allowed to go through the valley of his or her own "little deaths." By rising above his or her own hurt, he or she does not admit having been hurt. In a real sense, the person is refusing to mourn his or her loss. Eventually, though, it *will* surface. People who carry this unfinished business with them into their future experiences and relationships will suffer unrest, conflict and ongoing depression.[7]

Within delayed grief you may also find a residue of delayed anger. This needs to be admitted, identified and expressed. You might say to the person, "If I were in your situation, I would be quite angry." Help the person deal with his or her anger, but also help the counselee accept it as normal. Otherwise, he or she may experience excessive guilt over being angry.

Roy Fairchild's statement on delayed grief is very insightful:

> The refusal to mourn is the refusal to say goodbye to beloved persons, places, missed opportunities, vitality, or whatever has been "taken away," which is how many religious people view these losses. The refusal to mourn our earlier disappointments condemns us and rigidifies us, as it did Lot's wife. Genuine grief is the deep sadness and weeping that expresses the acceptance of our inability to do anything about our losses. It is a prelude to letting go, to relinquishment. It is dying that precedes resurrection. Our sadness reveals what we have been invested in; it is the cost of a commitment which has been shattered.[8]

Third, the worst grief is the one a person experiences personally. Suggest to the counselees that they not compare themselves with anyone else.

Fourth, grief is hard work. Effective grief work is not done alone. Find out who else they have in their lives who could help them.[9] Remember:

> Grievers cannot extricate themselves from their cistern called grief. They need a rope. Grievers need someone on the other end to pull. But they really need individuals to pad the ropes—not with pat answers or spiritual clichés or even Scripture promises but with hope.[10]

Last, the purpose of grief is to bring counselees to the point of making necessary changes, so they can live with their losses in healthy ways. It's a matter of beginning with the question, Why? Why did this happen to me? And then eventually moving to a new question, How can I learn through this experience? When the how questions replace the why questions, counselees have started to live with the reality of the losses. Why questions reflect a search for meaning and purpose in the losses, while how questions reflect a search for ways to adjust to the losses.[11]

MAKING NECESSARY CHANGES

What does your counselee have to do to get to the point of making necessary changes? There are four steps that can be followed for most types of losses.

Change the Relationship

First, they need to change their relationship with whatever they lost. If it was a person, they eventually need to come to the realization that the person is dead and that they're no longer married to or dating him or her.[12] They need to recognize the change and develop new ways of relating to the deceased person. They must learn to exist *without* the person the way they once learned to exist *with* the person. Memories—both positive and negative—will remain with them. They need to say good-bye to whatever and whomever they lost. Perhaps this can be called acknowledging and understanding the loss.

With some losses the development of a new relationship is relatively easy and clean, since in a short time there is a diminishing emotional effect of the loss. A lost opportunity, job, competition or pet or a wrecked car or stolen wallet may not have the same lasting effect compared to other experiences. One of the most difficult loss situations is a divorce in which children are involved and one of the spouses does not want the divorce. Because of the children, there is a continuing relationship over the years and a constant experiencing of past, present and future losses.

Get On with Life

Second, the counselee needs to get on with life, which involves several steps—some of which may come as a surprise. For purposes of this discussion, let's consider death or divorce as the loss.

One step is keeping the loved one alive as a memory in a healthy and appropriate manner. Another step is forming a new identity without the person's presence in your life.

As these steps are in process and the grief work is being completed, the emotional energy that was once invested in the person lost is now freed up and reinvested in other people, activities and hopes, which in turn provides emotional satisfaction once again.

Develop a New Relationship

Third, the question must be asked: How can someone develop a new relationship with the one they lost?

We keep people alive all the time in our society as we reflect upon who they were, their achievements and their impact upon society. Many ask the question, "I wonder what he would think if he were alive today?" or "Wouldn't he be surprised to see all of this?" People reflect on what their deceased spouse would do in a certain situation, using their memory of what the person would do as one of several options.

However, what is abnormal is the feeling that one must do things or see things just the way the deceased did. Sometimes in divorce, a spouse continues to allow the memory of a pressuring spouse to dominate present life. This is unhealthy. This allows the person to maintain an emotional investment in the other person. A phrase like "She would have wanted me to paint the house this color" could be indicative of continued emotional investment.

Get Real

Fourth, counselees needs to realize that sometimes when they lose something that has played a significant part in their lives—be it a job or person—their memory of the thing or the person becomes distorted. With the loss of a person, the usual response is to recall only the positive aspects. But in time, there must be realism. Thoughts and memories, both good and bad, positive and negative, and situations we're glad occurred—and those we wish had not—need to be reviewed realistically. By doing this, a balanced, realistic, accurate pool of memories develops. These realistic images are the ones needed to develop the new relationship with the person. The images will generate accompanying feelings as the person faces the recognition that the "lost" person is no longer with them.[13]

Relationship Loss

It's helpful to suggest to counselees that they write a relationship history graph about the person they lost (especially a spouse in death or divorce) and identify the positives and negatives of their relationship. See figure 4 for such an example:

Figure 4

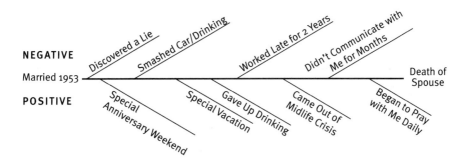

Step One

On the bottom portion of the graph, positive events and experiences are listed. It is good for counselees to first list 5 to 15 separate events. The length of the vertical line indicates how much the particular event meant to the person. Above the line, negative, upsetting or hurtful experiences are identified, and again, the length of the vertical line indicates the intensity of the experience.

Step Two

After counselees have sketched out their graph, suggest that they write a paragraph giving as much description as possible for each event—including both positive and negative events.

It's important for them to allow their feelings to emerge. Some of their feelings may include regrets or "if only" statements.

The following are some feelings from one person's descriptions:

- My feelings are all mixed up. I wish they were clearer.
- I'll never forget the times we prayed together. That meant so much.
- I'm glad we have pictures and a video from our anniversaries.
- I'm still hurt over the drinking. I wish it hadn't ever been a part of our marriage.
- I'm sorry for my angry outbursts.
- I'm angry you died so young. I feel cheated. Our marriage was getting better when you died. We needed more time.
- I wish we could have talked more. There's so much more I wanted to tell you.

Some of these statements may bring to mind thoughts such as, *I wish things could be different; I wish things had been better; I wish we had spent more time together; I wonder what would have happened if . . . .*

It helps to ask your counselee, "Can you think of any regrets or 'if only' statements you have about your relationship?"

The following is a list of one person's regrets and "if only" statements that were written over the loss of a relationship:

- I regret that I became bitter toward you.
- I regret that I didn't tell you how much I cared for you.
- I regret our busy and separate lives.
- If only we hadn't quarreled the day before you died.
- If only we had taken more time to play together.
- If only you hadn't worked so much the last several years.

These statements reflect a critical attitude toward what was done and not done and what the deceased person did or didn't do. If a person remains in this critical stage, inaccurate memories of the relationship begin to emerge. And the more this happens, the more difficult it is to complete the grief work. Therefore, discuss each regret with them: "How would your life be different if . . . ?" "Describe how you would have preferred to act." "What could we do now to overcome this lost opportunity?"

What a person discovers through this evaluation can bring them out of any pattern of denial and help them recover. It may seem like the pain is too much and unnecessary, but it is very important for developing this new relationship.[14]

Step Three

What about recalling how a deceased person died? Is that necessary or normal? Repetitious reviewing helps a person realize that his or her needs, hopes, expectations and dreams of continuing to be with the deceased person are not going to be fulfilled. He or she simply cannot be with this person the way he or she used to be—whether it be a loss by death or divorce. If the loss is by death, each time the person reviews it and the surrounding events, his or her understanding of it will increase and perhaps add more meaning. The counselee may tend to resist this, since the memories bring pain; but each time he or she does recall, the person will discover that he or she has a lot more control over the memories than the person thinks.[15]

Step Four

The next step is for counselees to develop their own self and life to encompass and reflect the changes occurring because of the loss. This will vary depending upon whether the loss involved a job, an opportunity, a relationship, a parent or a spouse.

Step Five

The fifth step is discovering and taking on new ways of existing and functioning without whatever it was that was lost. This involves taking on a new identity, but without totally forgetting the lost thing or person. Some people never seem to relinquish what they lost. They hang on and dwell upon what they never had or what they lost, and unfortunately, it dominates their entire lives. Often they become bitter. After the death of a child, some parents create an enshrinement. They keep their child alive by keeping his or her room just the way it was when he or she was alive. This can go on for many years and prolongs the grief.

Others respond with the opposite reaction. After the loss occurs, they act as though it never existed. They seem to block its existence from their memory and attempt to move on. Neither of these approaches reflects a healthy response. There is a balance. There is a way—especially in the loss of a person—to keep a loved one alive appropriately.

> **In healthy remembrance, counselees will find themselves having thoughts or doing, saying and feeling things that show that the other person continues to influence them.**

There are healthy ways to hold on to something that was lost. In healthy remembrance, counselees will find themselves having thoughts or doing, saying and feeling things that show that the other person continues to influence them.

As a counselor, you can say, "Your first step is recognizing that the other person is gone and you are still alive. At first you may not feel as though you're very much alive." Sometimes people say they can't go on or don't want to go on without the one who left or died. Yet there does come a time of emotionally letting go and reinvesting in life in a new way.

Step Six

Another step is deciding what there was about life with the other person that can and should be retained. It's deciding what is healthy to retain. In the case of the loss of a spouse, will they continue to

- go to the same coffee shop each morning for breakfast?
- go on an evening walk around the park?
- display special items they either made or purchased together?

- maintain any of the daily or weekly routines the two of them shared together?

The other question to ask is, What will you purposely relinquish from life with your partner? Attending the monthly couple's Bible study and potluck dinner might not be continued, even if some encourage him or her to go back once in a while. It might be too painful for some, yet I've heard of others who continued in spite of the discomfort. Many of the couple's activities, however, will be dropped.

For the counselee to relate to the deceased in a healthy manner, he or she could

- learn more about the deceased's favorite activities and involvements;
- look at home movies or videos, listen to tapes of the deceased or reflect on some of his or her stories to bring back memories; and
- decide to try some of the deceased's favorite foods or engage in his or her former activities just to experience what he or she did.

Memories are preserved by visiting the deceased's childhood school and work and going to the cemetery. I've said to some, "It's normal to talk about someone you lost; do things based on what you learned about your loved one or reflect on memories. Part of who you are today and how you respond today is based upon your relationship with your loved one. Perhaps he or she taught you new insights, perceptions, skills, appreciations or values. Your loved one left an indelible mark upon you, didn't they? Sometimes you may even be surprised as you discover yourself solving problems or responding in a manner that your loved one did." And often they nod in agreement.

During this process, there may be a change in identity from "we" to "I." This can be one of the most painful transitions of all, especially in the loss of a spouse. Counselees will see the world around them differently. Some of their friendships may change as well. They'll retain old friendships but adjustments may occur. Their identity may have been as a couple and most of their friendships were couple relationships. But now they're alone. Their time with couples will diminish. They'll need both some old and new relationships with people who share portions of their new identity with them.

Step Seven

Finally, after taking these practical steps, counselees will discover new directions for the emotional investments that they once had in the lost object, situation or person.[16] The recovery stage involves reinvesting emotional energy in something new that can give satisfaction and fulfillment, since the relationship with the person or object lost cannot. However, we are not talking about a replacement. A new cat cannot replace the old cat; a new dog cannot replace the former dog; a new person is not a replacement for the former person, and any attempts to make them into replicas are unhealthy responses. In the loss of a person, counselees may benefit by reinvesting, not in another person right away, but perhaps in a service organization, ministry or new career. It could be something immediately tangible or the pursuit of a goal.

These are the steps. This is the task. It's not easy. It's not without pain. But lives go on—different and new. Yet how lives go on, how different lives go on and what is new in life depends on the counselees' grief work.

These steps may sound simple, but they're not, since all of grief involves work, effort and pain. At the appropriate time, discuss with your counselees some suggestions for accomplishing each of the seven steps.[17]

THE GRIEVING PROCESS

Helping people acknowledge and understand their loss is essential to starting the grieving process. Depending upon the severity, some losses will soon be faint memories, whereas others—such as the death of a child or spouse—may never be completely settled. This process, though, does encourage counselees to integrate the losses into their lives.

Face the Loss

In time, counselees need to overcome the shock and denial and face the painful reality of what occurred. It means saying, "Yes, unfortunately this did happen." Facing their loss means they don't

- attempt to postpone the pain,
- deny that it actually happened, or
- minimize their loss.

If they do any of the above, they intensify their pain and drag it out. Instead, it may be helpful for them to admit that they do want to postpone or deny their loss. These are normal protective responses. A common myth of grieving is to bury feelings. Expressions like, "Don't cry," "Don't feel bad—after all, he's with the Lord now" and "Don't feel bad, you can handle it" are damaging myths. Often they're expressions made by people who feel anxious when a loss occurs because they never learned what to say. But no matter what the reason, these are nonsupportive statements. Warn your counselees that they might hear these. Your task is to help them experience the eight facets of facing their loss.

Facet One. To assist in the grieving process, at some point, it may help to have counselees make a list of the effects of their loss. This is one step in facing their pain. In addition, you can have them write each of these four statements on a 3x5 card or make them a card in advance. Ask them to concentrate on one statement each day. On the back of the card, have counselees outline what they think the statement means for their grief experience. The following are the four statements:

1. I believe my grief has a purpose and an end.
2. I will be responsible for my own grief process.
3. I will not be afraid to ask for help.
4. I will not try to rush my recovery.[18]

Facet Two. Another step in the process of facing a loss is to tell others about it as soon as possible. Call it by its name: "It was a loss and I am grieving." Suggest that counselees keep track of who they told, the date they told them and that person's response. Some have found it helpful to tell at least one or two people each day during the first week of their loss, but this varies from person to person. In addition, people need to share in moderation and not overdo it.

For your counselees, it means making the conscious decision that they are going to face the loss and feel the pain. The best way to describe this kind of pain is intense emotional suffering. You're going home to the uninvited guests of anger, denial, fear, anxiety, rage, depression and many other emotions. And they will cry! If crying is difficult for them, suggest a programmed cry.[19]

Depending on the severity of their loss, their numb reaction can be a slight down feeling or an incapacitating numbness. After it lifts—usually 24 to 36 hours later—the pain is faced and the feelings surge like the seasons of the year. There are seasons of depression, anger, calm, fear and eventually hope. However, they don't follow one another in a progressive way. The feelings overlap and often are jumbled together. Just when counselees think they're finally over one emotion, it comes bursting through the door again. This is normal. This is necessary. This is healing.

The best description I've read of this healing process is by Scott Sullender:

> The griever's suffering is never constant. The waves of pain are alternated by lulls of momentary rest. Initially, of course, in acute grief situations the waves are intense and frequent. Gradually, as one is healed the waves are less intense, less prolonged and less frequent. One can almost imagine the wave patterns charted on a graph, like radio waves. Each peak represents a mountain of pain, each valley a resentful lull. Initially, the peaks are high and long, the valleys are narrow and short, and the frequency is high. Gradually, ever so gradually, the storm quiets. Yet months and years later an isolated wave can still come crashing ashore. On sentimental holidays for example, the memories of lost loved ones are often raw. "Every Christmas," says a widowed, middle-aged woman, "after all the busyness is over,

I sit down and have a good cry." Periodically, an isolated wave of grief washes against the shore of one's soul.[20]

If the loss involves a trauma, the grief process can go on for years. When the first anniversary of 9/11 occurred, many in New York felt like a scab had been lifted and once again there was an open, raw wound. For many people, all of the television programs, memorials and ceremonies reactivated the depths of their wounds.

What most of us don't realize is the intensity of feelings in the pattern of peaks and valleys of grief. Consider the intensity of grief as indicated by figure 5:

Figure 5

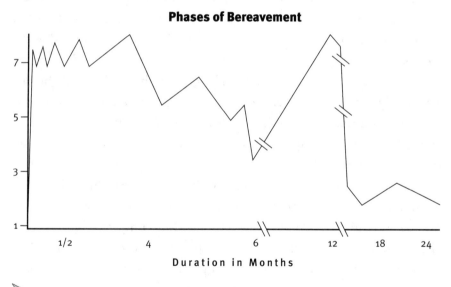

Phases of Bereavement

Duration in Months

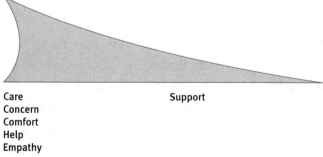

Care
Concern   Support
Comfort
Help
Empathy

Notice the jagged peaks. The pain and grief actually intensify at three months and then gradually subside—but not in a steady fashion. They go up and down. Most people don't need a reminder of the first-year anniversary of the loss of a loved one. The intensity of grief comes rushing in with an intense pain that rivals the initial feelings of loss. Notice how the amount of support diminishes just at a time when it is needed the most. If anyone attempts to tell your counselee that they should be "over it by now" or "feeling better" at any of these times, they may get upset, which is understandable. It's also understandable that others will lack understanding of the process of grief unless they've been through it themselves. Share this chart with them and let them know that their feelings are normal.[21]

Facet Three. How long will grief last in the loss of a person? Who the person was has much to do with the response. The response to any loss is directly related to the knowledge of the person who has died; it is the nature of the attachment. The intensity of grief is determined by the intensity of the attachment. The more intense the love relationship, the more severe the grief reaction. The greater the presence of the one who died to the sense of well-being and self-esteem of the counselee, the more intense the grief reaction. We call this the security of the attachment. In all relationships, there are both positive and negative feelings. Usually, the positive feelings far exceed the negative feelings. However, in the case of a highly ambivalent relationship (negative feelings that coexist in almost equal proportion to the positive ones), the grief reaction will be more intense. There is also a tremendous amount of guilt associated with highly ambivalent relationships, often expressed as, "Did I do enough?" There may also be intense anger at being left alone. The history of conflicts—as well as more recent disagreements—will be an important determinant of the grief response.

Facet Four. How a person died will also say something about how the survivors grieve. Traditionally, deaths have been catalogued under the NASH categories: natural, accidental, suicidal, homicidal. The accidental death of a young child may be grieved differently from the natural death of an older person. The location of the death—whether it happened close or far away—is also important and can also determine the grief response.

Another factor is advance warning. Was there some advance warning, or was the death unexpected? Studies suggest that survivors of sudden deaths—especially young survivors—have a more difficult time one or two years later than people with advance warning.

My mother lost two husbands. Her first husband died at work. Mom was 33 years old. She was driving to town when a car approached from the other direction. When the other driver saw her, he slowed his car until he came alongside, leaned out the window and yelled, "Your husband, Paul, is dead." Twenty-seven years later the police came to her door to inform her that her second husband, my father, had been killed in a car accident driving home from work. Her grief—as a result of both deaths—lasted for years.

> **As you minister to people in grief, the more you know about their past, the more helpful you can be in assisting them.**

Facet Five. What about the circumstances surrounding the death? Sometimes, the circumstances make it easy for survivors to express their anger and blame, especially in the case of accidental deaths. In circumstances where the survivor killed the person—be it accident or homicide—guilt will obviously be a key factor in coping with the loss.

As you minister to people in grief, the more you know about their past, the more helpful you can be in assisting them. There are some key factors that can assist you in predicting how a person might grieve. You need to know if they had previously lost someone and how they grieved. Were their previous losses grieved adequately, or are they bringing unresolved grief to the new loss? A person's prior mental history also is important to consider. This is especially true of people with a history of depressive illness. They will often have a more difficult time grieving than those without such a history.

Facet Six. Life-changing events that occurred in the past six months to one year are important to recognize. An assessment of how the person views the impact these changes have made is important for determining how a person will respond to a loss.

As you work with grieving individuals, there are a number of other factors to take into consideration in order to understand their response to loss. Factors you should consider are age and sex; how inhibited they are with their feelings; how well they handle anxiety; how they cope with stressful situations; how dependent they are; how much difficulty they have forming relationships; and whether or not they have a borderline or narcissistic personality disorder.[22]

In addition, you will need to be aware of each counselee's individual social structure of life. These structures are a form of a subculture and provide us with guidelines and rituals for behavior. In order to understand how the person is going to grieve, you have to know something about his or her social, ethnic and spiritual background. How much emotional and social support is available from others? This includes those inside and outside the family. This support can be significant in the bereavement process, and it's not just how much is available but how it's perceived by the grieving person. Most studies find that those who do not recover well have inadequate or conflicted social support.

Facet Seven. Were you aware that some people derive benefits from grieving? A survivor might get a lot of mileage in his or her social network because of grieving, and this will have an effect on how long the grieving goes on.

Facet Eight. Finally, what are the other stresses occurring at this time? Other factors that affect grief recovery are the concurrent changes and crises that arise following a death. Although some change is inevitable, there are those individuals and families that experience a high level of disruption following a death—including serious economic reversals. These, too, need to be considered.[23]

Communicate the Loss

It is alright for people to take charge and let others know what they need and don't need at this time in their lives. Your task as a helper is to give them permission to do so. That doesn't mean that others will perfectly comply, but they can try. Unfortunately, counselees may have to educate others around them about grief. They can tell others that they want them to call, to ask how they're doing and not to be put off by their tears or anger.

Many have found it beneficial to prepare a set of instructions to give to others as a guideline on how to respond to them. If they have to explain their loss to several people each day, it becomes not only wearisome but also painful to go over the loss again and again. Silence, as well as stumbling and hurtful comments from others, will add to their pain. The following letter describes three things:

1. what has happened;
2. what kind of responses to expect from the writer; and
3. what others can do to help them.

It's a road map teaching others how to respond.[24]

Dear Friend,

Recently I have suffered a devastating loss. I am grieving, and it will take months and even years to recover from this loss. I wanted to let you know that I will cry from time to time. I don't apologize for my tears since they are not a sign of weakness or a lack of faith. They are God's gift to me to express the extent of my loss, and they are also a sign that I am recovering.

At times you may see me angry for no apparent reason. Sometimes I'm not sure why. All I know is that my emotions are intense because of my grief. If I don't always make sense to you, please be forgiving and patient with me. And if I repeat myself again and again, please accept this as normal.

More than anything else, I need your understanding and your presence. You don't always have to know what to say or even say anything if you don't know how to respond. Your presence and a touch or hug lets me know you care. Please don't wait for me to call you, since sometimes I am too tired or tearful to do so. If I tend to withdraw from you, please don't let me do that. I need you to reach out to me for several months.

Pray for me that I would come to see meaning in my loss someday and that I would know God's comfort and love. It does help to let me know that you are praying for me.

If you have experienced a similar type of loss, please feel free to share it with me. It will help, rather than cause me to feel worse. And don't stop sharing if I begin to cry. It's all right, and any tears you express as we talk are alright, too.

This loss is so painful, and right now it feels like the worst thing that could ever happen to me. But I will survive and eventually recover. I cling to that knowledge, even though there have been times when I didn't feel it. I know that I will not always feel as I do now. Laughter and joy will emerge once again someday.

Thank you for caring about me. Thank you for listening and praying. Your concern comforts me and is a gift for which I will always be thankful.[25]

DEFENSIVE MODES

Sometimes the person you're counseling discovers different ways to negate the pain of his or her loss.

Denial

One of those ways is denial. When the loss is rejection, abandonment or death, denial is the usual defense. It's the expression, "No! That's not true. It can't be true!"

Denial is a common companion in loss. Unfortunately, some choose to live in a world of denial most of their lives. Those who come from extremely dysfunctional families are more prone to this. When they deny, they emotionally avoid realizing that a loss has occurred or is going to occur. The most serious kind of denial is denying not only the reality of what has occurred but also the effects of the loss. Everything is blotted out of a person's mind at this time.

Grieving is moving through several levels of denial. Each stage brings home the reality of the loss a bit deeper and more painfully. First, we accept it in our heads. Second, in our feelings. Finally, we adjust our life's pattern to reflect the reality of what has occurred. Yet if we prolong denial, there's a price to pay. The energy expended to keep denial operating drains us, and in time, we are damaged emotionally, thus delaying our recovery.

Rationalization

Rationalization is another defense against loss: "It really didn't hurt that bad. There are better men out there. After all, I only went with him for two years." Other responses might be: "That job wasn't the best", "Who needs a BMW?" and "Well, she lived a good long life and now she won't have to suffer anymore." These statements have one basic purpose—to help us cope with the pain of the loss. They attempt to lessen the impact. However, if counselees live with rationalization too long, they'll begin to believe it.

Idealization

A third defense people use to handle loss is idealization. This is a way to distort reality by idealizing what was lost. It is when negative characteristics or aspects are overlooked—whether it is the loss of a job, the death of a family member or an unwanted divorce.

PRACTICAL EXERCISES

There will be those who resist, fight or hate grief. This, too, is normal. Just as in heart surgery, you'll find those who would like to have a grief bypass.

Communicating with Your Grief is a helpful experience that can be used with just one person or in a group. This exercise allows the grieving people to take charge of their grief.[26] It dispels the notion that grief is a six-headed monster that will get you if you mention its name. The task here is to communicate with your grief as though it has a personality of its own. You will talk to your grief and you will listen to your grief.

You are going to write two letters. Use whichever stationery you normally use for writing to friends or family.

The first letter is from you to your grief. Use the following form:

Date: _____   Time: _____

To Grief:

Sincerely,

Before you write, ask yourself: *If I could tell my grief what I am thinking and feeling, what would I say? What do I want my grief to know about its impact on my life?* Be as frank as you can. Write the letter and sign it.

Approximately 24 hours later—but no less than that—write the second letter. This one will be from your grief to you. Use the same format as the first letter, except address it to yourself and sign it, "Sincerely, Grief." Before writing, ask yourself: *What do I think my grief is telling me? What does it want from me?* As frankly as possible, write to yourself on behalf of your grief.

Put the letters aside for a day or two, and then read them both out loud to yourself. What do the letters reveal about your attitude toward the experience of grief? What new thing can you learn about yourself from your letters?

Find someone with whom you can share the letters and talk about your discoveries. If you are in a support group, this is an excellent activity to share with one another.

The following is an example of the first letter:

Dear Grief,

You are a rascal. You take our energy, our organizational abilities, our brains and do strange things with them. I was prepared for the immediate grief and to feel the loss of my spouse for a long, long time. I was not prepared for the laziness, low energy level and stress.

I am impatient with it all. You take so much out of us when we really need to be able to function well. I do not understand why.

I must confess, though, that you've done good things for me. I am more compassionate, understanding and tolerant. You have given me new ways to be of service, and God will show me those ways. Perhaps after I've had more time to look back, I will feel differently about you, but for right now, you are not one of my favorite friends. I am a better person because of you and I must not lose sight of that.

Sincerely,

Irene

A day later Irene wrote the following letter to herself from her grief:

Dear Irene,

I'm sorry I've caused you so much pain. Remember what your pastor said at the funeral: "Grief is the noblest emotion of all." It truly is the last gift of love you can give to your husband. So experience it in a normal way. Let your own time frame happen. I know you are working hard to get through this phase of your life. I commend you for that. But I also want to say, "Let go and let God." Just put it in God's hands. I suggest you read the verses on death in the Bible. Remember, there is an atomic bomb of hope waiting to explode between the front and back covers of your Bible. I sense your excitement as you search through those Scriptures. You may be truly amazed at what you find.

Begin to use your time more wisely. Get extra sleep once or twice a week. You'll be alright. Soon your energy level will return. You may even lose the weight you've been trying to lose for some time. In time you will walk lighter. You will sit lighter. You will feel great.

I am your friend. I am a part of life. There is a purpose for me. You will see.

Sincerely,

Grief[27]

APPROPRIATE EXPECTATIONS TO HAVE IN THE GRIEF PROCESS

To assist someone in grief, you must first and foremost help the counselee understand what to expect. Therefore, use this sample listing of appropriate expectations. Either go over these one by one with the counselee or give it as a homework assignment for him or her to read and to bring back to the next discussion.

You can expect the following:

- Your grief will take longer than most people think.
- Your grief will take more energy than you would have ever imagined.
- Your grief will involve many changes and will continually develop.
- Your grief will show itself in all spheres of your life.
- Your grief will depend upon how you perceive the loss.
- You will grieve for many things both symbolic and tangible—not just the death alone.
- You will grieve for what you have lost already and for what you have lost for the future.
- Your grief will entail mourning, not only for the actual person you lost, but also for the hopes, dreams and unfulfilled expectations you held for and with that person, and for the unmet needs because of the death.
- Your grief will involve a wide variety of feelings and reactions, more than just the general ones often depicted with grief, such as depression and sadness.
- Your loss will resurrect old issues, feelings and unresolved conflicts from the past.
- You may have a combination of anger and depression, such as irritability, frustration, annoyance and intolerance.
- You will feel some anger and guilt—or at least some manifestation of these emotions.
- You may experience grief spasms—acute upsurges of grief that occur suddenly without warning.
- You will have trouble thinking about memories, organizational tasks and intellectual processing, and making decisions.
- You may feel like you are going crazy.
- You may be obsessed with the death and preoccupied with the deceased.

- You may find yourself acting socially in ways that are different from before.
- You may find yourself having a number of physical reactions.
- Others will have unrealistic expectations about your mourning and may respond inappropriately to you.

In summary, your grief will bring with it—depending upon the combination of the above factors—an intense amount of emotion that will surprise you and those around you. Most of us are unprepared for the global response we have to a major loss. Our expectations tend to be too unrealistic, and more often than not, we receive insufficient assistance from friends and society.[28]

Remember, there is no shortcut in grief, but with your assistance it will be easier for the griever.

RECOMMENDED RESOURCES

Resources to Recommend and Give to Others

Deits, Bob. *Life After Loss*. New York: Fisher Books, 1999.

Kinnaman, Gary. *My Companion Through Grief*. Ann Arbor, MI: Servant Publications, 1996.

Mitsch, Raymond R., and Lynn Brookside. *Grieving the Loss of Someone You Love*. Servant Publications, 1993.

Sittser, Gerald. *A Grace Disguised: How the Soul Grows Through Loss*. Grand Rapids, MI: Zondervan Publishing House, 1998.

Wright, H. Norman. *Recovering from the Losses of Life*. Grand Rapids, MI: Revell, 2000.

Resources to Give to Handle the Holidays

Smith, Harold Ivan. *Journaling Your Decembered Grief*. Kansas City, MO: Beacon Hill Press, 2001.

Zonnebelt-Smeenge, Susan J., and Robert C. DeVries. *The Empty Chair: Handling Grief on Holidays and Special Occasions*. Grand Rapids, MI: Baker Book House, 2001.

CHAPTER 6

HELPING A GRIEVING PERSON RECOVER AND SAY GOOD-BYE

PRACTICAL STEPS

There are many positive steps that aid a person in recovering from a loss. We've talked about several steps already in chapters 4 and 5, but we will focus on the final step here—learning to say good-bye.

What can be done to help a person move on? The general approach is to help him or her identify and express his or her feelings. For some this is easy. Others struggle with trying to figure out what they are experiencing as well as talking about it. Yet many counselees have been helped by this visual definition of grief:

Figure 6

Grief—A Tangled Ball of Emotions

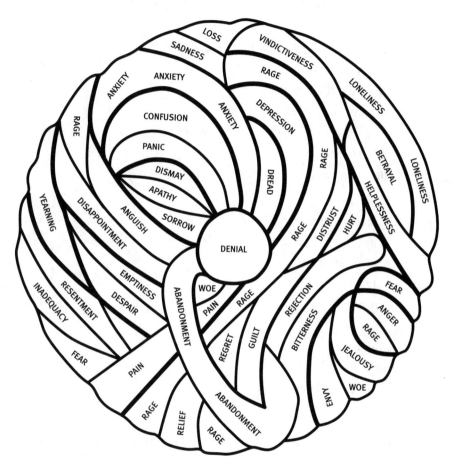

This ball of grief comes in handy. Suggest that your counselees use it to help them identify what they are experiencing. The feelings described in this image are what most everyone experiences; it's definitely normal to experience them.[1]

EVALUATE FEELINGS

From time to time, it is beneficial to help counselees look closely at an emotion in order to determine its extent and describe what it feels like.

Depression

Consider depression. The following chart with three questions has been helpful because of the way the questions were constructed:

1. What is it like when you feel depressed?
   - a slate-gray afternoon
   - a cold, drizzling rain
   - a hot, oppressively humid day
   - a freezing morning with a bitter wind
   - a dull, overcast sky
   - a season of ankle-deep mud and slush

2. Right now, what type of weather forecast best describes where you are in the spiral process of dealing with your loss?
   - stormy conditions
   - partly cloudy
   - heavy rain
   - a thaw
   - chilly days
   - sunny days ahead
   - gentle spring breezes are blowing

3. Where on the scale would you place your current grief process?

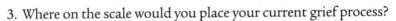

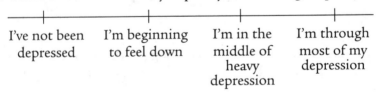

| I've not been depressed | I'm beginning to feel down | I'm in the middle of heavy depression | I'm through most of my depression |

Anger

Anger is another common response. When we lose things or people, we can become angry. There are many reasons for anger. Anger and even rage are common reactions to the loss of a loved one, as people think about what they have lost and how life has changed overnight. The following are some more specific reasons why people may get angry:

- They may be angry at the person who died and has left them behind to face a lot of legal work and loneliness.
- They may be angry at themselves for not doing enough.
- They may be angry because of the change in lifestyle inflicted upon them.
- They may be angry over role changes that have to be made within their family.
- They may be angry for what is perceived to be a loss of control in their life.
- They may be angry that family and friends have gone back to their normal lives and aren't thinking about their grief.
- They may be angry that the rest of the world busies itself around them as though nothing has happened.
- They may be angry with God.

As you work with the grieving person, it may be helpful to initially ask, "Could it be that there is some anger because . . ." (complete your sentence with any one of the previous reasons that you deem appropriate).

Anger is a warning sign. Anger may be the first emotion a person is aware of, but it is rarely the first emotion one experiences. The emotions that most frequently precede anger are *fear, hurt* and *frustration*. Not only are they painful, but they also drain a person's energy and increase one's sense of vulnerability.

> **Anger can camouflage, or at least minimize, pain. It even may be possible to influence or change the source of anger.**

At an early stage of grieving, counselees might notice that anger can divert their attention from these more painful emotions. Anger can camouflage, or at least minimize, pain. It even may be possible to influence or change the source of anger. It doesn't take a person long to learn that it's easier to feel anger than it is to feel pain. Anger provides an increase of energy and decreases a sense of vulnerability. Help your counselee to ask himself or herself, *What is the pain behind my anger? What can I do with the anger?* and *How can it be managed as well as dissipated?* This is what one man did for himself that was very beneficial:

I finally realized that holding on to my anger kept me victimized. As much as I wanted someone to pay, I knew it wouldn't happen. So I decided on a 90-day plan. I would allow myself to keep 10 percent of my anger, since I know I'm human and won't be perfect. But each day for 90 days I would give up 1 percent of my anger. The fact that I had a goal and then developed a plan really encouraged my recovery. Each day I spent 15 to 20 minutes identifying who or what I wanted to avenge. I wrote it out each time and then put it in the form of a brief letter. I stood in a room and would read it out loud unedited. Sometime it wasn't pretty. And sometimes I read it to a friend because it helped having a live body there.

Each day I wrote the phrase, "I forgive you for . . ." and then put down the first reason I could think of for not forgiving. It was like I was full of rebuttals against forgiving. I would always end the morning by reading a praise psalm out loud. Then I would lift my hands to the Lord and give Him my anger for the day. I thanked Him for what He was doing, even if I did feel bitterness. It kept me pinned down and stuck. I didn't want to forgive. They didn't deserve it.

But I kept at it. I wondered after 30 days if I'd even make 3 percent improvement. But by the time 60 days were over I felt ahead of schedule. I was improving. I was growing. I got well. Sometimes the anger and grief still hit me. I can live with that even if it's a companion the rest of my life. I have days and weeks when I feel whole again. Praise God for this.

Anger can be used positively and creatively in many ways. The following are several ways in which anger has been used positively:

- A relative of an accident victim *convinced* the hospital chaplain staff to establish new and improved procedures for helping survivors of sudden accidental deaths.
- A parent *proposed* that warning signs be posted at the pond where his son drowned to help reduce similar accidental deaths.
- A grandmother *requested* that parents of cancer victims be provided printed information about cancer as well as the location of support groups.
- An adult son who lost his elderly father *organized* programs for a local convalescent home.
- A young mother who lost her preschool-age daughter *solicited* toy contributions to give to a local pediatric ward.

Notice the action words in italics: "convinced," "proposed," "requested," "organized" and "solicited." They reflect how these people not only redirected their anger but also brought relief and a sense of control to their lives.[2]

IMPLEMENT WAYS TO CONTROL FEELINGS

There are many more positive steps people can take that will help both them and everyone else who learns of their loss cope better.

Construct an Explanation Letter

Too often others don't know how to respond or what to say to another's loss. Therefore, it helps for those who have lost to express themselves.

One creative way of letting others know about their situation is through a weekly update on their answering machine. A man I counseled for two years shared this idea and his own personal experience with me. The following is an example of three messages from a husband whose wife died of cancer on January 25, 1997. He continued these messages over a period of four years and transcribed each one so that he has a written record of his grief journey. Many would call purposely when he was at work just to get the weekly update. This was his way of letting others know how to pray for him. It also helped to answer his adult daughter's questions and brought a new closeness to his family.

March 7, 1997

Hi, this is Dave.

I'm feeling overwhelmed and lost. And I'm feeling the great loss of all the dreams Irene and I have worked for over the years, gone. My fear of the future is like a deep sharp pain. I wasn't ready for this to happen. Please pray that we can do what it says in Proverbs 3:5-6: "Trust in the LORD with all your heart and lean not on your own understanding; in all your ways acknowledge him, and he will make your paths straight."

April 19, 1997

It's been five months since I've been able to really hold Irene in my arms and hug her.

There were many times after her surgery when I wanted to comfort her with a hug. But all I could do was hold her hand and rearrange her pillows into a different position for her. I feel great loss and am really sad about that.

I know there are others who are in stressful circumstances and relationships. So if you'll leave your name, I'll pray for you. Because I'm reminded of what God—through Isaiah—says about comfort for His people: "Do you not know? Have you not heard? The LORD is the everlasting God, the Creator of the ends of the earth. He will not grow tired or weary, and his understanding no one can fathom. He gives strength to the weary and increases the power of the weak" (Isa. 40:28-29).

August 12, 1997

Hi, this is Dave.

I'm having lots of ugly thoughts and worldly feelings, and I'm filled with shame, because I struggle with taking them to the Lord and leaving them at the foot of the Cross.

So my prayer request is to help us remember the words of the psalmist: "The LORD is gracious and compassionate, slow to anger and rich in love. The LORD is good to all; he has compassion on all he has made" (Ps. 145:8-9).

Designate a Crying Time

There will be those who say to you, "I just can't stop crying. What can I do?" For some, tears and crying seem to consume their day. If this is the case, suggest that they use a designated crying time. Some have found it helpful to establish a specific time to cry. Have counselees set a timer for 30 minutes, sit, and cry over the pain and loss until the timer goes off, and then have them get into some activity that's productive.

If the tears come back, suggest to counselees that they interrupt the tears—as best as they can—and remind themselves that tomorrow they'll have another opportunity to cry. The next day have them do the same, but set the timer for 29 minutes. The day after that have them do the same, but set the timer for 28 minutes and so on, until the 30 days are up. By this time, most people feel their lives are no longer dominated by tears—there is now more of a balance.

Create a Remembrance List

One of the concerns that many people struggle with is not remembering the details of their lost loved one's life. If this is the case, they may want to consider creating a collection of 1,000 one-line statements. The husband previously mentioned, who lost his wife after 35 years to cancer, suggested the following: Every time you think of something about the person you want to remember, write it down in one line. When you have 1,000 one-line statements, you'll probably have most of what you want to remember. By doing this activity, you'll find that it will help you with your grief.

Start Journaling

Many have heard of daily journaling as a means of recovering. There are various ways in which to do this. The following are steps that were taken by the same man who taped messages and recorded one-line statements. You may want to duplicate the following steps on how to begin journaling and give them to those you're counseling:

1. Date every entry.
2. Start writing, drawing or doodling.
3. Be honest.
4. Be open.
5. Be willing to risk—remember, it's private.

In addition, you can share the following 20 journaling styles that can help your counselees through their recovery:

1. Captured Moments
   Write about an event or place that triggers memories or feelings for you.
   Examples: Revisit a special place; recall something your loved one did or you did together; remember conversations with others.
2. Stepping-Stones
   Write about times in your relationship.
   Examples: what you did; where you met; where you vacationed; places you went on dates; holidays you celebrated.
3. Topic of the Day
   Number down on a page the days of the month. Beside each number write a subject topic that needs to be thought out and written about.
   Examples: 1/1 Job; 1/2 Money; 1/3 House; 1/4 Parent or Child.
4. Character Sketch
   Try to see yourself as others see you.
   Examples: Journal on a particular Scripture, such as Matthew 7:3-5. What are the planks in your eye? What do people (or a particular person) do that angers you or makes you crazy?
5. Current Milestones
   Write about current events.
   Examples: moving; selling the house; making big purchases.
6. Write Letters to God, Lost Loved Ones, Yourself or Others
   A good time to write letters is when there is unfinished business

with the person who is gone or when there is a desire to experience closure of unresolved issues. The key is not to send them. This makes the letter a safe, nonthreatening atmosphere. Examples: Write letters that express deep emotions (i.e., anger, grief, hostility, resentment, opinions and affections).

7. List Opposites

   Under each word, make a list of things that come to mind when you think of a particular emotion.

   Examples:

Glad	Mad	This is what	This is what
Happy	Sad	makes me glad	makes me sad
+	-		
Positive	Negative		
Best	Worst		

8. KISS—Keep It Short and Simple

   Example: I'm scared and I feel like I'm going to break.

9. Theme Word for the Week

   Choose a word or topic and write about it every day.

   Examples: loneliness; confusion; change.

10. Quick Starts

    Begin with a question or statement and write about any thoughts or feelings it triggers. Keep a list of possible questions or statements on a page in your journal.

    Examples: I'm excited about . . . ; I'm alone and it's . . . ; My secret . . . ; I wish . . . ; I'm afraid of . . . ; I always . . . ; I never . . . .

11. Trigger Memories

    Use photograph albums or other objects to trigger thoughts, feelings and memories. Write about them freely.

12. Visit a Favorite Place

    Let the thoughts and feelings flow. Write about them as they come. Don't worry about grammar, spelling or composition.

13. Clustering

    Use both sides of the brain; use a keyword or phrase to trigger thoughts, feelings and memories; and then write about each cluster.

Keep it simple. It's okay to repeat yourself. Nonsense is okay. Poor grammar is okay. Try to complete your thoughts in one sitting. Just write them down.

Figure 7

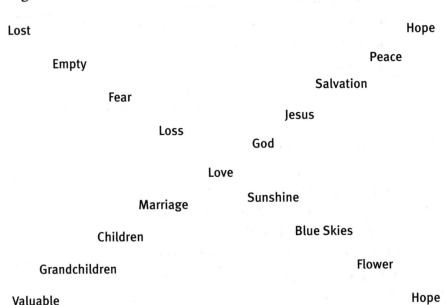

14. Secondary Losses
    Write about other losses you have experienced related to the loss or your loved one.
    Examples: friends; identity; income; house; activities.
15. Peripheral Events
    Write about events that led up to or surrounded the loss.
    Examples: illness; fight; poor communication.
16. Make a Card
    Write out or make a card for a special occasion such as a birthday, anniversary, Mother's Day.
    Example: Make or buy a Mother's Day card and write about what kind of mother she was or what you remember about her being a mother.

17. Write about how you feel about writing or how you feel about what you are writing.

18. Time Line

Begin with a date or range. Do a blessing time line, listing blessings in chronological order. Start with the earliest blessing you remember receiving. The same format can be used for other topics such as losses.

Example: Try combining a loss and blessing time line. Start with your losses, then add the blessings.

19. List of 100

Using a topic or sentence starter, list as many responses as possible.

Examples: Things I like about . . . ; Things I don't like about . . . ; Things that have changed . . . ; Things that I fear . . . ; Things that are blessings . . . ; Things I remember about . . . .

20. Egg Symbol

Select one picture to represent your feelings about your loss. Redraw it periodically over time.

Example: Draw an egg. At the beginning of your loss, it might be in a thousand pieces like Humpty Dumpty, who fell off the wall. As time passes, sometimes it will look put back together and sometimes it will be in more pieces.[3]

All of the previous suggestions are part of the process of helping a person take that important step of saying good-bye.

Say Good-Bye Beforehand

Being able to say good-bye helps those in grief move toward a sense of closure. It also brings back some of their feelings of control over their life and circumstances that were diminished by the loss.[4]

When people say good-bye, they are acknowledging that they're no longer going to share their life with whatever they lost. They will always have the memory, but now they acknowledge that they will live without whatever it was they lost.

What helps one person through grief may not be meaningful to another. Some parents who experience miscarriage simply move on with their life and have no real need for good-byes, whereas others have a memorial service. It all depends on the individual and how he or she copes with grief.

In her book *Brainstorm* (Macmillan, 1980), Karen Brownstein describes her ordeal of having a brain operation. It may sound strange, but prior to the attendant's shaving a portion of her head for the exploratory operation, Karen stood in front of the bathroom mirror, held and caressed her long hair and said good-bye to it. Later, when she underwent radiation therapy for an inoperable, malignant tumor and subsequently lost all of her hair, it was easier for her to accept the loss because of having held a brief good-bye ceremony.

Being able to anticipate a loss usually makes it easier to handle. It's not uncommon to hear someone exclaim in anger, "They left, and I never got a chance to say good-bye!"

Being able to say good-bye prior to the loss will help the grieving process.

There are even those who have returned to the location of a former place of employment, stood in front of the building and said good-bye. Sometimes their farewell was out of a storehouse of positive memories and other times out of anger.

Ask your counselee, "Who or what have you said good-bye to in your life?" Then ask, "Is there something or someone you need to say good-bye to in your life?" Recently I said good-bye to a home stored with 31 years of memories. It was a positive decision, but reflecting and saying good-bye helped sever the tie.

Write More Letters

One of the better ways of saying good-bye to many kinds of losses is in writing. Writing a letter is both a way to say good-bye as well as a way to express intense feelings of loss. It may be an angry letter or one that is full of joy and sadness.

• One person wrote to a friend who was about to die of cancer, expressing his great appreciation for his friend.

- Another person sent a good-bye letter to her elementary school teacher, who she had hoped would teach her own children but who was now retiring.
- One former addict wrote a farewell letter to his drugs, telling them good-bye and describing what a problem they had been for him.
- Many women have written good-bye letters to one of their breasts before or after a mastectomy. This has helped them cope with a loss that is very traumatic for a woman, especially a younger woman. It is a loss that is usually accompanied by an extended time of depression and mourning.
- Over the years, numerous people have written letters to a deceased friend, spouse, child, parent, brother, sister or any other significant person.[5] It helps to bring home the reality that the person is gone.
- It could also be a good-bye letter to a significant person during one of life's major transitions.

Saying good-bye is not morbid, pathological, a sign of hysteria or of being out of control. It is a healthy way to make the transition into the next phase of life.

> **Saying good-bye is not morbid, pathological, a sign of hysteria or of being out of control. It is a healthy way to make the transition into the next phase of life.**

TAKE THE STEPS TO SAY GOOD-BYE

How do you go about saying good-bye? Ask the one you're counseling this question. First of all, help the person identify what he or she thinks needs to be expressed in the good-bye. What are the actual words he or she wants to say? What words would express appreciation and regrets or would complete something that was never finished with whomever or whatever was lost?

Suggest to counselees that they write a good-bye letter or talk out loud to the person or object they lost. One divorcee actually wrote a letter to her marriage and addressed it as though the loss were a real person. This may be different, but it was very helpful.

They can address a good-bye letter to a lost dream, a lost hope, a lost business or even a change in their vocational life. The more regrets and "if only" thoughts they have, the more important their letter is, since this is their opportunity to express what was never verbalized.

It helps to let a letter rest for a day and then read it aloud to themselves or to a trusted friend.

In writing a good-bye letter, it is crucial to be as honest as possible. Remind them that their intention is to complete their emotional relationship with whatever or whomever they lost. Timing is also very important. It shouldn't be done prematurely. If there are still resentments existing in their relationship with the person or object lost, these need to be identified and relinquished.

Suggest to them that before writing the actual letter, it is helpful to identify incomplete business. This could involve

- making amends,
- offering forgiveness, or
- expressing significant emotional statements.

Making Amends

The first step in helping counselees overcome the death of a loved one is to help them identify how to make amends. Making amends is not only saying they're sorry but also changing their responses. Ask the question, "What positive or negative events or situations did you not make amends for? You can be sorry for something you did or for something you wished you'd done or said. Can you think of any at this time? If there was a negative behavior that you wished you could have changed earlier, what are you doing about it now?" One man said, "I wish I had been less negative and critical and more verbally appreciative. Now I'm making sure that

I give two or three affirmations or compliments for every criticism or concern I express."

A woman said, "I wish I had told you more often how special you were to me. At least I've started doing this more with other people."

Offering Forgiveness

The second step is identifying those areas where forgiveness is needed. Many people struggle with this and have a number of reasons for not forgiving.

It's important to identify the reasons for not forgiving someone or something. You could suggest that one way to do this is by identifying in writing the objections to forgiving the other person. Suggest that they take a piece of paper and write the person's name at the top. Then below the name write a salutation, as in a letter. Under the salutation write, "I forgive you for . . . " and then complete the sentence by writing down everything that has bothered them over the years. Encourage them to try to capture the immediate thought that comes to mind after writing the statement of forgiveness. Often it's a rebuttal or objection to forgiving the other person. Write the statement opposite the "I forgive you" statement. Continue the exercise by writing "I forgive you" statements followed by their immediate thoughts—even if they are contradictory. Have them repeat the process until they have drained all of their pockets of resistance and resentment. When they come to a place that they can write "I forgive . . . " several times with no objections or rebuttals, then forgiveness is occurring.

Expressing Emotion

The last step involves significant emotional statements that usually involve things the person wishes they could have said. It's as though they want one last conversation with the person. Talk with them about this. To help them, suggest the following sentence starters and say, "If you could complete these statements to that person, what would they be?" Statements could include the following:

- I appreciate you for . . .
- I was so proud of you for . . .

- It meant so much to me . . .
- Thank you for . . .
- You were so special at . . .

Some have also found it helpful to recall the last conversation with a loved one and then to share what can be remembered of it.

At the conclusion of your counselee's exercises, suggest that he or she say good-bye. This involves every aspect of the relationship: Good-bye to any emotional and physical incompleteness, pain or lack of forgiveness. Say good-bye to every part of the relationship.

Another variation of this is writing a "Letting Go" prayer:

Dear Friend,

Your death has left a gaping hole in my life and heart, producing an emptiness I know will never be filled. I miss your voice, the sound of your laughter, those funny endearing things you did and those moments when I was infuriated at you. I miss the dreams I had for and with you. I miss the future we will never have and the past which, no matter how long it may have been, will never be long enough.

I have wept for you as well as for myself. I have raged in anger at you, at God, at the world, at anyone and anything which seemed to be an appropriate target. I have tried to understand why you are no longer with me, why I have to struggle through this world without you. Some people have reached out to help me; others have turned away, unable to bear the pain I carry. I do not ask them to share it with me, only to listen as I talk and cry. I have waited in the darkness for some sign that you are in a better, safer place, and even when I may have received it, I could not help but question how it could be better if I am not there with you. And I have wanted to join you so often when the aloneness threatened to overwhelm me.

Through all of this turmoil and doubt, I have managed to come this far. I have not yet achieved my goal, but at least I can now recognize that I am on the road to recovery. I am not sure

how I will go on without you; no matter how many other important people may be in my life, you have always held a special
place, and it is hard to imagine you not with me.

Will you walk beside me now as a friend, comrade, loving
companion? I cannot come to you at this time; I can only trust
that we will be reunited in God's love and compassion. But my
life must go on; it is time for me to begin to live my life for myself
and others. As I think of letting go of you, I must now ask that
you also let go of me. Your new life must seem as strange to you
as my new life seems to me; perhaps the memory of me is as comforting to you as your memory is to me. Let us, then, agree to
explore these new existences, these new spheres of reality, knowing that we carry the other with us, not with chains, but with loving, open hands.

I let you go, my dearest. I know you will never leave my side,
as I will never leave yours. Thank you for the wonderful, unique
relationship we shared. When we meet once more, I look forward
to sharing these new experiences with you. I love you. I miss you.
I will never forget you.[6]

There are other ways to express good-byes. Sending a contribution
to a church or charity in the name of the person can be an acknowledg-
ment. Some people set up a living and lasting memorial by donating
a scholarship or painting, by planting a flower garden or a tree or by having a plaque made. At one of the largest Christian conference grounds
in Southern California, it is possible to dedicate a tree in the name of
a loved one. They also can talk with God about how much they miss
their loss and share with Him what they want to say in their good-byes.

LOOK OUT FOR THOSE IN GRIEF

Many in grief drift just as the homeless do. We as believers need to be
alert for the signs of grief and for the life situations that lead to grief.
You can't wait for people to come to you. We need to reach out to them.
Who are they? Consider the following:

- those who do not have a church home
- those who have stopped attending church because of a congregational situation or tension
- those who do not speak English or Spanish
- those whose loved one died while away from their home community, while traveling on business or vacation
- those whose loved one was undergoing treatment in a specialty medical center in another city
- those who have recently relocated or are in transition
- those who have been abused by organized religion
- those who are members of highly dysfunctional families
- those who have been marginalized by society
- those who cannot be involved in church due to health reasons or a disability
- those with mental disorders and disabilities
- young children
- ex-spouses or in-laws[7]

We as Christians need constantly to be on the lookout for those in need. We need to live life extending grace and aid through God's strength and not on our own.

CHAPTER 7

WHAT IS A CRISIS?

When you hear the word "crisis," what pictures or words pop into your mind? "Urgent." "Upset." "Helpless." "Nonfunctional." "Hopeless." "Anxious." "Numb." "Hysterical." "Dangerous." "Out of control." Perhaps it's all of these.

The Word of God describes many people in a state of crisis. Paul was one of them.

Now Saul, still breathing threats and murder against the disciples of the Lord, went to the high priest, and asked for letters from him to the synagogues at Damascus, so that if he found any belonging to the Way, both men and women, he might bring them bound to Jerusalem. And it came about that as he journeyed, he was approaching Damascus, and suddenly a light from heaven flashed around him; and he fell to the ground, and heard a voice saying to him, "Saul, Saul, why are you persecuting Me?" And he said, "Who art Thou, Lord?" And He said, "I am Jesus whom you are persecuting, but rise, and enter the city, and it shall be told you what you must do." And the men who traveled with him stood speechless, hearing the voice, but seeing no one. And Saul got up from the ground, and though his eyes were open, he could see nothing; and leading him by the hand, they brought him into Damascus. And he was three days without sight, and neither ate nor drank (Acts 9:1-9, *NASB*).

This is one of the most famous accounts of a sudden religious conversion, and frequently, such a conversion can precipitate a crisis. It is an excellent example, depicting some of the characteristics of a crisis. This experience affected Paul in many ways. First, it affected him physically, for he could not see and had to be led by the hand into the city. Second, he was changed spiritually, for he became a believer and reversed his whole pattern of responding to Christians. Third, he was affected mentally and emotionally, for he didn't eat or drink for three days. His conversion caused a crisis, or turning point, and in his case, for the better.

> **Crises are turning points where counselees can possibly move toward growth, enrichment and improvement, or they can move toward dissatisfaction, pain and, in some cases, dissolution.**

We have talked about the word "crisis," but to minister to others properly we need to become expert in understanding its meaning. Webster defines crisis as a "crucial time" and "a turning point in the course of anything."[1] This term is often used for a person's internal reaction to an external hazard. It's an upset in a person's baseline level of functioning. It's a disruption of the balance of his or her life. Anxiety, depression and tension increase.[2] A crisis usually involves a temporary loss of coping abilities, and the assumption is that the emotional dysfunction is reversible. If a person effectively copes with the threat, he or she then returns to prior levels of functioning.

The Chinese character for "crisis" is made up of two symbols—one for despair and the other for opportunity. When doctors talk about a crisis, they are talking about the moment in the course of a disease when a change for the worse or better occurs. When some counselors talk about a marital crisis, they are talking about turning points when the marriage can go in either direction—it can possibly move toward growth, enrichment and improvement; or it can move toward dissatisfaction, pain and, in some cases, dissolution.

CAUSES OF A CRISIS

When people are thrown off balance by an ensuing event, they are then experiencing a crisis. The term is frequently misused. It is applied incorrectly to even everyday annoyances. The terms "stress" and "crisis" are used interchangeably but incorrectly. Keep in mind that underlying a crisis is a loss of some kind; therefore, crisis and loss go hand in hand. But there is a difference between a crisis and trauma, which will be discussed later in chapters 10 and 11.

A crisis can be the result of one or more factors. It can be a problem that is too great or overwhelming, such as the death of a child; or it can be a problem that, to most people, is not serious but, for a given person, has special significance. Because of this, it becomes overwhelming for the individual. It can also be a problem that comes at a time of special vulnerability or when the person is unprepared for it. Ordinarily, people handle a stopped-up sink with no problem, but if it happens when they are sick, they may feel overwhelmed. It can occur when the person's normal coping mechanisms are not functioning well and when the person does not have support from others whom he or she needs. Often, a crisis is just one step away from a trauma.

Crises are not always bad. Rather, they represent a pivotal point in a person's life. Therefore, it can bring opportunity as well as danger. As people search for their methods of coping, they may choose paths of destruction—but they may also discover new and better methods than they previously had available.

FOUR COMMON ELEMENTS OF A CRISIS

A Hazardous Event

A hazardous event is an occurrence that starts a chain reaction of events that culminates in a crisis. For example, a young wife who prepared seven years for her career now discovers she is pregnant. A college senior who, in order to be selected by the pros, devoted himself to football during school now shatters an ankle while hiking. A widower raising five preadolescent children loses his job in a very specialized profession. All of these people have much in common, and it is important for the person in crisis and for their helpers or counselors to identify the precipitating events. As you read the characteristics of a crisis, think about the elements and the purpose of crisis counseling. Jane Crisp states:

> Crisis intervention is a process used to interrupt and/or positively impact a person's immediate crisis reactions. Sometimes called "emotional first aid," crisis intervention involves the use of verbal and nonverbal communication to encourage, empower, and build confidence in those who experience a crisis.[3]

The Vulnerable State

The person must be vulnerable for the crisis to occur. Even going without sleep for two nights can make a person vulnerable in a situation that he or she would usually handle without difficulty. Being ill or depressed also lowers coping mechanisms. Recently I talked with a woman who was depressed over the threat of another loss in her life. She wanted to give up her foster child, cancel an important fund-raising event and quit her business. I asked her not to make any decisions during her time of depression, because such decisions often are regretted later.

The Precipitating Factor

The precipitating factor is the straw that broke the camel's back. Some people seem to hold together very well during a time of extreme loss or heartache and then fall apart over a broken dish or a dropped glass. These apparently minor events are the last straws, and the reaction and tears are in response to the serious loss.

The State of Active Crisis

When a person can no longer handle the situation, the active crisis develops. The following are four indications of this state.

1. *Symptoms of stress—psychological, physiological or both.* These could include depression, headaches, anxiety, bleeding ulcers and so on. Some type of extreme discomfort is always present.

2. *An attitude of panic or defeat.* The people may feel that they have tried everything and nothing works. Therefore, they feel like failures—defeated, overwhelmed and helpless. There is no hope. They have two ways of responding at this time: (1) becoming agitated—with behavior that is unproductive (e.g., pacing, drinking, taking drugs, fast driving or getting into a fight); or (2) becoming apathetic—for example, excessive sleeping.

3. *A focus on relief.* "Get me out of this situation!" is the concern and cry. Their feelings are similar to the psalmist who said, "Have mercy on me, O God, have mercy! I look to you for protection. I will hide beneath the shadow of your wings until this violent storm is past" (Ps. 57:1, *NLT*). They want relief from the pain of the stress. They are not in a condition to deal with their problem in a rational way. Sometimes people in crisis may appear to be in a daze or even respond in bizarre ways. They are somewhat frantic in their efforts and will look to others for help. They may become overly dependent upon others to help them out of their dilemma.

4. *A time of lowered efficiency.* People in active crisis may continue to function normally, but instead of responding at 100 percent,

their response may be at about 60 percent. The greater the threat from the person's appraisal of the situation, the less effective the coping resources will likely be. They may be aware of this, which further discourages them. The appraisal aspect of any situation is an important part of the crisis sequence. The appraisal is what people make of an event. Every person has his or her own way of perceiving an event. The person's beliefs, ideas, expectations and perceptions all come together at this time to evaluate a situation as a crisis or noncrisis. At this time, it is important to help people try to see the event through their eyes, not yours. For example, the death of a close friend is appraised from several points: how close the relationship was, how often they were in touch with one another, how the person responded to other losses and how many losses there have been recently. A widow deeply involved in her husband's life perceives her loss differently from the man's close friend, a business associate or the uncle he saw once every five years.

BALANCING FACTORS

Most people experiencing a crisis perceive the loss or threatened loss of something that is important to them. Even a job promotion can bring a sense of loss that precipitates a crisis. Consider this example:

John enjoyed the camaraderie with the other salesmen in the car agency. Then he was promoted to sales manager. This gave him status, more money and changes in his relationships. He was not on the same level as the salesmen anymore, and in fact, he now had to push and urge them to make their sales quotas. John did not like this. He became so dissatisfied that he began to call in sick to avoid the conflicts.

Some people feel that a problem will not lead to a crisis unless there are deficiencies in one or more of the balancing factors of a person's life.

Adequate Perception

This is the way a problem is viewed and the meaning it has for the person. For example, if a couple's daughter gets a divorce, the couple could feel that this is the greatest possible tragedy and a negative commentary on their ability to raise their daughter. On the other hand, another set of parents may not feel this way at all.

Adequate Network

This involves having a group of friends, relatives or agencies that provide support during a problem. The Body of Christ has the potential of being one of the greatest support groups ever available, if the members know how to respond to the person in need.

Coping Mechanisms

Most of us learn this balancing factor. If these mechanisms do not function well or break down, a crisis can be experienced. These mechanisms involve rationalization, denial, new knowledge, prayer, reading Scripture and so on. The greater the number and diversity of coping methods, the less likely a person will experience a crisis.

Limited Duration

People cannot exist in a crisis state for an extended period of time. Something must be done; there must be some resolution. Experience and research show that a crisis ends and balance is restored within a

> **Experience and research show that a crisis ends and balance is restored within a maximum of six weeks.**

maximum of six weeks. This means that help needs to be available during this time frame, or the person may choose solutions that are detrimental or counterproductive. Therefore, there seems to exist only a short window of opportunity after a crisis in which help can occur. This is the most appropriate time for a crisis intervention model to be applied. Positive responses are active therapy, support, replay of events, exposed pain, released feelings, validated experiences and identified personal schemes in flexible collaborative relationships. After this window closes, the people adapt on their own and cover over and return to friendly defenses or styles. In some cases they work, while in others they don't. If chronicity takes over the counselee, your goal can more appropriately be described as one to arrest his or her decompensation process and to provide an alternative maladaptive response.[4] The equilibrium may be different from before, but at least there is some balance. The crisis is an opportunity for change.

According to Morton Bard and Dawn Sangrey, "Minutes of skillful support by any sensitive person immediately after the crime can be worth more than hours of professional counseling later."[5] In other words, individuals who utilize crisis intervention skills can help people reconstruct their lives and reduce the need for longer-term psychological intervention later.[6]

It is sometimes easier to help the person who is in the state of active crisis, for those who are hurting the most are often motivated to make significant changes in their lives.[7]

LIFE'S TRANSITIONS

Not all crises are unexpected. Another type of crisis is the predictable event. It is an event that is part of the planned, expected or normal process of life, which leads to a crisis. Life is full of many transitions. A transition is a "period of moving from one state of certainty to another, with an interval of uncertainty and change in between."[8]

"It's like traveling from one island to another. We leave solid ground in order to move on. Usually we are vulnerable while traveling between islands."[9] The Bible sees all of life as a pilgrimage:

By faith Abraham, when called to go to a place he would later receive as his inheritance, obeyed and went, even though he did not know where he was going (Heb. 11:8).

Many transitions occur throughout life that have the potential of becoming crises: the transition from being single to being married; the transition from the 20s to the 30s and the 30s to the 40s; the transition from being a couple to being parents; the transition from being parents to having an empty nest; the transition from having an empty nest to becoming grandparents; and the transition from being employed to being retired.

Many of these events we see looming closer on the horizon. And a person can prepare for them and even rehearse mentally what he or she will do when they arrive. New information can be gathered to assist in the transition process. For example:

One teacher, who realized he would have to retire in 10 years, began to expand his interests. He started to take courses at the local college in subjects he thought he might have an interest in, so he took up photography and began to read in areas he had never considered before. He began developing a list of projects he would like to tackle—health and finances permitting—upon retirement. As there would be a significant loss in his life—his job and livelihood—he planned in advance for a variety of replacements and worked through some of those feelings of loss. He developed hobbies and interests that could be enjoyed whether his health was good or poor. Through anticipation he eliminated the possibility of seeing this transition become a crisis.

If moving through the various stages of life occurred smoothly and everything was predictable, life would be fairly easy for most mature people. But two factors must be considered. First, many people are not mature enough or able to take responsibility because they are stuck at an earlier stage in their development. Second, many changes are not so predictable and do not occur at the time we have planned.

New Roles

Consider for a moment the additional changes that can occur as we move through life. We may take on new roles, such as becoming a part-time student while continuing as a homemaker or full-time employee. We may become foster parents while still parenting our own children. We might get divorced and so give up a spouse. We may graduate from school and become a full-time employee.

We give up roles and, at times, do not replace them with others. These include retiring from work without finding a fulfilling role in retirement, losing a spouse without remarrying and giving up being a parent (the empty nest) without taking an outside job or becoming a grandparent.

Geographical Changes

We can also experience geographical changes, such as moving from one country to another, from the rural South to the urban East Coast or from the city to the suburbs.

Socioeconomic Changes

Socioeconomic shifts include shifting from the lower to the middle class or from the upper to the lower class.

Physical Changes

Physical changes include going from being a hearing person to being a nonhearing person, from being confined to a wheelchair for years to regaining the ability to walk or from being obese to becoming trim.

Remember, transitions can be swift or gradual and can have a positive or a devastating impact. All transitions, however, have the potential of being a crisis, depending upon the person involved. Even the experience of a person's spouse becoming a Christian has been the catalyst for a crisis in some families.

Midlife Crisis

Midlife is one of those disruptive transitions. Much has been said and written about this stage of life. The midlife years can be a time of reminiscence, growth, challenge and delight or a time of pain, frustration, frantic searching and anger. Because we see book after book written about male midlife crisis, we have come to believe that a crisis is inevitable for every man. The fact is, it is not. Only a minority of men experience a midlife crisis, whereas all men go through a midlife transition, which is a normal process.

The term "male midlife crisis" literally means changes in a man's personality. These changes usually occur rapidly and are substantial, thus appearing both dramatic and traumatic. At this time, a man becomes aware of how he is changing physically and mentally, and even his values change. He reacts to these changes with other changes. For some, the changes are threatening. For a Christian, they present an opportunity to apply his faith and develop further toward maturity. It is not a burnout time of life, but a time of both harvest and new beginning, a time of enrichment and stability. Our interpretation of life and its events can change. The dismay and despair of confronting disappointments and unreached expectations can be shifted to realistic acceptance. As we learn from the past, the future can be different.

David C. Morley puts it this way:

To the Christian these middle-life changes have a different meaning. The change that is so threatening to the nonbeliever is an opportunity for the Christian to exercise his faith and to experience the process of true Christian maturity. The mature Christian is a person who can deal with change. He can accept all of the vicissitudes of life and not deny nor complain about them. He sees them all as the manifestation of God's love. If God loves me, then He is going to provide an experience that makes life richer and more in line with His will. To the Christian, "All things work together for good to them that love God . . . " (Romans 8:28). How often we hear that Scripture quoted. How little we see it applied to real-life experiences. What God is really saying is that we should comfort ourselves with the thought that what happens in our lives, victory or defeat, wealth or poverty, sickness or death, all are indications of God's love and His interest in the design of our lives. If He brings sickness to us, we should be joyful for the opportunity to turn to Him more completely. So often in the bloom of health, we forget to remember the God who has provided that health. When we are in a position of weakness, we are more likely to acknowledge His strength, we are more likely to ask His guidance every step of the way.[10]

The ideal is that a Christian should be able to respond positively to the changes at midlife. But unfortunately that does not always happen. Why? In most cases it is because too many of those in our churches are not aware of the various transitions of life—especially midlife. They have not been prepared for these transitions in order to prevent a crisis. It is possible for a man to avoid the crisis by preparing for midlife in the following ways:

1. building his sense of identity upon a solid basis and not upon his occupation and how well he does there;
2. becoming more complete in his humanity by experiencing, accepting and expressing his feelings;
3. developing strong and close friendships with other men;
4. preparing for life's changes and crises by incorporating God's Word into his life.

The ministry of churches—if we are going to lessen some of life's crises—is to prepare our congregations in advance for the changes they

> **The ministry of churches—if we are going to lessen some of life's crises—is to prepare our congregations in advance for the changes they will experience.**

will experience. This involves educating them about these stages of life and the actual transition they will go through. In addition, they need help in applying God's Word so that they are better able to handle life's sudden as well as predictable changes.

PEOPLE'S NEEDS IN A CRISIS

What are people likely to want from you when they seek you out at a time of crisis? People's needs vary. Do not be surprised by the wide range of requests you hear. In many cases, people will expect you to be the miracle worker. You are their last hope, and their expectations are excessive, unrealistic or both. When you cannot produce what they want, don't be surprised if they become disappointed or angry. You will be able to help in other ways that will meet some of their needs.

Types of People

What are some of the types of people who will seek you out for counseling? Aaron Lazare and his associates conducted a survey of the types of patients who visited a psychiatric walk-in clinic. They were able to isolate 14 different categories that represent the wide variety of types of counselees who need crisis intervention work:

1. Counselees who want a strong person to protect and control them. "Please take over for me."
2. Those who need someone who will help them maintain contact with reality. "Help me know that I am real."
3. Those who feel exceedingly empty and who need loving. "Care for me."
4. Those who need a counselor to be available for a feeling of security. "Always be there."
5. Those ridden with obsessive guilt who seek to confess. "Take away my guilt."
6. Those who urgently need to talk things out. "Let me get it off my chest."
7. Those who desire advice on pressing issues. "Tell me what to do."
8. Those who seek to sort out their conflicting ideas. "Help me to put things into perspective."
9. Those who truly have a desire for self-understanding and insight into their problems. "I want counseling."

10. Those who see their discomfort as a medical problem that needs the ministrations of a physician. "I need a doctor."
11. Those who seek some practical help such as economic assistance or a place to stay. "I need some specific assistance."
12. Those who credit their difficulty to ongoing current relationships and want the counselor to intercede. "Do it for me."
13. Those who want information about where to get help to satisfy various needs, actually seeking some community resource. "Tell me where I can get what I need."
14. Unmotivated or psychotic persons who are brought to the counselor against their own will. "I want nothing."[11]

People Who Cope Poorly

Of the various people who seek your help, some will cope quite well with their crises, and others quite poorly. It is possible to predict which will be which.

Emotional Weakness. Individuals who are emotionally weak prior to the crisis respond in a way that makes matters worse, but from their perspective, they are doing the most efficient thing possible. This is because they are already hurting emotionally.

Poor Physical Condition. Those who have some type of physical ailment or illness have fewer resources to draw on during a crisis. If you notice poor coping skills during difficult times, recommending a physical examination is important.

Denial of Reality. Those who deny reality have a hard time coping with a crisis. Denying reality is their attempt to avoid pain and anger. They may deny that they are seriously ill or financially ruined or that their children are on drugs or terminally ill. Even well-educated, professional people sometimes respond in this manner.

Magic of the Mouth. A Harvard psychiatrist, Dr. Ralph Hirschowitz, has created a term for the fourth characteristic. He calls it magic of the mouth: the tendency to eat, drink, smoke and talk excessively. When difficulty enters these people's lives, they seem to regress to infantile forms of behavior, and their mouths take over in one way or another. They are uncomfortable unless they are doing something with their mouths most of the time. This attempt not to face the real problem can continue after the crisis is over. The person is actually creating an additional crisis for himself or herself.

Unrealistic Approach to Time. People who use this coping mechanism crowd the time dimensions of a problem, or they extend the time factors way into the future. In other words, they want the problem to be fixed right away, or else they delay and delay. Delaying avoids the discomfort of reality but enlarges the problem.

Excessive Guilt. These people tend to blame themselves for the difficulty. By feeling worse, they immobilize themselves even more.

Blame. These individuals do not focus on what the problem is but instead turn to who they believe caused the problem. The approach is to find some enemies—either real or imagined—and project the blame on them.

Excessive Dependence or Independence. These people either turn away offers of help or become clinging vines. Those who cling tend to suffocate you if you are involved in helping them. Overly independent people, on the other hand, shun offers of help. Even if they are sliding down the hill toward disaster, they do not cry out for assistance. When the disaster hits, they either continue to deny it or blame others for it.

Theology. A person's theology will affect how he or she copes with a crisis. Our lives are based upon our theology, yet, so many people are frightened by that word. Our belief in God and how we perceive God is a reflection of our theology. Those who believe in the sovereignty and caring nature of God have a better basis from which to approach life.

A book that has spoken to me repeatedly is Lewis Smedes' *How Can It Be All Right When Everything Is All Wrong?* His insights and sensitivity to life's crises and God's presence and involvement in our lives can answer many of our questions. One of his own experiences describes how our theology helps us move through life's changes:

The other night, trying to sleep, I amused myself by trying to recall the most happy moments of my life. I let my mind skip and dance where it was led. I thought of leaping down from a rafter in a barn, down into a deep loft of sweet, newly mown hay.

That was a superbly happy moment. But somehow my mind was also seduced to a scene some years ago that, as I recall it, must have been the most painful of my life. Our firstborn child was torn from our hands by what felt to me like a capricious deity I did not want to call God. I felt ripped off by a cosmic con artist. And for a little while, I thought I might not easily ever smile again.

But then, I do not know how, in some miraculous shift in my perspective, a strange and inexpressible sense came to me that my life, our lives, were still good, that life is good because it is given, and that its possibilities were still incalculable. Down into the gaps of feeling left over from pain came a sense of givenness that nothing explains. An irrepressible impulse of blessing came from my heart to God for his sweet gift. And that was joy . . . in spite of pain. Looking back, it seems to me now that I have never again known so sharp, so severe, so saving a sense of gratitude and so deep a joy, or so honest.[12]

Chuck Swindoll always talks so realistically and hopefully about life's crises:

Crisis crushes. And in crushing, it often refines and purifies. You may be discouraged today because the crushing has not yet led to a surrender. I've stood beside too many of the dying, ministered to too many of the broken and bruised to believe that crushing is an end in itself. Unfortunately, however, it usually takes the brutal blows of affliction to soften and penetrate hard hearts. Even though such blows often seem unfair.[13]

Remember Aleksandr Solzhenitsyn's admission:

It was only when I lay there on rotting prison straw that I sensed within myself the first stirring of good. Gradually, it was disclosed to me that the line separating good and evil passes, not through states, nor between classes, nor between political parties either, but right through all human hearts. So, bless you, prison, for having been in my life.[14]

Those words provide a perfect illustration of the psalmist's instruction:

Before I was afflicted I went astray, but now I obey your word. It was good for me to be afflicted so that I might learn your decrees (Ps. 119:67,71).

After crisis crushes, God steps in to comfort and teach.[15]

FINAL THOUGHT

And teach He does. What about you? What are the crises you've experienced in your life? What has been your response to them? What have you learned through your crisis experiences that will help you to help others? After all, this is the way we can benefit from our crisis experiences.

We all need to remember:

The LORD hears his people when they call to him for help. He rescues them from all their troubles. The LORD is close to the brokenhearted; he rescues those who are crushed in spirit (Ps. 34:17-18, *NLT*).

CHAPTER 8

THE PHASES OF
A CRISIS

Sometimes, models of grief are used to describe crisis stages, stages such as shock, denial, disorganization and reorganization. *The Phoenix Phenomenon* (Jason Aronson, 1999), by Joanne Jozefowski, identifies five phases of grief: impact, chaos, adaptation, equilibrium and transformation. Jozefowski's model reflects other models in order to describe the stages or phases of a crisis, including the ones that will be covered here.

The following figure of the phases of a crisis is based upon Lloyd Ahlem's description in *Living with Stress* (Regal Books, 1978). The figure is simple and is easy to comprehend visually. It has been helpful to many in a crisis state.

THE IMPACT PHASE

The first phase of a crisis is the impact phase, which is usually very brief. You know immediately that you have been confronted with a major happening. For some people, it is like being hit with a two-by-four. It is becoming aware

Figure 8

The Normal Crisis Pattern

Emotional Level (dashed curve rising from bottom-left to top-right)

TIME

	PHASE I Impact	PHASE II Withdrawal Confusion	PHASE III Adjustment	PHASE IV Reconstruction/ Reconciliation
	Hours to Days	Days to Weeks	Weeks to Months	Months
Response	Should you stay and face it or withdraw?	Do you feel intense emotion or feel drained? Are you angry, sad, fearful, anxious, depressed, raging or guilty?	Your positive thoughts begin returning along with intense emotions.	Hope has returned. You are more self-confident.
Thoughts	You are numb and disoriented. Your insight ability is limited, and your feelings overwhelm.	Your thinking ability is limited. It is uncertain and ambiguous.	You're now able to problem solve.	Thinking is clearer.
Direction You Take to Regain Control	You search for what you lost.	You are bargaining—wishful thinking. Detachment is involved.	You begin looking for something new to invest in.	Progress is evident and new attachments are made to something significant.
Searching Behavior	You often reminisce.	You are puzzled; things are unclear.	You can now stay focused and begin to learn from your experience.	You may want to stop and evaluate where you've been and where you're going.

Based on a similar figure by Ralph Hirschowitz, "Addendum," *Levinson Letter* (Cambridge, England: The Levinson Institute, n.d.), p. 4.

of the crisis and experiencing the effect of being stunned. This period lasts from a few hours to a few days, depending upon the event and the person involved. In a severe loss, tears can occur immediately or a few days later. The more severe the crisis or loss, the greater the impact and the greater the amount of incapacitation and numbness.

It is possible for the impact phase to linger on and on, as in the case of a divorce proceeding. During this phase, the person has to make a decision whether to stand and fight the problem through to resolution or to run and ignore the problem. Psychologists call this the fight or flight pattern. During this impact stage, we are usually less competent than normal, and our usual tendency of handling life's problems will probably emerge. If our tendency has been to avoid problems, we will probably run from this one.

However, fighting and attempting to take charge in the midst of a crisis seems to be the healthier response. Running away only prolongs the crisis. And because each of the succeeding phases is dependent upon the adjustments made in the previous one, avoiding reality does not make for good judgment. Pain is prolonged instead of resolved.

Thinking Capability

During the impact stage, our thinking capability is lessened. We are some-what numb and disoriented. It is even possible for some to feel as though they cannot think or feel at all. It is as though their entire system shuts down. Insight is lessened and should not be expected at this time. The fac-tual information that you give these people may not fully register at this time and may have to be repeated later. You may explain something to them, and they in turn ask a question that indicates they never heard one word. Because they are numb and stunned, they may make unwise deci-sions. Unfortunately, at this time, important decisions may be necessary and postponing them may not be an option. This is where they need the help of other people and what is suggested needs to be in writing.

The Lost Object

During the impact phase, a person actually symbolically searches for the lost object. His or her thought process is directed toward the loss. For example, it is common for a person who loses a loved one in death to take out photographs and other items that remind him or her of the person who died. When something that means a great deal to us is lost, we hold on to our emotional attachments for a while. It is very normal to search for the lost object or a replacement, and the searching is greater when we are not aware of what is happening to us.

> **If you are feeling discomfort when you counsel a person in crisis, instead of having the counselee shut down his or her feelings, take time to discover the source of your own discomfort.**

Reminiscing about the loss is in proportion to the value of the object or person. A person needs to be listened to and have his or her feelings accepted at this point of the crisis. Feelings rejected delay the resolution of the problem. Feelings should not be buried or denied at this point. The person may even feel strange about the feelings and thoughts that he or she is experiencing, and negative comments from others don't help. If you are feeling discomfort when you counsel a person in crisis, instead of having the counselee shut down his or her feelings, take time to discover the source of your own discomfort. For in doing this, you will become better able to respond to life yourself and to help others.

The Emotion of Guilt
The emotion of guilt frequently accompanies change and crisis. People feel guilty for so many reasons—from failure to achievement. Many people have difficulty handling success. They wonder if they deserve it, or they see others who do not succeed and, in their empathy, experience guilt over their own success. Children of parents who divorce sometimes feel guilty, as though they are responsible for the destruction of the marriage. Those who witness accidents or catastrophes experience guilt.

"Why was I spared?" and "Why did my young child die and not me? He had so many more years left than I did!" are common reactions.

People who experience guilt have several choices available to them to alleviate the guilt. They can rationalize their way out of the guilt. They can project blame onto others. They can attempt to pay penance and work off the guilt. Or they can apply the forgiveness available where there has been genuine sin and violation of God's principles. God can and does remove true guilt, although there will be other feelings of guilt that have no basis in truth. People who live on their emotions most of the time will be more guilt-prone during a crisis than others. Those who have negative patterns of thinking or of self-talk will exhibit guilt more than others. Forgiveness from God is not usually needed for false guilt, but what is needed is help in changing their perspective or self-talk. This will take time and will probably not be accomplished during the impact phase. Our role, therefore, is to be there for counselees. This is a time to be responsive to people's safety and security needs, especially if you feel they could be in danger. At this point, they may need help with practical everyday matters. But don't make all the decisions for them; keep them involved in simple decisions.

> One of the most helpful ministries you can ever engage in at this time is to help normalize what the person is experiencing.

Before we go on to the next phase, here is how the use of the crisis sequence chart has been helpful in counseling people in crisis. Often people in crises feel overwhelmed and wonder if their responses are normal. On many occasions, I show people the complete chart, describe the various stages and ask them to indicate where they are on the chart. They respond by first identifying the stage they are in and then by saying, "You mean my response is normal?" By discovering the normalcy of their response, they feel relieved. Then they are able to see where they will be heading, which further alleviates their anxiety. I usually wait until the next phase to share their direction, as they seem to comprehend it better at this time. One of the most helpful ministries you can ever engage in at this time is to help normalize what the person is experiencing.

THE WITHDRAWAL-CONFUSION PHASE

The second phase of a crisis is the withdrawal-confusion phase.

Emotional Turmoil

One of the key factors in this phase is turmoil in the emotional area. With some counselees, you'll see something like a caldron churning with one emotional expression after another. The emotions are on the surface. However, there are some who are so numb during the initial phase that they're unaware of the caldron of feelings. The individuals may feel as if they have died, but the feelings haven't.

During this second phase, some who have already experienced their feelings may feel *worn out emotionally or depressed.* The person has no more feelings to experience. If you look back at the crisis sequence chart, you will note that each phase becomes progressively longer. Keep in mind that the various phases can overlap. Not only that, a person may shift back and forth from one phase to another.

During this phase, the tendency to *deny one's feelings* is probably stronger than at any other phase. Feelings now become the ugliest. Intense anger occurs toward whatever happened, which in some cases brings forth guilt for having such feelings. Shame then results, and the pain of all the various feelings can bring the tendency and desire to suppress all feelings. Christians and non-Christians alike refuse to let the process of grief occur. This denial leads to emotional, physical and interpersonal difficulties in time.

How do people actually *feel* when confronted by a crisis? What goes on in their emotional spectrum when they find that they are unable to adjust to life's major difficulties? The following are nine disruptions that signal a person's inability to cope in his or her usual way:

1. A sense of *bewilderment:* "I never felt this way before."
2. A sense of *danger:* "I feel so scared—something terrible is going to happen."
3. A sense of *confusion:* "I can't think clearly—my mind doesn't seem to work."
4. A sense of *impasse:* "I'm stuck—nothing I do seems to help."
5. A sense of *desperation:* "I've got to do something, but I don't know what to do."
6. A sense of *apathy:* "Nothing can help me—what's the use of trying."
7. A sense of *helplessness:* "I can't cope by myself—please help me."
8. A sense of *urgency:* "I need help now."
9. A sense of *discomfort:* "I feel so miserable and unhappy."[1]

Knowing these emotions will assist you in relating to the person. You might ask questions or make statements such as:

- Could it be that you just can't think clearly, like your mind isn't working?
- Could it be that you feel stuck, like nothing you do seems to help?
- Perhaps you feel immobilized and you're thinking, *Why try? Nothing I do seems to help.*

If our shared feelings begin to shock and alarm our friends, we tend to repress them. But they are never hidden from God. He both understands and accepts our emotional state. Feelings need to be expressed, which means that friends, relatives or some other type of social support system needs to be available. Unfortunately, the availability of friends and relatives might not coincide with when a person needs help. While meals, gifts, cards, time and prayers come during the impact phase and the beginning of the withdrawal-confusion state, the support system usually diminishes in a few weeks, and that is when it is needed the most.

Extra Support

Over the years I have come in contact with more and more churches that have developed an ongoing ministry for those who have experienced the loss of a loved one. The church arranges for families to minister to the bereaved person in some way each week for a period of two years. This not only involves many from the congregation but also supports the person over an extended period.

A minister who attended one of my crisis seminars shared that following a funeral or memorial service, he writes the name of the family on his desk calendar every three months for the next two years to remind him to continue to reach out and minister to them over that period of time.

During this phase, people do not need or benefit from spiritual and psychological insights or teaching. Their emotional state—whether it be anger or depression—interferes with the information. We can only hope that they will be able to draw on what they have already learned, since they will find it difficult to incorporate anything new. Scripture and prayer also can bring comfort.

Good Organization

One of the best ways to aid people during this phase is to give them some help organizing their lives. They need assistance in arranging appointments, keeping the house in order and other such routine responsibilities. They need this help because they may be suffering from some paralysis of the will.

Above all, when you work with a person in phase one or two, use sustainment techniques. These are basic and simple—listening, reassurance, encouragement and reflection. These approaches will help to lower the person's anxiety, guilt and tension and to provide emotional support. Your task is to assist the counselee to restore equilibrium.

Self-Pity

Another tendency at this phase is self-pity. It is not uncommon for the people to appear confused. This may be evident because they will begin some task or start to approach people and then retreat. They may approach new people and situations as a type of replacement for what was lost but then retreat to reminiscence. Making a decision during this phase to replace what was lost—such as finding and marrying a new spouse—is not a good idea. The person is not ready, for whatever or whoever was lost has not yet been fully released.

Counseling Guidelines

Remember, crisis counseling is *not* therapy. It's a skillful intervention, and it follows a definite format. This is why professional counselors, ministers and trained laypeople can all be effective in helping others at a time of crisis.

During phase one, as well as two, the following two guidelines will help the person in crisis:

1. As you ask questions and make statements, keep them short and concise. Ask only one question at a time. Open-ended questions are best unless you need specific, factual information. Ask them to describe their memories of what happened, such as where they were, what they saw, smelled, felt, heard, and above all, let them tell *their story.*[2]
2. Be sure to tend to any stress, pressure or tension in your life prior to attempting to help in the situation. Being calm can provide stability. Be sure, in a calm, quiet way, that you provide structure, set limits and guide the outcome. Sometimes, using repetitive questions or statements when a person strays can help.

Verbal Effects

When a person is in a crisis or traumatized, our words, tone of voice and suggestions have a far greater impact than at other times in life. Even offhand comments can have an effect. What you say to people in crisis or to traumatized people can calm and lower their blood pressure or it can increase their anxiety. When you don't know what to say, don't! It's better to say nothing than to fill the air with words.[3]

The authors of *The Worst Is Over: What to Say When Every Moment Counts* talk about verbal first aid. It's not a process meant to take the place of good medicine but rather to make a good medicine better. The focus of this insightful book is

How to generate support that begins the communication, how to give suggestions for pain relief that actually supports the body to produce chemicals that support healing and how to create an atmosphere that helps to turn fear into hope and pain into calm.[4]

> **What you say to people in crisis or to traumatized people can calm and lower their blood pressure or it can increase their anxiety.**

What do we often do when we're called into a crisis or emergency situation? We see those who are upset, and in an attempt to bring a sense of calm into their lives and into the situations, we say, "Everything is going to be alright." We don't know that. It's a false assurance. It could jeopardize our credibility. Something bad or terrible already has happened to these people. We could say that the worst is over or the worst is over for now. That is true. These words have an effect on the chemical process in the body. These words can reduce panic and fear and bring a sense of relief. It's a suggestion to bring healing.[5]

Dutch Sheets, in one of his recent books on hope, shared the story of his brother, Tim, who was allowed to witness an open-heart surgery. He sat in an elevated section reserved for physicians and medical students. During the surgery, the patient's heart had been stopped from beating. When it came time to restart it, the doctor massaged it, but nothing happened. Despite repeated attempts and using several procedures, the medical staff was unable to get the heart to beat again. Their anxiety and concern were apparent. Finally, although the patient was unconscious, the surgeon leaned over and said into the patient's ear, "We need your help. We cannot get your heart going. Tell your heart to start beating." Immediately—as incredible as this sounds—the patient's heart began to beat again.[6]

Essentially, we need to be careful of what we say in the presence of others. Even the statements, "This is going to be so difficult for them" or "You'll probably be depressed in a few weeks" can end up not only being a suggestion but a negative self-fulfilling prophecy. Sometimes the mind wraps itself around what you say, and your words become reality. Before we say anything, we need to think and pray. We also need to be willing to learn and change some of our former approaches:

1. When silence occurs, just let it happen. Those in crisis have slowed reactions. Often, their ability to respond to questions is impaired. If their personality preference is introversion, they need to think quietly on their own in order to formulate their response.

2. It's alright to interrupt gently if necessary, especially if the person is stuck on rambling. A gentle "I just wanted to be certain I'm hearing you correctly" is appropriate.

3. Listen with your eyes as much as with your ears. You may pick up more information this way, or it may contradict what is being verbalized.

4. If the person dumps on or vents to you, don't take it personally. You may be the first safe person they've met for a while.

5. As you listen, prioritize the problems in your mind as well as on paper with a few notes. Help them discover if the crisis is interfering with their lives.

6. Help the person generate options.

7. Be sure you have the following at your fingertips:
   a. Books and resources that deal with different problems. Keep books and tapes in your office to sell, rather than sending your counselees out to a bookstore that may or may not have what they need. If people purchase a resource, they are more likely to follow through and read or listen to the material.
   b. Have phone numbers of local and national agencies available.
   c. Have a listing of various support groups available.

8. If you will see this person again, discuss how they'll be able to keep their appointment. Do they have transportation or friends to provide it?

9. Work together to see what options work for this person. Does he or she think it will work? That's what's important.

10. Put the plan in writing for both of you. Let counselees describe what they will be doing.

11. Is there any potential or indication of possible suicide or homicide?[7]

Assessment

As you work with people in crisis, it's important to determine how well they were functioning prior to the crisis event. Focus on previous coping patterns and any unresolved personal conflicts. Understanding these can shed light on how an event led to crisis.

Once this is done, there are five areas in which you need to make an assessment. These areas have been defined as the five BASIC modalities.

B refers to the behavior patterns of the people in crisis. What do you look for? How has their working, eating and sleeping been impacted by their crisis? You need to know how the current pattern is different. If you hear, "I'm just not sleeping well at this time," you could ask, "How is that different from before this happened?"

A is for their affective functioning. What feelings or inner responses have they experienced? This is where using feeling words, such as those listed on the ball of grief (see chapter 6), can be beneficial, since some people don't have a feeling vocabulary. For others, this is a time when it's difficult to connect feelings with words. When feelings are identified, look for how they have been translated into behavior.

S stands for any physical symptoms created in response to the crisis. Are they new or have old ones intensified?

I relates to the interpersonal category of functioning. How has this crisis impacted the other people in this person's world? What kind of support system does he or she have?

C stands for cognition. What are the thoughts, shoulds and should nots, dreams, thought distortions or destructive fantasies?

When you have this information, you'll be better able to help the person move forward.[8]

THE ADJUSTMENT PHASE

The third phase of a crisis is the adjustment phase, which takes longer than the others. The emotional responses during this time are hopeful. Some depression may remain or may come and go, but positive attitudes have started. Things are looking up. People talk with hope about such future possibilities as enjoying a new job or a new location, rebuilding a fire-destroyed home or considering remarriage. Counselees have just about completed their detachment from what was lost and are now looking for something new to which they can become attached.

Climbing Out

What is occurring in the people's worlds begins to take on new importance. They have been through the depths of the valley and are now climbing out. What they begin to attach to holds special significance, although the outsider may not see the same significance and may feel that the people are making a mistake by choosing a new job, new home or new partner. People do not need their counselors as critics, for they are responding from a perspective different from their counselors. As counselors, we need to see life through their eyes and not our own.

The one area in which we do need to caution counselees is selecting a new partner. At this phase, it is usually too soon. I encourage those who are going through a divorce to wait at least a year following the divorce to begin dating. Recovery needs to occur first; or they'll select a new partner from a position of weakness, and the baggage they bring from their previous relationship interferes with the new one.

Gaining Hope

Remember that people at this time are hopeful, but it is not a consistent sense of hope. They fluctuate and will have down times. They still need someone to be close or available. Because insight is returning, they can be objective about what has occurred and now can process new information and suggestions. They can gain new insights spiritually at this point, and their values, goals and beliefs may be different and have a greater depth.

THE RECONSTRUCTION PHASE

The fourth phase of a crisis is the reconstruction phase.

Spontaneous Expression of Hope

A characteristic of this phase is the spontaneous expression of hope. There is a sense of confidence—plans are made out of this sense of confidence. Doubts and self-pity are gone, because the person has made a logical decision at this point not to engage them anymore. The person takes the initiative for progress, and reattachments are occurring. New

> A crisis is an opportunity for the person to gain new strengths, new perspectives on life, new appreciation, new values and a new way to approach life.

people, new places, new activities, new jobs and new spiritual responses and depths are now in existence. If there has been anger and blame toward others or if relationships were broken, this is now the time for reconciliation. Helpful gestures, notes, meals shared together or doing a helpful act for others may be the form of reconciliation.

Reflection of Newness and Growth

The final resolution of a crisis is a reflection of the newness of a person. A crisis is an opportunity for the person to gain new strengths, new perspectives on life, new appreciation, new values and a new way to approach life. I have experienced the four phases of crisis in my life. Sometimes it is possible to work your way through the four phases in less time than indicated. At other times, one or two of the phases may take more time because of the experienced or threatened loss.

A number of years ago, I experienced some strange physical symptoms. These included vertigo, pressure experienced in the back of my head and headaches. These symptoms persisted for about seven weeks, during which time the doctors had some theories but nothing concrete. There was a real uncertainty, and my own concerns and worries about what this might be added to some of the feelings I experienced.

Finally, after going through further examination, including a CAT scan, the symptoms disappeared. As we pieced together what had occurred, we felt that the physical symptoms were brought on by too many strenuous seminars with no recuperation time in between, coupled with a cold and some altitude changes. Physical exhaustion was one of the greatest culprits. But this experience—especially at the age of 47—caused me to think, reevaluate and consider some changes. I didn't necessarily like what I went through, but I grew because of it and felt it was necessary.

Crises and trials can become the means of exciting growth. I have always been impressed with William Pruitt and his response to a physical problem he conquered. In many ways, his crisis did not go away but was with him for the rest of his life. In his book *Run from the Pale Pony,* Pruitt uses an analogy to describe what happened in his life:

About thirty years ago, one of my joys as a boy was to ride a white horse named Prince. That proud, spirited stallion carried me where I wanted to go, wherever I bid him to and at the pace which I chose. I don't have to explain to horsemen the feeling of strength, even authority, which comes from controlling such a powerful animal. Nor need I expand upon the excitement I felt when I galloped him at full speed, or about the quiet pride that came when I twisted him through the corkscrew turns of a rodeo exercise. After all, he was mine and I trained him. Those experiences are a part of my heritage.

My cherished white horse was gone and seldom remembered about fifteen years later. It was then that I encountered a completely different kind of horse. When I first became aware of the specter, its shape was too dim to discern. I know only that I had never seen anything like it before. Too, I know that I had not sought any such creature, yet something different was with me wherever I went and that shadow would not go away. I told myself, "Really, now, you're much too busy to bother with something that seems determined to disturb you, get rid of it." And I tried to will it away. No matter what I did though, the specter followed my every move. Furthermore, the harder I tried to lose it, the clearer the creature's form became to me.

My uneasiness changed to anxiety when I realized that this unwanted shadow had a will of its own. The chill of fear came when I understood that it had no intention to leave me alone. Without further warning, it began to communicate with me openly one day, and in a harsh voice which was almost rigid with animosity, it spat out, "You can no longer go where you want to go when you choose at the speed you pick. That's true because I will give you weakness instead of strength. Excitement and pride? Never again will you have them like before. I plan only confinement and disability for you. And I will be your constant companion. My name is Chronic Illness."

At the time I heard it speak, I shrank back from actually seeing it face to face. It spoke harshly of miseries which were inverse to joys with my white horse named Health and the bitter irony was reflected in the form of a malicious creature. Chronic Illness took the shape of a stunted misshapen pony. Its shaggy coat was pale in color, streaked with ages old accumulation of dark despair. But, unquestionably, the most frightening feature of the animal was its overwhelming glare—its glare-eyed stare which held me helpless. The pony's wild eyes stared restlessly from side to side, yet strangely were unblinding. This book is written first of all for those people who have met the pale pony face to face.[9]

The pale pony might come in many possible forms—serious physical or mental illness, injuries from war or other sources, to name a few. Whatever shape the pony takes, the results can be quite similar. William Pruitt's pale pony was multiple sclerosis. He sensed that the disease was increasingly affecting his life, but his story is the story of hope. He realized that he had a number of years before he would be completely disabled; and realizing that he wouldn't be able to carry on the type of work he was in, he went back to college in a wheelchair. He earned a Ph.D. in economics and began to teach on a college level.

Pruitt's book is not a book about giving up but rather about fighting back and winning. It is a very honest book, telling of the pain, hurt and turmoil. Yet its emphasis is on faith and hope.

What causes a major crisis to become a restrictive, crippling, eternal tragedy rather than a growth-producing experience in spite of the pain? *Our attitude.*

Many people who work through their crisis find that they can then minister in a much better way to others. Out of our difficulties, we can feel with others and walk through their trials with them in a new manner.

ADDITIONAL QUESTIONS

Look back at the crisis sequence chart and answer the following questions:

- At which phase(s) would you pray with a person in crisis?
- At which phase(s) would you share Scripture with a person in crisis? Identify which passages you would share for each phase. What is your purpose in sharing each one?
- If you were to pray at the impact phase, write out what you would say in your prayer. Do this for all four phases. Your own comfort level will be enhanced by considering these questions and planning in advance.

RECOMMENDED RESOURCES

Resources for Counselees

Jeremiah, David. *A Bend in the Road.* Nashville, TN: Thomas Nelson, 2001.

Macintosh, Mike. *When Your World Falls Apart.* Colorado Springs, CO: Cook Publications, 2002.

Wright, H. Norman. *Will My Life Ever Be the Same?* Eugene, OR: Harvest House Publishers, 2002.

Resources for Counselors

Acosta, Judith, and Judith Simon-Prager. *The Worst Is Over: What to Say When Every Moment Counts.* San Diego, CA: Jodene Group, 2002. Chapters 1, 4 and 6 will challenge your thinking and the importance of what to say.

Resources for Laypeople

Crisis Care: The Victory videocassette series and *Crisis Care II: The Victory* videocassette series. Both series are designed to train laypeople to help others at a time of loss or crisis. Available through Christian Marriage Enrichment at (800) 875-7560.

Wright, H. Norman. *How to Help a Friend.* Minneapolis, MN: Bethany House Publishers, 2003.

Resources for People Looking for More Information on Life's Transitions

Sheehy, Gail. *New Passages.* New York: Random House, 1995.

———. *Understanding Men's Passages.* New York: Random House, 1998.

CHAPTER 9

THE PROCESS OF CRISIS INTERVENTION

There are several steps for you to follow to help a person in crisis. This is a long and extensive chapter, but these steps are applicable to various types of crises, and you will need to be sensitive and flexible in their application. Remember that each person and his or her specific concerns are different; therefore, you need to adapt to the individual. We will look at eight steps of crisis counseling adapted from Douglas Puryear's *Helping People in Crisis* (Jossey-Bass, 1980).

STEP 1: IMPLEMENT IMMEDIATE INTERVENTION

The first step in crisis counseling is *immediate intervention*. Crises are perceived as dangers. They are threatening to those involved, and there is a time limit to the opportunity for intervention. This is a time of turmoil with a high level of distress.

The vulnerable or disturbed state of the person is his or her reaction to the initial impact. Each person will respond to the problem in a different way. Some see it as a threat to their needs, security or control of their own lives. Others may see it as a loss. Still others see it as a challenge to growth, mastery, survival or self-expression.[1]

The Waiting List

Every minister has his or her own schedule. Many ministers have set aside specific times for counseling. When a call comes in to the church, either you or the church secretary will need to determine if this is a crisis that requires immediate attention or if it can wait until later in the day or for your next opening.

Some people handle an accident, the discovery of child abuse or sexual molestation, an affair or a job loss quite well. Others fall apart. The waiting list, however, has no place in crisis counseling. The preparation of a message, a committee meeting, luncheon engagement or golf game must be interrupted. People in crisis may be hesitant to reach out if they see you as exceptionally busy. They may hesitate to interrupt you and will need your reassurance that they did the right thing by contacting you. They need to know that you are glad they did. Let them know that their issue takes priority. If you have a trained crisis team in place, this is where it is advantageous for everyone to work together.

Keep in mind that people cannot tolerate the stress of a crisis for long. In one way or another, they will resolve it within a period of six weeks. In this time frame, they're pliable like clay, but in time, a hardness sets in. A state of equilibrium must be achieved. If they must wait to see you, it shouldn't be for more than one night. And if there is a wait, at least talk with them briefly over the telephone, because the way people in crisis achieve equilibrium may or may not be healthy. They may be so overwhelmed that they become self-destructive if they don't receive immediate help. You need to act quickly because your assistance can make the crisis less severe. It may even help protect the person from inflicting harm upon himself or herself.

In a crisis there is tension, a sense of urgency, misperceptions and lowered efficiency. Therefore, many attempts for quick relief that the

person makes will not be well thought out. They could even be counterproductive by worsening the problem or crisis.

Sustainment Techniques

During the beginning phase of helping a person in crisis, it is important
to use sustainment techniques to lower anxiety, guilt and tension and to
provide emotional support. All of these efforts help restore equilibrium.

Reassurance. Reassurance is one technique used to help someone
who is worried about cracking up. While too much reassurance may
eliminate all the anxiety—some anxiety is needed for positive change to
occur—the right dose helps the counselee overcome his or her feelings of
helplessness and hopelessness.

Direct Influence Procedures. Procedures of direct influence are
other techniques used to promote desired changes in a counselee. These
are used more often in crisis counseling than other types of counseling
and include encouraging new behavior as well as reinforcing what the
person is already doing.

When a person is depressed, confused or bewildered, he or she may
need more forceful techniques. You might advocate a definite course of
action or warn the person of specific consequences if he or she acts a certain way. For example, a suicidal person needs direct intervention.[2]

> **If you are going to have an effect upon the life of a
> person or family, it will be at the time of a crisis.**

Some of the most severe outcomes of a crisis are suicide, homicide,
running away, physical harm, psychosis or a family's breakup. Cutting
oneself off from acknowledged emotional ties of a family is a disaster for
both the person and the family members.

Therefore, one of our goals in crisis counseling is to *help avert a disastrous outcome* with beneficial direct influence procedures.

During crisis times, you have a tremendous opportunity to help and
minister. The unsettled state of a crisis is a time of change and flexibility,

because the counselee usually is more open to growth, is more accessible and is less defensive. Because the person is unsuccessful in his or her typical ways of responding and coping, he or she will most likely be open to trying something new. If you are going to have an effect upon the life of a person or family, it will be at this time. This is why crisis counseling is so important for those in ministry.

As I mentioned earlier, you may need to talk with the person on the phone first, if you are not able to meet immediately. Ask questions to help you determine the urgency of the situation and if it really is a crisis. I have had some people call and declare an emergency or crisis, only to discover the problem has been in existence for months. While on the phone, arrange for the first meeting and determine who is to be present. Try to gain enough information to formulate a tentative idea about the problem and to make some simple plans for the first meeting. By doing this, you are not totally unprepared for your first meeting. It is also important to know if the crisis necessitates having several people who are affected or who can be a support group come to the counseling session.

In addition, be sure you maintain control of the conversation over the phone. You may need to limit it. It is alright to let the person know you have a few minutes to talk in order to arrange for the first meeting. If you get too involved, the counselee might want you to solve the dilemma over the phone. If you hear too much of the story at this time, the person may be hesitant to discuss it again. You are expected to remember the details. This conversation is simply to make contact and establish the beginning of a relationship.

However, if for some reason you are unable to see the person immediately, during the initial phone conversation arrange for him or her to be seen by someone else. (If at all possible, develop a team of lay caregivers to assist in your ministry.) This may mean finding a minister or worker from another church if you do not have anyone else available. Church or denominational loyalties are unimportant during a person's crisis.

Basic Intervention Procedures (BIPs)

No matter what crisis phase your counselee is in, these procedures need to be followed and are foundational for what you do and whether you'll be of assistance. Whenever I'm in the process of learning a new approach to counseling, I've found it helpful to list all of its steps on a 3x5 card, laminate it to make it somewhat permanent, carry it with me, read it over until it's locked into my mind, rehearse the principles in different scenarios in my mind and then use them as often as possible.

The following model of responding, from Joanne Jozefowski's *The Phoenix Phenomenon* (Jason Aronson, 1999), is an excellent guide for working with those in crisis. No matter what model of grief or crisis you use, the following principles can be used at each stage or phase in the model.

Listen. Listen and listen some more—with your heart and your eyes, not just with your head and your ears. Your listening will let you know the person's level of functioning and coping. Listen for any indications of bodily, as well as emotional, complaints. Hear his or her own struggles and challenges, and then adjust and adapt. Listen to discover what he or she needs to know.

Assess. Throughout every session, you need to assess their needs as well as their progress. Using the grief or crisis model will help you do this. What you discover will help you determine what tasks need to be accomplished or can be completed.

Normalize. Use your counselees' own words and descriptions to describe where they're at in their crisis or grief. Above all, they need to know whatever they're experiencing is normal for this stage or phase. Physical, emotional and spiritual struggles will come and go; they are normal. Validation brings reassurance and encouragement. Give counselees copies of the crisis chart, grief charts or listings of symptoms—anything that might help them through the crisis. Let them know that grief comes and goes. It will drop in for unexpected visits as an unwelcome guest.

Reassure. Let them know they will be able to work through the process, even though they may not feel like it. Assure them there will be others available to work through it with them. Never leave them isolated.

Support. Support any effort they make, no matter how small—you may need to reframe growth for them. Any ideas they come up with need to be affirmed by you to help them see that they're capable of moving ahead.

Plan. Planning is always in the foreground or background as you counsel. Remember to

1. make realistic, attainable plans—don't overwhelm;
2. prioritize needs and the most important plans;
3. codesign the plans—don't do it all yourself.

Educate. When appropriate, provide printed information. Let them hear from others who have grown in similar situations. What you share early on may be learned later when concentration is better. You will need to repeat yourself.

Monitor. Be on the lookout for decomposition, depression, regression, withdrawal, suicidal intention or anger that the counselee might act out. Listen to your hunches and ask questions. Be prepared to intervene when needed. It's better to refer too soon than too late.

After each of the eight steps listed in this chapter have been followed, stop and ask yourself, *Which of the BIPs need to be employed at this time?* This is one way to make these a part of your mind-set.

STEP 2: TAKE ACTION

The second step of crisis counseling is *action*. Something needs to start happening right away. People in crisis tend to flounder, and we need to move them toward meaningful, purposeful and goal-directed behavior. They need to know that something is being done by them and for them.

> **People in crisis tend to flounder, and we need to move them toward meaningful, purposeful and goal-directed behavior.**

They need to feel this right from the first session. This is not the time to have them fill out questionnaires, take a personality test, explore their history or establish rapport. You, as the minister or counselor, need to be very active. You will need to participate in, contribute to and direct this first session. Remember that listening is an important part of gathering information.

During this time, help the person understand the crisis. Usually the crisis is related to some event, but he or she is not able to bridge the two. The person needs to bring his or her feelings of despair together with the event. Encourage the person to express his or her thoughts and feelings.

Consider Prior Crises

Even though crisis counseling does not focus much upon the past, it is important to determine how the person was functioning prior to the crisis. It is not necessary to do a structured investigative inquiry, but listen for significant information through the interaction process. You are looking for indications of the previous emotional state, behavioral patterns, thought processes, relationships with other people and any physical problems. In a sense, you are endeavoring to discover what happened, who is involved, when it happened and so on. The questions who, what, when, where, why and how will be your guide. This is usually accomplished by having the person tell his or her story.

Significant issues need to be discovered and considered, such as: What are the person's strengths? What are the weaknesses or deficiencies (i.e., low-paying job, poor self-image, few friends and so on)? Why did their problem-solving ability break down at this time? Has anything similar to this ever occurred before? These questions are necessary because in crisis theory there is a basic premise: Most people involved in a crisis have experienced some type of precipitating event and it needs to be determined. As the person tells his or her story, listen to how he or she feels. What impact has this crisis had on the person's work, friendships, family life and physical health? Is his or her daily routine the same or has it been altered? What are the person's thought processes like? Is his or her thinking intact and clear? Are there excessive fantasies? Dreams?

As you work with someone, give attention to both his or her strengths and weaknesses. Many people in crisis have aspects of their lives that are not affected. Look for these, as well as the weak areas. As you discover strengths or abilities that are a part of the person's lifestyle, you then can encourage the person in that direction.

For instance, one counselee was involved in a physical exercise program. He was encouraged to continue this regularly because it served as a basis for building self-confidence and energy and it was a distraction from his problem. For others, family members and friends can be a source of strength. It is important to keep these questions coming: Does the counselee have an available support system? Is there an indication of dangerous behavior to the person or someone else?

Besides looking at a counselee's past, be sure to look at any potential future difficulties for the person or his or her family. Some might need help in telling parents or children what has occurred, or an abused spouse may need a safe place to stay.

As you are gathering this information from the person's story and your questions, you are seeking to discover the answers to the following questions:

1. What issues in the person's life need to be attended to immediately?
2. What issues can be postponed until later?

Help the person make this determination, because often people in crisis are not aware of what can wait and what must be handled now. As you work more and more in crisis situations, you will discover that you seldom have to conduct a question-by-question approach to derive this information. The person will volunteer most of it. However, as you discuss the situation with the person, *be sure to keep all these questions and issues in mind.*[3]

Consider Communication Skills

Be aware of the person's level of alertness and his or her communication capabilities. Attempt to identify the cause of the crisis with questions or statements, such as: "What has happened to make you so upset?" "Can you tell me the reason you're so upset? I would like to hear what you have to say" or "I'd like to hear what happened." (The guidelines for conducting a critical incident stress debriefing, CISD, can be put in use here as well. See chapter 11.) Those in a crisis sometimes have difficulty clearly stating what they want to say. When this occurs, you will need to be very patient. Any verbal or nonverbal indications of impatience, discomfort or urging the person to hurry will be detrimental. Allow for pauses and remain calm. Remember that especially during the impact phase of the crisis, there is a stage of confusion and disorientation, and the mental processes are not functioning as they normally would. Some of the pain is so extreme that words will not come easily.

As you listen to the person, notice if any important themes are being expressed. You usually can detect them through repetitive statements or intense statements. These are clues to the person's point of stress.

Filter. On occasion, you will need to channel the direction of the conversation. Some crisis situations need action taken *immediately* rather than tomorrow or next week. You can reinforce statements that are related to the crisis and avoid responding to unrelated topics such as rambling statements that deal with the past or peripheral events. You might say, "What you have just said sounds important to you, and in the future we can talk about it. However, right now, it doesn't seem directly related to your real concern. Let's come back to that." This focusing process helps filter out any material that is irrelevant to the crisis but that the person may not realize is meaningless.

Clarify. If you're confused by what is said, don't hesitate to ask for clarification. When people are able to express themselves fairly well, help them explore the available alternatives to deal with the situation. A helpful question is, What else might be done at this time? Discover what type of support system the person has—spouse, parents, friends, fellow workers or even people in your congregation whom you have trained to be a support for an isolated person. The person you're counseling may be the new person in town with no contacts or roots in your area. You will need to help create a new support system in addition to whatever help you can personally give.

Consider Perception

A person in a crisis will interpret his or her environment as something that is difficult to manage. The person sees confusion and perhaps even chaos. Try to determine if you might be able to bring a greater sense of order to the person's environment. If you can assist in bringing a sense of calm and stability, you will help him or her a great deal. Perhaps the person needs to stay at a different location for a while. He or she may need some space and quiet. Even those who are attempting to help might actually be adding to the confusion by their inappropriate attempts.

As the person is talking, assess what he or she is telling you and compare it with the problem as you see it. A crisis is triggered by the person's perception of what has occurred. You may experience times when you feel the counselee is overreacting, but remember that what he or she is reacting to might not be the main problem. Some people fall apart over an insignificant occurrence that is really only a trigger mechanism. They may have a blocked or delayed response to a crucial problem.

For example, a mother appeared to be functioning quite well after a major accident that killed one person and critically injured her son. But while doing dishes in her kitchen, she dropped a plate and immediately she fell apart. She alternated between hysterical weeping and intense anger. A relative visiting in the home could not understand this reaction to the simple breaking of a plate. The minister who worked with her later in the day, however, was able to bring all the factors together.

Ministers and lay counselors alike often ask, "How do I know how much action to take?" A rule of thumb is this: Only if circumstances severely limit the counselee's ability to work through the crisis do you take extensive action. If you do take action, you want to move the person to an independent role as soon as possible.

Consider a Facilitative or Directive Role

It has been suggested that you take either a facilitative or a directive role in helping the person deal with the crisis.

If the crisis creates danger for the person or for others, if the person is so emotionally overwhelmed that he or she has no capability to function or take care of himself or herself, if the person is on drugs or alcohol or if he or she has been injured, then you take a *directive role*.

When the person is not a danger to others or to himself or herself, when the person is capable of making phone calls, running errands, driving and caring for himself or herself or others, your role is *facilitative.* While the counselee and you make the plans together, the counselee carries out the plans. You may even want to work out a contract with the person, detailing how the plans are to be carried out.

If your action is directive, the two of you need to work out the plans together—the action involves both of you. The agreement or contract agreed upon also can involve others such as a friend, spouse, parent, child, agency or church deacon. You need to be involved to the extent that the next step will be carried out by the person and the support people.

Whether you are taking directive or facilitative action, *listening* and *encouraging* are primary tools.

Since advice falls under facilitative action, you might say, "You know, I am concerned about what's happening to you at this time. Let's do this for now . . . "

With facilitative action, you can advise new approaches and actions. You can also advise a new way of thinking or looking at the situation. Often I have people come in with statements such as, "I'm cracking up"; "I think I'm going crazy"; "I must be the only person to feel this way"; "Other people don't have this much pain, do they?"; "I am really a crummy Christian, aren't I?" and "If I had more faith, I wouldn't be responding this way." What are these people really saying? What are they really feeling? They're saying, "I'm out of control. I'm afraid." They are trying to figure out what is happening to them, and this is their attempt to understand their predicament.

This is your opportunity to offer realistic reassurance with statements such as, "It's common to feel this way, but in reality, it's doubtful you're going crazy. Your reaction and feelings are normal considering all that you have experienced." Or you might say, "With all you've been through, I'd be a bit concerned if you weren't reacting in some way." Helping them realize that their feelings and reactions are normal can be a source of relief. Normalizing accomplishes so much.

At this point, I show counselees the crisis sequence chart described in chapter 8, which helps relieve pressure. Consider the implications of thinking you are going crazy or cracking up. Would this pattern of thinking help you recover or hinder the progress? Subtly and perhaps unconsciously, it becomes a blockage. Relabeling what is occurring is a part of the process of building hope.

When you're involved in helping a person with direct action, keep in mind the specific laws and legal procedures of your state and community. For example, do you as a minister, professional counselor or lay counselor have the status of privileged information or confidentiality when you counsel? What does the law state if the person talks specifically about suicidal or homicidal intent? Can someone in your county be involuntarily confined in a hospital for observation if the person appears emotionally distraught or suicidal? What if a parent tells you that he or she physically abused his or her child four years ago? What if an adolescent tells you that she has been sexually abused? You need to know the law and any recent changes.

Unfortunately, because of time constraints, their own personality or lack of available training, many ministers tend to take direct action too often. Before you take action, ask yourself questions such as:

- *Is this something the person could do for himself or herself?*
- *What will this accomplish in the long run?*
- *How long will I need to be involved in this way?*
- *Are there any risks in doing this? If so, what are they?*
- *How could this person be helped in a different manner?*

Consider Alternative Action

Because the feeling of helplessness is so strong during a crisis, you can counter this feeling by encouraging the person to create alternatives and take action. It will also help the person operate from a position of strength rather than weakness. One way of doing this is to ask the person how they've handled previous difficulties. Once again, remember to have the counselee do as much work as possible in order to have him or her build self-esteem.

Coach the person to consider the possibility that there are alternatives. Some statements can be structured in this way: "Let's consider this possibility. What if you were to . . . ?"; "What might happen if you would . . . ?"; "What do you think someone else might try at this time?"

and "Let's think of a person you feel is a real problem solver. What might that person do?" Be sure to help the person anticipate any obstacles to implementing the plan. We cannot assume that the person will follow through without first considering the obstacles.[4]

STEP 3: RESTORE BALANCE

The third step is to start achieving the *limited goal* of crisis counseling— to *avert catastrophe and restore the person to a state of balance.* This is not a time to attempt personality changes. You must first help the person achieve some type of limited goal. There should be a bit of challenge to it, but it must also be attainable. A person who just lost his or her job may be able—with your help—to make a list of his or her qualifications, abilities and job experiences. Just the simple task of completing an action can provide a sense of relief.

The following are two ways to help a person restore balance:

First, look at the information the person is giving you about the situation. Does he or she see the complete picture or only selected aspects? Does he or she have all the facts? Is the person distorting the situation because of his or her emotions or biases? Does he or she understand that certain responses and feelings are normal during times of crisis?

Asking pertinent questions and prodding for informational answers can help the person in two ways:

1. You can help to fill in some of his or her informational gaps.
2. The person's fears and overconcerns can be diminished as he or she receives accurate information.

Both of these steps help to restore equilibrium.

STEP 4: FOSTER HOPE AND POSITIVE EXPECTATIONS

Since people in crisis feel hopeless, it's important to *foster hope and positive expectations.* Don't give them false promises, but encourage them to solve their problems. Your belief in their capabilities will be important.

This is a time when they need to borrow your hope and faith until their own returns. You expect the crisis to be resolved in some way at some time, and you expect them to work and be able to solve problems. It is your approach and interaction with them that usually conveys this rather than blanket statements you might make.

The problem-solving approach—rather than giving false reassurances—is a positive step. As the anxiety level of the person drops, he or she will see the situation in a more objective manner. When this occurs, the person can reflect on what has happened and what is now occurring.

> **Don't give counselees false promises, but encourage them to solve their problems. Your belief in their capabilities will be important.**

In addition to considering what the person in crisis is dealing with, note how he or she is interacting with the objective situation. How does the person grasp the choice of action open to him or her in light of the recent changes in life (such as the loss of a job or a spouse)? What options are left open to this person (such as caring for the children if a spouse has died or left)? Help the person consider the choices and the consequences of any decision to himself or herself and others who may be involved. Examining choices and consequences and then selecting a path enable a person to cope both now and in future situations.

As the counselee gains greater strength and capability, he or she will be able to examine his or her own part in the situation and his or her response of feelings and behavior.

STEP 5: PROVIDE SUPPORT

The fifth step in counseling a person in crisis is to *provide support*. One of the reasons why a problem develops into a crisis is the lack of an adequate social support system. Intervention in a crisis involves giving support, and initially, you may be the only one giving it. Just being available to talk by phone is a good source of support.

Telephone Calls

The knowledge that you are praying for the person each day and are available to pray with the person over the phone is a source of support. Do not be surprised by a number of "urgent" calls during the early stages of a crisis. These need to be returned promptly and often. It is important to return calls promptly, but that is not the same as immediately. If you drop everything you are doing to call back within a few minutes, a dependency relationship might be encouraged. If, however, a half hour goes by, the person has the opportunity to do some thinking on his or her own. The person may calm down, and by the time you do talk to him or her, the problem or issue is no longer as critical. This is important because it takes you out of the "magical, miracle worker" role. If the person is highly suicidal, of course, then you need to call immediately. You also need to provide him or her with the phone numbers of other agencies and ask for his or her commitment to call them if you are not available.[5]

At some point, you may need to set some limits on the phone calls as a person becomes better able to handle his or her life. To express limits, you can tell the person that, because he or she is better handling the situation, you want him or her to exercise his or her capabilities a bit more and you want the person to call only during your office hours. Set a time limit on the calls, and perhaps suggest that he or she begin to try to let a day go by between phone calls. If you know he or she will probably call, suggest a time when it would be more convenient for you to respond. Sometimes I have suggested to counselees that they give me a call at a specific time on a specific day. I explain that I have a brief break in my schedule at that time, and I would just like to know how the person is getting along.

Support System

The best way of supporting the person is to expand his or her support system as soon as possible. This reduces demands on you, and it helps the person through the crisis now. It can also help to prevent a crisis in the future. More and more churches are training and equipping laypeople to become involved in counseling. And since crisis counseling is short-term, this is one of the best types of counseling to prepare them for: counseling that assists, supports, helps with funeral arrangements, aids in victim relief and so on.

Be sure you give some specific guidance to the support people. They are not to give a lot of verbal advice, which may be well intended but is unnecessary and not beneficial at this point. Note how the person is stabilizing with this support and, as soon as possible, gradually withdraw the support. We do not want counselees to expect and depend upon others living their lives for them over an extended period of time.

Other Important Cues

If you have a crisis counseling session that involves either a couple or a family, the following are some other principles to follow: When the couple or family comes to your office, take the initiative to go out, greet them by courteously introducing yourself and invite them into your office. Indicate where they are to sit. Speak to each one and show equal interest and friendliness. Let them know your purpose for the session and how much time you will be spending together.

You will be the most important element involved in setting the atmosphere for the joint or family sessions. Tell them that you want to help them and that they have the freedom to tell you how they perceive their current situation. Tell them that everyone will have the opportunity to talk and that you will help them look at the problem as it now exists and assist them in choosing a better way of handling the issues. It is also important to create a healthy atmosphere of communication. This may involve setting some specific guidelines, such as:

1. Only one person at a time should speak. Each one is listened to for the purpose of understanding his or her perception of the issue and how he or she is feeling. It's okay to ask questions.
2. Each one needs to speak for himself or herself and not for others. Any assumptions about another person's thoughts or feelings need to be checked out and verified.
3. A definite distinction will be made between thoughts and feelings and between facts and opinions.
4. Anything expressed that may be vague will be clarified so that all those present understand the specifics.

5. There will be differences in opinions, which is alright. The points will be clarified rather than argued. Some issues will be resolved and others may not be. Some issues raised may be dropped because they cannot be resolved.

6. When a person is speaking, he or she may do so without being interrupted, but monologues will not be acceptable. A monologue causes others to lose interest, and the person talking gains control. Further, as the person continues to talk, it may cause his or her own feelings to escalate or may bother the others. You can interrupt the monologue to clarify a point, ask another person what he or she is hearing, comment upon someone else's nonverbal responses or even say, "You know, you've brought up so many good points that I want to stop and clarify some of them."[6]

Regarding the last point, there may be occasions when it is difficult to stop the person. In this case, lean forward, raise your hand a bit and say, "Let's stop for a minute," in a definite, firm voice, which should keep you in control. I remember a very volatile family conference with five adults. The anger had escalated and people were rudely interrupting, each trying to outtalk the others. I listened a bit to see if they would gain control and then in a loud, firm voice said, "Alright, hold it!" They stopped and looked at me in shock. I went on to say, "Not one of you is listening, and you are getting nowhere. Now, this is what we are going to do if we are going to get anywhere." And I proceeded to again establish the guidelines and also stated that if there were a violation, I would interrupt the person to keep him or her on track. This does not happen too often, but you need to be firm if it does.

STEP 6: FOCUS ON PROBLEM SOLVING

The sixth step, *focused problem solving*, has been called the backbone of crisis counseling. You and the counselee try to determine the main problem that led to the crisis, and then you help the person plan and implement ways to resolve it. You may discover other side issues and problems along the way, but you need to stay focused on this one problem until it is resolved.

Think of yourself and the counselee as a team. You will work together. Dr. William Glasser, author of *Reality Therapy* (HarperCollins, 1989), uses the word "we" in his counseling: "What can we do?"; "How can we figure this out?"; or "Let's see what we can develop as we spend this time together." Involving the counselee in the plan accomplishes two things:

1. It increases his or her chances of following through.
2. It helps to develop self-reliance.

Set Goals

During the problem-solving phase, focus on setting goals, looking at the resources available to solve the problem and brainstorming alternatives. Make a list of the alternatives that could be used. If the person is running dry on ideas, which often occurs, you can suggest some alternatives. You are not giving advice or telling him or her what to do; rather, you are offering other possibilities from which he or she can choose.

Be Sensitive to Current Values

Help the person look at the consequences of each action, both negative and positive. A major question is, Will this alternative in any way counter the person's sense of values? For example, a husband who is having financial difficulties but who highly values time with his family and having his weekends free for church involvement may struggle with taking a second job that requires him to be out four nights a week and work three weekends a month.

Look for conflicting values by asking each counselee what the possible consequences of a decision are and his or her feelings about each of those possibilities. Let the counselee give his or her perception of the consequences first, and then—if you have additional, valid information—offer other possible suggestions.

I once talked with a woman whose divorce was to be final soon. She experienced an unexpected crisis during the Christmas holidays. As we talked, she indicated her tendency of wanting to return to her husband because of the emptiness of being alone. Through some simple questions, she was able to evaluate what had occurred in the marriage and whether her husband was willing to change if they got back together.

I also discovered that the woman had not clearly expressed to her husband, in writing, the changes she needed in the relationship to consider stopping the divorce. This was posed to her as a possible course of action, along with reading Jim Smoke's book *Growing Through Divorce* (Harvest House Publishers, 1995) and seeking out a divorce recovery group for assistance. When she left the 45-minute appointment, she seemed to be in better control. Since she now had some tangible steps to follow, she was no longer immobilized.

Select a Course of Action

After you evaluate the various alternatives, help the counselee select a course of action. You may need to encourage and even urge him or her to do so. Ask the person for a commitment that covers what, how and when he or she will do it. Go through the process step-by-step and in detail, and try to anticipate any roadblocks or ways the person may inadvertently sabotage the process.

You may become frustrated if the person says, "Oh, I've tried all of these things that we've talked about and they've never worked before" or "Oh, yes, I know what to do. I've had these plans before, but somehow I never get around to completing them." Your patience, your belief in his or her capabilities and your help to construct a workable plan may make the difference. It might help to ask for a commitment in writing, which spells out the details of the plan for both of you to remember.

I talked with another woman who had three specific alternatives to use for her difficulty, all of which she had used before. When these were implemented, her difficulties began to subside. This was a case where she said, "Oh, I know what to do, but I don't know why I don't follow through." I suggested, "Let's put those three steps into action this week. Will you take the medication your physician prescribed, follow the reading exercises recommended by your treatment program each day for this next week and then evaluate how you are feeling?" She agreed to do so, and I was confident she would follow through.

Any of the plans that develop may need to be refined through a reviewing process. You may need to help the person redefine the problem. A man may say that his problem is that he lost his job. Your interpretation of that could be that he has not yet adjusted to the loss of his job or he has yet to consider a new source of employment. An older person may be shattered by the loss of a 17-year-old dog who was a constant companion. The problem seems to be that the dog died, but you would interpret it as that she has not yet adjusted to this loss in her life.

Whatever the crisis at hand, be sure you don't make either the problems or the solutions appear overly simple. Information may resolve the problem, but not always. Remember that you need to be an expert, not in solving a person's problems, but in the process of problem solving and helping him or her solve the problems himself or herself. This will be noted by your attitude and approach. As you begin working with someone, first focus on the problem so that it is properly defined and identified, and then turn to problem solving.

Face the Problem

Part of our task is to help counselees face the pain, but this must be done gradually, so they're not overwhelmed. We can create an environment in which they feel safe and comfortable enough to face their situation fully.

One of the best ways to respond to emotions is to use *active* listening. (This is one of the BIPs.) This type of listening involves being alert for the underlying, or latent, message and then checking it out to see if you have heard correctly.

Counselee: I just don't think it's worth the time and effort.
Minister: You're feeling kind of hopeless about it and doubting if it's worth trying.

In a sense, we sometimes guess about counselees' feelings to help them clarify them. We are guessing at the meaning of what they are saying. Even if we are wrong, our listening will help counselees clarify their problems. When you are listening in this way, you are making statements rather than asking questions. This approach keeps the problem within the counselee's responsibility, but he or she feels your support as he or she seeks to discover a solution. It conveys respect and acceptance as well as your expectation that the person will be able to solve the problem. This approach is useful when talking with someone who has a problem, but it should not be used in other circumstances.

Monitor Feelings

Monitor the anxiety level in each person and attempt to regulate that level. There will always be some amount of anxiety, and some is necessary for the person to be motivated to face his or her problems. However, we want to keep it from overwhelming the person. One way to accomplish this is to regulate the amount of emotion expressed and how it is expressed. When you work with couples or families, anger is the most common emotion. Your tone and example can be helpful in regulating the level. Note how each person may be responding by his or her posture and the intensity of his or her verbal responses.

Within the process of problem solving, feelings are important. If these are short-circuited, they will tend to short-circuit the problem solving later on. There are no shortcuts to helping a person in crisis. In many crises, there is a grief over loss. It is common to equate grief with the loss incurred in the death of a loved one. But the loss of a job, a home, a valued object, a friendship, a family member (through divorce or separation), an opportunity, hope, ambition, as well as impending bad news, all bring grief. Therefore, encourage the person and help him or her work through his or her feelings of loss. It is necessary that the grief work be accomplished. If you become upset or overwhelmed by an upset person, you will not be able to help. Your tendency may be to try to stop him or her from getting upset.

In reality, counselees will express many feelings. You can help them sort out their feelings and identify those that are most acute.

As counselees share their hurt, you may feel it to an extreme degree and even feel like crying with them. But perhaps they need your strength at that point and just want you to be a good listener. I remember a woman who made an appointment for counseling. When she came in, she said that her husband had been killed in a steam shovel accident two weeks earlier while working on a job.

All of a sudden, I knew what the woman was talking about, for I remembered seeing the newscast showing the accident. She went on to describe—through tears—her feelings for her husband and what each of the children said about him after his death. She relived their hard times and their good times. She mentioned that the night before his death he had attended church with her and given his life to the Lord. As she expressed the feelings and gave me all this information, I had to fight back my own tears and struggle to maintain composure. She could sense my feelings with her, but she did not need to handle the intensity of my emotions at that time.

On another occasion, a young husband described his feelings of being stuck in life with nowhere to go and with no hope. I could feel his hurt and despair and I said to him, with tears in my eyes, "I can feel your hurt and wish there was more that I could say or do." He said, "I know and thank you."

On the flip side, though, take note of the person who is *not* experiencing or showing grief when grief should be the normal response. I have seen several people who appeared quite composed and seemingly in control. They even expressed the fact that they are "handling everything quite well." You might say something like, "I guess if I were in your situation, I would be hurting and feeling the loss like an empty spot in my life. I wonder what you might be feeling at this time?" Or you might say, "There will be a time when you feel the hurt and loss and you'll probably weep. Maybe this isn't yet the time to weep, but it will come."

With this last statement, I have seen the composure break and the tears flow as the pain is experienced. This was not hard-heartedness but a loving gesture on my part. It was an invitation to feel the hurt and to share it with another person who would be there during the time of grief.

In crisis counseling, think about feelings in this way: They're steps that must be dealt with before the real work of problem solving can occur. These can be handled by good listening procedures. In time, move from relating the feelings to the problem-solving or thinking process. This means moving from the ventilation of feelings to rational evaluation and resolution. This occurs whether the crisis situation involves a family or one person. If you see a family in crisis, there may be blaming, anger and attacks. Sometimes feelings can escalate and get out of hand if you do not help them make the connection between feelings and solutions. Encourage the person or people to begin the thinking process as soon as possible. At this time, you may be functioning like a guide bringing the person or persons to their destination.

STEP 7: UNDERSTAND AND ASSESS SELF-IMAGE

It may sound strange to bring in the subject of self-concept within the context of crisis counseling, but this seventh step is one of the most important. It involves (1) assessing and understanding the person's self-image and (2) discovering how the crisis affects it and how what you do affects it. This is a time both to protect and to enhance the self-image. During crises, there are both anxiety and low self-esteem.

The following are some typical responses of people who have feelings of low self-esteem:

- anger at other people or even at you,
- desperation that involves demanding help, and
- passivity that involves sitting back and waiting for help.

Sometimes the person who seeks your help is the one experiencing the crisis, or it may be someone who is trying to help a person in crisis but is not succeeding. Either one may have the same struggle with self-esteem. Be aware of the person's tendency to blame in order to protect his or her self-image. The blame usually will be coupled with anger. Anger sometimes gives a person a sense of control or of being in charge again. And even if it is irrational, it feels better than the state of hopelessness.

Some ministers and students have told me of their shock at the extent of the antagonism and belligerence that has been shown toward them as they have tried to help. We don't have to be thrown by this if, in our own minds, we can say, *It is all right for them to feel this way, and I do not have to take it personally. It is their protection against their feelings of failure and helplessness.*

Expect negative feelings and see them for what they are—a camouflage against the pain of feeling bad about the situation and not feeling too good about oneself either.

Your task, then, is to be consistent in helping the person elevate feelings about himself or herself. It also involves helping the person protect his or her self-image. Treat the person with respect and courtesy, and do not be condescending. It sometimes helps to show an interest in some untroubled areas of his or her life.

Avoid Labeling

If you are working with a family and a particular individual is identified as the problem person, determine the effect of this labeling. Unfortunately, when families come in with a crisis and point the finger at one person, they fail to realize their own contribution to the problem and the ways they reinforce the behavior they do not like. In this situation, you may need to divert attacks of family members by reinterpreting what they are saying, helping them see the positive points or strengths in the person and moving toward a solution rather than lingering on the blame. You can focus on the attacker and talk about his or her feelings and responses, or you can change the subject and begin asking, "What can we try at this time to change this situation? I would like a couple suggestions from each of you, and I would like to know why you feel your suggestions would work."

Help them see how they have resolved difficulties before. When they say, "I can't handle anything; I can't even get through the day," respond with something like, "I saw you come into my office by yourself, and you have been a big help by being able to provide so much information about your difficulty." If someone says he or she has difficulty expressing himself or herself, you could say, "You're concerned that you are not communicating well, but you are very clear and doing very well in telling me the problem."

Thus, one of your goals is to express to the counselee your perception of him or her. You need to believe that he or she has value, worth and capabilities and at the present time is simply overwhelmed by the difficulty. Your assessment of the person may be more positive than his or her assessment, and eventually, he or she may accept your assessment.

> **You need to believe that the counselee has value, worth and capabilities and at the present time is simply overwhelmed by the difficulty.**

In regard to handling the difficulties, many Christians believe that they *should* be able to handle anything and that if they had more faith or a stronger relationship with the Lord, they would not be floundering. This mind-set tends to produce more guilt, bad feelings and lower self-esteem. Hopefully at some point later in the recovery phase, they'll be able to recall that many of the people God used in Scripture went through times of trouble as well.

As counselees perceive that you believe in them and see them as capable people, they will catch the fact that you have expectations for them. Again, the idea of teamwork needs to be emphasized, because you will brainstorm together, plan together, pray together and solve the problem together.

STEP 8: INSTILL SELF-RELIANCE

Along with helping to strengthen the person's self-image, we work through the final stage to *instill self-reliance*. Remember that a person in crisis is at the end of his or her rope. And because of this, the person's behavior may be regressive—he or she may respond at an earlier level of functioning. The person wants to be rescued and healed instantaneously by you. Do not respond to this need, however, for it will lower the counselee's self-esteem and, in time, create hostility toward you.

To keep a person from becoming too reliant on you, you need to make it clear that you do not have all the answers. You expect effort from the counselee. Make sure the person is beginning to do things and is doing them successfully. This means that small steps should be undertaken or the person will become overwhelmed. This is especially true for anyone in depression, for any failure sends him or her two steps back down the ladder.

As stated before, you are developing a team effort in planning and evaluating the situation. Self-reliance comes from the counselee's involvement in the planning.

If you are working with someone who is, for the most part, a dependent person, it will be more difficult to get him or her to take responsibility. Others who know this person may alert you to this fact.

Assign Responsibility

One of the most basic principles to follow in crisis counseling is this: *Do nothing for the counselee that he or she can do successfully.* If there is a choice between you or the counselee making a phone call and if the counselee has the capability of doing it, have him or her do it. As Douglas Puryear puts it:

> You are attempting to convey by your entire approach, your attitude that the client is a capable, decent person who has been temporarily overwhelmed by extreme stresses, and who will use your help to cope with these stresses and get back on track.[7]

Let's dissect Puryear's sentence: "convey by your entire approach" means to convey better than just verbally; "is a capable, decent person" indicates support of the counselee's self-image; "temporarily overwhelmed" means the crisis situation is temporary—this provides hope and expectation; "who will use your help to cope" means to define your role (the counselee will cope with your help; you can't cope for the person, but you can offer your support to his or her problem solving); and "get back on track" is the goal of returning to equilibrium.

Deal with the Emotions at Hand

When people attempt to cope with their stress, their emotions run deep. They may have to cope with the threat to their source of past security and sense of competence and self-esteem. If these have been shattered, they have to deal with feelings of loss and longing.

You may be surprised by the person's reaction if you have known him or her over a period of time. You may have seen the individual as alert, strong and very capable. Now you cannot understand why he or she is falling apart. You may be shocked, threatened and overwhelmed yourself. You may be angry because you are seeing a strong person become so weak. The person's reaction may threaten your own sense of security, which may be solid or fragile. If he or she can fall apart, perhaps you, too, have that same capability under stressful conditions. It can happen to any of us!

Cope with a New Role

In addition, new anxieties and frustrations will emerge. Because of the upheaval of the crisis, the person has to make new decisions, devise new solutions and find new resources. The individual also may have to move into a new role of some sort. And the new solution or role, once selected and implemented, may carry with it some stress of its own. Adjusting to the new solution and role will occur because of shifts in position and status in the family and community. It involves acceptance of the new solution and the level of satisfaction with the solution—learning to live with being less than satisfied until the new solution or role is stabilized.

It all comes down to this: You are the helper God has called to walk people through these transitions.

RECOMMENDED RESOURCES

Resources on Critical Incident Stress Debriefing (CISD)

Lewis, Gerald W., Ph. D. *Critical Incident Stress and Trauma in the Workplace.* Muncie, IN: Accelerated Development, 1994.

Mitchell, Jeffrey T., Ph.D., and George S. Everly, Jr., Ph.D. *Critical Incident Stress Debriefing: An Operations Manual.* Ellicot, MD: Chevron Publishing Corporation, 1997.

Resources to Equip Your Congregation

Crisis Care: The Victory videocassette series and *Crisis Care II: The Victory* videocassette series.

Kuenning, Delores. *Helping People Through Grief.* Minneapolis, MN: Bethany House Publishers, 1987.

Lampman, Lisa Barnes, ed. *Helping a Neighbor in Crisis.* Carol Stream, IL: Tyndale House, 1997.

Schweibert, Pat, and Chuck DeKlyen. *Tear Soup: A Recipe for Healing After Loss.* 2nd rev. ed. Portland, OR: Perinatal Loss, 2001. This outstanding book and video for all ages is the ideal tool to show in the home, in schools, in churches and in companies. It affirms the bereaved, educates the unbereaved and is a building block for children. This is a must-have resource for any person working in the field of grief recovery.

Wright, H. Norman. *Helping Others Recover from Losses and Grief.* Orange, CA: Christian Marriage Enrichment, 1998. This is a teaching curriculum with reproducible transparency patterns, which can be used in classes, church or community or for preaching.

———. *How to Help a Friend.* Minneapolis, MN: Bethany House Publishers, 2003.

The above material for your congregation can all be ordered through Christian Marriage Enrichment, P.O. Box 2468, Orange, CA 92859, (800) 875-7560.

WHEN TIME
DOESN'T HEAL ALL
WOUNDS

Trauma. It began in the Garden with Adam and Eve. Their act of disobedience led to their banishment and the ensuing consequences. The losses they experienced were life changing and overwhelming (see Gen. 3). And as often happens when trauma touches one family, there is a ripple effect upon other members, as was the case with Adam and Eve's direct descendants Cain and Abel.

Another biblical man, Job, lost his family, farm and health in a sudden and violent fashion (see Job 1:13-19). David also was a trauma survivor. He's usually remembered as a hero and not a victim, but as you read the Psalms you will see vacillations in his spiritual and emotional life. He had a battlefield career, killed thousands and witnessed unbelievable human slaughter. He went from anxiety and sorrow to emotional numbing, or detachment. His own losses were extensive. And the ripple effect continued. David's daughter Tamar was raped by her half-brother, Amnon (see 2 Sam. 13:10-15); Amnon then was killed at the command of David's other son, Absalom, who later died a violent death (see 2 Sam. 13:28; 18:9-15). But through all of this, David learned to trust in God:

In the LORD I take refuge. In you our fathers put their trust; they trusted and you delivered them. They cried to you and were saved; in you they trusted and were not disappointed (Ps. 11:1; 22:4-5).

Other biblical incidents include gang rape (see Judg. 19); Jonah's shipwreck and being swallowed by a whale (see Jon. 1:15-17); Paul's beating, imprisonment and three shipwrecks (see 2 Cor. 11:23-28) and Christ's experience of crucifixion on the cross (see Luke 23:26-49). Jesus' journey started on a Thursday night. Jesus and three of His disciples came to the garden to spend time praying. The disciples didn't know what was coming—only Jesus did. He hoped for their support during this time of fear and dreaded anticipation. During this difficult time, He became quite depressed and possibly experienced anticipatory anxiety. It also could have been terror, since His body perspired drops of blood. His disciples didn't know what to expect, and due to their fatigue, they fell asleep. We read these stories and they seem so factual, but each one is filled with trauma:

And He took with Him Peter and James and John, and began to be struck with terror and amazement and deeply troubled and depressed. And He said to them, My soul is exceedingly sad (overwhelmed with grief) so that it almost kills Me! Remain here and keep awake and be watching (Mark 14:33-34, *AMP*).

Trauma continued to be noted throughout history. It occurred in the Middle Ages and during the Civil War. Shakespeare wrote about it in *Henry IV*. It's been called tunnel disease, nostalgia, soldier's heart, nervous exhaustion and De Costa's syndrome. But it wasn't until World

War I that the term "shell shock" was coined. Later it was called war memories. It came to the forefront after the Vietnam War and became known as post-traumatic stress disorder, or PTSD. It's also referred to as trauma or aftershock, which are new names for an old problem.

It's been a constant in our country since day one, but largely overlooked. Most occurrences were individual or family traumas, or perhaps a fire, earthquake, tornado or hurricane. They lingered in the media for a few days and then vanished. We were vaguely aware of ongoing trauma in places like Bosnia and other countries, which for the most part didn't affect our day-to-day lives. However, that all began to change in the '90s.

First, in 1993 at the World Trade Center, then in 1995 in Oklahoma City and in Atlanta during the 1996 Olympics, followed by Columbine High School in Littleton, Colorado, and Wedgewood Baptist Church in Fort Worth, Texas, in 1999 and then New York City on September 11, 2001—no longer did the horrific traumas only take place in foreign countries. Americans now faced a new type of disruptive trauma in our lives, and ever since the 9/11 attack, we've been stunned. We experienced a twenty-first-century day of infamy—life in the United States has been altered forever. People will suffer the aftermath of this for years. And due to the extended TV exposure, many will experience secondary trauma for years. It's called CNN stress. We now have more than a passing acquaintance with trauma.

TRAUMA—IT IS MORE THAN MEETS THE EYE

Trauma is the response to any event that shatters your safe world so that it's no longer a place of refuge. Trauma is more than a state of crisis. It is a normal reaction to abnormal events that overwhelm a person's ability to adapt to life—where you feel powerless.

The word "trauma" comes from a Greek word that means "wound."[1] It's a condition characterized by the phrase, "I just can't seem to get over it." This experience is not limited to those who have gone through a war. I've seen it in the father who saw his daughter fatally crushed in an accident years ago and in women who were sexually abused as children or who experienced an abortion. I've seen it in the paramedic, the chaplain, the nurse, the survivor of a robbery, the traffic accident or rape victim and in those subjected to pressure or harassment in the workplace. I saw it in the faces of those in New York after 9/11.

> **When you experience trauma, you're thrown about like a rodeo steer. Your world turns wild, out of control, crazy.**

If you've ever been to a rodeo, you've probably seen a rider pursuing a steer. He guides his horse next to that galloping steer and, at the precise moment, leaps from his horse, grabs the steer's horns and pulls it to a dusty halt. With the right amount of pressure at the right time, he literally throws that steer to the ground. When you experience trauma, you're thrown about like that steer. Your world turns wild, out of control, crazy.

What we used to see as a safe world is no longer safe. What we used to see as a predictable world is no longer predictable. Most people overestimate the likelihood that their life is going to be relatively free from major crises or traumas; they underestimate the possibility of negative events happening to them. People never dreamed that the things that happen to them were ever going to happen. Perhaps that's why they're so devastated when bad things do happen to them—and what about us as helpers? What beliefs do you hold about life? What will happen to those beliefs if you experience trauma? It's important to ask yourself these questions before trauma enters your life, as it has the lives of so many.

If one lives with a feeling of invulnerability—the "it can't happen to me" mentality—trauma will not only wound him or her and destroy this belief, but it will fill his or her life with fear. Invulnerability is an illusion. We didn't have to be a victim of the bombing in Oklahoma City or the terrorist attack in New York to have our vulnerability snatched away. Just viewing the continuing vivid pictures on TV or the still photographs in the paper were sufficient to take us from the role of spectator to participant. We all ended up feeling that if it can happen there, it can happen here.

We see it all the time on TV. Most newscasts carry several stories with trauma potential. We see snatches of the tragedy, usually with a scene from the memorial service, a few anguished words from a family member or victim, and then the scene quickly shifts to another tragedy. It may be the last we see or hear of it and perhaps the last we think about it. But it's not over for those involved—it's just beginning. For some, the trauma will go on for years. For others, it will go on forever. Whenever I now see a tragedy, my first thought is to ask how many people were traumatized and how many of them will get the help they're going to need.

TRAUMA—HOW WIDESPREAD IS IT?

Perhaps you've asked the question that most people ask: How widespread *are* traumatic events in our country? How many people *are* exposed to traumatic events, such as natural and technological disasters, accidents, crime, abuse and war?

At one time, 75 percent of the general population in our country have been exposed to some event that meets the criteria of a trauma. Now it's even higher. The good news is that only about 25 percent of those exposed to such events become traumatized.[2]

TRAUMA—IT AFFECTS SOME AND NOT OTHERS

Not all trauma cases are the same. They can be mild, moderate or severe. It depends on the person's personality, spiritual or religious beliefs, culture and the meaning they ascribe to the trauma and event itself (man-made or natural disaster).[3]

You can experience a crisis and not end up traumatized. I was seven miles from the epicenter of the Whittier, California, earthquake, in a racquetball court watching the walls sway back and forth, but I wasn't traumatized by that.

I've been in intense winds and lightning and electromagnetic storms on lakes but wasn't traumatized.

The office of the American-Arab Anti-Discrimination League was 100 yards from my counseling office. One morning when I wasn't there, it was blown up by a terrorist bomb and the director was killed. I saw the results on television, but I wasn't terrorized.

When I was a teen, my family was saved by our collie barking and alerting us to a fire in our home, but none of us were traumatized.

There are other people walking around today who think and feel that the state of trauma they are in is just the way life is meant to be lived, but it's not.

I was a witness to a train wreck in which a speeding train devastated a Volkswagen that had tried to bypass the traffic gates and sneak across. In fact, I could see it happening in my mind before it occurred, because of my proximity, but I was powerless to stop it. I was secondarily traumatized by this experience.

Physical trauma can affect a person in two ways. First, trauma can affect some part of the body when a powerful impact damages the body's natural protection, such as skin or bones. It is also trauma when the body can't prevent the injury and the body's normal, natural healing capabilities can't mend the injury without some assistance.

Many of those you and I will counsel won't be able to put into words what their lives of trauma are like.

What's not so obvious is the emotional wounding of trauma. Your psyche can be so assaulted that your beliefs about yourself and about life, your will to grow, your spirit, your dignity and your sense of security are damaged. You end up feeling helpless. You can experience this to some degree in a crisis and still bounce back, but in a trauma, you have difficulty bouncing back because you feel derealization—Is this really happening?—and depersonalization—I don't know what I really stand for anymore. In essence, trauma is indescribable.

Elie Wiesel, a Nobel Peace Prize recipient and a survivor of Auschwitz, and his wife were in a taxi in Manhattan when the first tower of the World Trade Center was hit on September 11, 2001. They went home and turned on the television. He said, "We watched the first pictures. They were both surreal and biblical: the flames, the vertical collapse and the disappearance of the world's two proudest towers. Many of us were stunned into silence. Rarely have I felt such a failure of language."[4] Many of those you and I will counsel won't be able to put into words what their lives are like.

TRAUMA—NEUROLOGICAL AND PSYCHOLOGICAL EFFECTS

As the result of trauma, something happens in your brain that affects the way you process information. It affects how you interpret and store the event you experienced. In effect, it overrides your alarm system. Trauma has the power to disrupt how you process information. When you can't handle the stress, you then activate your survival techniques.[5]

What is normal when trauma hits? Often a person spontaneously enters into what is called an altered state of thinking and feeling, as well as something called experiencing their environment. These are called dissociative states, and they're involuntary. There are various physical indicators—the pupils dilate and breathing, pulse and blood pressure fluctuate.

The psychological symptoms include the distortion of time (time shrinks or expands), fixation of attention, a phenomenon called negative hallucination (not seeing or hearing what's going on right in front of them), a distortion of sensory experiences and age regression. The only benefit there might be is, with time shrinking, people might not see all the mayhem around them.[6]

Many have tried to help those traumatized, through counseling or critical incident debriefings, without ever understanding the reason the person is reacting and responding the way they are. We need to take a careful look at our mind and body. This next section may seem like a lesson in physiology and perhaps it is; but when you grasp it, you'll know the answer to the question, Why is he responding that way? Then you'll be better equipped to help.

Trauma—Physiological Effects

The brain is a creation at the hand of God. It is unique in its design, purposeful in its creation and wonderfully made (see Ps. 139).

Left Side Versus Right Side

This is what we know at the present time about our brain:

The left side has its own unique functions, as does the right side. The thinking pattern of the left side of the brain is analytical, linear, explicit, sequential, verbal, rational and goal oriented. It holds your beliefs, values and expectations. This hemisphere controls language and reading skills. It will gather information and process it logically in a step-by-step fashion. Some individuals are extremely left brained in their approach to life, while others seem to go through life reflecting just the right side. Others have a mixed dominance.

The right side is spontaneous, intuitive, emotional, nonverbal, visual, artistic and spatial. It's a picture album. The left side does the thinking and the right side has the pictures. It stores memories as pictures. Many are imbedded with energy and power, so just talking about the pictures doesn't remove the image. The language here is not words but a picture. This is where post-traumatic stress disorder (PTSD) pictures come from. Traumatic memory is like a series of still snapshots or a silent movie. There is no music or words.[7] This side processes patterns of information. It's the host of our emotions.

Figure 9   **The Brain**

Analytical	**L**	**R**	Spontaneous
Linear			Intuitive
Explicit			Emotional
			(women excel)
Sequential			Nonverbal
Verbal			
			Visual, artistic
			(women stronger)
Concrete			
Rational			Holistic
			Spatial
Goal-Oriented			(men stronger)

Parts of the Brain

There is a connector between the two sides of the brain, the corpus callosum, and it is how the two sides communicate. The corpus callosum integrates the emotional and cognitive aspects of our existence. Women have up to 40 percent more of these nerve bundles than men, which means that women are able to use both sides of their brain at the same time, whereas men have to switch from one side of the brain to the other, depending upon what they need. Women can enjoy more cross talk between both sides of the brain, since they use their brains holistically. This is why they can handle several tasks at one time and can read earlier than boys. However, humans need the functions of both sides to have balance and to derive the most out of life.

We've also given names to other sections of the brain (see figure 10); each section has different functions. Three other portions are as follow:

1. **Thalamus.** Receives incoming information through our senses of sight, smell, hearing, touch and taste and then passes it on to the other part of the brain for processing.
2. **Hippocampus.** Interprets emotional valence (vigor), controls emotional response by transforming sensory stimuli into emotional and hormonal signals and then refers this information to other parts that control behavior. It is analytical and *calms* down the emotional part of the brain: *No, the fact that he is a large person doesn't mean he'll hurt me. He's just large and eats a lot.* Also, when fear comes, it remembers where you are and what you are doing.
3. **Frontal Cortex.** Acts as the supervisory system of the whole process of integration of emotional and cognitive functions.[8]

When the brain functions the way it's supposed to, we function well. The problem with trauma, though, is that it can change all the proper functioning. Trauma is a wound. It's a wounding of the brain. It overwhelms the ordinary adaptations to life. Trauma creates PTSD. It is not just an emotional response to troubling events; it's the expression of a persistent deregulation of body and brain chemistry. And brain chemistry can

Figure 10

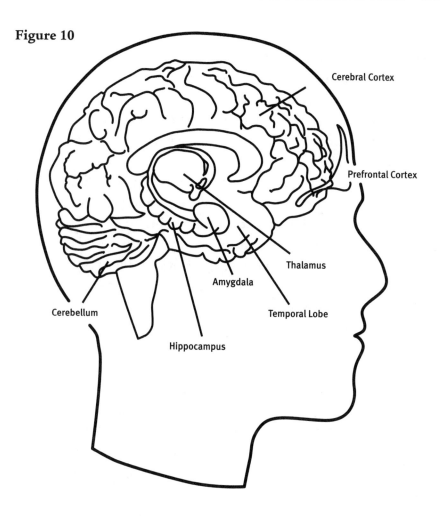

be altered for decades. With this change, arousing events can trigger flash-backs.[9] Trauma creates chaos in our brain and causes an emotional as well as a cognitive concussion:

> Entering the world of trauma is like looking into a fractured looking glass. The familiar appears disjointed and disturbing. A strange new world unfolds.[10]

In addition, if trauma occurs to a child, it hardwires the experience. In other words, the trauma can permanently affect the brain and all its functions.

The Amygdala

The amygdala is a small, almond-shaped portion of the brain. It looks like two small clusters of grapes, one on each side of the brain. It is the emotional part—the primitive part—of the brain. It interprets messages that declare danger or safety. It knows nothing about reasoning or cognitive functions. It deals with feelings and emotions. And it remembers what you're afraid of.

It is also the alarm portion of the brain. Every bit of information that enters your senses also flows through the amygdala, which is the early warning system. It constantly monitors this huge stream of information, trying to detect any signs of danger. For example, as you read this book, your eyes focus on the page. However, the amygdala scans those parts of your visual field that you are not paying attention to, such as the edges of your visual field—the corners of your eyes. It searches for possible threats, a sudden movement, a looming shadow. It monitors every sound your ears pick up, including background noises to which you are consciously oblivious. At night you rest, but the amygdala doesn't. It continues to monitor your sensory information for any sign of threat. If there's an earthquake or a door slams shut or the cat knocks a vase to the floor, the amygdala will instantly detect the menacing noise. It then activates its connections to the startle response so that you leap out of bed—heart racing—ready to protect yourself.[11] It also becomes highly active during and while remembering a traumatic incident. It controls your behavior. When you've been in trauma, it becomes hypersensitive and overreacts to normal stimuli. It sees a large person and feels, *He's going to hurt me. Oh no!*

Trauma—It Freezes Thinking

It is as though trauma causes the left side (the cognitive) and the right side (the emotional) to become disconnected from one another. Usually our body, emotions and thoughts are all connected, but trauma separates these from one another. Left brain and right brain have to pull together, otherwise just one side is in charge. And they do until trauma enters the picture. It splits them up. You may have vivid, graphic thoughts about what happened but have no emotion. Or you may experience intense emotions without the thoughts or actual memories. As one man said, "I feel like my brain was disrupted, and one part transmits the AM and the other the FM. Sometimes there are holes in my memory like a slice was taken out. Other times I can't get those intrusive, unwanted memories to stop. I want them evicted! I can't remember what I want to remember and I can't forget what I want erased." This struggle is shared by many.[12]

What this man described is called disassociation—a separation of the elements of the trauma experience which reduces the impact of the experience.[13]

Figure 11

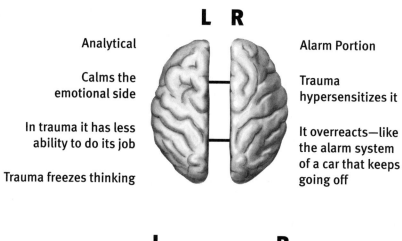

L   R

Analytical

Calms the
emotional side

In trauma it has less
ability to do its job

Trauma freezes thinking

Alarm Portion

Trauma
hypersensitizes it

It overreacts—like
the alarm system
of a car that keeps
going off

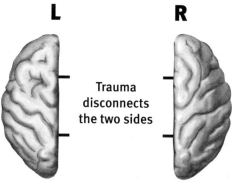

L   R

Trauma
disconnects
the two sides

Trauma is intrusive. It interrupts your current life. It can also constrict and limit your life. Sometimes you alternate between the two—you find yourself caught between amnesia and reliving the trauma; between floods of intense, overwhelming feeling and arid states of no feeling whatsoever; between irritable, impulsive action and complete inhibition of action.[14]

Traumatized people have alterations in their brain. The hippocampus is reduced in size. Memory is affected, which creates lapses, deficits in verbal recall and short-term memory deficits.

The frontal cortex ability is decreased; therefore, the brain is *less able* to do left-brain functions. It can't distinguish a real threat from a false threat. It also limits people from putting into words what they feel. *They may think there is danger when there isn't danger,* because the section of the brain that is supposed to analyze this isn't working.

The right side—the alarm section—reacts *too much. It's activated to danger when there isn't any.* It's like a car alarm system that keeps going off, even when there's no danger, and the owner with the key isn't around to turn it off. With a brain scan there is a lot of lighting up on the right side and very little on the left, which implies that people are not necessarily thinking as much with the left side of their brain.[15] So if they don't remember or their stories don't line up . . . Everyone is a bit ADD after a trauma.

Intense stress or trauma is accompanied with the release of hormones. A nerve running out of the brain to the adrenal glands triggers adrenaline and noradrenaline secretions. Adrenaline and noradrenaline surge through the bloodstream, causing the heart to beat faster and priming the body for an emergency. Then these hormones activate receptors on the vagus nerve running back to the brain. This causes the heart to continue to beat faster but also signals various parts of the brain to supercharge intense emotional memory. These hormones assist the individual to mobilize in the event of emergency. They also sweep through the body, return to the brain and trigger the release of more equally powerful hormones (cortisol, epinephrine and norepinephrine, oxytocin, vasopressin and endogenous opioids). This flood of hormones produces the fight or flight response in most people. When a trauma occurs, up to 70 percent of your brain-bound oxygen is diverted into your muscles in order to propel you somewhere else.[16] But for a few individuals, it produces a freeze mode. In this instance, all those hormones rushing through the body have no appropriate physical response. The stressor has paralyzed the victim, and the problem comes when the next emergency arises. The physical, biological body remembers and responds the same way it did before—without any decision-making process from the lessons learned by the intellectual brain in the last emergency.[17] In addition, traumatic events are remembered differently than nontraumatic events. They're free floating in time. It's experienced as *now* and not just a past event.[18]

The next time you interact with a traumatized person, remember what has happened to his or her brain. Don't hesitate to describe this to the person. I do this in recovery seminars, debriefings and one-on-one counseling. Many times those hearing this respond as if someone just turned on a lightbulb. It makes sense and helps to normalize their experience.

TRAUMA—WHAT FACTORS CAUSE ONE TO EXPERIENCE IT?

Are some of us more susceptible to being traumatized than others? If I were emotionally healthy, if I came from a healthy home, if I were a strong Christian, would I be immune to this disorder? We're all susceptible to trauma; we're all at risk. Your previous mental stability, race, gender, level of education, previous emotional disorders or lack of emotional disorders seem to make no difference, although your ability to handle life's ordinary stresses and your personally developed coping skills can help. Yet trauma overwhelms all of us.

Stress

What does make a difference—more than anything else—is the intensity and degree of stress. Studies have identified 58 general vulnerability factors that contribute to a person's becoming traumatized. But researchers are still puzzled about which responses assist a person in adapting best to a traumatic event.[19]

If you end up traumatized, it's *not* because of a defect in you. Your reactions are normal, in response to an abnormal event. Your personality doesn't alter the outcome of experiencing trauma, but trauma does impact your personality. Yes, we do vary in our responses and our capacity for endurance. Some have better coping skills than others. Those who have a strong faith in Jesus Christ and an accurate understanding of life through the Scriptures have more resources to help them cope. But for all of us there comes a point at which our defenses are overrun.[20]

Natural Versus Man-Made Disasters

There's one last factor to consider. Those who are involved in natural catastrophes seem to experience shorter and less intense PTSD than those involved in man-made disasters. As mentioned earlier, if a natural disaster can be seen as an act of nature or God—"That's just life"—the survivors don't lose as much trust in others as they would if it were a man-made disaster. Another word for man-made disasters is "atrocities." That's why the Oklahoma City bombing, the Columbine shootings and the 9/11 attacks have impacted us so much. Additionally, those who experience one trauma usually recover more quickly than those who have experienced multiple traumas.[21]

Other Factors

What experiences qualify to create traumas in our lives? There are a multitude of events. As you read the list, consider the people you know—including yourself—who may have experienced such natural catastrophes as earthquakes, fires, floods, hurricanes, tornadoes, volcanic eruptions, landslides or life-threatening windstorms.

Sometimes there are community or work-related disasters such as a chemical spill or explosion.

Trauma can occur in the survivors of a refugee or concentration camp.

Many people have become traumatized through sexual or physical assault, and some have gone through satanic ritual abuse. By the age of 18, 25 percent of girls have been sexually abused and 18 percent of boys. For some children, trauma is not Oklahoma City; it's going home at night.

Children who were physically mistreated by excessive beatings, spankings, confinement or deprivation of food or medical care can be affected.

You can be traumatized by witnessing a death or serious injury in a car accident; the beating, rape, injury or death of a person in a crime; an uprising, riot or war.

The murder of a close friend or family member is traumatic. Children, who have even less capability than adults to handle significant events in their lives, can be more easily damaged. At risk is any child who has witnessed the murder, suicide, rape or beating of a family member, significant adult or friend. The number of traumatized children who experience the aftermath of gang violence in our society is growing.

Many of the conditions mentioned so far pertain to being a witness. When it happens to you, it's even worse. The list of events is extensive.

Being a combatant, prisoner or medic in war creates the potential for trauma. Anyone who has been burglarized, robbed, mugged, abducted, raped, kidnapped, terrorized or injured in a vehicular accident experiences trauma. Any situation in which you feel that you or another family member could be killed or hurt gives you cause to experience trauma.

Those involved in the helping profession are open to trauma if they've been involved in just one of the following situations:

- witnessed death and injury;
- experienced a threat to their own safety and life;
- made life-and-death decisions;
- worked in high-stress conditions.

This last situation includes long work hours and an unsafe environment. Paramedics, rescue teams (for example, the rescue workers in the burned-out hulk of the federal building in Oklahoma City, the divers searching for bodies underwater amidst the torn fuselage of TWA flight 800 or the various personnel at Ground Zero), police officers, firefighters and medical personnel all are at risk.

My son-in-law, who is a firefighter, has experienced first- and second-degree burns fighting fires. He has witnessed numerous deaths and made many significant life-and-death decisions. Firefighters frequently have to operate on very little sleep and sometimes work 48-hour shifts.

If someone you know has experienced any of the above events, then that person has experienced trauma. This doesn't mean that PTSD or being traumatized is a result. But the *event* that leads to this problem has occurred.[22] Keep in mind that sometimes what is traumatic to one person may not be to another.

TRAUMA—IT TAKES ITS TOLL

Trauma has many effects. It shatters a person's beliefs and assumptions about life, challenges their belief that they have the ability to handle life and tears apart their belief that the world is a just and orderly place to live. You will hear the following from those you counsel:

Trauma leads to *silence:* "I don't have the words to describe it."
Trauma leads to *isolation:* "No one seems to understand or enters into the experience I had."
Trauma leads to *feelings of hopelessness:* "There was no way to stop what happened or the memories of what happened."[23]

Traumatized people's level of optimism begins to crumble. They feel depersonalized. Even their rationality turns against them. Basically, our rationality is good and necessary. In a trauma, however, it can turn against us. Robert Hicks, in *Failure to Scream*, wrote:

When trauma hits, our rationality becomes a curse. We are not like animals that, after sniffing a dead carcass, can walk off with no apparent feelings of remorse, anger or regret. Humans are more complex. We are *Homo sapiens* (Latin for "thinking man"). We think about our tragedy, and our thinking can drive us crazy. The replay of the event, the flashbacks, even the smells, bring up reminders of the trauma. As rational beings we seek the rationale in the trauma. When none is found, the traumatic blow is heightened. The meaninglessness of the event can drive one into despair, compulsive activities, or addictive relationships, which are all possible quick fixes for the pain. All of these feelings illustrate the depth to which our rationality has been attacked and how shattered our world has become.[24]

You and I and the traumatized person are all alike. We all want a reason for what happens to us. We want to know why, so we can once again have a sense of order and predictability about life. But sometimes we must live our lives with unanswered questions.

> **We all want a reason for what happens to us, but sometimes we must live our lives with unanswered questions.**

If we believe in a morality that says that right will always prevail and so will justice, what do we do when traumatic events that seem unfair drop into our lives? What do we do when we expect the good guys always to win and the bad guys always to lose, but it doesn't turn out that way?

We won't be the first or the last to cry out against injustice. Listen to Job:

If I cry out concerning wrong, I am not heard. If I cry aloud, there is no justice (Job 19:7, *NKJV*).

We want answers, we expect answers, we plead for answers, but sometimes heaven remains silent. That's when our faith undergoes a crisis, in addition to whatever else is impacting us. Perhaps along with C. S. Lewis you end up asking,

Where is God? This is one of the most disquieting symptoms. When you are happy, so happy that you have no sense of needing Him, so happy that you are tempted to feel His claims upon you as an interruption, if you remember yourself *and* turn to

Him *with* gratitude and praise, you will be—or so it feels—welcomed with open arms. But go to Him when your need is desperate, when all other help is vain, and what do you find? A door slammed in your face, and the sound of bolting and double bolting on the inside. After that, silence. You may as well turn away. The longer you wait, the more emphatic the silence will become. There are no lights in the windows. It might be an empty house. Was it ever inhabited? It seemed so once. And that seemingly was as strong as this. What can this mean? Why is He so present a commander in our time of prosperity and so very absent a help in time of trouble?[25]

Trauma—It Affects Who We Are

Trauma also affects how we see ourselves; it affects our self-identity. We all have a picture of ourselves. We may see ourselves as rational, strong, take-charge, in-control people. A trauma can change all that.

When Trauma Is Reexperienced Through Thoughts and Pictures

One of the main indicators that trauma may be part of a person's life is reexperiencing the trauma. Thoughts and pictures of what occurred in the form of dreams, nightmares or even flashbacks may take up residence in your life. Sometimes they slip into your mind like a video stuck on continuous replay. This sensitivity can become so extreme that an event can trigger a flashback and make you feel and act as if you were experiencing the original trauma all over again. Again and again trauma interrupts life. It stops the normal progress of life by its constant intrusion. It's as though time stopped at the moment of trauma and locked itself into the memory.[26]

One fireman said:

After the twin-towers disaster I heard about others who died, and it was like a carousel of faces running in front of me. There were classic pictures that will be in my head forever. I knew 30 guys that aren't here anymore. I can see them, feel them, taste them. I don't know what to make of it! There's just no language to describe what you see and feel. It's like a nightmare you can't wake up from. I see a lot of destruction, but this was magnified a million times. I'm just trying to grab on to life.

A friend of mine who is a Vietnam veteran often experiences this kind of trauma at a police funeral as he sees the flag-draped coffin. I've been with those who can't watch certain movies on TV because of the effect it has on them. I've been with a person who, when the loud rumbling of a truck goes by, reacts as though it were a major earthquake hitting again, such as the one that traumatized him.

A combat veteran walks down a street and hears a car backfire. He dives behind a car to hide from the enemy and recalls the memories of his friends who were blown up in front of him. A victim of rape or sexual abuse has a flashback when making love to his or her spouse. An accident victim has a flashback at the sight of a car wreck or blood. Someone sees an object falling from a building and once again he or she sees people jumping from the World Trade Center.

Reminders or triggers can include the anniversary of the event. As the date draws near, the intensity of the actual trauma can intensify. Holidays and other family events can create strong emotional responses. It's possible for a traumatized person to be set off by something they see, hear, smell or taste. In the case of abuse, a confrontation with the abuser may bring back emotional or physical reactions associated with the abuse.

Even the system that is designed to help the victim can cause a person to relive the painful event. It could be the court system, the police, the mental health system or the sentencing process. Certainly the media doesn't help, with their graphic descriptions of the worst incidents in life, nor does the extent of violence portrayed in movies. These portrayals can bring back the memories of a traumatized person's victimization.[27]

In a flashback, it's as though you leave the present and travel back in time to the original event. It seems so real. You see it, hear it and smell it. Sometimes a person begins to react as if he or she were there. Many times a person is hesitant to admit this to others for fear of their reaction. A flashback is like a cry of something that needs to come out and does so in the only way it knows how. When survivors can talk about the trauma, write about it and bring it to God in a very honest and real way through worship, there isn't as great a need for this memory to be so intrusive in nightmares, images or flashbacks.

Some reexperience the trauma through dreams, nightmares or insomnia. A person may shake, shout or thrash about during the dream. Even though the dream may not be remembered, the terror and fear experienced may be. Dreams can be replays of the event, be similar in theme or just contain the feelings of fear, anger, grief or helplessness that the victim felt. For some, sleep is evasive. I've talked to people who wake up 10 to 15 times a night and other people who take several hours just to fall asleep. Focusing on Scripture has helped those suffering from sleep-related problems:

> If I'm sleepless at midnight, I spend the hours in grateful reflection (Ps. 63:6, *THE MESSAGE*).

> When you lie down, you will not be afraid; when you lie down, your sleep will be sweet. Have no fear of sudden disaster (Prov. 3:24-25).

Watching relaxing and inspiring videos such as *In His Presence* by Moody has also helped.

Sometimes a person reexperiences trauma not through memories or images but through painful and angry feelings that seem to come out of nowhere. These feelings occur because they were repressed at an earlier time. Now the emotions are simply crying out for release. This state reminds me of the following poem by C. S. Lewis:

> Out of the wound we pluck the shrapnel
> Thorns we squeeze out of the hand.
> Even poison forth we suck, and after the pain we ease.

> But images that grow within the soul have life
> Like cancer often cut, live on below the deepest of the knife

Wanting their time to shoot at some defenseless hour
Their poison, unimpaired, at the heart's rot

And, like a golden shower, unanswerably sweet,
Bright with returning guilt, fatally in moment's time
Defeat our brazen towers long-built;

And all our former pain and all our surgeon's care
Is lost, and all the unbearable (in vain borne once)
Is still to bear.[28]

You inevitably will minister to someone who has experienced what Lewis
has described.

When Trauma Is Reexperienced Through Numbing and Avoidance

Another way people reexperience trauma is through numbing and
avoidance. It's painful to reexperience trauma. For some, it's agonizing.
They want it to go away and disappear forever; but it doesn't, so the
body and the mind take over to protect against the pain. This is done
by emotional numbing. Their defense system kicks into gear to help
them adjust. When numbing occurs it can create a diminished interest
in all areas of life. They may feel detached from others around them,
even the ones they love the most. Often there is no emotional expression because they've shut down everything. They tend to reduce their
involvement in life.[29]

When a person reexperiences trauma, he or she may end up feeling
some of the emotion that the person didn't experience at the time of the
event because of the numbing that took place:

Sometimes situations of inescapable danger may evoke not only
terror and rage but also, paradoxically, a state of detached calm,
in which terror, rage and pain dissolve. Events continue to register in awareness, but it is as though these events have been
disconnected from their ordinary meanings. Perceptions may be
numbed or distorted, with partial anesthesia or the loss of

particular sensations. The time sense may be altered as though it slowed down. One woman said, "It didn't seem real, more like a bad dream. I just hoped I would wake up soon."[30]

This is referred to as constriction. Now when feelings of rage, anger, guilt, anxiety, fear or sadness emerge, he or she wonders, *Where did these come from? They hurt! I don't want them!* He or she shuts down again so that he or she won't feel as if he or she is going through a series of out-of-control mood swings. Then the person begins to avoid situations he or she feels may trigger this condition. The person will retreat from other people, family and even from life. He or she will do this mentally, socially, physically and often spiritually.

It's interesting to see a traumatized person swinging back and forth between intrusion and constriction. These two contradicting symptoms keep the person from integrating the traumatic event. Often a person feels caught between reliving the trauma and amnesia, between floods of intense feeling and no feeling at all.[31]

Individuals find themselves staying away from places where the problem occurred. If a person was robbed in a restaurant, he or she may avoid restaurants. Firefighters, police officers and medical personnel may seek different lines of work. A friend of mine was a counselor for a group of hospice nurses and patients. He told me that in one year he had lost 45 people who were terminally ill. He said that for his own sanity he was going into another profession. It had become too much for him to handle.

People who have experienced trauma have their own sets of triggers that can activate the memories of what they experienced. The effort to avoid these situations can make a person a prisoner as well as create difficulty in interpersonal relationships.

When Trauma Is Reexperienced Through Increased Alertness

Another characteristic of trauma involves a person's increased alertness, usually referred to as hyperalertness or hyperarousal. The strong emotions one experiences—fear, anxiety, anger—affect his or her body, particularly adrenaline output.

When people say they are pumped up, it's usually because of an adrenaline rush that puts the body into a state of hyperalertness. Adrenaline increases blood pressure, heart rate, muscle tension, blood sugar and pupil dilation. Because the blood flow to their arms and legs decreases and the blood flow to their trunk and head increases, they can think and move better. This occurs because of the increase of adrenaline. If too much adrenaline pumps, they end up in the freeze response. They end up moving and thinking in slow motion. Everything seems to shut down. It's like an instantaneous freezing in a block of ice.

This condition is often evident by symptoms such as insomnia, periods of irritability, lack of concentration, anxiety about being in crowds and the tendency to be easily startled.[32]

After being a spectator to a train wreck, I became hypervigilant. About a block before any train crossing, I would think about how I would safely cross it. This lasted for years.

During a traumatic event, when the heart begins to race, breathing is difficult and muscles tighten, it's easy to label these responses as catastrophic. Some, in their attempt to make sense of what is happening, mislabel their bodily responses. You'll hear them say, "I'm going crazy"; "I'm going to collapse"; "I'm going to have a heart attack"; or "I'm dying." Some never correct the way they label these bodily responses. Therefore, anytime their heart pounds or it's hard to breathe, they misinterpret what is happening and end up in a panic attack.[33]

Sometimes, emotions—like fear—feel as though a dam has collapsed and the raging waters are totally out of control. I work with many people who are paralyzed by fear. Sometimes they fear making a decision, trying to gain another's approval or taking a stand. They may fear that other people don't like them. And even worse, they fear breaking out of this pattern that they are trapped in.

Physical paralysis is a terrible thing. To be locked up or immobilized so that your body can't function and respond to the messages of your mind is frustrating. But it is even more frustrating when the paralysis is the limitation or immobilization of the mind. This happens with trauma.

CONCLUSION

This chapter on trauma is basic. The information is meant to alert you to the fact that trauma exists and is perhaps closer to you than you realize. If you are counseling someone who displays the characteristics of trauma, keep the following in mind.

There is another side to trauma. The current research on those traumatized indicates that the majority of victims say that they eventually benefited from the trauma in some way. These are people who experienced as much pain as those who didn't fully recover. How did they benefit? There was a change of values, a greater appreciation for life, a deepening of spiritual beliefs, a feeling of greater strength and an appreciation and building of relationships:

> The most important element in recovering is to remain connected to other people.[34]

The following are three final statements that I would like to leave you with:

1. *Being traumatized is not incurable; recovery is possible,* but it is a slow process.
2. *A person will need to work with a professional,* someone who is equipped to assist those experiencing trauma. This could include a highly trained minister, chaplain or therapist.
3. *Healing comes through understanding.* The more a person learns about trauma, the more he or she will feel in control of his or her life.

RECOMMENDED RESOURCES

Resources to Use with a Traumatized Person

Macintosh, Mike. *When Your World Falls Apart.* Colorado Springs, CO: Cook Publications, 2002.

Wright, H. Norman. *Will My Life Ever Be the Same?* Eugene, OR: Harvest House Publishers, 2002.

CHAPTER 11

HELPING THE TRAUMA VICTIM

If there is ever a time to help immediately, it is when a trauma occurs. The longer you wait, the greater the imprint upon the brain.

Those who work with others in crisis or trauma follow the *wet cement theory*. This approach tries to help a person as soon as possible. Just as it is easier to smooth out the rough spots in cement before it hardens, working with a person's mixture of thoughts, feelings and emotions is generally easier when everything is fresh in the person's mind. It's easier to teach and reframe misconceptions, wrong impressions and information before the person permanently locks in wrong thoughts.[1]

CISD APPROACH

During the past 15 years and especially since 9/11, one of the main immediate interventions in a crisis or traumatic event is the critical incident stress debriefing (CISD) approach. Although there are several models of this intervention, the one developed by Dr. Jeffrey Mitchell is the most widely used. The various debriefing models vary in terms of goals, content and technique. From its inception, it was used for helping emergency personnel (firefighters, EMTs, police personnel, soldiers and so on), but it is now used in just about every traumatic situation, both in group and individual settings.

Traditionally, debriefing is a facilitator-led, group-oriented intervention, in which major elements of a trauma are reviewed by the participants shortly after the event, once they are out of immediate danger. Even though it is a group process, the focus is usually on individuals and their reactions and not on the group per se. This approach is used to educate, normalize reactions and hopefully prevent PTSD from occurring. It is best used within 24 hours after the event.

Most CISD programs use a seven-step phase model—both in a group and one-on-one setting. The following is a brief overview of the seven phases of this approach. I would recommend to anyone counseling those in trauma that they take both the basic and advanced training seminars. I've taken seminars on several occasions, including approaches other than the Mitchell model. On each occasion what I learned was invaluable.[2]

Introductory Phase

The seven phases begin with an introduction. This is to introduce yourself (and others, if it's a team approach), explain the process and clarify expectations as well as ground rules. During this phase you're tapping into the person's thinking, or cognitive, realm.

Fact Phase

The second part is the fact phase, which allows people to describe the traumatic event from their own perspective. You're asking them to tell you who they are, what their role in the incident was and what they saw or heard. Questions or statements to use include the following: Can you tell me what happened? Can you tell me what you've been through? I'd like you to describe for me what you experienced. You're still in the cognitive domain, focusing on facts, although feelings may slip in at this point. This is especially true when working with women or adolescents.

Thought Phase

Next is the thought phase, in which the people are asked to describe their cognitive reactions to the event. This will provide the transition to the affective, or feeling, domain. Questions and statements to focus on include the following: I'd like you to describe what your first thoughts were in response to what happened. What were your thoughts when you saw what was happening? What was going through your head? What was the first thought you had when you went off autopilot?

Reaction, or Feeling, Phase

The fourth phase is the reaction, or feeling, phase. Here you're trying to help the people identify the most traumatic part of the experience. You're helping them recognize the strong emotions that accompany their experience. This is the time to normalize and legitimize the feelings. It's a normal response to an abnormal experience. No one would be prepared to experience what they experienced. Questions may include What was the worst part of the experience for you personally? When this happened, how did you feel? What was it like for you? What did you feel at the time? What are you feeling now?

Symptom Phase

The next part is the symptom phase. This brings the people out of the feeling domain and back into the cognitive. It helps to ask about their reactions right after the event, which is usually the initial 24 hours. Helpful questions and statements include the following: What physical or psychological reactions have you noticed? Have you experienced any signs of distress since this happened? What are some of the stress responses you've experienced? I've found it helpful to ask, "Could it be that you've experienced . . . ?" and describe several possibilities. Not only do people connect with this, but they often ask, "Is that normal?", which opens the door to normalization.

Teaching, or Educational, Phase

The sixth phase is the teaching, or educational, phase, which is again in the cognitive domain. In this phase, as well as the previous phases,

I use the trauma recovery guidelines (see the end of this discussion). I go over these guidelines with the individual or group to normalize and help them anticipate what they may experience. During the teaching phase, suggestions are given to reduce the negative effect of the responses. For example, I've encouraged them to watch their driving following a traumatic experience. This is a time when they're prone to get in an accident or receive a ticket, since their minds aren't working as well. They may go over and over the trauma in their minds while driving, which isn't the best thing to do. I'll also show them the pictures

> **Alerting a person to a future anxiety can help to diminish the tension. If you try to help them take charge of future triggering events, the recovery is enhanced.**

of the brain to explain trauma's impact on it (see chapter 10). When I conduct a briefing for bank employees following a robbery, I've learned to ask, "Which door did he come in and how will you react when you hear that door slam? Since the robbery occurred Thursday at 11:00 o'clock, how might you respond next Thursday at 11:00 o'clock?" Alerting a person to a future anxiety can help to diminish the tension. If you try to help them take charge of future triggering events, the recovery is enhanced.

In addition, counselees are encouraged to exercise, structure their time, talk and share feelings with others, journal, not make any major life decisions, avoid alcohol, eat well, pray, read Scripture and devotional material and so on.

Reentry Phase

The last phase is the reentry phase, which brings closure to the CISD process. This is a time to answer questions and summarize what was covered. Remember that the people probably won't remember much of what you say because of what they experienced, so use handouts. In a group setting, this process takes anywhere from one hour to two-and-a-half hours, depending upon the group as well as the number involved.[3]

This is just a brief overview. Be sure to take the training seminar, read the resources, observe as many demonstrations as possible and then *practice, practice, practice* this process until it's locked into your thinking. It can be used anywhere and anytime. Whenever you minister to people who have experienced trauma, have them tell their stories.[4] The following are questions from several categories to both assist and show you the value of insightful questioning.

1. Questions that are designed to help the counselee *tell his or her story:*
   * Can you tell me what you've been through?
   * Can you tell me everything that you feel I need to know in order for you to know that I understand?
   * If your emotional pain could speak, what would it say?

2. Questions that are designed to assess the *lingering impact* of traumatic events:
   * Could you take a few moments and describe the situation you are in now?
   * Could you give me a description of what has been happening to you in recent weeks?
   * What is the _____ or the memory of _____ (robbery, rape and so on) preventing you from doing in your life now?

3. Questions that are designed to help the counselee *reframe* the traumatic events:
   * Although what you experienced is a terrible thing, can you think of anything positive, even a small thing, that has come out of this experience for you?
   * Was the stressful experience as bad as it could have been, or could it have been worse?

4. Questions that are designed to help the counselee *attend to* his or her *coping strengths:*

- Can you recall a time when you were nearly overtaken but instead you managed to cope?
- Can we use any of the information to change the way you are handling the situation?
- What would help you recognize little signs of recovery?
- What do you need to remember to tell yourself in order to feel okay and in order to cope better?

5. Questions that are designed to help the counselee *establish treatment goals*:
   - What advice would you have for someone else who is in this situation, has experienced a similar problem or is having difficulty with the memory of this?
   - What goals do you think you should be working on in treatment or training?
   - How will you know when your goals have been achieved?

6. Questions that are designed to help the counselee *take a different perspective*:
   - Do you know of any other people who have had a similar experience (or people who are in a similar situation)? Who? How did they handle it?

TRAUMA RECOVERY GUIDELINES

The following guidelines are provided to those individuals who have experienced trauma. Even though the event you've experienced may be over, you may now be experiencing or may experience later some strong emotional or physical reactions. It is quite *normal* for people to experience emotional aftershocks when they have passed through a trauma.

Sometimes the upset or stress reactions appear immediately—a few hours or a few days—after the trauma. In some cases, weeks or months may pass before the stress reactions appear.

How long do they last? It could be a few days, a few weeks, a few months and occasionally longer, depending on the severity of what has been experienced. With the understanding and support of others, stress reactions usually pass more quickly. Occasionally, the traumatic event is so painful that professional assistance from a counselor may be necessary. In no way does this imply craziness or weakness. It's just that the particular event was too powerful for you to manage by yourself.

Common signs and signals of a stress reaction are seen in four categories:

Physical	Cognitive	Emotional	Behavioral
Chills	Confusion	Fear	Withdrawal
Thirst	Nightmares	Guilt	Antisocial acts
Fatigue	Uncertainty	Grief	Inability to rest
Nausea	Hypervigilance	Panic	Intensified
Fainting	Suspiciousness	Denial	pacing
Twitches	Intrusive images	Anxiety	Erratic move-
Vomiting	Blaming	Agitation	ments
Dizziness	Poor problem	Irritability	Change in social
Weakness	solving	Depression	activity
Chest pain	Poor abstract	Intense anger	Change in
Headaches	thinking	Apprehension	speech
Elevated blood	Poor attention/	Emotional shock	patterns
pressure	decisions	Emotional	Loss or increase
Rapid heart rate	Poor concentra-	outbursts	of appetite
Muscle tremors	tion/memory	Feeling over-	Hyperalertness
Shock	Disorientation	whelmed	to environ-
symptoms	of time, place	Loss of emotion-	ment
Grinding of	or person	al control	Increased
teeth	Difficulty identi-	Inappropriate	alcohol
Visual	fying objects	emotional	consumption
difficulties	or people	response	Change in usual
Profuse sweating	Heightened or	Startled	communica-
Difficulty	lowered	response	tions[5]
breathing	alertness		
	Increased or		
	decreased		
	awareness of		
	surroundings		

SAFETY FIRST

Remember what trauma is and does. Trauma is a thief. It steals from people. It takes away their sense of well-being, security, predictability and safety. Understanding this helps guide anyone wanting to help a traumatized person. To begin with, they need an atmosphere of safety.

Dr. Babette Rothschild has suggested several steps to take in helping a traumatized person. The first is to help the person feel safe inside and outside the counseling office.

When you work with traumatized people, giving them reasons for their symptoms and normalizing them can provide some of the relief they are looking for.

> **Trauma is a thief. It steals from people. It takes away their sense of well-being, security, predictability and safety.**

By understanding that the way they react now is tied to changes in their brain, people can realize that what they're experiencing now does *not* mean they're in danger. It's still upsetting, but not as upsetting as the actual event.

Making Sense of Flashbacks

Flashbacks were described as disturbing and threatening in the previous chapter. One positive step you can take in helping others with their flashbacks is to indicate that their flashbacks are memories. They are unlike other memories because they're often accompanied by intense, painfully charged emotions, such as feelings of terror and dread. When a flashback occurs, it means an old memory has been triggered by some event. It could have an inconsequential resemblance to the past, sometimes a symbolic resemblance. It's unpredictable and can come in the form of something seen, heard, swallowed and so on.

When flashbacks occur, it's not just a neutral experience. Often, extreme emotional and physiological arousal will accompany the flashbacks. This experience may make a person feel immobilized to the extent that he or she may become unaware of immediate surroundings. But once again, all this is normal for what has transpired. Inform the person that his or her flashbacks are a form of memory and that memories are a form of acting—telling a story. Trauma tends to keep the memories frozen. They freeze the person so that he or she is often unable to take any further action.

Our task is to help the individual *normalize* and *reframe* flashbacks in an attempt to *heal* from the traumatic experience so that he or she can move forward in life. They may have been offered, or may already believe, the advice that forgetting is the only way to cope, that time heals all wounds, that this will be behind them soon, that it is only in their head or that they should just move on. However, when a person grasps the concept that a flashback is the mind's attempt to *make sense* of a very important and significant life-transition event and that it's normal and a way of adapting, some of the pressure is relieved.

I heard the illustration of a person's mind being like a railway station. One day the person is standing on one end of the platform. He can't control what trains come into the station. On some days there may be special trains to take people to a special event or location. The trains that come into the station depend upon what is going on in the outside world. Yet he can choose whether he boards a train, ignores it or waves good-bye to whomever is on the train. When he tries to stop his intrusive thoughts, it is as if he's jumping on the railway track to try and stop the train. We all know that won't work. Perhaps he should calmly greet the thoughts like he greets the train and then wave them good-bye. He could practice a calm approach to the thoughts. It is impossible to force a physical wound, as well as a psychological wound, to heal quickly. Healing takes time. In either case, he will have to flow with the healing process, rather than fight it.[6]

It may help to ask the following two questions:

1. What would give you a greater feeling of safety at this time in your life?
   They may have an answer, or you may need to provide them with suggestions.

2. What gave you a feeling of safety before this trauma occurred? Ask what it looked like, smelled like, sounded like and so on. When this is identified, it may be helpful for them to visit it in their imagination.

Dwelling on and reminiscing about a safe place can be relaxing as well as beneficial.[7]

TRIGGERS

Triggers are a big part of a traumatized person's life, and they need to be addressed. We all have them to a certain degree. To help the counselee understand what his or her life is like, it may help for you to identify triggers you've experienced in your life.

Helping the counselee means identifying and removing as many of these triggers as possible. When they are removed, they lose their power, and then the person can return to his or her "normal" life with little effect.[8]

> **The brain is like a video camera: it tapes and stores not only what it sees but also what it feels.**

Remember, the brain is like a video camera: it tapes and stores not only what it sees but also what it feels. A trigger recalls the events *and* feelings. That's why it can dominate a person's life.

It comes in all shapes and sizes. It may be an anniversary or something they have seen on TV or heard in a conversation. Triggers make people fear losing control and going insane; they take away their safe feelings.

Therefore, it's important to identify triggers. Ask the person to list several items that they identify as triggers. Their first task is to divide their trigger situations into four categories. Ask them the following questions:

1. Which triggers can you handle now?
2. Which triggers do you feel you might be able to handle after a few more months of healing?
3. Which triggers do you feel you might be able to confront in a few years (maybe)?
4. Which triggers do you plan to avoid for the rest of your life?[9]

Desensitization

What can a traumatized person do to desensitize himself or herself to these triggers? There are numerous relaxation techniques including deep breathing, muscle relaxation, exercise and so on. Self-talk also is a very effective approach, for we all internally talk to ourselves. What is said during this internal dialogue can either be healing or destructive.[10]

Another approach used among many mental health professionals is the eye movement desensitization and reprocessing (EMDR). This is an eight-phase treatment approach that uses eye movements or other left-right stimulation. It has been quite successful in helping trauma victims reprocess disturbing thoughts and memories. Yet it can only be administered by those who have been trained and certified in the process.[11]

Defensiveness

Those who have been traumatized develop many ways to cope with the aftermath of the trauma. Some of these are methods or defense mechanisms that the person has used much of his or her life but that now have intensified. A defense usually is used for self-protection, which is healthy. However, the problems abound when a person sticks with his or her defenses instead of discovering others that could serve him or her better.

Questions to consider are

• Is it best to leave the defense as it is?
• Is it best to replace it?
• Is it best to see the value in the defense?

The author of *The Body Remembers: The Psychophysiology of Trauma and Trauma Treatment* suggests not removing the defenses but developing its

opposites for balance and choice.[12] The problem with coping mechanisms, or defenses, is not in what is being done but in the fact that a
person continues to use that choice and nothing else, thus limiting the
possibilities of discovering something better. Consider some of the following defenses:

- Don't most of us withdraw at one time or another? Yes, but if
  that's the only method of coping used, it's limiting our recovery process and most likely our interaction with others.
- If anger is the method used to defend oneself, it may work, but
  at what cost?
- If anger can't ever be expressed—in order to keep everyone else
  happy—there is a cost to this as well.
- Retreating into a daydream may feel safe, but it doesn't bring
  any permanent solution.

Many are reluctant to give up their defenses, for to do so might be
an admission that they're not good, and what else would they have to
use?[13] Thus, people need to be affirmed for what they're doing now and
then taught new choices and defenses that expand their repertoire.

For instance, when I've worked with perfectionistic clients, I've not
asked them to give up their perfectionism but to keep it. But in addition
to that trait, they learn another way of responding so that they have
another approach to use and weigh against their current approach.

Recovery Process

If you are working with people who have been traumatized, it is best to
err on the side of caution.

Gauge the Speed

Go slow and be safe. Don't push the individuals. They need to face their
symptoms, as well as the trauma, slowly. Dr. Rothschild and others liken
a traumatized person to a pressure cooker. My mother cooked with one.
One day she and I were out, and she called home to tell my brother to let

some steam off or turn it off. He told her she was too late; it was all over the walls and ceiling, because it exploded. With your counselee, you need to open his or her lid slowly and let the pressure off a little bit at a time. If not, he or she may explode in your face. If you try to have a traumatized person open up too soon, his or her explosion might appear in a myriad of ways such as decompensation, breakdown, serious illness or suicide.[14]

Aphrodite Matsakis, author of *I Can't Get Over It!* has done extensive research work with those suffering from PTSD. She takes a very positive approach to the healing process. For healing to occur, she says, people need to stop seeing themselves as diseased or deficient. It isn't their personalities that are abnormal, but rather the event or events that they experience. The event is so out of the ordinary that it overwhelms them— as it would anyone.[15]

Determine the Stage

According to Dr. Matsakis, there are three stages in trauma recovery: the cognitive stage, the emotional stage and the mastery stage.

The Cognitive Stage. The cognitive, or thinking, stage is when the person fully faces the trauma, remembers it and even reconstructs it mentally. This isn't a matter of dwelling in the past but of taking fragmented and disconnected memories and pulling them together in order to make sense of the present. Sometimes this stage involves talking with others, re-creating the scene or reading written accounts of it. When this is accomplished, the counselee will be able to view what happened from a new perspective—an objective view rather than a judgmental view.[16]

In the cognitive stage, counselees need to look at what happened to them as a detached observer (even though it may be difficult), not as an emotionally involved participant. If they're able to work through this stage, they'll acquire a new assessment of what their real choices were during their traumatic experience. They'll have a better understanding of how the event has impacted the totality of their life and be able to reduce the self-blame that most experience. Finally, they'll gain a clearer understanding of who or what they're angry at.[17]

The Emotional Stage. This stage deals with the way people mentally heal and recover. This stage necessitates dealing with any repressed feelings caused by the trauma. Counselees must experience their emotions at the gut level. This can be difficult, because many people have a fear of feeling emotion as well as fears of hurting and losing control. However, it's important for them to remember that they don't have to act on the feelings, nor will the feelings take over their lives. But they do need to face their emotions. These emotions include anger, anxiety, grief, fear and sadness—the list goes on and on.[18]

The Mastery Stage. The final stage is the mastery stage. This is when people find new meaning through their experience and develop a survivor perspective, rather than continue to see themselves as victims. People who have a relationship with Jesus Christ and a biblical worldview have the greatest potential to become survivors.

Mastering the trauma involves people making their own decisions instead of allowing experiences, memories or other people to make decisions for them. This is a time of growth, change and new direction in life. What they learn because of a trauma they probably could not have learned any other way. Look at what Scripture says about this:

> Blessed be the God and Father of our Lord Jesus Christ, the Father of mercies and God of all comfort, who comforts us in all our tribulation, that we may be able to comfort those who are in any trouble, with the comfort with which we ourselves are comforted by God. For as the sufferings of Christ abound in us, so our consolation also abounds through Christ. Now if we are afflicted, it is for your consolation and salvation, which is effective for enduring the same sufferings which we also suffer (2 Cor. 1:3-6, *NKJV*).

Persevere Through the Tough Times

I've had people ask me, "How do I know I'm growing and getting better?" First of all, they have to develop a new way of looking at progress. Again, it will be slow. There will be regressions. They need to focus on the improvements rather than on the times of feeling stuck. One man told me that he rated his progress each month on a scale of 1 to 10, which helped him understand his own progress.

It's important to initiate the discussion of the possibility of lapses and relapses. If something is tried and it doesn't work, don't fret; it may prove helpful. It's not a failure. It is like a scientist who performs an experiment. Sometimes it works, which is wonderful; but sometimes it fails. When does the scientist learn the most? Often when the experiment doesn't work, but it is a choice to see it this way.

Picture teaching a child to ride a two-wheel bike. At first the parent runs alongside, holding on to the bicycle seat. After the child develops some confidence, she says, "It's okay, let me go. I can do it." So the parent lets go. Sometimes the child rides by herself, and sometimes she falls; but when does she learn the most? Often when she falls. Why? Did she go too fast? Did she turn the wheels too quickly? Was the ground wet and the bike slid out from under her? If the bad things didn't happen, then she wouldn't learn to ride well.

Recovery Goals

As you work with traumatized individuals, remember that your goal is not to help them get back to normal; this won't occur. Instead, a new normal will need to be created, and your real goal is to help them move along on the path to recovery.

Recovery includes but is not limited to the following:

- reduced frequency of symptoms,
- reduced fear of symptoms,
- reduced fear of insanity, and
- rechanneled anger and grief.

There are numerous changes that occur. The traumatized individuals change from being victims to survivors. Many never believe this could happen. There is a change from rigidity to flexibility and spontaneity. Their appreciation of life increases, along with the return of a sense of humor. Those who have suffered develop a profound empathy for others who suffer. Their lives can reflect what Paul said in 2 Corinthians 1:3-5.

Judith Herman talks about recovery in her book *Trauma and Recovery* (Basic Books, 1992). She suggests that it unfolds in three stages. The first stage is to establish a safe environment. No other recovery goals can be set until this occurs. This needs to be restored because trauma strips a person of a sense of power and control.

The second stage is remembrance and mourning, in which the traumatized person confronts what happened in the trauma and tells the story in the safe hearing of the counselor and in living color. This is not to eliminate the trauma but simply to integrate it. Telling the complete story turns it into testimony.

The third stage is reconnection with life and with people. Part of this involves finding a survivor mission, which is the recognition of a political or religious dimension in people's tragedies. It is also people discovering how to transform the meaning of what they've experienced by making it the basis for social action. Dr. Herman says:

> The trauma is redeemed only when it becomes the source of a survivor mission.[19]

RECOVERY PROGRESS

Is recovery ever complete? Not really. The issues can be reawakened from time to time.[20]

Fears Will Diminish

How can a person tell if they're progressing? First of all, they can expect to see a reduction in the frequency of symptoms. In addition, the intensity of fear they struggled with over the presence of these symptoms will diminish. One of the fears that is so disheartening is the fear of going crazy or insane. This fear will also diminish.

Anger Will Subside

Anger and grief, which exist hand in hand, will lessen. What remains can be directed into positive directions. Candy Lightner, whose daughter was killed by a drunk driver, founded Mothers Against Drunk Driving

(MADD). A friend of mine, traumatized by the Vietnam War, each week spends time and energy to help the men in our local veterans hospital. He and his Alaskan husky take the men to worship service and other activities. He's even taught his dog to talk. I mean, actual people words! I've heard him, and it's amazing. He's been on many major talk shows on television. He and his dog provide a great deal of entertainment and laughter to those in need. Another great direction to take is to write letters to congresspeople and state senators—in a properly assertive and consistent manner—to bring about change.

However, there will be times when the only way counselees will get rid of their anger and feelings of revenge is to face the fact that they can't change the past nor prevent the future. They can learn to give up a portion of their anger or resentment each day (see chapter 7). Taking positive steps like this will help them make the shift from victims to survivors. Believing that they can become survivors will accelerate the process.

Rigidity Will Decrease

As they move through their journey to recovery, the rigidity that helps them cope will diminish. They'll gradually discover the value of flexibility and spontaneity to a comfortable degree, which is based upon their own unique personality type.

Appreciation Will Abound

One of the delights of recovery is developing a new appreciation of life. Counselees begin to see what they weren't seeing before, to hear what they couldn't hear before, to taste what was tasteless before.

Some people rediscover their sense of humor and all its healing properties.

They'll discover a new and deeper sense of empathy for the wounded around them. In a real sense, they will become wounded healers and have greater compassion for others. Romans 12:15 (*NKJV*), "Weep with those who weep," will take on a new meaning.[21]

Improvements Will Be Noted

A common struggle in the recovery process is the ability to see and measure one's progress. For years I've had people keep a daily or weekly journal in which they explicitly write out what they are experiencing or feeling. Some keep a time line of recovery. Some do both. These records, over time, make people more aware of their progress in a tangible way.

A time line is a simple way to record the peaks and valleys of the recovery process. The counselees use a monthly calendar and plot the days on the bottom, with a scale of 1 to 10 on the left. At the end of each day, they indicate where they are for that day. This might go on for months or years, but over time they'll discover that they are growing.

When people experience trauma, sometimes it's all they can remember. They think, *What would happen if I were able to leapfrog over that event back to what my life was like before the trauma?* We call this looking at their life as it was. What were their lives like? What did they do each day? Have them answer the following questions to help them recapture the time before the trauma:

- What was your biggest struggle then?
- What fulfilled you?
- What did you enjoy the most?
- What did you look like then? (It helps to be very specific about this. Sometimes pictures and videos help the process.)
- Who were your friends?
- What did you like and not like about yourself?
- Who did you get along with?
- Who didn't you get along with?
- What did you believe about God then?
- What were your Christian practices, such as prayer?
- What were your beliefs about life then?
- What were you realistic about? Naive about?
- What did you want out of life then?
- What were your goals or dreams for yourself then?
- What are your goals or dreams for yourself now?
- Why would you like to be different now?

As they look at what they write, they discover what specifically is different now. What alternatives can they come up with to make their life more the way they want it to be? Have them make a list of all the things that they would like to happen now, and then check off what possibly could happen if they choose to pursue this avenue. Ask, "What would keep you from growing and changing?" For many, it's the lack of a plan. Dreams can fade without a plan. Help them with this part of the exercise.

In the *NIV Worship Bible*, there is a section entitled "My Beloved," which is a page of Scripture passages that are paraphrased into a personal letter from God to the reader. It is encouraging to hear and meditate on these words several times a day. You could give the selection listed here to the traumatized person at an appropriate time. Often when a person reads this out loud, the truth and comfort of Scripture begin a healing process in the individual.

> Have no fear of sudden disaster. When it comes, proclaim that I am your Refuge and your Fortress, your God, in Whom you place your trust. Then I will save you from the impossible places . . . places where death is waiting to take you. I will cover you with My feathers, and under My wings you will find refuge. I will protect you from trouble and surround you with songs of deliverance.
>
> I will demonstrate My faithfulness to you and to those around you. The knowledge of My love for you will protect you physically and emotionally. And when you have discovered this shelter . . . stay there. You will always be safe if you do what is righteous and speak the truth from your heart.
>
> You will no longer fear the terror that the night brings, nor the violence that walks the streets, nor the evil that stalks in darkness, nor even an untimely death.
>
> I will command My angels to guard you in all your ways. Then you will go on your way in safety, and your foot will not stumble, when you lie down, you will not be afraid, when you lie down, your sleep will be sweet. I alone will cause you to dwell in safety. For I am your God (Pss. 4:8; 15:2; 32:7; 91:1-6,11; Prov. 3:23-36).[22]

Final Thought

Our task is to assist the counselees in their journey and to encourage them in their faith. Overcoming trauma is a process—a journey. No one travels the journey alone; the Lord is with all of us:

> The Spirit of the Sovereign LORD is on me, because the LORD has anointed me to preach good news to the poor. He has sent me to bind up the brokenhearted, to proclaim freedom for the captives and release . . . for the prisoners (Isa. 61:1).

> When Jesus spoke again to the people, he said, "I am the light of the world. Whoever follows me will never walk in darkness, but will have the light of life" (John 8:12).

> You, O LORD, keep my lamp burning; my God turns my darkness into light (Ps. 18:28).

RECOMMENDED RESOURCES

Resources for Your Understanding of Trauma Counseling

Herman, Judith, M.D. *Trauma and Recovery.* Grand Rapids, MI: Basic Book House, 1992.

Matsakis, Aphrodite. *I Can't Get Over It!: A Handbook for Trauma Survivors.* Oakland, CA: New Harbinger Publishers, 1992.

Meichenbaum, Donald, Ph.D. *A Clinical Handbook/Practiced: Therapist Manual for Assessing and Treating Adults with Post-Traumatic Stress Disorder (PTSD).* Waterloo, Ontario: Institute Press, 1994.

Rosenbloom, Dena, Ph.D.; Mary Beth Williams, Ph.D.; and Barbara E. Watkins. *Life After Trauma: A Workbook for Healing.* New York: Guilford Press, 1999.

Rothschild, Babette. *The Body Remembers: The Psychophysiology of Trauma and Trauma Treatment.* New York: W. W. Norton, 2000.

CHAPTER 12

THE CRISIS OF DEATH

On Sunday morning, you notice a man sitting in the congregation who has been attending for several months. He has kept to himself pretty much, although he is friendly when spoken to. This morning, though, you seem to notice an air of depression hanging over him. Following the service, you speak to him and ask how he is doing. His response surprises you, "I guess I'm a bit angry and confused right now. I'm wondering where this God is that you're always talking about. I need Him now, but He sure isn't helping me or answering my prayers. I've been praying and reading Scripture, but nothing has changed. My doctor told me three weeks ago that I have cancer. It's terminal. I've been given six months. I don't want to die! Where is He?"

Your ministry with this person begins at that moment. How will you reply, and what will you do? Will you be able to handle his feelings without being overly threatened? Can you handle his depression and anger? Can you handle your own feelings of mortality, which you will be forced to face as you watch this man die? What are the stages he is going to experience?

On Monday morning, you receive a call from one of your board members. He's in tears and you can hardly understand him. As you listen, you begin to understand that his wife and 14-year-old daughter were killed this morning in an automobile accident. He wants you to come over and be with him. He and the two younger children are at home. As you leave, you wonder how he will handle this loss. How will he handle the children and care for them? How will the children handle the loss of their mother? What should you expect from them during the next two years? How can the members of your congregation minister to them at this time?

These are the type of questions that need to be asked and that require concrete answers when dealing with the crisis of death.

WHAT IS DEATH?

Death is the permanent, irreversible cessation of the vital functions of the body. Not all functions stop at the same time. It used to be that the lack of heartbeat was considered final evidence of death, but now the attention has shifted from the heart to the brain for a reliable indication of when death has occurred.

The Scriptures have much to say about death:

Precious in the sight of the LORD is the death of his saints (Ps. 116:15).

And as it is appointed unto men once to die, but after this the judgment (Heb. 9:27, KJV).

And God shall wipe away all tears from their eyes; and there shall be no more death, neither sorrow, nor crying, neither shall there be any more pain: for the former things are passed away (Rev. 21:4, KJV).

People live much longer today than they used to. We strive for not only the good life but also the long life. In 1900, the infant mortality rate was much different from what it is today. At that time, for every 1,000 live births, 100 infants died. In 1940, for every 1,000 live births, 47 infants died. In 1967, for every 1,000 live births, 22.4 infants died. A significant decline in the death rate of mothers giving birth has also been noted.

WHY IS DEATH FEARED?

Why is it that we fear death so much? Modern man denies death; we shrink from even discussing it. We criticize the Victorians because of their attitude toward sex, but they were very aware and dealt openly with death. Today we have just the opposite attitude: Our society is very open about sex but closed about death. Robert Burther said, "The fear of death is worse than death."

We also fear physical pain and suffering and the unknown—the things we do not understand. We fear leaving loved ones and friends. It has been estimated that the average person can go through a 20-year period of time without being exposed to the death of a relative or friend. Today, 80 percent of people in our society die away from home or familiar surroundings. This in itself creates a fear response, because we do not want to be alone when we die:

> Men fear death because they refuse to understand it. In order to understand death, we must deal with our fears of it.[1]

You will be working with death and dying more than you want. The mode of death, as well as those who die and are grieved, will surprise you. You will probably be called upon to conduct death notifications; therefore, it's important for you to understand some of the most significant deaths in the family life cycle. You will be aware of several, but it could be that you haven't given the others any consideration. Before continuing, take the time to complete the following survey:

Looking at My Own History of Losses

William Worden developed an extensive survey for use with counselors preparing to work with grieving people. Answering the questions below and spending some time reflecting on your answers with a friend or colleague can pay dividends later in helping to make you more effective in your own work.

1. The first death I can remember was the death of _____.
2. I was age _____.
3. The feelings I remember I had at the time were _____.
4. The first funeral (wake or other ritual service) I ever attended was for _____.
5. I was age _____.
6. The thing I most remember about that experience is _____.
7. My most recent loss by death was (person, time and circumstances) _____.
8. I coped with this loss by _____.
9. The most difficult death for me was the death of _____.
10. It was difficult because _____ _____.
11. Of the important people in my life who are now living, the most difficult for me would be the death of _____.
12. It would be the most difficult because _____ _____.
13. My primary style of coping with loss is _____.
14. I know my own grief is resolved when _____.
15. It is appropriate for me to share my own experiences of grief with a counselee when _____.[2]

WHAT ARE SOME DIFFERENT TYPES OF DEATH?

Your way of coping with the death of a loved one may be different from the ways of the people you are called upon to help. How will others cope with the death of a loved one? It depends on whether the death was sudden or anticipated, as well as on other factors.

Accident or Disaster

An accident or disaster can lead to either a sudden or anticipated death. When someone loses a loved one in this way, there are several issues that arise that will probably be discussed in your presence. One issue is preventability. It seems that those who lose a loved one handle it better if it was a natural disaster (i.e., tornado, flood, earthquake, hurricane) than if it was caused by human events (i.e., an automobile or airplane crash). In a natural disaster, there's no one to blame. Yet those that are preventable take a toll on the survivors, whose energy and time are devoted to discovering the cause and whom to blame, dealing with the unfairness and trying to regain control. If they weren't there, they imagine the worst. Legal and insurance issues are difficult to deal with, as is survivor guilt.

Homicide, Suicide and Death by Natural Causes

Another type of death is homicide. This is a preventable death. The same issues with accidents or disasters are also present. There can be intense rage as well as additional victimization by the court and legal system.

> It seems that those who lose a loved one handle it better if it was a natural disaster than if it was caused by human events.

Suicide is one of the most difficult deaths to deal with. It's sudden, and it was a choice on the part of the one who is dead. Feeling angry and intensely guilty, going over and over the missed cues, not understanding the act and even wondering if this is a family tendency cloud the recovery.

A death by natural causes alleviates the survivors from dealing with someone or something responsible for the death. Some causes may be indirect or direct, but often the death is far more acceptable. Often there is a satisfaction that the loved one didn't suffer.

HOW DO FAMILIES GRIEVE?

Within a family, family members will grieve differently over the same person. Family grief is not easy. For example, when the oldest child in this family died, it represented different things to each family member:

- the parents lost the firstborn—the star child;
- the father lost the one who would carry out his own frustrated dreams;
- the brother lost the buffer for his family expectations; and
- the sister lost a domineering sibling, whom she resented.

Each feeling is real for each person, and some feelings contradict each other. Even if the feelings are the same, the timing may be different. One person may be angry when another is sad; while another is in shock, struggling with anxiety over the loss.[3]

Each family member will cope with the loss in a personal way, which makes it difficult for each individual to find the support he or she needs. Some will blame everything and everyone except themselves, which is a form of narcissism. The following are some of the things people say to cope with their loss:

- "We'll never speak about this again."
  This is reflective of a family that operates on threats and intimidation.
- "Well, you can talk about it . . . just not with me."
  In this family, the members grieve, but they grieve alone.
- "Our faith is going to sustain us and see us through."
  This can be true, but if there is no room for sadness, there is denial.
- "We are all fine, just fine, but we appreciate your asking" or "Darn! This is just one more thing to have to deal with."
  Some families seem to live in a perpetual state of crisis and disruption.
  Some don't say much, but internally their body is grieving and bodily symptoms begin to appear.
- "I think we all need some help."
  It would be helpful if each person felt this way, but too often the family is a mixture of responses.[4]

As you minister to families following a death, you may want to discover the answers to the following questions:

- What were the roles that the deceased assumed in the family (e.g., scapegoat, peacemaker, clown or hypochondriac)?
- Did any one individual assume the deceased's role?
- Who was aligned with whom in the family system? (The level of family functioning should increase as more and more distance occurs after the death of the loved one.)
- How are the dates of the death remembered?
- Who in the family can talk about the death and who cannot?
- Are there both positive and negative memories available?
- How was the news about the death handled by each family member?
- Who told whom about the death?
- Were any family members present at the death?
- Did all family members see the body at the funeral home? Who did not?
- Were there unresolved issues between any family members at the time of death?
- How were funeral arrangements made and who was present?
- Were any family members alienated from one another?
- Was there a will?
- Does anyone visit the grave?
- What happened to the deceased's clothes, jewelry and so on?
- Are there any secrets about the death?
- What dreams were shortened by the death?
- Did the death occur by AIDS, suicide, homicide or automobile crash?
- What are the family members' beliefs about an afterlife?
- How is life different since the person's death?[5]

HOW DO PEOPLE RESPOND TO THE BEREAVED?

This ministry is one that needs to continue for months and, in some cases, years.

Prayer and Support Ministry

It is important to pray continually for the bereaved for two to three weeks after the death. However, it is important to show continual support and concern for the bereaved in tangible ways for two to three months after the death—sending cards, making phone calls or taking an occasional meal to them.

> **It is important to show continual support and concern for the bereaved in tangible ways for two to three months after the death—sending cards, making phone calls or taking an occasional meal to them.**

Unfortunately, at the time when the bereaved most need support, people usually discontinue their ministry. It might be better if churches would develop a program of ministry wherein 12 families commit themselves for a period of two months, each to minister to the bereaved over a two-year period of time and, thus, help them through the hurt process. A number of pastors and laymen I know do the following: After the memorial service of a friend or acquaintance, they write the name of the family on their calendar every three months for two years to remind them to reach out to the family for two years.

Counseling Ministry

Counseling others when a family death occurs can be a complex matter. It's not just a matter of knowing how to respond but of understanding how the immediate and long-range impact will direct what you do and say. A number of guidelines will be presented, using the death of a spouse as the basis for this discussion.

The death of a spouse can occur at any stage of the family life cycle. Widowhood is the conclusion for all marriages unless the couple dies together.

In fact, each year 800,000 individuals experience the death of a spouse. About one-fourth of them are men and three-fourths are women. The

United States Census Bureau indicates that seven percent of the population in this country is widowed. About 400,000 of those widowed are under the age of 45, and 6.1 million widowed persons are between the ages of 45 and 60. Of the persons over the age of 65, 50 percent of the women and 14 percent of the men are widowed.[6]

When a spouse dies, the identity of the one left behind changes. His or her sense of self and security is disrupted. The comfort zone is disrupted, since the one who knew the person best is gone. The one remaining now operates in the world as one-half of a pair. Many widowed people describe themselves as *alone* and *incomplete*. What is it like for a person to lose his or her spouse? In order to help, you need to enter his or her world of loss. What are a widow or widower's concerns and feelings? The following statements are what they may say:

- "I feel as though I've lost my best friend."
  They've lost a companion who shared activities, a familiar and shared language, daily physical contact and loyalty. The companion is gone.
- "I'm angry."
  The widowed person feels abandoned and robbed of his or her future. It can be directed toward the one who left, himself or herself, the doctor, whoever caused the death and so on.
- "I feel guilty for things I did or failed to do."
  The guilt arises over what wasn't done or what the widowed person thinks wasn't done, over new financial gain or over not providing the kind of care that may have made a difference.
- "I think about my own death more frequently."
  When a spouse dies, the reality of one's own death takes on a new meaning. Thoughts about mortality increase.
- "I feel old."
  This often is a companion to thoughts about death.
- "I feel sick all the time."
  Many have health changes following the death of a spouse. Symptoms often reported are insomnia, tiredness, anorexia, headaches, indigestion, chest pains and heart palpitations.

- "I am afraid."

During the first few months following the death, the widow or widower may experience fear as a companion. Fears seem to come out of nowhere and multiply. It could be fear of driving, shopping, being alone and so on.

- "I worry about money."

There is usually some financial upheaval following the death of a spouse. Financial matters are probably not in order, and the surviving spouse may have little or no knowledge of the finances. There may not be a will (50 percent of property owners don't have a will), finances may be insufficient and distribution may be unfair to some.

- "I am going through an identity crisis."

Remember that a wife can no longer call herself a wife and a husband can no longer call himself a husband. Friendships with other couples will change and the survivor will feel excluded. A young widow shared with me her experience after the first anniversary of her husband's death. She went to a new doctor and, in filling out the required information, discovered there was no place to indicate her status as a widow—it was either married or single. Her response was, "I am not really married and I'm not really single. They don't have a place for me to check. If I had to choose I would have said married, because I don't feel single. I still have one foot in the marriage. It's only been 14 months."

- "I feel relieved after the death."

This happens, and it's a normal response. It can be for several reasons. The one who dies was terminally ill, in great pain or an accident victim whose quality of life had diminished. Or perhaps the deceased was a violent abuser, incarcerated in prison or in a mental institution or suffered from a chronic addiction. Many struggle with their feelings of relief, but such feelings do occur.[7]

Your counseling ministry is to address these issues with the person. You could take each one and ask, "Could it be that you've thought or felt . . . ?" You're once again giving them permission to admit and discuss their thoughts and feelings. There may be a need for a good resource system as you discuss these issues. In addition, some issues may require a specialist.

Keep in mind that there will be certain adjustments that are common to most people who have lost their spouse. You could ask if these have occurred yet and, if not, tell counselees that they shouldn't be surprised if they do.

Unpleasant Memories. Many will struggle with recurring unpleasant memories. These can be related to the death or to the marriage itself. When a spouse is terminally ill, a bad marriage tends to get worse and a good marriage tends to get better. Help them identify their good and bad memories. Talk and write about the memories. If they want to get rid of any of the reminders or sell the house immediately, discuss the reasons as well as the benefits and detriments of doing this.

Some people will avoid certain rooms to avoid memories. It's alright to do so for a while and not feel obligated to enter them. Yet in time, the pain will diminish and the room or car or chair won't seem to be so off-limits anymore.

Hallucinations. Some experience hallucinations. We call this the-face-in-the-crowd syndrome, and it often lasts up to 18 months. Many experience seeing or hearing something or sensing the presence of the other, but they won't tell anyone. They don't want to appear crazy. We don't know why, but the sensations are real to the person experiencing them.

Personal Effects. Many will struggle with what to do with personal effects. Discuss this with the counselee. There is no right or wrong time to deal with personal effects, only when the counselee is ready and has the energy. If family members begin to pressure the widow or widower for some of the deceased's effects, encourage him or her just to say, "It's too soon. I'm not ready."

As you bring up these issues and concerns, you'll be helping the griever anticipate and normalize the process. There is no real preparation for the loss of a spouse. You learn as you experience the painful process.[8]

How Do the Bereaved Overcome Their Loss?

One aspect of grief is called surviving and rebuilding. Because women live longer than men, you will probably have more of a ministry with widows than widowers. So we will relate this stage to the widow.

The three periods involved in surviving and rebuilding are (1) bridging the past; (2) living with the present; and (3) finding a path into the future.

Even with the pain of loss, during the first few days of the loss, significant decisions have to be made by the widow. The funeral, financial matters and so on have to be taken care of, and it is the widow's primary responsibility to do so. She may decide to have others make these decisions for her, or she may act as though she were still her husband's wife, in the sense that she carries out decisions and arrangements as she thinks her husband would have wanted her to do. In the latter case, she does not think of herself as a widow at this time.

The widow will still need to function in other areas such as buying groceries, preparing meals, caring for children, pets and the household, and perhaps even functioning at work or in the family's business. This is where family and friends can be of assistance.

Bridge the Past

The primary task in this period is for the widow to loosen her ties to her deceased husband and begin to accept his death. This involves breaking the threads of shared experiences with her husband and translating them into memories. It also includes learning to use the word "I" in place of "we."

Live in the Present

The second period is living in the present. After the funeral, a shift in the family structure needs to be made. Various roles need to be reassigned in order to take care of daily, routine tasks. Changes in expressive tasks also need to be considered. Children will need to be comforted by their mother, even while she is involved in her own grief. This involves her sharing her pain and sorrow with the children just like she, at other times, has shared her joy and delight with them. Children need support and security from their mother during this time of losing one parent.

A mother cannot function as both a mother and a father. She will wear herself out attempting to fill both roles. Ministers should be careful in what they say to the spouse and children at this time. Statements such as, "You will have to function now as both mother and father" are not healthy. Telling a son he will have to take the place of his father and be the man of the house is not realistic. It is better for the remaining parent to work on being a better parent, rather than to attempt to fulfill both roles. Family members will have to accept the fact that some changes must be made and that all the father's duties will not be assumed by the mother. Other family members or relatives may be able to fill in some of the vacant places, but not completely.

Role changes will affect everyone. Some of the changes will be unfamiliar, such as a widow's having to handle mortgage payments, inheritance tax, bank statements, investments, settlement of debts, her husband's business problems and so on.

The issue of housing arrangement also is crucial at this time for the widow to remain living in the present. The home may have so many memories that the spouse will make or be forced into making a hasty decision to sell and move. Your counsel at this time may be important. The widow may be in a panic to ease the pain and the potential financial burden, but good decisions usually are not made at this time of intense emotion. Counsel her to wait, if at all possible, and to consider the consequences carefully. Many widows have regretted selling too soon—they and their children do need the familiar setting. Several months should elapse before significant decisions are made.

Living in the present is a time of giving up old habits and establishing new ones. Many widows report that their ties with their children become stronger at this time. Don't be surprised, however, by conflicts that occur over the will, possessions or family functions.

Significant signs of living in the present are seen as the person goes shopping alone for the first time, takes a job, goes out on a date, redecorates the house and so on.

Find a New Path

The third period is finding a path into the future. During this time the widow finds stability in functioning and is now able to reorganize her life without her spouse. She has developed new roles and can operate independently in a new fashion.

She seeks to develop new relationships, not to replace the original spouse, but to refocus her own life or find a parent for her children, to ease economic strains and to have the comfort and companionship she desires.[9]

What can you say or do at this time of grief?

Begin where the bereaved person is. Do not begin where you think she should be at this point in her life. Do not place your expectations for behavior upon her. She may be more upset or more depressed than you feel she should be, but that is her choice.

Clarify her expressed feelings with her. This can be done by restating her words in your own words. Help her bring her emotions to the surface. You might say, "You know, I haven't seen you cry for a week. If I were in your situation, I would probably feel like crying." If she is depressed, be near her and assure her that it will pass in time. She probably will not believe you and could even ask you to leave. Do not be offended by this.

Empathize. Feel with her.

Be sensitive to her feelings. Don't say too much. Joe Bayley gives this suggestion:

> Sensitivity in the presence of grief should usually make us more silent, more listening. "I'm sorry" is honest; "I know how you feel" is usually not—even though you may have experienced the death of a person who had the same familial relationship to you as the deceased person had to the grieving one. If the person feels that you can understand, he'll tell you. Then you may want to share your own honesty, not prettied-up feelings in your personal aftermath with death. Don't try to "prove" anything to a survivor. An arm about the shoulder, a firm grip of the hand, a kiss; these are the proofs grief needs, not logical reasoning. I was sitting, torn by

grief. Someone came and talked to me of God's dealings, of why it happened, of hope beyond the grave. He talked constantly, he said things I know were true. I was unmoved, except to wish he'd go away. He finally did. Another came and sat beside me. He didn't ask leading questions. He just sat beside me for a hour and more, listened when I said something, answered briefly, prayed simply, left. I was moved. I was comforted. I hated to see him go.[10]

As we've said again and again, let them know their feelings are normal. Some of them will apologize to you for their tears, depression or anger. You will hear comments such as: "I can't believe I'm still crying like this. I'm so sorry" and "I don't know why I'm still so upset. It was unfair of them to let me go after 15 years at that job. I know I shouldn't be angry, but I guess I really am. It seems so unfair."

You can be an encourager by accepting their feelings and the fact that they have feelings. Help by normalizing what they're experiencing. Give them the gift of facing their feelings and expressing them. There are many statements you can make to them:

- I don't want you to worry about crying in front of me. It's hard to feel this sad and not express it in tears. You may find me crying with you at times.
- I hope you feel the freedom to express your sorrow in tears in front of me. I won't be embarrassed or upset. I just want to be here with you.
- If I didn't see you cry, I would be more concerned. Your crying tells me you are handling this in a healthy way.
- If I had experienced what you have been through, I would feel like opening my eyes and letting the flood of tears come pouring out. Do you ever feel like that?

Anger is another feeling that is difficult for many people to express. Use comments such as:

- It is natural to feel anger and hostility toward everyone and everything that had to do with your husband's death. I feel angry, too.
- You must be very angry that your baby has suffered and that you can do nothing about it.
- It is normal and reasonable to be angry and resentful when you have lost your baby and others have live and healthy babies.
- You have lost your daughter, and you have a right to be angry and frustrated.
- It must be hard to find the words to express your anger, helplessness and frustration.
- It is important that you allow yourself to express your anger and rage, no matter how much others try to discourage you.

Your encouragement will help grieving persons understand that their expression of feelings will not cause you to withdraw from them. Reassure them that you are not going to leave because of their feelings or try to talk them out of feeling the way they do. Your support is going to remain.

Another positive way of responding to the bereaved is through touch. Be sensitive to people you are ministering to who may not be as comfortable with touch as you are. If they seem to reject your physical gestures, such as hugs or touch, be sure to respect them.[11]

Don't use faulty reassurances. Assurances such as, "You'll feel better in a few days" or "It won't hurt so much after a while" do not aid counselees through recovery quicker. How do you know that?

Remember not to give up helping the person too soon:

It seems when the initial paralyzing shock begins to wear off, the bereaved slowly returns to consciousness like a person coming out of a deep coma. Senses and feelings return gradually, but mingled in with the good vibrations of being alive and alert again is the frightening pain of reality. It is precisely at this time when friends, assuming the bereaved is doing just fine, stop praying, stop calling, and stop doing all those little kind things that help so much. We need to reverse this trend. In fact we must hold the bereaved person up to the Lord more during the first two years of grief than in the first two weeks.[12]

WHAT GOALS SHOULD THE BEREAVED SET IN PLACE?

Someone, whether it is you or another concerned person, will need to help the grieving person accomplish several tasks. These tasks are especially applicable in the loss of a loved one and will be accomplished over a period of time.

Identify Secondary Losses and Resolve Unfinished Business

For many people, their losses are never identified or grieved over. It could be the loss of a role, the family unit, the breadwinner, the social life and so on. Sometimes saying aloud what a grieving person never said or had an opportunity to say to the deceased helps to complete some of the unfinished business.

Experience Grief for Any Dreams, Expectations or Fantasies

This is sometimes difficult or even overlooked, as dreams, expectations and fantasies are not usually seen as losses, because they never existed. Yet each constitutes a loss, because it is highly valued.

Discover the Bereaved's Capabilities and Where They Might Be Lacking in their Coping Skills

It is important to help the bereaved handle the areas where they are struggling. Encourage their positive steps, such as talking about the loss. When they do something unhealthy, such as avoidance, alcohol or over-medication, provide them with other alternatives.

Provide Helpful Information Concerning What They Are Now Experiencing

Most people do not understand the duration and process of grieving. You want to normalize their grief without minimizing it as well as let them know that their grief responses will be personal. They should avoid comparing themselves with anyone else. Don't let them equate the length and amount of grieving with how much they loved the person.

Let Them Know You Understand That They May Want to Avoid the Intensity of the Pain They Are Presently Experiencing

Your empathy, understanding and respect will do much to assist them in knowing that their grief is normal. Encourage them to go through the pain of the grief. There is just no way to avoid it. If they don't face the pain, it will explode at another time. They may need to be reminded that even with the present intensity of their pain, in time it will diminish.

Help Them Understand That Their Grief Will Affect All Areas of Life

Work habits, memory, attention span, intensity of feelings and response to marital partner will be affected. This is normal.

Help Them Understand the Process of Grief

Understanding that their emotions will vary and that progress is erratic will help alleviate the feeling that there is no progress. Help them plan for significant dates and holidays in advance. Encourage them to talk about their expectations of themselves, and help them evaluate whether they are being realistic.

Help Them Find Ways to Be Replenished Spiritually, Socially and Physically

Be aware of their eating and exercise habits. Don't let them forego their own regular checkups. Alert them to the possible diminished capacity of the immune system that occurs several months after a major loss.

Help Them with the Practical Problems Following a Loss and Assist Them in Preventing Unwise Decisions

Such practical items as helping to arrange for meals, transportation, financial consultation and eventually training or education needed for survival may be part of your task.

Sometimes grieving people will make major decisions too early, which creates additional losses. Some plan to sell their house or move to new cities, but this may eliminate their roots or a needed support system. Making major changes during the first year should be discouraged if at all possible. These changes may appear to be wise, but they also bring another sense of loss.

Over a longer period of time, you may be able to assist grieving persons with a number of tasks. Help them discover their new identity separate from the one they lost and the new roles that they must either develop or relinquish. These changes must be identified so that things such as lost portions of identity (from married to single) and roles can be grieved.

Encourage New Relationships

You may be the one to bring up the fact that a healthy new relationship with the lost person must be developed.[13] This thought will be foreign to many, but it is a major adjustment for anyone who has lost a loved one. It is helpful to ask them how they plan to keep parts of their former life, such as special times, routines or mementos, alive and how reminiscing can be helpful.

There is wisdom in what Professor Morrie Schwartz said in *Tuesdays with Morrie*: "Death ends life, not a relationship."

One of your future tasks will be helping grieving persons reinvest in new lives. They will be able to start this process at their own time and pace. Some will need direction in getting back into the mainstream of life, especially if they cared for a chronically ill person for a period of time or if they placed an elderly or handicapped person in a convalescent home. There can be a tremendous sense of loss and resulting adjustment to life following such a drastic change.

Sometimes finding support groups or other means of social support will end up providing lasting relationships. You need to be sensitive to the ability and desire of people to get back into the mainstream of life. Be sure you don't encourage them into new relationships too soon. Be especially careful of trying to promote new dating activities for those who have lost spouses through death and divorce.

Provide Growth Opportunities

At some point, you will have the opportunity to talk with people about what they have learned through their loss. There can be growth and gain, but these are not seen immediately. Additionally, it does not mean that we deny the significance of the loss in any way, but we do come to the place where our loss becomes an opportunity for spiritual growth and learning.[14]

The following are some helpful suggestions to provide to the bereaved as you minister:

- As soon as they feel ready, they can reread sympathy cards and other correspondence. Looking up Scripture references and trying to memorize helpful sayings, stories and verses have helped many.
- Suggest that they take an inventory of other expressions of sympathy, such as flowers, meals and visits. Help them recall who supported them during the initial days of their grief, and encourage them to keep up their end of those friendships, if that is important.
- It may be helpful to listen to the funeral tape monthly. They need to allow themselves time alone to cry, reflect quietly, be angry or get in touch with other feelings. Often a person is so numb at the funeral that their true feelings are masked or suppressed. Some have listened again to the funeral meditation and outlined it for future reference.
- Encourage them to write down significant, comforting statements made by others.[15]

WHAT IS DIFFERENT ABOUT EXPECTED LOSSES?

Another crisis ministry will be to those who know they are going to die. The terminally ill person has special needs and responses during his or her last days.

What do people experience when they know they are going to die? It is important for us to know what they are going through for two reasons: (1) some of us may be aware prior to our death that we are going to die; and (2) in order to minister to another person who is in this state, we need to know the stages.

Dying means change. Even when we think we are prepared, we also live with the fear that we will not be able to cope. We are afraid of the kinds of changes that will occur in us and also what these changes will do to others. When a person knows he or she is going to die, he or she usually expresses five different stages of emotional response. His or her loved ones go through these same emotional reactions as well.

Stage 1: Denial and Isolation

The first reaction is, *It can't be. They're wrong. It's not me they are talking about.* Some people make statements like, "They'll find that someone in the lab made a mistake, and then they'll come and tell me that I'll be alright." Or the person may go to doctor after doctor, seeking another diagnosis and a ray of hope. Not only does the person not want to hear that he or she will die, but also his or her relatives and loved ones do not want to hear it. The disciples didn't want to hear Jesus speak about His dying, but again and again he told them about His betrayal and crucifixion.

Often a person experiences a shock reaction upon hearing the news. One way shock manifests itself is through denial. Denial has been called the human shock absorber in time of tragedy. Through denial, our emotions are temporarily desensitized. Our sense of time is somewhat suspended because of our attempt to delay the consequences. Not only can the denial aspect of shock manifest itself in a reaction such as, "Not me! No, I won't believe it," but in some cases denial can take the form of displaced concern. Some relatives who are shocked with the news about their loved one may try to act as though they are emotionally detached. Yet denial freezes the emotions, and they must be thawed eventually.

What do we do to help a person at this time, as we visit him or her at home or in a hospital? Don't judge him or her for what he or she says, no matter how difficult it seems. Do not expect too much response on the first, second or even third visit. He or she may not feel like talking. Do not become discouraged and quit visiting the individual. Eventually the person will respond because he or she needs someone with whom to share his or her loneliness. Perhaps the example we find in Job can be a pattern for our response to the person (see Job 2:13).

Stage 2: Anger

In the second stage, the person experiences anger, rage, envy and resentment. *Why me, God? Why me? Why not someone else?* The person is angry at those around him or her who are well—friends, relatives, doctors. The person is angry at the doctors who cannot make him or her well. The individual is angry at God for allowing this to happen and for not immediately healing him or her.

In Job 7:11 (*NKJV*) we read, "Therefore I will not restrain my mouth; I will speak in the anguish of my spirit." Perhaps this is what the person is experiencing at this point in his or her life. You may become the object of the person's anger simply because you are there, but don't take the anger personally. Nor should you become judgmental and say that he or she should not feel this anger. Anger is part of the normal process that any person will experience. Through the person's anger, he or she could be demanding attention; therefore, honest and open communication can help him or her feel understood.

Stage 3: Bargaining

"Spare me, Lord! Let me recover and be filled with happiness again before my death" (Ps. 39:13, *TLB*). This is the prayer of so many people facing death. The person makes promises: "If I can get well, I will serve the Lord more than ever." The person bargains: "If only I can live until June to see my son get married." Then, if the person lives until June, he or she may say, "If only I can live to see my grandchildren," and the bargaining goes on and on. This stage usually lasts only a brief while, but it can be intense while it lasts.

Hezekiah, a man noted in the Old Testament, was told by the Lord:

Set your affairs in order, for you are going to die; you will not recover from this illness (Isa. 38:1, *TLB*).

When Hezekiah received the news, he turned his face to the wall and bargained with God. He reminded God of how he had served and obeyed Him, and then he broke down and cried (see Isa. 38:3). Hezekiah's prayer was heard by God, and he was given 15 more years to live.

Hezekiah's response to this experience was:

Yes, now I see it all—it was good for me to undergo this bitter-ness, for you have lovingly delivered me from death; you have forgiven all my sins. For dead men cannot praise you. They can-not be filled with hope and joy. The living, only the living, can praise you as I do today. . . . Think of it! The Lord healed me! (Isa. 38:17-20, *TLB*).

Part of the bargaining process may reflect our reaction to death and to God. We feel that God doesn't know what He is doing in some cases, and we need to straighten Him out. Joe Bayley writes:

Death for the Christian should be a shout of triumph, through sorrow and tears, bringing glory to God—not a confused misun-derstanding of the will of God to heal.[16]

Our ministry to the terminally ill is to be a listener. James 1:19 (*AMP*) states that we are to be "a ready listener." This is a time to listen and not to give the dying person false hope. False reassurances do not help the individual. Simple reflection, a touch and a listening ear will minister and speak volumes.

> **Our ministry to the terminally ill is to be a listener. Simple reflection, a touch and a listening ear will minister and speak volumes.**

Stage 4: Depression

When denial, anger and bargaining don't work, the individual facing death concludes that nothing works. Then depression sets in, which has two parts: (1) reactive depression—thinking about past memories and (2) preparatory depression—thinking about impending losses. This is a time when the person needs to express sorrow—to pour it out. You can minister best at this point by sitting silently with the person, holding his or her hand and letting the person know that it's alright to express his or her feelings. Do not argue or debate with the individual, for the consequences can only be negative.

Stage 5: Acceptance

At the final stage, the person now rests in the knowledge of what will happen. This is a somewhat peaceful acceptance of the inevitable death. There is nothing else to do but accept the inevitable. The person may lose all interest in what goes on around him or her at this point and even may become less talkative. You need to be honest with the person. The individual may ask how long he or she has to live, but you should never give a time limit. People vary with their responses. My pastor friend knew he had less than a year to live. He said, "My calling now is to teach my congregation how to die."

The authors of *The Worst Is Over* said that if we want to help a person who is terminal, it is best to take their spiritual temperature. The purpose of this is to discover whether they are *living* with their condition or *dying* from it. Some have given up and are waiting for the end, whereas others are ready to experience life each day to whatever extent they can. If you understand which position you are dealing with, it will help you choose your words and response to the individual.[17]

HOW DO FAMILIES COPE WITH EXPECTED LOSSES?

Family members of the terminally ill need as much or more help and support as the ill person. They may not want the person to be told he or she is terminally ill, but it is better for all concerned that the person be told.

When death comes from a chronic and/or terminal illness, the circumstances can be a blessing, a curse or a combination of both, depending on the characteristics of the illness, such as length, type, the amount of pain and the type of treatment. Others' reactions to the illness and death, including those of your own family members, affect the impact. Economic issues also play a part.

There may be time for anticipatory grief and closure on unfinished business. However, a person also experiences a sense of powerlessness to stop the death from occurring as well as the progressive deterioration of a person they love.[18]

A terminal illness creates a multitude of problems that many family members never consider. Some of the special problems include the following:

- Numerous remissions and relapses, so loved ones are on an emotional merry-go-round.
- Lengthy periods of anticipatory grief.
- Increased financial, social, physical and emotional pressures.
- Family disruption that goes on and on.
- The varying emotional responses of each family member to the progressive decline of the loved one. Rarely is every family member on the same page when it comes to grieving.
- Uncertainty, which continues more than anyone wants.
- Various treatments, which are accompanied by their side effects and are sometimes futile.
- Dilemmas over decisions such as hospital costs, treatment plans and so on.[19]

Expected death usually is gradual and dominates all aspects of a family's life. As one person said:

I thought this would be easier than a sudden death. It wasn't. From the day of the diagnosis to the day of death I was totally out of control. It was worse for me to see the daily decline of someone I knew as strong and capable. Not only that, I was supposed to take care of the rest of the family at the same time. I'd feel torn between their needs and my husband's, who wouldn't be here much longer. And I really couldn't take care of myself. So, what do I do with my own health? And what about my guilt and anger and sorrow? I'm exhausted. I have regrets. I wish I could have done more. I have relief that it's over but that brings up some guilt as well. I want to grieve. I really do. But I don't have the energy. My life is different now. It's empty and lonely. I was needed before and now I'm not. I lost some friends and social involvements, but I don't have the energy to invest. Where do I go from here?

These are questions you'll hear again and again. Your help is needed for a long time.

Avoid Abandonment

Family members should be encouraged to face their crisis of life with patience. They should not isolate the circumstances. One of the problems that can occur is the abandonment syndrome, which is when dying people express the fear that their condition will make them so unacceptable to others around them that they will be abandoned. Unfortunately, many case studies have confirmed their worst fears. The following are some of the ways abandonment occurs:

1. *Giving brief and formal monologues.* A relative or even a doctor may come in and ask a few rhetorical questions and then leave without letting the person express his or her inner fears and hurts. People breeze in but seem to respond only on a superficial level. Other people come in and inform the person how he or she ought to be feeling; they promise to come back but never return.

2. *Treating the person as though the disease or accident has turned him or her into a nobody.* The person feels badly when others talk in front of him or her as though he or she were not there any longer. Even some unconscious people can hear what is being said. Many who have survived a coma have said that the faithful, verbal prayers of others were heard and meant so much to them. You should pray with the person whether or not you know that he or she can hear.

3. *Ignoring or rejecting the cues that the person attempts to give.* The person may want to talk about what is happening. What would you

say to the person who says, "I think I am going to die soon?" Many respond with, "Nonsense. You're going to live for many years." That is not what the person needs to hear. The counselee's feelings and interpretation are important to him or her.

4. *Literally abandoning the person.* Sometimes people in nursing homes, as well as terminally ill patients, are actually abandoned. Some people say that they want to remember the person as he or she used to be or that the person will receive better care at the nursing home than they can provide. Often, this is a reaction to their fear of their own death. Because of the implications of the loved one's death, they try to separate themselves from him or her in some way. It also has been observed that some loved ones initially have close contact with the terminally ill person, such as kissing him or her on the lips. But then they begin to kiss the person on the forehead and then on the hand, and finally they simply blow a kiss from across the room. The patient senses this form of rejection.

Pertaining to abandonment, should the person return to his or her home to die? For some people, this may be the best way, should they so desire, but others feel more comfortable staying at the hospital. It is important that they stay where they feel the most secure and where they are in an honest atmosphere and receive the best care.

Provide Options

More and more people who are terminally ill are having their memorial service prior to their death. This gives the dying person the opportunity to hear what others would say about them. It also gives the person the opportunity to give a blessing to their children and grandchildren as well as to say farewell to their friends.

WHEN IS THE APPROPRIATE TIME TO GRIEVE?

In regard to those losing a loved one, many people do much of their grief work in advance of the death of a terminally ill family member. They experience the same grief stages as the terminally ill person. Ministers can help such people by having them actually visualize the sequences of the death, the funeral, the mourning and the people involved prior to this time. It is an act of preparation that is needed.

I have talked to many people who are unaware of the process of grieving before the death. Recently, a distant relative experienced the death of her mother. She was a bit taken aback when her father remarried eight months after her mother's death. Yet, he had grieved during the last three years of her impending death and was able to readjust and go on with his life in a brief period of time.

Grieving over a loss that you know is going to occur may be less severe than grieving following a sudden, unexpected death. The following are four basic stages in anticipatory grief:

1. *Depression.* This depression occurs following the diagnosis.
2. *Heightened concern for the ill person.* In an unexpected death, often there is guilt over such things as not being kinder, not showing sufficient love, having argued with the person and so on. In anticipatory grief, much of the guilt can be eliminated through the opportunity to increase love, concern and compassion for the person. Personal business can be concluded with the person prior to his or her death.
3. *Rehearsal of the person's death.* It's very common for the person to rehearse in his or her mind what he or she will do when the family member dies. The individual anticipates how he or she will feel, be comforted, react and so on. Many arrange for the funeral in advance, which also helps prepare for the person's death.
4. *Adjustments to the consequence of the death.* Those who are left after the death adjust to life without the family member and begin to consider the future.[20]

FINAL THOUGHTS

Remember the following three points as you minister at this crisis time:

1. A bereaved person, no matter what his or her age, needs *safe places*. The person needs his or her own home. Some people prefer to withdraw, because their home reminds them of their loss, but giving up the home and moving create more of a loss. A brief change may be alright, but familiar surroundings are helpful.

> **A bereaved person, no matter what his or her age, needs safe places, safe people and safe situations.**

2. The bereaved also needs *safe people*. Friends, relatives and a minister are necessary to give the person the emotional support he or she needs. It is better to visit the person four times a week for 10 minutes than to come once a week for one hour. This is a continual support without becoming exhaustive.
3. Finally, the bereaved needs *safe situations*. Any kind of safe situation that provides the bereaved person with worthwhile roles to perform will benefit him or her. The roles should be uncomplicated, simple and stress free. One pastor called upon a home in which the woman had just lost her husband. He could tell that people had been coming in and out all day long and that she was tired of receiving them and their concern. As he came in he said, "You know, I've had a tiring day. Would it be too much to ask you to make a cup of tea or coffee?" She responded and fixed the coffee. When he was leaving she said, "Thank you for asking me to make you the coffee. I started to feel worthwhile and useful again."

Perhaps what most people need in order to minister effectively to others is a clear understanding of what death is. For the Christian, death is a transition, a tunnel leading from this world into the next. Perhaps the journey is a bit frightening because of leaving the security we feel now for the unknown, but the final destination will be worth the present uncertainty. John Powell said:

> This book is gratefully dedicated to Bernice. She has been a source of support in many of my previous attempts to write. She has generously contributed an excellent critical eye, a cultivated literary sense and especially a confident kind of encouragement. She did not help with the preparation of this book. On July 11 she received a better offer. She was called by the Creator and Lord of the Universe to join the celebration at the banquet of eternal life.[21]

RECOMMENDED RESOURCES

Resources for Counselors and Counselees

Ford, Janice Harris. *No Time for Goodbyes: Coping with Sorrow, Anger and Injustice After a Tragic Death.* Pathfinder Publishing of California, 2000. Comprehensive and very helpful, including assistance on the criminal justice system and financial adjustments.

Mitsch, Raymond R., and Lynn Brookside. *Grieving the Loss of Someone You Love.* Servant Publications, 1993.

Sittser, Gerald. *A Grace Disguised: How the Soul Grows Through Loss.* Grand Rapids, MI: Zondervan Publishing House, 1998. A profound book from a man who witnessed the death of three of his family members.

Wright, H. Norman. *Recovering from the Losses of Life.* Grand Rapids, MI: Revell, 2000.

Zonnebelt-Smeenge, Susan J., and Robert C. DeVries. *Getting to the Other Side of Grief.* Grand Rapids, MI: Baker Book House, 1998.

CHAPTER 13

DEATHS YOU WILL ENCOUNTER

As we travel through the family life cycle there will be deaths that are predictable, even expected. There will also be others that "shouldn't have occurred." Most of the situations you encounter will fall into the following categories.

THE DEATH OF A PARENT

The most commonly expressed statements uttered when a parent dies are

- I feel like an orphan.
- Now I'm closer to death.
- I feel vulnerable.
- I'm frustrated because there was something more I needed to say or do.
- I am released from a burden.[1]

These reactions come about because most of us never really think our parent's death is actually going to occur. Yes, we know it will, but a part of us denies it. When a parent dies, the child feels the protection of his or her own life dissolve. One man in his 40s said, "When my mom died, I felt like my home had been taken away. I was cut adrift."

If the person's parent were older, he or she already may have experienced a role reversal. Their father or mother became the child and they became the parent. This is usually done to protect the parents and can be sudden or gradual. Either way it's one of life's losses.

Reacting to the Loss

When a parent dies, there are four factors that affect the way a person will react to the loss. A person should ask himself or herself the following questions:

1. *How did the parent die?* An unexpected loss will be more of a shock than a gradual one, although the pain is the same in either.
2. *What was the quality of the relationship with the parent? Was there any unfinished business?*
3. *What is the amount of support the person received during the grief process?*
4. *How will a person's past experiences with loss affect this loss?*[2]

Sometimes a death brings a sense of relief and a feeling of safety a person never experienced before. If a parent was a dominating bully or an abuser, this is often the case, but there is still grief. And some of that grief is over the relationship the person never had with his or her parent. I've talked with those who never had the parent they would have loved to have loved.[3]

The death of a parent is like the beginning of a child's own death. "If my dad could die, then so can I." This is a concept to work through during grief counseling. The death of parents is the most common form of bereavement for adults. Depending on the relationship, the response can range from deep sorrow to ambivalence. One of the main factors influencing grief is the age of the parent and the age of the child. There is a major difference in losing a parent when the child is in his or her 20s and the parent is middle-aged than when the child is in his or her 50s and the parent is 85.

Losing a Parent at a Young Age

I lost my father when I was 22 and he was 72. Yes, he was older, but the manner of his death was overwhelming. He was killed in an auto accident. One writer said:

> The fact that you weren't there when he died can also be a source of long-lasting regret. The fact that *no one* may have been there can also be stressful. You may have to deal with the lengthy, painful mental process of second-guessing. *If only* your father had taken a later train, *if only* your mother had consulted a doctor earlier and so on. Sudden deaths are often bizarre, like nightmares, because they are so unexpected.[4]

My mother died at 93 and I was 54. But in her case, it was a progressive, deteriorating illness and I was prepared.

If you are working with someone in their 20s who has lost a parent, keep in mind the following:

- Those in their 20s and 30s are experiencing transitions and changes in their lives. They still may be separating from their parents and becoming more independent. Reliance upon their parent who died has come to an end. The parent is robbed of years but so is the adult child. If both parents died, the person feels orphaned. All these and other developmental factors create additional crises and losses.
- What if the parent was living life to the fullest? It makes death even more untimely. If a parent was elderly, senile or just waiting to go home to Jesus, some of the feelings are those of relief as well as "it was a blessing."
- Is this the first or second parent to die, and how many deaths has the person experienced before? If it's the first, not only can the

shock be intense, but there also will be concern for the remaining parent.

- When both parents die, there is no longer a generation between the adult child and death. The buffer is gone and now *this* person is the older generation. Their thoughts and feelings need to be explored so that they are able to accept this new position.

Some of the adjustments that can occur with this loss are as follows:

- Their opportunities are lost to resolve past unpleasantness.
- They can no longer help their parent in a way they wanted. If they are now in a position to return favors, it can't be done.
- If the adult child had not separated emotionally from his or her parents and couldn't make decisions without their approval, now what?
- If the child wanted his or her parents dead and hated them, what is their reaction now?

Staying Connected

When children lose a parent, they usually try to stay connected in some way. The activities vary but include the following:

- They attempt to imagine the parent in some distant place; it seems to help them make sense of their experience.
- They experience the deceased by believing that their parents are watching them, perhaps through their dreams.
- They reach out to the deceased parent by visiting the cemetery or talking to them. Their waking memories—such as thinking about them in very literal terms—are very common.
- Some use what we call linking objects, such as carrying around an object that the deceased owned. This tends to keep the child living in the past, but it also becomes a transitional object.[5]

Changing Relationships and Personalities

A common result of the death of a parent will be the change in relationships with siblings. It can build or destroy relationships. Some individuals feel the burden is on them, or there may have been internal fighting to protect a family member. One of the greatest sources of conflict with siblings is the will and estate. Often family estrangement occurs with parental death and the aftermath.[6]

When a parent is terminally ill, children may see a personality change. This can come from pain, medication or the knowledge of their impending death. There may also be an absence of personality, especially if there is dementia or Alzheimer's disease.[7]

Questioning to Follow

With careful questioning you will be able to help the person sort through his or her issues. As you work with someone through the process of grieving over the death of a parent, there are several questions that can be addressed at an appropriate time:

- Could you describe the relationship you had with your parent?
- What were the most important aspects of this relationship?
- What was your parent's perception of you? How would he or she have described you—personality, character and so on? Do you feel he or she really knew you? What else do you wish he or she knew about you?
- What is your strongest emotional response to the death? What words or pictures come to mind? What's the reason for the feelings?
- What do you wish he or she had said or done? We call this unfinished business. How can you take care of this now to bring some resolution to it?
- Describe what you really miss at this time. Talking? Resolving problems? A regular phone call? Having to attend a mandatory dinner?
- What will you or your children miss in the future because of his or her absence?
- What's the best memory you will always have of him or her? If he or she were here now, what would you like to say to him or her?[8]

The Death of a Sibling

What happens when a sibling is lost as an adult? It's been said that there is no other loss in adult life that is so neglected, even though most of us will experience it at some time. In fact, sibling losses may outnumber

> **There's an assumption that the loss of a parent or spouse is the most distressing, but for some adults, sibling loss is the hardest.**

other losses. My mother experienced the loss of all six of her siblings before she died. There's an assumption that the loss of a parent or spouse is the most distressing, but for some adults, sibling loss is the hardest.

Why Is Losing a Sibling So Significant?

Consider John. He had two brothers, one who was two years older and one who was two years younger. Their parents died when the brothers were in their 20s, which is also the time when they all married. By the time John was in his 50s, he'd had his parents for half of his life and he'd been without parents for about half of his life. However, when his older brother died, he lost someone who had been a part of his life from the very beginning. John's future with this brother was gone. No longer would they share the memories, family traditions or birthdays. A constant was gone from John's life. His brother's death made him feel older and much more mortal. His family of origin had shrunk by one third. He found himself wondering if he, too, would die when he reached his brother's age. The bell that tolls for a sibling may keep on tolling with the message, "You're next."

When a sibling dies, very few take into account the depth of a bond that can occur between two siblings. Often it seems that others make light of such a loss. If the loss is an adult sibling, insensitive responses such as, "Just be glad it wasn't your child or your spouse," may be expressed. It's as though the death of a sibling is dismissed, since a brother or sister is not considered one of the central characters of a person's life. Therefore, in addition to losing a sibling, there is the loss of the support of others during the grief process. The loss may not have the same impact on members of the immediate family. The remaining sibling becomes a forgotten griever. There are other names for it as well, such as the lonely mourner, and indeed, one does feel like a lonely mourner.[9]

What Does a Childhood Loss Have to Do with It?

If a person is close in age to his or her sibling when he or she dies as an adult, the person will experience many of the same losses as if this event had occurred in childhood.

Many begin this struggle with a loss in childhood. A century ago there wasn't much reaction to the death of a child as there is today, because the child mortality rate was much higher. At the end of the last century, as many as 100 out of 1,000 infants under the age of one year died from various diseases. Families usually had several children so that some would survive. As childhood mortality has declined, the thought of a child dying seems remote. Therefore, when it does occur, there is a greater impact than ever before on families, including the parents and siblings, no matter the age.

What Does Guilt Have to Do with It?

Just as guilt can come to a child who loses a sibling, it can come to adults, perhaps for different reasons. It may begin with remembering how close one was when they were younger. Then the person finds themselves wishing he or she had done more to perpetuate that closeness, but he or she didn't, and now it's too late. Or maybe there were unresolved issues that he or she now wishes had been settled. Perhaps the adult wonders why his or her sibling died first, which activates survival guilt. All of these feelings may be compounded with the additional loss of not being included in decisions about the funeral arrangements, because all of that was left to the surviving spouse and children.

If a sibling had a terminal illness, other siblings may experience old rivalries as time, attention and financial resources of parents and others are directed toward that sibling. This and other issues can generate resentment, which later may come back to haunt the siblings after their sibling dies. The obvious door to guilt opens wide.

What About Changing Roles and Relationships?

With a sibling gone, the roles and relationships with other family members may need to undergo a change. This, too, may entail more loss and stress, as it did in Ted's case. Ted was the second of two sons; he lived in the shadow of his older brother. After his brother died, he received more attention and recognition for his achievements, but he also had to assume his deceased brother's role of being responsible for his elderly parents.[10]

Perhaps the various aspects of losing a sibling as an adult can best be described by a woman who lost her younger brother, Bob:

I grieved for Bob, my brother, who was not only a member of my family but someone who knew me, who understood me, who felt with me, in a way no one else on this planet ever did or would. Someone who, more than I had ever dared know, was me. My brother-double.

And I grieved, too, still more deeply, for all that now would never be. For except in brief, nervous flashes, my brother and I had never been able to truly convey to each other the emotional kinship between us. We had never really been able to express it, enjoy it, sustain each other through it, make anything of it in our lives. We may have wanted to—and I think, as we grew older, that both of us truly did—but we just couldn't manage it. There had been too much history between us, too many cruel gibes, and long silences, too much fear. And that was why, whenever we said hello, we were already edging away, already saying good-bye.

And when I finally understood all of this, fully and deeply, I was able to forgive both of us the chance we had missed with each other and would never have again. Given who we were, and given the world in which we found ourselves, Bob and I had done the absolute best we could. And as that recognition deepened within me over the next weeks and months, I felt my grief lifting. A measure of peace and energy returned to me. And unexpectedly, as the pain receded, I began to feel Bob's presence more vividly. While before I had been able to think of my brother only with sadness and longing, I was now beginning to remember him also with amused affection, to be able to enjoy memories of his con-man charm, his absurd humor, his breathtaking, unstoppable energy.

I did not stop missing my brother then. I still miss him greatly, and I expect that I always will. But sensing Bob's spirit nearby—chortling, manic, ready for the next high-stakes game—helps me fill the space where he once was.[11]

What can you do amidst this change? You can educate others about the importance and impact of sibling loss. You can show through your responses that you understand the significance of the loss and validate either the intensity of their feelings over this loss or in some cases their ambivalence.

The Death of a Friend

What do you call a friend who has lost a friend in death? There are no labels really. A wife is a widow and a husband a widower, but there is no term to describe those who grieve friends.

Friends will die. We will probably lose more friends than relatives. The deaths of friends accompany us throughout our lifetime and shape our lives. Harold Ivan Smith voiced a sentiment that most of us think but rarely say:

My friends, although dead, fill the bleachers of my memories.[12]

What is this loss like? Perhaps you, too, will identify with the following words, as many of your counselees will:

I am again a traveler,
wandering through a landscape for which Fodor

has no guidebook—a land called grief.
Experiencing my friend's death has depleted my heart.
My heart lies, collapsed, like a party balloon
the mourning after the celebration.
No one understands my grief.
I guess that's what I get for taking friendship so seriously.[13]

The first death I ever experienced was the death of a friend. We were in high school. My youth pastor came to school and told us Ned died. He fell over dead of walking pneumonia in choir. We didn't know how to respond.

The second death came a couple of years later. One evening I opened the newspaper and saw the picture of one of my brother's closest friends. Both of them were in the air force. My brother's friend had died the day before when his fighter jet plunged into the ground. We all grieved.

It's important to keep in mind that intimacy among friends is often higher than in many other social relationships. For a friendship to develop and last, there is a great investment of trust, openness, vulnerability, affection and warmth. Therefore, when a friend dies, something has been ripped away. There can be a mixture of feelings, including the sense of unfairness if you're young. There is the feeling of that could have been me or the relief that it wasn't.

The death of a friend also impacts other friendships or social groups. These groups need to be rearranged if they're going to survive, but often there's a gaping hole.[14]

Friends Have the Right to Grieve

In our society, we have denied a very large group the right to grieve, to be recognized as people in grief, to assist them and to walk with them and give them their proper place—and this group encompasses all of us, for we have all lost friends and will continue to do so. Friend grievers have as much right as any grievers to grieve and be socially supported in the process.

A friend who is grieving really has little or no identity or role recognition and little function with respect to the deceased. Kenneth Doka in *Disenfranchised Grief* describes the typical scenario:

The social meaning of the grief period is that the recognized griever is not able, expected, or allowed to function in a normal manner. The family is expected to behave as mourners, experiencing sadness and crying in amounts deemed appropriate. They are expected to perform a variety of functions such as planning the funeral, greeting guests, dealing with funeral directors or clergy. There are prescribed, socially acceptable rules on clothing, places to sit, things to do. These mourners are released from the daily tasks of work and play. Not so the friend.[15]

However, some friends are fortunate, or so we think. They are given what we call an honorary family membership, but what they do is still prescribed by the family members. For example, what about the funeral arrangements or memorial service? Family members are given a special place to sit up front, but the audience is made up of friends—many of whom were closer and had healthier relationships than some of the family members. Usually the minister's remarks are often directed just to family who may or may not be experiencing the deepest grief. I have seen this in services. It's so unfortunate:

The difficulties triggered by the death of a close friend may be severe, and in some cases more severe, as those found in the loss of an immediate family member.[16]

Basically, "the person who has a relationship to the deceased is the one who suffers the loss of that relationship, and the degree of intensity of that relationship is the degree to which the survivor(s) feel the loss."[17]

Friends Can Be Called Upon as Chief Supporters

And then you have the question, Who is the chief supporter? This is a key person for many reasons. Some are quite visible, while others are doing their work behind the scenes. This individual does the recruiting and coordination of support for the chief mourners. He or she communicates, interprets or could even defends the wishes and desires of those closest to others.[18]

However, what if there's a conflict over who the chief supporter is? What if a friend of the deceased is at odds with the spouse of the deceased? What if someone was a friend of the deceased but not of his or her spouse? Harold Ivan Smith says:

> Suppose a husband dies. Legally the chief mourner will be the widow. The chief mourner tends to be the person(s) who stood in the closest legal and social relationship to the deceased. Once that role or privilege is determined, either implicitly or after something of a challenge, or these days, negotiated, all other mourners—especially the friends—are expected to support that chief mourner. When one funeral director was asked, "Who is the chief mourner?" he responded, "Check the limos" (in some areas called "family cars") referring to the order: family first.
>
> The issue can become conflicted if the deceased has been previously married or has children by different spouses or partners, when there is a large estate, or if a person is still legally married but is living with a romantic partner, say during divorce proceedings. Now who is the chief mourner? To whom does the friend offer support? Spouse or lover? Both? If the issue is confused, some friends distance themselves or limit themselves to minimal support, saying, "It's best not to get involved."[19]

A conflict surrounding who should be the chief mourner is never easy. However, often a friend jumps in and becomes the chief supporter, since family members might not be as functional. In doing this, a friend may overlook his or her own grief as he or she tries to help others, which in turn triggers delayed grief. For instance, sometimes those who have a few close friends find that when one of those friends dies, they feel friendless; therefore, they end up with the problem of delayed friend grief.

Plain and simple, friends are expected to be there to help—to meet physical, emotional and sometimes even funeral needs or other needed support. Not to do so creates suspicion concerning the friendship.[20]

One author said:

A friend often becomes something of an emotional midwife.[21]

A supportive friend (sometimes friends aren't certain what they should do) can be called upon by the family to send flowers, bring food, volunteer, fulfill specific requests, help with announcements, provide dates and, if asked by the chief mourners, offer advice on decisions, the eulogy and so on. I've been asked to conduct the service of a friend, read the eulogy and a personal letter, call others and so on. Friends can provide immediate, short-term and long-term support.[22]

Friends Need Support

If you are working with someone who lost a friend, talk with the person about his or her experience. Did the person feel he or she was able to help? Was the person ignored or slighted in any way? Did the person feel that if anything was to be accomplished he or she had to do it? Had the person had an opportunity to grieve? If not, what was keeping him or her from it at this time?

> **One of the ways that you can help everyone in your church and community is to talk openly about friendship grief and its normalcy and appropriateness.**

Encourage this person to grieve and to remember his or her friendship. Encourage the person to write explanation letters to give to others.

One of the ways that you can help everyone in your church and community is to talk openly about friendship grief and its normalcy and appropriateness. In counseling, a man or a woman can find a safe place to remember his or her friends. Why couldn't this be done in classes? A time of friendship remembrance is very healing. There are numerous questions you can use to ask people about their friends:

- Who encourages you to remember your friend?
- Who discourages you from remembering your friend?
- How are you remembering your friend?
- What do you miss about your friend?
- What are you not missing about your friend?[23]

Friend grief is a far more common experience than both the professional and the layperson realize. It's a disenfranchised grief in that it's not usually openly acknowledged, validated or publicly mourned. You, as a pastor or clinician, can change this. Perhaps the first step is to look at friendship loss in your own life. You can normalize friendship grief and encourage others to talk about this grief. Help friends find new ways to verbalize their grief for a friend. Sometimes obituary notices say, "friends are encouraged to attend," but perhaps they also should be encouraged to grieve.

Help those who lose a friend identify and prepare for the secondary losses. How will they handle the other losses such as their friend's spouse remarrying or moving away? When someone loses a friend, he or she will probably need assistance from you in knowing what to say if he or she is involved in the memorial service as well as in handling the death, no matter what stage of life they're in. One woman shared her dilemma:

At 25, we should not be planning a memorial service for a friend. There is little in our experience to guide us, and little in other sources for us to follow. There are no rituals for mourning friends, no ready-made readings that say what we need to say.[24]

Like others, all a friend has left of the friend who has died is the memory:

As friends move on with their lives, we see that, like other mourners, this loss has changed them. They carry with them a new appreciation and sensitivity for life, and their friend remains an important part of who they are. They learn to live with the paradox that their friends are gone, yet still live on.[25]

Your task in helping someone with the loss of a friend is as Harold Ivan Smith wrote:

Helping take the death of a friend and stir it into the emotional batter of their lives.[26]

It also may help to ask, "Do you think or feel that the loss of your friend has been recognized by others?" "How would you like others to recognize your loss?" "Has anyone said, 'It was *only* a friend?' and if so, how can you respond to that?"

The best response you can make is "tell me about your friend." It's difficult for many to handle and integrate a friend's loss into their life. You as a minister, caregiver or counselor can provide a safe place for people to "audition words, to try out thoughts and to have the words, the narratives and the emotions witnessed and valued rather than analyzed and critiqued."[27] Your task and mine is to help the person in grief find an appropriate place in their emotional life and learn now to live with a memory rather than a person.

THE UNRECOGNIZED LOSS— THE DEATH OF A PET

The loss of a pet ranks right up there with the loss of a person for many. Those who have a close connection with a pet will understand the feeling of loss that occurs at this time.

Pet loss occurs when the pet runs away, is stolen, killed or even lost in a custody battle. Those who divorce sometimes become involved in as intense a custody battle for their pet as for a child. One of my clients had visitation rights and another paid $800 a month in support and an additional $25 in dog support.

One of the worst losses is a missing pet because of the animal's unknown whereabouts, which can cause a lack of closure as well as the tendency to blame oneself for leaving the pet unattended, a gate unlatched, a door open and so on.

Another difficult and unique problem you may encounter is the euthanasia decision. A person may be facing this prospect, or perhaps it has already occurred. It's not easy to be placed in the position of making a life-or-death decision. It's a decision laced with a moral and ethical dilemma or even a crisis. You'll have to help the pet owners work through the loss of their pet as well as their feelings about euthanasia. The word "euthanasia" literally means "mercy killing." It's not the pet's choice; it's the pet owner's choice. Isn't it interesting that we refer to this practice as putting pets to sleep instead of calling it what it is—putting them to death. Remember, it's not just a pet that will be gone, it's a relationship.[28]

Pets Are Family

It is not unusual when a pet dies that a person grieves more deeply than for a human companion. Why? Pets often give us something that others cannot—unconditional love.[29]

Studies show that in recent years pets have become even more important to people. Seventy percent of those who share their lives with a companion animal see their pet as their child. A recent study indicated that 99 percent of cat and dog owners view their pets as family members.[30]

When we lose a person, we are usually surrounded by others who share this grief. This is seen as a significant loss, and sympathy and support are available. Yet the same supportive conditions are not as available when someone's pet dies. Often family and close friends can't grasp the depth and extent of a person's bereavement involving pet loss. The pet owner runs into the problem that his or her loss of a pet is often unrecognized by others. To others it's insignificant and minimized. Yet our task is to validate their loss and reinforce the fact that it is significant. Putting them in touch with other pet owners who have incurred a similar loss can be beneficial.

For many, the companionship received from a pet is often stronger than that from another person. While you may or may not be an animal lover, a pet loss still needs to be recognized, acknowledged and mourned.

It is the elderly for whom the loss of a pet can be especially devastating and from which it may be difficult to recover. For some, their pet may be the last friend they have, since relatives and friends may be sick, deceased or unavailable. It may be difficult for them to grieve properly because of the lack of a support system:

> Bereaved elderly pet owners are often overwhelmed by the loss of a pet who provided them with love and support through other losses in their lives. Without their animal companion and other family members, they may be unable to cope on their own. This can intensify feelings of despair, loneliness and isolation. The elderly person who has lost a pet may become depressed or even lose the will to live. He or she may experience feelings of social isolation and abandonment. The current loss almost always awakens memories of past losses, compounding feelings of sorrow and loneliness.[31]

The morning of the day I was putting the final touches on this chapter, my dog Sheffield died. He was more than a pet. He was a companion. I took him fishing, hunting, into the counseling office to comfort those who were hurting and into the convalescent homes to bring a moment of joy to the lonely. Since Sheffield came into our lives eight months after the death of our son, he was with us through our journey of grief. The bond was very deep. Sheffield's loss was one of the last links we had with Matthew. He was a member of our family.

We watched our dog slowly deteriorate and knew for several days that his death was imminent. Even our other dog, Aspen, seemed to sense something was amiss. We said good-bye to him and thanked him for what he had brought into our lives. There was a loss, a time of sorrow and tears. Many friends and acquaintances also felt this loss, as he was special. Two close friends called to talk and reminisce and pray with me. What a difference it makes when others understand.

THE DEATH OF A CHILD

The death of a child is unlike any other loss. It is a horrendous shock, no matter how it happens. It's important to comprehend the impact this has on parents in order to understand why they respond to the remaining children in the way they do.

Children die for many reasons. I worked with a mother whose son fell off a roof and lingered for six days before he died. Another mother came to get counsel because her five- and six-year-old sons were murdered by her husband. Another family lost their child in a drowning accident. When there is a miscarriage, stillbirth or infant death, it is called the *loss of possibility*. Children die because of abortion, kidnapping or running away.

A friend of mine lost his 18-year-old daughter one morning. She just died. There was no reason or cause that anyone could find. She just died. No matter how, it's one of the deepest hurts of life. And when parents receive the news of a terminal disease, they're overwhelmed. With a terminal illness parents feel the end of hope:

The worst moment is the diagnosis. There were symptoms that puzzled you that rest and fluids and aspirin could not resolve. There were tests, too many of them: repeated finger pokes and blood draws; hours in impersonal waiting rooms; x-rays and CAT scans; too many unfamiliar doctors, some kind, some brusque and mechanical. Then the appointment with the specialist, from whom you hoped to hear that it's all been a mistake. You and your child can go home now. Instead, there are the words that blind, pierce and scar. Most agree that learning of their child's diagnosis is the worst moment. The doctor's words come with the force of a death notice. The shock and disbelief that follow are much the same as that which other parents experience when they are told that their child has died.[32]

Nineteen percent of our adult population has experienced the death of a child. Miscarriage is the most common form of death following accidents. In fact, miscarriages, stillbirths and deaths of children over 30 account for around two-thirds of all children deaths.[33]

Grieving the Lost Child

One of the most difficult and disturbing issues to handle is the "wrongness" of a child's death. It just shouldn't happen. It doesn't make sense. It's death out of turn. The parent often feels, *Why should I survive when our child, who should have survived, didn't?* Death violates the cycle of the young growing up and replacing the old.

Grief over the loss of a child is disabling. It will be more intense and last longer than grief over the loss of anyone else. The death of a child has been called the ultimate bereavement.

Even for someone who has experienced other losses, there is no precedent for losing a child. Nothing prepares a parent for such a tragedy. The loss of a child casts a shadow on the parent's life.

> **One of the most difficult and disturbing issues to handle is the "wrongness" of a child's death. It just shouldn't happen. It doesn't make sense. It's death out of turn.**

When parents lose a child, they also lose what the child represented to them. They feel victimized in so many ways. They feel as though they've lost part of themselves—even part of their physical body. The loss of those features in the child that bore resemblance to either parent seems to magnify the loss.

Parents miss the physical interaction as well—the sight, sound, smell and touch of their child. If they were still in the hands-on, caregiving stage with their child, this absence would be terribly painful.

In so many words, the child embodied their connection to the future, a future that no longer includes the child here on Earth. If the child was old enough to respond to them, they've lost a very special love source. That love was based on need, dependence, admiration and appreciation, but now it's gone. They've lost some of their own treasured qualities and talents as well, for they saw those that they valued most in their child. Further, they've lost the expectations and dreams they had for their child as he or she grew older. The anticipated years—full of so many special events—were ripped away.

Shadow Grief. Ronald Knapp gives an insightful description of shadow grief, which is often experienced by parents who have lost a child:

Shadow grief reveals itself more in the form of an emotional "dull-ness," where the person is unable to respond fully and completely to outer stimulation and where normal activity is moderately inhibited. It is characterized as a dull ache in the background of one's feelings that remains fairly constant and that, under certain circumstances and on certain occasions, comes bubbling to the surface, sometimes in the form of tears, sometimes not, but always accompanied by a feeling of sadness and mild sense of anxiety. Shadow grief will vary in intensity depending on the person and the unique factors involved. It is more emotional for some than for others.

Where shadow grief exists, the individual can never remember the events surrounding the loss without feeling some kind of emotional reaction, regardless of how mild.[34]

Often others don't understand the loss of a child and how the parents feel. Think about this:

When does a parent stop being a parent? Death does not seem able to sever this bond. Yet, bereaved parents are often misunderstood when they continue to include their dead child as one of their offspring and include the child in their lives.[35]

My wife, Joyce, and I understand shadow grief. It still hits us, even after all of these years. Our son Matthew died in 1990 at the age of 22. We had lived a continuous life of loss with him, since he was born profoundly mentally retarded as well as brain damaged. We still remember the diagnosis that prompted his surgery and two weeks in the hospital and the day the hospital message was, "You need to be here as soon as possible." We remember the words of finality spoken by the doctor, the good-byes and his home going. Matthew changed our lives by his life and his death. Through this experience Matthew shaped the direction of our lives and ministry both before and after his death. Fortunately for us, we grew and learned from our experiences and, through this, have a new direction for ministry.

Remember that each parent's bereavement experience is different. It will be colored by many unique factors. It is a mistake to lump all bereaved parents together, an error to assume that all bereaved parents are alike merely because they have lost a child. The following factors must always be taken into account when attempting to evaluate or understand a bereaved parent's response:

Characteristics and Meaning of the Loss Sustained and Relationship Severed

- The unique nature and meaning of the relationship severed
- The individual qualities of the relationship lost
- The roles that the child occupied in the family
- The characteristics of the deceased child
- The amount of unfinished business between the parent and the child
- The parent's perception of the child's fulfillment in life
- The number, type and quality of secondary losses for the parent

Characteristics of the Grieving Parent

- The parent's coping behaviors
- The parent's level of maturity and intelligence
- The parent's past experiences with loss and death
- The parent's social, cultural, ethnic and religious/philosophical background
- The parent's sex-role conditioning
- The parent's age
- The presence of concurrent stresses or crises in the parent's life

Characteristics of the Death

- The timeliness of the death
- The parent's perception of the preventability of the death

- Whether the death was sudden or expected
- The length of the illness prior to death
- The amount of the parent's anticipatory grief and involvement with the dying child

The Social Factors Influencing the Bereaved Parent's Response to the Death of the Child

- The parent's social support system and the acceptance and assistance of its members
- The parent's sociocultural, ethnic and religious/philosophical background
- The parent's educational, economic and occupational status
- The funerary rituals utilized

The Physiological Factors Influencing the Bereaved Parent's Response to the Death of the Child

- The parent's use of drugs and sedatives
- The parent's nutrition
- The amount of rest and sleep the parent receives
- The parent's physical health
- The amount of exercise the parent gets

Without an understanding of and appreciation for these variables and how they affect a particular parent's grief experience, *no* judgments can ever legitimately be made about the person's grief response.[36]

Feeling Guilt over the Lost Child

Parents also may see their child's death as a failure on their part. They may feel anger and frustration over their inability to exert some control over what happened to their child.[37]

With the death of their child a parent feels he or she has failed in the basic function of parenthood: taking care of the children and the family. A parent is supposed to protect and provide for their child. They are supposed to keep her from all harm. She should be the one who grows up healthy to bury her parents.

When one "fails" at this, when the child dies, the parents may feel that they have failed at their most basic function.

The death of any child is a monumental assault on the parents' sense of identity. Because they cannot carry out their role of preserving their own child, they may experience an oppressive sense of failure, a loss of power and ability, and a deep sense of being violated. Disillusionment, emptiness, and insecurity may follow, all of which stem from a diminished sense of self. And this can lead to the guilt, which is such a common feature in parental grief.[38]

Parental guilt can take many forms. Some parents experience survival guilt—the feeling that it's not right that they're still alive and their child isn't. There also can be illness-related guilt, where the parent thinks some personal deficiency caused the child's sickness and death. Some parents experience guilt over the belief that in some unknown way they either contributed to their child's death or failed to protect the child. And some experience moral guilt over the belief that the child's death was punishment for one or both parents' violation of some moral or religious code.[39]

Feeling Anger over the Lost Child

A parent who has lost a child will struggle continually with anger at what happened, anger at anyone they feel could have prevented it, anger at the unfairness of what transpired, anger at the disruption of their lives and anger at God. The anger will come and go for years.

However, the bereaved parents will have to grow up with the loss. Parents tend to mark their lives by the accomplishments and events involving their children. The dates when those events occur will still come around, even though their child won't be there to experience them. The sixth birthday, the first teen birthday, the times when the child would have received a driver's license, graduated, married and had children—all these things will bring a resurgence of grief when the parents least expect it. And it is all the parent can do not to get angry.

Suffering in Marriage over the Lost Child

Following the death of a child, some marriages tend to flounder. It's as though the very structure of family life is under attack. Parents may have to intervene with their other children as they react to the loss of their brother or sister. The parents may struggle with vocational pressures because of being distracted and absent from their jobs for an extended period of time. Because of their grief, parents' daily routines seem overwhelming and they may pick at each other when things seem left undone. There also may be new financial burdens because of the child's illness or the unbelievably high expense of a funeral. All of these elements add to marital tension.

We've heard estimates that 90 percent of all couples who lose a child face some kind of marital struggles within the first year after the death. Some say divorce rate is very high among couples who have lost an only child.[40] Statistics have indicated that in approximately 70 percent of the families where a child was killed violently, parents either separated or divorced after the death of the child.[41] However, many marriages that dissolve after such an experience were held together by a slim thread to begin with, and the event seemed to shred the remaining strands. It also could be that the parenting roles were more intense than the marital relationship itself.

Recently a survey from The Compassionate Friends has challenged these statements:

TCF has never found reliable statistics concerning divorce rates following the death of a child. To confirm or refute these claims, the survey included a series of questions regarding marital status. Based on the results, it is clear that the divorce rates quoted so often are erroneous. Overall, *72% of parents who were married at the time of their child's death are still married to the same person.* The remaining 28% of marriages include 16% in which one spouse had died, and *only 12% of marriages that ended in divorce.*

While this percent may be slightly understated due to sample composition, the undoubted conclusion is that the divorce rate among bereaved parents is significantly below the often-cited numbers.[42]

> **The death of a child does not have to lead to divorce. With the right approach, this tragic experience can become a time of mutual comfort, support and growth.**

The death of a child does not have to lead to divorce. With the right approach, this tragic experience can become a time of mutual comfort, support and growth.

FINAL THOUGHTS

Perhaps it would be helpful for you to reflect upon the deaths you have experienced in your life. Your own journey of grief can either hinder or add to your ministry to others. For the believer, death is a transition, not an ending. Even so, those who are still here need a comforter.

Praise be to the God and Father of our Lord Jesus Christ, the Father of compassion and the God of all comfort, who comforts us in all our troubles, so that we can comfort those in any trouble with the comfort we ourselves have received from God (2 Cor. 1:3-4).

RECOMMENDED RESOURCES

Resources to Use with the Loss of Parents

Guthrie, Nancy. *Holding On to Hope.* Carol Stream, IL: Tyndale House, 2002.

Hayford, Jack. *I'll Hold You in Heaven.* Ventura, CA: Regal Books, 1986.

Rosof, Barbara D. *The Worst Loss.* New York: Henry Holt and Co., 1994.

Vredevelt, Pam. *Empty Arms.* Portland, OR: Multnomah Press, 1994.

Wiersbe, David. *Gone but Not Lost: Grieving the Death of a Child.* Grand Rapids, MI: Baker Book House, 1999.

Wolterstorff, Nicholas. *Lament for a Son.* Grand Rapids, MI: Eerdmans Publishing Co., 1987.

Wright, H. Norman. *Recovering from the Losses of Life.* Grand Rapids, MI: Revell, 2000.

Ziglar, Zig. *Confessions of a Grieving Christian.* Nashville, TN: Thomas Nelson, 1998. A powerful story of the loss of an adult child.

Resource to Use with the Loss of Friends

Smith, Harold Ivan. *Grieving the Death of a Friend.* Minneapolis, MN: Augsburg Fortress Publishers, 1996.

THE CRISIS OF SUICIDE

I arrived home late Monday afternoon after spending the day at the lake with my daughter and nephew. Everything seemed fine at home, and we ate our dinner. As we concluded, my wife, Joyce, said to me, "Let's go into the other room. There's something I need to discuss with you." We went to the living room and sat down. Joyce looked at me and said, "Norm, a tragedy happened to a couple at church yesterday, and there was nothing you could have done about it." She went on to tell me that a distraught husband who was separated from his wife and two children went to see his wife on Sunday morning and demanded that she give him custody of the children. When she refused, he took out a revolver, killed her and then turned the gun on himself and committed suicide.

I had seen the man three days before for his first session of counseling. He talked with our pastor on two occasions. The day before the tragedy, he called and talked to me awhile on the phone.

We always feel stunned when someone we know of or have talked with takes his or her life. I appreciated the way Joyce informed me of the suicide incident, for she anticipated my reaction. I wonder how you would respond if something like this occurred?

SUICIDE CASES ARE EVERYWHERE

This family's specific incident was not an isolated experience, although I wish it were. Most of us hope we will not have to handle suicidal situations, but we will. Those of you in ministry will see a number of people

> **Those of you in ministry will see a number of people who are thinking about suicide or have already planned to take their own lives.**

who are thinking about suicide or have already planned to take their own lives. Some give you no warning, whereas others provide indication as their way of crying out for help.

Case 1

Prior to my appointment as the minister of education and youth at a church where I used to serve, there was a young man from the church who was attending college away from home. During his senior year, he failed to receive an A on a course for the first time in more than nine years. For some reason he could not handle that situation, so he jumped off of a 200-foot tower on the campus and died. Five years later, the boy's father put a gun to his head and ended his life. The other two sons were in our youth group, and I always wondered what went through their minds as they thought about how their brother and father were no longer with them. Fortunately, they seemed stable, and no additional tragedies struck the members of that family.

Case 2

On another occasion, I was asked to see the fiancée of a young man who had committed suicide. He had jumped off the Saint Thomas Bridge in

Long Beach, and his body was discovered after being in the water for two weeks. In talking with his fiancée, I soon discovered a high level of insecurity and low self-esteem in her. She had depended so much upon this young man, and now her world was shattered. She, too, was highly suicidal, to the extent that during the time I counseled her I was never sure that I would see her at the next session.

When she came to the second counseling appointment, I noticed her hand was bandaged. I asked her what had happened, and she explained that three days before a man had broken into her apartment and tried to kill her. She fought him and cut her hand. He proceeded to rape her and then fled. As she described this to me, I was taken aback by the quiet, determined, controlled rage in her voice as she said, "I hope the police don't find him. I want to find him, and I know what I will do to him."

I continued to work with her for a few weeks, but because the suicidal risk in her case was so high, I referred her to a psychiatrist.

As you minister to those in a suicidal crisis, you need to be aware that the crisis involves not only the person with the suicidal intent but also the family members or other loved ones who would be left behind.

Case 3

Many years ago, I was conducting a teacher training course in a church and noticed a man who was there for the day-long session but was not very involved. At the afternoon break he came up to explain to me why he was there. He told me that a month earlier, his 20-year-old son who was away at a state university took his life. His son was the most brilliant student to go through the school system in this large city, yet he had nothing to live for. He planned for his death very carefully. He went to the beach near the university and drank a beaker of cyanide. In his 20-page suicide note, which I was allowed to read, he said he wanted to be sure to take enough so that he would die, but not an excessive amount so that he would be unable to experience the death process. What would you say to that father? This is what our ministry is all about, reaching out to the hurting and suffering.

HELP NEEDS TO BE READY

I urge you to have every person in your church who has any kind of counseling responsibility read this chapter. Have your church secretaries, support staff and your spouse read it. They may have to be the one to handle a call or a visit by a person who is suicidal when you are not around. They cannot put this person on hold and tell him or her to wait for your return.

I learned the importance of preparing an entire staff years ago. I had counseled several suicidal people, and one night at the start of the evening service, I was called to the phone. One of my counselees had slashed her wrists and turned on the gas at home. I had her turn off the gas and also determined that the cuts were superficial, but I did need to go over and help. I asked someone to have my wife summoned from the sanctuary, and when Joyce walked in, I told her what had happened, handed her the phone and said, "It will take me 20 minutes to get there. Keep her talking about anything, but keep her on the line. See you later." With that I rushed out the door. I stayed at the home for two hours until the husband got there. In spite of her protests, he needed to be informed and become part of the support team.

Later when I returned home, Joyce said, "Norm, you're teaching the seminary students how to counsel the suicidal. I would really appreciate some of this teaching for myself." I understood her need and invested the time to train her. There have been times when she has been the person to handle the call whether she wanted to be or not. This will occur with your church staff and your spouse as well. Let's help them feel comfortable about ministering to others.

SUICIDE HAS OCCURRED THROUGHOUT TIME

In the Scriptures, we do not find any judgments on suicide, but we do find several instances of suicide recorded as historical fact. In the Old Testament, the following suicides are mentioned:

- Abimelech (see Judg. 9:54)
- Samson (see Judg. 16:28-31)
- Saul (see 1 Sam. 31:1-6)
- Ahithophel (see 2 Sam. 17:23)
- Zimri (see 1 Kings 16:18).
- Saul's armor-bearer (see 1 Chron. 10:5)

In the New Testament, we have the account of Judas Iscariot (see Matt. 27:3-5). In addition, there are many extrabiblical accounts of suicide. Perhaps the most famous account is the mass suicide of those at Masada after holding out for several years against their Roman attackers.

For several centuries the Church did not say much about suicide. Augustine was one of the first to speak concerning it. He felt that suicide was generally unlawful and indicated a weak mind. Thomas Aquinas in the thirteenth century stated that the commandment "Thou shalt not kill" refers to the killing of oneself as well as the killing of others.

In the year A.D. 452, the Council of Arles became the first church conclave to condemn suicide. The Second Council of Orleans in A.D. 533 ordered that offerings or oblations be refused for suicides. The Council of Brage in A.D. 563 denied religious rites at the burial of suicides. The council of Toledo in A.D. 693 punished attempted suicides with exclusion from the fellowship of the church for two months.

During the Middle Ages, civil law began to follow the teaching of the Church and prohibited suicide. Desecration of the corpse of a suicide became standard practice. Bodies of suicide victims were dragged into the street. Stakes were driven through the heart of the victim, and the bodies were sometimes left unburied at a crossroads for animals and birds to consume. Or they were hung on the gallows and allowed to rot. Superstition and fear were greatly in evidence. If the death took place in a house, the body could not be carried out through the door but only through a window, or a portion of a wall had to be taken down. In Scotland, it was thought that if the body of such a suicide victim were buried within sight of the sea or cultivated land, it would be disastrous to fishing or agriculture. In England, the last body to be dragged through the streets and buried at a crossroads was in 1823.

In 1882, Britain ordered that suicides could have normal burials, but the strong feeling and reaction toward this kind of death has lingered for many centuries. Today both Judaism and the Christian Church have softened their harsh stand against suicide. There is an emphasis upon support for the survivors. And the belief that suicide victims go to hell has changed. There is more of an acceptance that the person was under stress or strain and that only God knows their motives and heart.

SUICIDE IS SELFISH

Suicide is a deliberate act of self-destruction in which the chance of surviving is uncertain. It is a major problem. More than 34,000 people kill themselves in the United States each year. On an average day, close to 2,000 people attempt suicide.[1] These only account for the suicide attempts we know about, because many suicides are not reported or go

> **Estimates indicate that suicide is the tenth leading cause of death in our country.**

undetected. Estimates indicate that suicide is the tenth leading cause of death in our country. The death rate from suicide is as high as 100,000 a year, and there are more than 5 million attempts each year. Between 10 and 20 percent of those who make a suicide attempt eventually kill themselves.[2] About 500,000 people commit suicide each year worldwide.[3] In the 15- to 19-year-old age group, suicide is surpassed as a cause of death only by two other factors—accidents and cancer. On some college campuses it is the leading cause of death.[4]

What Causes People to Take Their Lives?

The best description is psychological pain, or *psychache*. Edwin Schneidman, founder of the American Association of Suicidology, gave this description:

Psychache is the hurt, anguish or ache that takes hold in the mind. It is intrinsically psychological—the pain of excessively felt shame, guilt, fear, anxiety, loneliness, angst, dread of growing old or dying badly. When psychache occurs, its introspective reality is undeniable. Suicide happens when the psychache is deemed unbearable and death is actively sought to stop the unceasing flow of painful consciousness. Suicide is a tragic drama in the mind.[5]

Psychological pain manifests itself in different ways. Dr. Schneidman has identified five clusters of psychological needs that aren't being met, which account for suicidal acts:

1. Some take their life because their need for love, acceptance and belonging has been thwarted.
2. Some people's needs for control, predictability and arrangement have been fractured, which are related to their needs for achievement, autonomy, order and understanding, which also are not met.
3. Some feel their self-image has actually been assaulted; they are trying to avoid shame, defeat, humiliation or disgrace; they don't feel any affiliation.
4. Some people's key relationships have been ruptured, which is often tied into frustrated needs of nurturance and affirmation.
5. Some have excessive anger, rage and hostility—when this occurs you often have a person whose need for dominance and aggression has been blocked.[6]

When you are working with a suicidal person, look for these concerns. You are looking for a suicidal state of mind. There is one sign that is characteristic of the suicidal state of mind—constriction. The best way to describe constriction is a narrowing or tunneling of the person's focus of attention. And there is one word to listen for that is the most dangerous word in all of suicidal intent—"only." 72 hours

- It is the *only* thing I can think of.
- The *only* solution is . . . .
- It's the *only* way I can solve the problem.

When you hear these statements, you need to talk about the constriction and help them discover other alternatives. Dr. Schneidman talks about "widening the blinders," because if you do this, you'll come up with other options.[7]

> **The suicidal person sees suicide as their only solution. Help them discover other solutions.**

Remember, the suicidal person sees suicide as their *only* solution. Help them discover other solutions.

SUICIDE HIDES BEHIND MANY FACES

As you counsel people struggling with thoughts of suicide, you will soon recognize various patterns of suicide. Let's explore four of those patterns.

Depression

One pattern of suicide is depressive suicide. The person is sitting on a high level of unacceptable rage that has developed because of a series of events in life over which he or she has no control. Eventually this repressed rage is turned against himself or herself in suicide. Within our churches, we have depressed people who are "suicides waiting to happen." You don't recognize them because they repress their depressive symptoms as well as their rage, and when they die, everyone is taken by surprise and shocked.[8]

Relief of Pain

Many people commit suicide for relief of pain. People who have a low threshold for pain and experience chronic pain are candidates for suicide. Those with high levels of pain usually have three choices: a psychotic distortion that reduces the pain, drugs or alcohol, or suicide. They often say, "I don't want to die, but I don't know any other way out—I just can't stand it."[9]

Revenge

Others commit suicide for revenge. Some teenagers feel overwhelmed by hurt or rejection from another person. Their desire to hurt back is stronger than the desire to live. For others, the death of a loved one, family member or friend is too much to handle. Many of the sick and elderly indicate in suicide notes that they couldn't handle being a burden upon others.

Hopelessness

Twenty-five percent of those who commit suicide do so after giving it quiet consideration and weighing the pros and cons of living and dying. They decide that death is the best option. It may seem strange to us that there are people who think this way. Perhaps this factor can motivate those of us who know the good news of Christ to share it with those who have no hope.

MYTHS ASSOCIATED WITH SUICIDE

Understanding some of the common myths will help us appreciate what suicide is and is not.

Myth 1: Suicide and Attempted Suicide Are the Same Class of Behavior

Suicide is committed usually by someone who wants to die, whereas attempted suicide is carried out usually by someone who has some desire to live. Attempted suicide has been called a cry for help. People who attempt suicide are intent on changing something. Most are hoping to be rescued.

Some people carelessly plan their attempts at suicide and die not really wanting to. One wife attempted suicide about once every six months in an attempt to control her husband. She would turn on the gas shortly before he was to arrive home, and he would find her just on the verge of unconsciousness. Naturally she received much attention from him after that, but it would slowly dissipate until she would again perform her act. One time, however, her husband was two hours late in arriving home. Her miscalculation led to her death.[10]

Myth 2: Suicide Is a Problem of a Specific Class of People

Suicide is neither the curse of the rich nor the disease of the poor. It is no respecter of persons in socioeconomic class, race or age. Teenagers under stress who come from poor families do commit suicide, but this is a result of isolation, not poverty. There appears to be a slightly higher rate among white males as compared to black males. Males outnumber females in committed suicides, whereas females make many more attempts. At age 15, there are 64 attempts for each girl actually committing suicide. There are less than six attempts for each 15-year-old boy who commits suicide. Many of the adolescent attempts are for attention.

Myth 3: People Who Talk About Suicide Don't Commit Suicide

About 80 percent of those who take their own lives have communicated their intention to someone prior to the act. Any threats or hints about suicide must be taken seriously, for most acts are preceded by a warning. Part of the problem, though, is the signs they give aren't always obvious until after the act. Unfortunately, many warnings have gone undetected or have been ignored because no one wanted to believe that the person was serious about his or her intention. Take it seriously; it is the distraught person's cry for help. The person feels hopeless and is trusting you with his or her plea.

Ben P. Allen, professor of psychology at Western Illinois University, says:

> Ignoring a person who talks about suicide isn't the best solution. Threatening suicide should always be taken seriously. It is a very important warning signal. There may be cases where that's all it is, but no one should make that assumption, even if it was just an attention getter. How do you ever know that?[11]

Myth 4: Once a Person Is Suicidal, He or She Is Suicidal Forever

This is not true. Many people who have thought of or attempted suicide have discovered the answers to their problems, and they are no longer suicidal.

Myth 5: Suicide Is Inherited or Runs in Families

If another family member has committed suicide, this fact could cause a person to be afraid of his or her own future behavior.

Many survivors of suicide report that they feared they might take their own life following the suicide of a loved one. There are several reasons for this. The first is that suicide has been added to their frame of reference whereas previously they may not have considered it. The second is that they may be genetically susceptible to depression or mental and emotional instability, which can lead to suicidal thoughts. Finally, even if there is no initial physical predisposition toward depression, it is natural for them to be depressed about their loved one's suicide. Clearly, there is much more research needed on this.[12]

Also, the family environment and examples of others may be influencing factors.

Myth 6: If a Person Is a Christian, He or She Will Not Commit Suicide

This, unfortunately, is not true. Some have said that if a person commits suicide, he or she is not really a born-again person—a true believer could never become so unhappy that he or she would think of such an act. Yet Christians as well as non-Christians experience all kinds of physical and emotional disorders. Because of the many factors that cause a person to consider suicide, we need to remember that no one is immune.

Myth 7: Suicide and Depression Are Synonymous

Most people who attempt suicide are experiencing stress, yet others experience stress without thoughts of suicide. The statement, "I can't understand why he did this; he didn't seem unhappy or depressed" indicates the belief that suicide occurs only when there is unhappiness or depression. Depression is not a sign of suicidal thoughts. However, whenever a person is depressed, we should be on the lookout for any thoughts or indications of the possibility of suicide.

Myth 8: Improvement After a Suicidal Crisis Means That the Risk of Suicide Is Over

Studies by the Los Angeles Suicide Prevention Center indicate that almost half of the persons who were in a suicidal crisis and later actually committed suicide did so within three months of having passed through their first crisis. The period of time immediately following a suicidal crisis appears to be critical. If a person immediately states that his or her problems are solved and seems overly happy, we ought to be concerned.

As has been indicated, it is sometimes difficult to obtain accurate statistics on suicidal rates. It could be that the actual rates are twice as high as we know them. However, the following are some statistics that may show who is at high risk.

The suicide rate is much higher for men than for women at all ages. Men over 65 account for America's highest suicide rate—38 per 100,000, a rate that escalates as they grow older, peaking at 60 per 100,000 around the age of 85. And in California, it is 103 per 100,000 for those 85 and older. This is in contrast to 12 per 100,000 for the general population.[13] Why is this happening?

Older people are often tired, sad, lonely and ill. Men especially have lost much of the meaning of life, for they no longer have their occupations. One of the problems in our society is that men place too much emphasis on their occupations. To them it is their source of identity and self-esteem. And with no other pillars to give them this meaning, letting them retire is like letting the air out of a balloon. Nothing is left. This is reflected in their depression and increased suicide rate.

How can you help the elderly? Evaluate the person carefully. Is he or she ill? Depressed? Mentally stable? Does he or she have sufficient finances, or has the individual been denying himself or herself some of the necessities of life? Has the person been forced to give up his or her independence by living in a care unit or with a relative? How does the individual handle frustration? Does he or she talk about the future or live for past memories?

The elderly give hints of their intentions, as do others. If they begin to clean up everything and dispose of property—including treasured keepsakes—be alert. If someone has been depressed over a long period of time and now is suddenly cheerful, he or she could also be a high risk.

Elderly people also may need a physical examination. Help them feel useful and give them encouragement and compliments. They need to hear that someone appreciates their situation. Help family members include them in their activities. Set up a support team from the church to give them contact with others on a continual basis. One of my concerns about some retirement homes and centers is the refusal to let those living there have pets. A loving cat or dog is appreciated by the elderly and may keep some of them living longer. Whatever you can do, endeavor to alleviate their loneliness. Your task is to get them to say yes to life again. Help them focus on what they can do and have instead of what they cannot do and do not have.

SUICIDE IS COMMUNICATED

In working with counselees or through contact with people in our everyday lives, it is important to be aware of the verbal and nonverbal hints people give about their suicidal thoughts.

1. *The suicidal attempt.* This is the most clear and dramatic cry for help. One who has attempted suicide needs immediate help and support.
2. *The suicidal threat.* Any kind of threat should be taken seriously. The majority of those who talk about suicide do attempt it.
3. *The suicidal hint.* Some people who consider killing themselves are unclear in communicating their intent. They may make statements such as, "You would be better off without me"; "Life has lost all meaning for me"; or "It's just that I hate to face each day more and more." Some who express keener-than-usual interest in suicide may be hinting at suicide. A Christian may ask, "Does a person who commits suicide lose his salvation?" or "What does God really think of a person who takes his own life?"
4. *The suicidal activity.* There are many kinds of suicidal activity. Making sure all the bills are paid, making out a will or making arrangements as though the person were going on a long trip could be clues that the person is considering suicide. It is important, however, not to be analyzing every person's activity and seeing suicides behind every bush!

5. *The suicidal symptoms.* A long, serious illness could bring a person to the point of despair, especially if there is no immediate hope or if the illness is terminal. Another symptom is sudden changes in personality such as becoming easily upset, moody, anxious or agitated. Remember, too, that among alcoholics there is a high incidence of suicide. Agitated depression is one of the most serious signs that a person may attempt to take his or her life. The depressed person who becomes withdrawn by staying indoors for long periods of time, keeping to himself or herself and shutting off contact from others may be a definite risk. A person thinking of suicide may be bothered by physical symptoms such as loss of appetite, sexual drive, weight fluctuation and so on. Watch for significant and sudden behavior changes.

6. *The recent crisis.* Many suicides have occurred in response to some immediate and specific stress. Each person evaluates stress in a different manner. A crisis might be the death of a loved one, failure at work or school, marital or home problems, loss of a job, a broken romance, financial reversal, divorce or separation, or a rejection or loss of any kind that involves people whom the person cares about. Any of these may cause the person to question the value of living.

CONCLUSION

When you come into contact with a person who is suicidal, definite intervention is needed. A person's life is at stake, and whether or not you want to be involved, you are! Your initial task is to help the person stay alive. Second, help the person gain insight into how he or she came to this place. Third, guide him or her to make the necessary changes to ensure that it will not happen again.

Remember, too, you are not omnipotent and this person's life is *not* on your shoulders. Your role simply is to be as much help as possible.

CHAPTER 15

HELPING THE SUICIDAL PERSON AND HIS OR HER FAMILY

Many people who are contemplating suicide call a friend, church or agency for assistance. Thus the procedure suggested here focuses on a plan to minister to those who call. The same principles can be used in face-to-face contact with someone who in the midst of his or her counseling session indicates suicidal thoughts or intentions.

STEP 1: ESTABLISH A RELATIONSHIP, MAINTAIN CONTACT AND BUILD RAPPORT

For many people, suicide is a gradual process while under stress. They begin to seek solutions to their problems and try alternative one, then alternatives two, three, four, five and so on—all without success—before they arrive at suicide as a solution. Many struggle against this alternative by seeking the other alternatives, but if their way is blocked, they turn to

> A suicidal person is ambivalent toward life and death. The individual wishes to kill himself or herself and is tired of what is going on in life. At the same time, he or she wants to be rescued by someone.

this last choice as their solution. Remember, a suicidal person is ambivalent toward life and death. The individual wishes to kill himself or herself and is tired of what is going on in life. At the same time, he or she wants to be rescued by someone. When this person calls, it is important to develop a positive relationship. This relationship may be the reason he or she decides to stay alive. When the person calls, say something like:

- "You did the right thing by calling."
- "I'm glad you called."
- "I think there is help for you."

These statements are important because they assure the person that he or she made the right decision and that someone cares for him or her. This verbal approval communicates that the person can make other right decisions. The suicidal person needs you to talk calmly, confidently—with a voice of authority (but not authoritarian)—and in such a manner that he or she will not feel challenged. Caring, acceptance and genuine concern are very important.

As you talk, it is important to find some common ground upon which you and the caller can agree. A place to start is the fact that the caller has a problem and wants help, and you want to help him or her. Sometimes when a caller is unclear and ambivalent, it takes more work to discover a common ground. It is important to use the word "help" frequently in different contexts.

It also is important to show interest in the caller and attempt to discern his or her feelings. A relationship of trust needs to be developed. This can be done by giving straightforward answers to questions. You shouldn't be hesitant to identify yourself and your relationship with the church or organization if asked. If the person asks if you have ever helped a person in a similar situation and you haven't, be honest, but also let him or her know that you feel you have the resources and training to help him or her.

After you have identified yourself, try to get the person's name, phone number and address. These questions should be spaced throughout the conversation so the person is not unduly threatened. If the person is reluctant to give his or her name, don't pressure the caller at that point. Instead ask, "Could I know your first name so I have something to call you by? I would feel more comfortable with that." If he or she will not give an address, you could ask what part of town he or she is from. If the person gives you a general area, you could respond by saying, "Oh, that is out near . . ." This statement will perhaps stimulate the person to give more information. You should also attempt to obtain the phone number of other significant people who could help the person—relatives, neighbors, physicians and so on.

During a call, you may find that a person asks you to promise not to tell anyone he or she called. Professional counselors and ministers have the right to keep some information confidential. However, some state laws require you to contact authorities when someone threatens to kill himself or herself or someone else, and you *cannot* make a promise not to tell. However, you can assure the person that you won't do anything to harm him or her.

STEP 2: IDENTIFY, OBTAIN INFORMATION ABOUT AND CLARIFY THE PROBLEM

It is important first to hear the person's story with as few interruptions as possible. Then you can let them know that you care and that you've heard them by saying, "A person in your situation is usually hurting. What hurts?" Encourage the person to tell you:

1. What has led him or her to where he or she is now.
2. What is bothering him or her right now.
3. What has he or she tried before to cope with his or her situation.

Remember not to challenge what the person says in response to your questions. Statements such as, "You shouldn't feel that way" or "Things are not as bad as they seem" are setbacks to the person—they do not help.

> **You're probably looking for a guaranteed approach, but it doesn't exist. Sometimes just your being there is all it takes.**

As you read this, you're probably looking for a guaranteed approach—something that you can count on that's foolproof. But it doesn't exist. You may do everything perfectly and it still may not work. Sometimes just your being there is all it takes.

Identify the Problem

Your goal is to obtain information in order to identify the problem. Keep them talking. Ask as many questions as you can, but avoid why questions. If people talk, they are not taking their own life.

When obtaining information, you do not want to provoke the person. Therefore, if what you are saying through questions or statements annoys or agitates the person, go in a different direction. It's better to retreat.

What questions can be very beneficial. The following are informational questions that can assist you:

- What has happened in your life to bring you to this point?
- What's been going on in your life the past three months?
- What would need to be different for you to go on with your life?
- What would you need to help you?
- What is it you would like help with at this time?

- What would you like me to know about you?
- What would you like me to understand about you?

Also keep in mind the three *Hs* of a suicidal person. The following are three important words that are highly descriptive of the typical suicidal person, and coincidentally each begins with the letter *H*.

1. *Hopelessness.* The only people who kill themselves are those who have lost *all* hope. Therefore, whenever you work with suicidal people, do whatever you can to build in them as strong a component of hope as possible.
2. *Helplessness.* A concomitant of hopelessness is often helplessness.
3. *Haplessness.* Many suicidal people have had incredibly sad lives.

Obtain Information About the Problem

Suicide is a form of communication. The word "dirt" is used to help identify the risk factor:

D = Dangerous—The greater the danger in the attempt, the higher the current level of risk that the suicide is going to occur.

I = Impression (of the degree of risk)—If the person honestly believed that he or she would die because of what the person did to harm himself or herself during the attempt, then the present level of risk is still high.

R = Rescue—If the chances were good that the person would be rescued or if he or she assisted in his or her own rescue in any way, then the present level of risk is lower.

T = Timing—The more recent the attempt, the higher the current level of risk.

When you talk with someone who is thinking about suicide, don't ask, "Why would you want to do something like that?" Instead, begin your assessment by asking, "How would you harm yourself?" The answer to that question will let you know quickly if the person has a plan of attack.

Focus on what the person is feeling and assist him or her in clarifying his or her feelings. If the person has difficulty expressing his or her feelings, help him or her to label them. Try to reflect what you think the person is thinking and feeling, as this will help him or her to pinpoint the problem. The person's overwhelming helplessness can now be broken into specific problems, the solutions to which may be seen more easily. The person should be helped to see that his or her distress may be impairing his or her ability to assess the situation. When the person can see the problems, he or she can begin to construct a specific plan for solving them. And if you understand the nature of the problem the person is trying to cope with, then you can understand more about his or her strengths and weaknesses. You want to explore his or her reasons for wanting to die.

If a person calls and just talks about being down or depressed, statements and questions such as the following may help:

- You seem to be depressed much of the time.
- How much have you been depressed over the past few weeks?
- When do you get depressed?
- Have you ever thought that life just isn't worth living?
- Have you thought of ending it all?

These statements can help a hesitant person put his or her feelings into words. The actual threat of suicide needs to be out in the open for you to help the person.

When a person has trouble talking about suicide, he or she is usually relieved to find that you're not afraid to talk about it openly. At times this can relieve the person of his or her trapped feelings. Suicide should be discussed in an open and nonmoralistic manner. Suicide is not a moral issue for the suicidal person. For the most part, it is the result of stress. Many are already struggling with guilty feelings, and if a discussion of suicide as an immoral act occurs, it can add to this burden and cause further discouragement.

Dr. Keith Olson suggests another approach. If you are talking in person to an adolescent who is considering suicide, talk with the individual about his or her beliefs about death. Many adolescents have never seen a dead person or been to a funeral. They don't understand its finality. They may be thinking only of the attention they will receive. Helping them gain a realistic perspective of death may deter them.[1]

Does it help or hurt to discuss the suicide? Many feel it lessens the probability or defuses the intention. Your talking about it encourages the counselees to be more open about it. The following are numerous questions that you can ask:

- I appreciate your willingness to talk with me about this. I'm wondering if there are others you want to be notified about what you intend to do?
- What is it I should tell them?
- Do you want them just to be notified, or would you like them to come at this time?
- They'll probably ask me questions. What do you want me to say? They'll want to know your reason for wanting to do this.
- This might be a different question for you to consider. You're probably thinking it's best not to be around anymore. What will be better about it?

Also don't be afraid to ask questions regarding the aftermath of their proposed suicide:

- Will anyone miss you? (Be prepared for the answer, "no one.")
- If the answer is "no one," then ask, "Tell me how certain you are about that—70 percent, 80 percent or 100 percent?"
- Tell me about the time in your life when people would miss you if you were gone? Who were they? What changed? Who do you want to miss you now? What could turn this around for you at this time?[2]

Clarify the Problem

A number of factors are involved in making the evaluation of whether or not your counselee is a high risk for suicide. As you listen to the person, you will be receiving pieces of information that will assist you in making this determination:

1. *Age and sex.* Remember that the suicide rate rises with age and that men are more likely than women to follow through. Older single males are more vulnerable. Younger females are less likely to carry out their plan. Persons suffering from alcoholism are considered a high risk, and sporadic drinkers are more vulnerable to suicide than a chronic, heavy drinker. Alcohol often serves as a defense against pain and then becomes a source of new pain. If pain is unbearable in the sober state, suicide may be the choice.[3]

2. *History of suicidal behavior.* It is important to try to determine if this is the first attempt or if this is one in a series of attempts. The more recent the onset of suicidal behavior, the better is the chance to prevent it. Yet at the same time, the need is greater for active intervention. An extensive pattern of suicidal behavior will require long-term therapy from professionals. If the person has repeatedly attempted suicide, he or she will probably at some time succeed and actually kill himself or herself. The job of both the paraprofessional and the professional is to help break this suicidal circuit and help the person develop a plan for living.

3. *Evaluate the suicide plan.* The plan has three parts:
    a. *How lethal is it?* When a person has admitted planning to end it all, you can ask, "How are you thinking of killing yourself?" Sometimes the harsh words can bring home the reality of the situation. Shooting and hanging are considered the most lethal methods, barbiturates and carbon monoxide poisoning are second. The lethality of a method is measured by how abruptly the point of no return is reached. Other methods are explosives, knives, poisoning and drowning.
    b. *How available is it?* If a gun or bottle of pills is at hand, the risk is greater. Ask what kind of pills are available

to the counselee and where they are. If he or she plans to use a gun, ask, "Do you have a gun? Where is it? Do you have bullets for it?"

c. *How specific is the plan?* If the person has worked out the details very well, the risk is higher. If the person says, "I have 100 pills here and I am also going to turn on the gas. I have covered the cracks around the door and windows so the gas will stay in," then the suicide most likely is preplanned. However, if the person says that he or she has to go out and buy the pills or the gun or a hose for the car exhaust, the risk is lower.

Remember that even if you are talking with a person who has a well-worked-out plan, he or she still called, which indicates that some small seed of desire to live remains. If a person is in this situation and will not say who he or she is (or if the person has already started the process of taking his or her life), you may need to work out some system of getting the attention of a coworker. The coworker should notify the police, who will trace the call.

A person having a lethal and specific plan for suicide should alarm you. If the situation is serious, do not attempt to handle the problem by yourself. Responsible family members, a family physician or a professional counselor need to be included in the intervention.

4. *Stress.* This must be evaluated from the caller's point of view. To you it may not seem significant, but to him or her it is. If the person has experienced losses, reversals or even successes, it could be creating stress or strain.

5. *Symptoms.* What are the symptoms in this person's life? Is there depression? Alcoholism? Agitation? Is the person psychotic? Remember that agitated depression is the worst symptom. Its stress factors and symptoms are high; therefore, your actions must be fast.

6. *Resources.* What resources does this person have available to help him or her? Are friends or relatives nearby? Are counseling

services available to the person in the community or at work? Does the person have a place to stay? A lack of resources makes the risk factor higher. If the person is remaining at home, and it is a sick environment, it would be better for him or her to be cared for elsewhere. The person may need to get away from a parent or spouse who is contributing to the problem. A person living in a depressogenic environment (a negative environment where the person's self-esteem is constantly under attack) would be better off out of its influence.

7. *Lifestyle.* What is the person's lifestyle? If it is unstable, such as a history of changing or losing jobs, changing living locations, drinking, impulsive behavior and so on, the risk is higher.

8. *Communication with others.* Has the person cut himself or herself off from other people including friends and family? If so, the person could be at higher risk. If he or she is still in touch with others, you can use them to help.

9. *Medical status.* If there are no physical problems, the risk is less. If there is some illness or injury, talk about it and find out how serious it is. Is it really the case, or is it merely in the person's mind? Has the person seen a physician? Some who have a terminal disease may think of suicide as a way of eliminating the pain for themselves and the expense for their families.

STEP 3: FORMULATE A PLAN TO HELP THE CALLER

It is important to find out what part of the plan the caller has put into action and help the person reverse his or her course of action. If the person has turned on the gas and sealed the windows, have him or her turn off the gas and open the windows. *Do not let the person promise to do it when you hang up.* Give specific instructions and stay on the phone while the person carries them out. If the person has a gun, have him or her unload it. If it is an automatic, have the person take the clip out of the chamber and then take the bullets out of the clip. Next, the person should place the bullets in a drawer and put the gun somewhere difficult for him or her to get to in a hurry. If the person has pills, you might ask him or her to flush them down the toilet. If the person does not want to reverse the plan, continue talking until your relationship is built to the point that he or she will trust you.

Once you have built this trust, then get a commitment from the person. Ask the person to promise to call you if he or she has any other difficulty or if the person is tempted again to take his or her life. Professionals have found that this is quite effective. The person may let other obligations go, but he or she will keep his or her promise to you. Your word of encouragement on the phone may keep the person alive. Consider this example:

> One professional counselor stated that on one occasion when he was out of town, a counselee called and asked for him. The man was very depressed that night, and later it was discovered that he was planning to kill himself that same night. The counselor's wife replied by saying, "My husband is not here tonight, but I know that he wants to talk to you. I will have him call you as soon as he gets back, and I would also like you to call back again yourself. I will let him know, and thanks for calling." Later when the counselor saw this person, he said that those very words kept him alive that night.

Determine Positive Resources and Alternatives

Help the person determine positive resources and alternatives. If the person has committed himself or herself to you and agreed not to do anything, help the person widen his or her view of the problem in order to discover the resources that he or she has lost sight of during the crisis. Perhaps some other people can help the individual. In some cases, a person may need to be hospitalized. If the person is quite depressed, be sure to caution him or her that the process of recovery involves some ups and downs. Perhaps you know of some agencies where the person can obtain food, job leads or professional or legal assistance. Perhaps a neighbor can stay with the person or give him or her emotional assistance. In summary, be sure to convince the person that there are various positive alternatives to suicide. Assure him or her that by working together, the two of you can discover the alternatives. Make it personal by saying, "I could see you tomorrow at 11:00 A.M." or "I could have you see our pastor. Can you come over then?" Let the person know that you are looking forward to seeing and working with him or her.

Create a Committed Environment

When you see the suicidal individual in person, it may be helpful to have him or her sign an antisuicide agreement. Even though it is just a piece of paper, the person may feel more committed to following the guidelines because it is signed.

> **In suicide counseling, it is important to convey to the person that you care and are committed. It is also important to carefully work in the fact that God cares, as does His Son, Jesus Christ.**

In this type of counseling, it is important to convey to the person that you care and are committed. It is also important to carefully work in the fact that God cares, as does His Son, Jesus Christ. In some cases you may feel led to say this during the first telephone conversation. At other times it may be best to say it face-to-face. Whenever you decide to share, be careful that your approach and tone do not take on a preaching air. The truth of God's love should be explained naturally and honestly, using a direct leading of the Holy Spirit at the right time.

Communicate Your Intentions

The following are three elements that are crucial to the phone counseling approach discussed so far:

1. *Activity.* The person needs to feel that something is being done for him or her right now. This assurance can relieve his or her tension.

2. *Authority*. The counselor must set himself or herself up as an authoritative figure who will take charge. The caller is not capable of taking charge of his or her life at this time, so someone else must step in.

3. *Involvement of others*. If the caller realizes that others are now involved and caring for him or her, the person will be more apt to feel the care and concern and will more likely respond.

In order to be the best possible help to a caller, it is important to be aware of our own defenses that may hurt this ministry. Dr. Paul Pretzel of the Los Angeles Suicide Prevention Center outlines the following barriers to communication with people contemplating suicide:

1. anxiety on the part of the listener that makes him or her uncomfortable (and less of a listener);

2. denying the significance or meaning of previous suicidal behavior that the caller has not made totally clear or the listener has failed to determine;

3. rationalizing verbal and nonverbal suicidal cues. This is like saying to oneself, "This isn't what the person really means";

4. an aggressive reaction to suicidal hints or threats;

5. fear, which immobilizes the helper and prevents the person from really talking about the situation. It could also be a fear of becoming too involved with the responsibility demanded by another person;

6. manipulating a suicidal person who has "cried wolf" too many times and is no longer listened to by others.[4]

STEP 4: BREAK THE NEWS

Part of the process of counseling that most of us would rather avoid is notifying a family member or friend that a loved one has committed suicide. A friend of mine shared his first call as a volunteer firefighter chaplain. He was called out to a home during the middle of the night and was met by police officers. It was the residence of one of the fire captains he had met recently. The family's 12-year-old daughter had put a gun in her mouth and killed herself. When the father arrived home, my friend had to tell him. He shared that he didn't know what to do, so he just stood there holding the father and weeping with him. Later that night he and two others spent hours cleaning up the room where the girl had taken her life. That, as well as crying with the father, was an act of ministry.

Do you know what to do if you are called upon to break the news to someone? The following are some practical guidelines to follow:

- It's best to be gentle up front with the one you're talking to: "I wish I didn't have to share with you this news, but I need to inform you that _____ committed suicide." You may need to provide them with corroborating reports such as police or medical reports that give information about the cause of death.
- You may need to review the facts of the death, since when told of this kind of death many slip into denial. If there is a note, go over it with the family members or friends.
- It may be helpful to ask if anyone noticed any change in the deceased's behavior, attitude or emotions over the past 72 hours. Prepare to hear, "I should have seen this coming," which is an expression of self-blame and responsibility. Talk this through with them and let them know this is a normal expression. Talking about this can help to resolve these feelings. Take time to discuss any clues or indications of depression prior to the suicide. Were there ever any other attempts?
- Encourage, as you would with anyone else, the expression of their feelings and normalize them and their experience. When they take responsibility for not having seen and preventing the suicide, ask what do they think they could have done? How would it have changed anything? Once again, go over the facts.
- Ask them about the last time they saw one another. What was said? What did they wish they had said? When the why question arises, go back to the facts of the suicide. Explain that only the one who is dead knows the answer.

- Spend time educating them on what to expect. Discuss who else they want informed and what they want said. Some will want to hide the fact of suicide. Since this will come out at one time or another, help them evaluate the pros and cons of not fully disclosing. Are there any cultural or religious issues to be confronted because of suicide, such as burial, family shame or dishonor? If children need to be told, discuss how to tell them.
- Evaluate how they are taking the news. Is there any hint or a possibility that the suicide could trigger a similar response in another individual? Ask questions like, How has this left you thinking or feeling about yourself? Has anyone else in the family ever attempted this or actually completed the act?
- Create a climate in which all of their feelings can be expressed—especially anger. Using the ball of grief image from chapter 6 could be very helpful. Ask the person questions such as:
What is a pleasant memory you have of . . . ?
What is a sad memory you have of . . . ?
What is an angry memory you have of . . . ?

This also is a time to conduct a family and/or friend debriefing, asking each person to share how they heard the news (this could be now), their reaction and thoughts, the feelings or responses it left them with, how they think this will affect them in the future and so on. After the shock begins to subside, try to plan at least one additional debriefing session.

Encourage Survivors to Find Continual Support

Discuss with the survivors of the suicide victim how they can process this loss, and share with them the steps of grieving (see chapter 6). One unique feature to discuss is the economic impact. After the death, there may be less income, issues with life insurance and so on. Be sure to assist the people to become involved in a support group for survivors of suicide, such as Survivors of Suicide (SOS).[5]

What does a survivor of a family who has experienced suicide contemplate? Listen to this firsthand story:

There is a need to ask, "Why?" The questions must be asked, even though you may never find the answers. It is an enigma and it is part of the process of healing that we all go through. But, ultimately, if there are no answers, you may need to stop asking the questions, for to continue only becomes an obsession which can be destructive to yourself and those around you.

I found I only had partial answers and nothing really satisfactory. I will never know all the answers as to why my son chose to end his life, but I came to the conclusion that I didn't have to know in order to go on with my own living. I finally chose to let go of the question but only after I had asked it over and over and struggled with the "why." Had I not done that, I could have allowed mourning to become my lifestyle for the rest of my life.

I don't know why . . .
I'll never know why . . .
I don't have to know why . . .
I don't like it . . .
I don't have to like it . . .

What I do have to do is make a choice
about my living.
What I do want to do is accept it and go
on living.
The choice is mine.

I can go on living, valuing every moment
in a way I never did before,
Or I can be destroyed by it and, in turn,
destroy others.
I thought I was immortal, that my
children and my family were also,
That tragedy happened only to
others . . .

But I know now that life is tenuous and
valuable.

And I choose to go on living, making
The most of the time I have,
And valuing my family and friends in a
way I never experienced before.[6]

Practice Your Response

You're in a conversation with a person and they say that their father,
mother or child committed suicide. What's your first response? What
would you say to them? Had you ever thought about it? Most people say,
"Oh, I'm so sorry." Is that a good response? Not really.

When Children Respond. As a 10-year-old child was talking about
this, she told her mother she just hated it when people discovered her
father had committed suicide. They would say, "I'm sorry." When asked
why she didn't like that, she said, "Well, they didn't do anything wrong,
so why are they saying they're sorry? It would be better if they said, 'I can't
imagine how you feel.'"[7]

When responding to children, remember that your response is even
more crucial. The following are some facts to take note of when responding to children regarding suicide:

- Children have the same emotional needs as adults, but sometimes these needs are ignored or taken lightly. Many times
  adults are too full of grief to reach out to their children or they
  don't believe a child is capable of intense grief.
- You need to be honest with them. They need clear, correct facts
  about the suicide in a compassionate, loving way. Be careful
  not to overexplain.
- When you tell a child about the tragedy, keep in mind that
  whether the person who has committed suicide is a parent, sibling, grandparent, close family friend or some other important
  person in a child's life, the parents (or surviving parent) need to
  tell the truth about what has happened. This doesn't mean

explaining the suicide in the kind of detail you might use when talking to a close adult friend, but it does mean explaining what happened in clear terms a child can understand. And it means being prepared to answer in a direct way the questions that will inevitably follow.[8] An example of what could be said is, "Your father loved you very much, but you know that he was very unhappy and that he had emotional problems. The pain had become so great for him that he decided he couldn't go on any longer. He swallowed a lot of pills. The doctors tried everything they could at the hospital, but there was nothing they could do."[9]

- Listen carefully to their questions, then answer truthfully. It's not only important to remain consistent in *your* answers, but to have others convey the same message.[10]
- Be open about talking about the person who died.
- All of the children involved need to be told about the suicide, even the youngest ones, according to their level of comprehension.
- Encourage the children to share their feelings and questions with those they trust. Teach them to be selective about sharing the facts of the suicide.
- They will grieve better by seeing adults cry and crying with them. They need to know that crying is an acceptable and natural release for grief.
- Be sensitive to some possible feelings of guilt. Assure them that the suicide was not their fault. (See chapter 17 on children in crisis for details on children's grief response.)
- Be sure to discuss constructive ways of handling problems. They need to hear that suicide is a permanent solution to a temporary problem and problems can be solved. Even if a family member chose suicide, the children have other options.[10]

When Families Respond. Consider the impact of suicide on those remaining: Just as a suicide can devastate individuals, its impact on a family—the complex web that includes brothers, sisters, parents, friends, uncles, aunts and cousins—can be monumental. Some families are blown apart by the guilt and blame that can follow a suicide. Some are drawn together, rallying to support one another as they struggle through their individual and collective grief and confusion. Other families continue on in silence, pretending as best they can that nothing has happened or that the suicide was an accidental death.[11]

How a surviving wife or husband reacts depends a lot on the condition of the marriage and the circumstances of the suicide. But most often, a surviving spouse feels guilty for not having prevented the suicide, as well as rejected and/or abandoned. Even if their relationship was a good one, the suicide is likely to be interpreted as something of a referendum on their married life. The surviving spouse may also feel shame, fearing that others will look on him or her as having been so awful to live with that the spouse was driven to suicide.[12]

Parents are left wondering what they did wrong. Were they too strict? Were they not strict enough? Were they too attentive? Were they not attentive enough? Even parents of children who are well into adulthood are left wondering, *Was I a bad parent?*[13]

When Teens Respond. When a teen loses a friend to suicide, the following are the questions he or she is most likely to ask afterward:

- Why did he kill himself?
- Could I have prevented it?
- Did I do anything to cause it?
- Was it really a suicide?
- Whose fault was it?
- What am I supposed to feel?
- Why sometimes do I feel depressed?
- Could I commit suicide?
- Was she crazy?
- What happens to people when they die?
- Is suicide a sin?
- Is it wrong for me to feel angry?
- Why do I feel guilty?
- Why do people have to suffer so much that they kill themselves?

- How can I prevent another suicide?
- Is it okay to talk about his suicide?
- Do a lot of people kill themselves?
- Why do people kill themselves?[14]

FINAL THOUGHTS

What can you do (and encourage others to do) to help the family and friends of a person who commits suicide? At this more than any other time they need the support, love and concern of their relatives and friends. How would you feel as a survivor? Often they feel completely isolated. Their basic needs are for kindness and caring. With time—the understanding and the concern of their friends, as well as a support group—the survivors' feelings of grief will lessen. Keep in mind that suicide is not a comfortable topic, and many people tend to forget the survivors of a suicide death sooner than the survivors of a nonsuicide death. The following suggestions apply both to the time immediately after the suicide, including the funeral, and for as long as necessary afterward:

- Make an extraspecial effort to go to the funeral home, and encourage others to do so. The shock, denial and embarrassment are overwhelming for the survivors. They need all the support they can get. Often the coffin is left closed due to the cause of death.
- When going to the funeral home, do as you would normally do at any other type of wake. It will not be easy, since you sincerely want to comfort the bereaved person but really don't know what to say. Just a few words, such as, "This must be such a difficult time for you"; "Please accept my deepest and sincerest sympathies—my heart goes out to you" and "I wish I could do more for you at this difficult time," can be a help. When the person is close, take their hand, hug them and don't feel the need to say anything. It's your presence that counts.

- Remember that survivors tend to become more paranoid than the average person. Why? Guilt and shame. The guilt is so overwhelming, and when people do not attend the funeral or send a card, the guilt increases. All sorts of thoughts run through the survivor's mind. A note, phone call or visit in the weeks and months to come is a must.
- Don't try to comfort the survivors by saying, "It was an accident, a terrible accident." They're not sure. Some may think this is helpful, but it's more of an expression of one's own anxiety. The survivors need to start dealing with the fact of suicide.
- Don't say, "Oh, he or she was on drugs or drunk. They weren't really aware of what they were doing." You weren't there during the suicide, so how could you possibly know? It's not helpful or necessary to give reasons for the suicide. Talk with the survivors about what to say and how to respond when they hear these comments.
- Remember that with this kind of loss, a survivor's grief is so painful that sometimes it is easier to deny that it ever happened. You need to be patient and understanding. Sometimes the denial gives them a break from the pain before the reality sets in.
- Avoid saying that the suicidal person was not in his or her right mind or was insane or crazy. The majority of people who commit suicide are ambivalent and tormented. Even if a mental disorder is involved, it is up to someone else to determine at a later time. Telling the survivors that the person was insane may create worries of inheriting mental illness. Suicide is not inherited.
- Surviving family members and close friends have every right to feel sensitive. Unfortunately, there will be some people who deliberately avoid the survivors. They will cross the street or pretend that they didn't see the survivors. This adds to the survivor's grief and guilt. Such actions are not done out of malice but rather out of confusion about what to say. It's important to make every effort to befriend the survivor and to reach out on a continuous basis.

- Accept the fact that vicious and cruel remarks will sometimes be made, even in church. They hurt survivors deeply. If you hear any of these remarks, confront the issue and try to help the originators of the remarks to realize the hurt that they are causing those in grief.
- When you talk with the family, avoid discussing the signs of suicide. It's not helpful because the suicide is a fact. Telling them, "There must have been signs indicating depression" only lays more guilt on the survivors.
- The anniversary of a suicide is a very painful time. Relatives and friends should make every effort to be available, listen, call, visit, send a note and do other thoughtful acts.

In summary, be alert to the needs of people. For the most part, suicide victims do reveal that they are considering suicide; therefore, be equipped and prepared. And remember, the greatest help you can give this person is you—your concern, your interest, your listening ear and the love of Jesus Christ as reflected through you.

RECOMMENDED RESOURCES

Resources to Share with Others

Grollman, Earl A., and Max Malikow. *Living When a Young Friend Commits Suicide.* Boston: Beacon Press, 1999.

Robinson, Rita. *Survivors of Suicide.* Franklin Lakes, NJ: New Page Books, 2001.

CHAPTER 16

MINISTERING TO CHILDREN AT A TIME OF LOSS, CRISIS OR TRAUMA

You're a child again. Seven years old. Your parents have just moved, and it is your first day at a new school. It is strange and big and scary. You didn't sleep well. Your stomach doesn't feel good and you have to go to the bathroom a lot. As you walk down the hall to the room, you would rather turn around and run. The door opens and 35 strange faces turn around and stare at you. You're about to enter a crisis!

Perhaps for you as an adult that experience would not be a crisis (although imagine walking into a boardroom where 35 faces turn to see the new employee just hired). Yet in a child's eyes, each day can produce a miniature or major crisis. Moving, separated or divorced parents, rejection by a friend, loss of a pet, a poor grade on a test—these and many other events can produce an upset in such intensity that it jars the child's world.

The following are the most common losses—in the sequence most likely to occur—in a child's life:

- death of a pet;
- death of a grandparent;
- a major move;
- divorce of parents;
- death of a parent(s);
- death of a playmate, friend or relative;
- debilitating injury to the child or to someone important in the child's life.[1]

Did you ever experience one of these situations as a child? How did it make you feel?

Children experience many upsets and crises. Their fears and potential fears abound. Ministering to children also will involve ministering to their parents. It involves training all those who work with children in your church to identify the signs of crisis problems and then equipping them to help as much as they can. Some people assume they will never work directly with children. However, a crisis may occur with children where they are forced to help; therefore, all of us need to be prepared.

As a minister or lay counselor, you at times will see the parents initially. You may work through them, giving them guidance and suggestions in order to help the child. There will be other occasions when you will help the child directly. You need to be capable of doing both.

Several specific problems of children will be considered in this chapter. They tend to overlap in some cases, yet they are distinct. The suggestions provided will help you deal with the situations discussed and with other problems as well.

CHILDHOOD CRISES IMPACT ADULTHOOD

The way we learn to handle losses in childhood impacts our lives as adults. Adulthood losses actually may be compounded by unresolved childhood losses. These are brought into adult life like unwelcome baggage. Time after time I have seen the ungrieved losses of childhood interfere with an adult's ability to respond normally to life and relationships. And this, in time, can turn an adult loss into a crisis. The losses vary in their complexity and intensity. For instance, some children are never allowed or encouraged to grieve over the loss of a favorite pet. They are told, "Don't cry. It's just a cat" or "We'll get you a new goldfish tomorrow."

> **The ungrieved losses of childhood interfere with an adult's ability to respond normally to life and relationships. And this, in time, can turn an adult loss into a crisis.**

A friend saying "I don't want to play with you anymore" is a loss. Not making the Little League team or simply not getting to play can devastate a child. Not having a favorite dress available for a special day can be devastating for an adolescent girl. Not getting the part in a play can spoil an entire week for some kids. Therefore, we need to see the losses through the eyes of the child.

Unresolved crises in childhood can have long-lasting effects because it may make the child less capable of dealing with trauma in the future. They cope with crisis events in a different way than adults and are more limited in their coping skills.

Divorce

When parents divorce there is a major disruption. Children of divorce are more likely to drop out of school. They tend to carry a pattern of insecurity, depression, anxiety and anger into their adult years because of the extent of the loss. In divorce, children experience a multitude of losses. These not only include the disruption of the family unit but also the possible permanent loss of one of the parents, home, neighborhood, school, friends, standard of living, family outings and holidays, self-esteem, and the list goes on.

In addition, the mourning period after a divorce is open-ended. It comes and goes depending upon the involvement of the noncustodial parent. If the parent does not stay involved, the children wonder if mom or dad will ever come back. And if not, why not? The children will question what they have done to cause this situation. They aren't sure if the loss is permanent or temporary. The occasional birthday card, weekly phone call and infrequent visits and vacations keep the fantasy alive that the parent might return home.

Abandonment

Another damaging loss is abandonment. It is true that some children are physically abandoned, but many more children are emotionally abandoned. Often kids don't know why they feel so alone and abandoned. Their physical needs are met, but their emotional needs are neglected. They lack nurturing, hugging and emotional intimacy. The verbal affirmations they so desperately need are shrouded in silence. Soon they begin to think that something is wrong with them, and they carry this perception with them into adulthood. Teenagers are particularly vulnerable because they often seem to want to be left alone, which causes parents to withdraw. However, the truth is that teens need constant reassurance of their parents' love and attention.

CHILDREN'S CRISES HAVE TWO RESOLUTION STAGES

For children, there are two stages of crisis resolution.

Stage 1

The first stage involves the initial shock and then a high level of anxiety. Adults handle this better because of their previous experiences with crises. However, children usually do not have the mental or verbal ability or the life experiences to draw upon. They do not know that the problem will be resolved, and they feel as though they are in the midst of a tornado. The child's mind and emotional state are not yet developed enough to solve problems as an adult. It's less sophisticated and processes information about tragic events differently. Adults can fall back on resources and established routines; children fall back on chaos. In a way, they lose their identity or sense of self, and the chaos brings silence, isolation and a feeling of helplessness into their life.

Stage 2

The second stage is similar but less intense. The child's reaction is less crippling, and he or she is able to look at the crisis and evaluate it instead of just responding to it. Yet children often lack the verbal skills and the creative fantasy available to an adult. They may find a poor solution and cling to it even though it is not good for them. Children need to discuss and sort out their fears with an adult because they probably don't realize they have other options.

If a child remains anxious and does not live up to his or her potential, he or she is stuck in the second stage and probably has not yet resolved the crisis. In uncontrollable events, a child feels helpless. When the child experiences helplessness repeatedly, he or she learns to despair at the lack of control. Children with repeated experiences of loss of control soon lose total control. Some adults are capable of handling a crisis by restricting their activities in some way, but this approach is not available to children. They must face daily challenges. For example, they are not allowed to skip school, even if the bully continues to hurl insults.

CHILDREN NEED DIRECTION

One of the characteristic responses of a child in crisis is regression. When a child responds at his or her appropriate age level, the child knows how

> **A child in crisis is in danger of becoming extremely impaired emotionally.**

to use his or her skills and capabilities properly to relate to others and confront daily tasks. But if the child becomes upset, such as in a crisis, the child loses his or her capability to coordinate all of his or her abilities to meet the needs of the situation. The child becomes confused and disorganized. Those attempting to help the child may need to take charge of part of the child's life and guide his or her behavior.

When a child is in crisis, begin counseling immediately. Remember that a child in crisis is a time when he or she is in danger of becoming extremely impaired emotionally. Why? Because a child doesn't have an adult's abilities or resources. The person helping a child needs to be both concerned and competent. A child needs reassurance during a crisis. One of the ways this occurs is when the person helping models problem solving and helps the child sort out alternatives. As the helper demonstrates how to sort things out and takes action, a child will be able to function better.

In addition, it is vital to help a child realize that a crisis did indeed occur. If a child is defensive or engages in denial, don't accept this behavior, as it just prolongs the crisis. Lead the child out of denial by asking appropriate questions.

If the child engages in blaming, don't support or encourage this. The more a child engages in this behavior, the less they cope. They'll move ahead faster without blame—blaming encourages victim thinking. Each time you talk with a child, work toward the goal of coming up with actions the child can take. Your goal in crisis counseling is helping the child move to the place of taking action rather than being a passive victim.[2]

Above all, don't give false reassurance. You can't take away all of the child's pain, anxiety and depression. Discomfort is a part of crisis. However, you can give a sense of hope that eventually the child will overcome the crisis.

As you, your Sunday School staff or other lay counselors work with children in crisis, consider the following facts:

- Helping a child resolve a crisis can become a crisis for the person helping the child.
- Your tendency may be to put a lid on the child's crisis too soon and thereby hinder a proper resolution.

- You do not have any magical solutions, so do not convey to the child the idea that you do.
- Things may get worse before they get better. This is true in many types of counseling.
- In working with a child, you may vacillate between feeling confident and uncertain.
- If you have a greater investment in helping a child than the child has in being helped, the results will be negligible.
- A child will influence you as much as you influence a child. You may find yourself being friendly toward a friendly child and angry toward an angry child.
- A very anxious child will tend to agree with most anything you say. And a child can be led—simply by the structure of a question—to make false statements.
- You may struggle with your own limitations and your desire to provide follow-up help.
- Most people attempting to help a child will experience some or perhaps all of the above responses.[3]

CHILDREN FACE CRISES EVERYWHERE

It happens at school, in the streets and in the home. Children and teens are victims in many places like Oklahoma City, Columbine High School, Wedgewood Baptist Church in Fort Worth and now the World Trade Center. Can you imagine sitting in the premiere high school or elementary school in Manhattan and looking out the windows to see the planes crashing into the towers a few hundred yards away? Within minutes you're rushing out, hoping to escape far enough away from the destruction to survive. You survive, but then you learn that the sister of the principal of your high school, as well as others you know, died in the towers. When the elementary school reopens its doors, the students in one of the classes come to their classroom and just sit and stare. They aren't functioning. The father of one of their classmates works in the towers. They had seen him before, but they won't again. If we as adults struggle with intense thoughts, feelings and images, what must it be like for a child?

Other children experience trauma vicariously. In America, the media saturation of disasters via television, newspaper and radio has left its mark. New terms have been coined to describe the effect—"living room witnesses" or "CNN trauma."

We used to say that in the United States few children experience human-perpetrated disasters. Yet Oklahoma City began a change, which was greatly expanded by the twin-towers disaster of September 11, 2001. Between these two events, there are few children in this country who haven't been exposed to catastrophes through the media. The repetitious viewing of these events, especially the planes impacting the towers and the towers' collapse, tattooed images on the minds of the children. *USA Today* reported preschool children building towers out of Legos and then crashing toy planes into them again and again saying, "They're dead. All the people are dead." A mother on Long Island, New York, told me about her preschooler who built cardboard towers each day and silently crashed his planes into them. If children share their fears and concerns over these events with us during the day, think of how they must live with them at night.

TRAUMA THREATENS CHILDREN

Traumatic events of any kind turn the life of a child upside down. To a child, trauma is like an ongoing, festering splinter.

Trauma sends four messages to children:

1. Your world is no longer safe.
2. Your world is no longer kind.
3. Your world is no longer predictable.
4. Your world is no longer trustworthy.

If children or teens are involved in a disaster of any kind, they often experience a loss of innocence. Their entire world becomes less safe and secure. They are forced to face issues of loss and bereavement sooner than adults wanted them ever to have to experience. A disaster or traumatic event makes them a different person.[4]

The following are characteristics of children who have experienced trauma. These PTSD symptoms are unique to children:

- A child under the age of four tends to forget their experiences, although a few may remember. Those over this age do tend to remember the experiences vividly, whereas adults often deny reality or repress.
- Most children don't experience the psychic numbing common to adults. Yet if it's parental abuse, they do.
- Most children don't experience intrusive and disruptive visual flashbacks.
- A child's school performance usually isn't impacted by acute trauma for as long a time as adults' work performance is impacted.
- With a child, play and reenactment increases in frequency. And with a child you will find frequent time distortions.[5]

How to Help a Child Cope

What do children need in a trauma? An abundance of them need to be encouraged just to be patient with themselves. Most of all, they need to know it's alright to feel and express feelings.

Attempt to return a child to the world of childhood as soon as possible. They need the routine of school, recreation, bedtime, sports, church, clubs, parties and so on. A child responds better when he or she regains the environment that gives him or her back the security of routine. A child needs to be given permission to be a child again. Children need to do their usual playing or learning.[6]

When a Child Doesn't Cope

The following are some warning signs that indicate a child isn't coping well:

- A child consistently doesn't want or refuses to go to school, or the child's grades drop and don't recover.
- A child loses all interest or pleasure in what he or she used to enjoy.

- A child talks about hurting or killing himself or herself.
- A child hears or sees things other don't.
- A child can't eat or sleep enough to remain healthy.[7]

CHILDREN NEED EMPATHY

One of the main approaches with children is the use of empathy. Empathy means

- entering the private world of the child and becoming comfortable with it;
- realizing that the child's thinking and perception are different from yours as an adult;
- moving into the child's world for a time *without* making judgments;
- sensing the meaning of events of which the child is not aware;
- putting your thoughts and help into words the child can understand;
- not attempting to unravel and expose unconscious feelings for the child, which would be too threatening and counterproductive; and
- clarifying the child's jumbled feelings, for he or she may experience a number of confusing feelings all at the same time. Unraveling these will help the child solve problems according to his or her ability.[8]

CHILDREN NEED COMMUNICATION

Communication is a key in counseling children in crisis. If you have not talked with children for some time, you are going to feel like an alien invader from outer space trying to understand these creatures. Some of you think you can communicate with children, but do the children feel that you are communicating with them? Children have their own style of reasoning, meanings for words and connections for events. You must enter their frame of reference if you are going to be able to minister to them. A child's thought pattern will follow its own logic and not yours. What makes sense to you may not make sense to the child.

> **If you have not talked with children for some time, you are going to feel like an alien invader from outer space trying to understand these creatures.**

Children's Communication Stages

It is important to look at children's thinking and communication at different stages in order to minister to them in crisis. William Van Ornum and John B. Mordock (as well as others) have developed an interesting classification of children's thinking and communication.[9]

The Magic Years. The magic years (ages three to six) are the years of early childhood, nursery school and kindergarten. Children of this age do experience crises. We call this the time of magical thinking, because the child's belief at this age includes believing that his or her own thought processes can influence objects and events in the world outside himself or herself. The child is unable to understand how and why things happen, and how and why life is unpredictable, whereas adults accept sudden events as just a part of life. Scripture teaches us that life is uncertain and we should expect problems and upsets to occur, but children have difficulty grasping this concept.

Children at this age do not understand that their thoughts do not cause an event to occur. Children's thinking reflects omnipotence. They believe that they are at the center of life and can affect what happens. For example, children don't understand why they become ill. They become quite disturbed with the unfamiliar bodily changes that accompany illness, and they often believe that they caused the illness. They feel that they were bad and the illness is a punishment.

If this is how they think, how will you act if you are called upon to help? Sometimes it will be impossible to change the child's pattern of thinking fully. You need to accept this as a fact of life and lessen your own frustration. Helping a child fully express his or her inner thoughts and feelings is one of the best approaches. This helps the child gain greater self-control in a crisis event. When a child expresses his or her thoughts aloud, the child moves to a new position. You also will want to repeat your questions to the child patiently and encourage him or her to think aloud. Help the child discover the most probable or real reason for what occurred instead of giving the child a reason. Additionally, look for any indications of guilt the child may be experiencing. Look at this example:

> A young boy lost his mother through divorce, and he was now living with his father. The helper said, "You know, Jimmy, it could be there were times when you wanted your mother to go away. And now she has gone away. Tell me about those wishes you had." After the child related his feelings, the helper replied, "Your mother had several reasons for leaving, and none of those reasons had to do with you. Let's find out what those reasons were. Who could you ask?"

Young children are egocentric. They are centered on themselves and fail to consider the viewpoints of others. This has nothing to do with being conceited; it is just a normal part of the developmental process. Children of this age talk past one another. They have their own private speech and may not be talking to anyone in particular. They are not concerned whether the listener understands their words or not; they just assume their words have more meaning than there really is. They take things for granted and do not realize that other people need clarification. It is not until a child reaches the age of seven that he or she begins to learn to distinguish between his or her perspective and someone else's.

As a helper, you need to use the child's language and be flexible in your communication. You must actively guide your conversation with a young child or you will end up failing to communicate. Why? Because a young child takes things at face value—very literally. When a parent says, "I'm sick and tired of the way you are acting," what does the child think? The child catches the parent's anger but also believes that the parent is truly "sick" and "tired." Think of the other phrases we say that are misunderstood. "Keep your shirt on," "hold your horses," "that's cool" and so on. Try to enter the child's mind. If you actually heard what the child is thinking, you would be amazed!

A child puts two and two together and does not necessarily come up with four for an answer. A child's connections are unique; the connections make sense to him or her but to no one else. For instance, a child may see illness and going to a football game as related because his father became seriously ill the last time he went to a football game. The child may even become anxious himself and avoid going to a football game because of the connection he made between the game and his father's illness.

Young children often center on one aspect of an event to the exclusion of all the others. They cannot see the forest for the trees. If you throw too much information and too many events at a child in your conversations, he or she will not be able to handle it. Therefore, you need to introduce other aspects of the situation to a child gradually as he or she is ready to handle them. Your task will be to help the child see all the aspects, organize his or her thoughts and explore other reasons for what happened. One of the best descriptions I have heard is that helping young children is like working on a jigsaw puzzle. You help them by asking them to discover the other pieces, by pointing out some of the pieces and by helping fit the pieces together.

Whenever you are called upon to help a young child, remember the following four facts:

1. The child feels responsible for what happened;
2. The child makes different connections than yours;
3. The child is egocentric; and
4. The child centers on one event to the exclusion of others.

The Middle Years. Children ages 7 to 12 have changed considerably in their thinking. They have advanced in their ability to think conceptually. They are now able to work out problems in their heads instead of just by trial and error. They can see the viewpoints of other people as well as recognize the feelings of others. Even their world of fantasy has changed. They now fantasize about real people and events instead of so much make-believe.

Children in the middle years are usually enjoyable and uncomplicated, calm and educable. Yet they still have a difficult time dealing with anything that resembles a crisis situation. They prefer to avoid the problems and often will change the subject when you attempt to draw them into a discussion surrounding the problems. Why? Because they try to avoid the pain and anxiety. This is why so many who work with children of this age use games and playtime in the therapy process. Play allows children an outlet for what they are feeling and gives the counselor the information sought after. Communication toys such as tape recorders, phones, drawing materials and puppets are very helpful.

Even though these children have developed considerably in their thinking processes, they still tend to jump to conclusions without considering all the facts. In fact, children of this age group have a tendency to listen to contradictory information and not see the inconsistency. Often they don't understand what they are hearing. At other times, these children will not understand adults who are talking to them, and the problem is that the adults do not realize that they are not being understood. As you work with a child, you need to make your statements very clear and even rephrase the statement several times. Repeat and repeat again. What may be clear to you may not register with the child.

MORE COMMUNICATION APPROACHES

Based upon the way children think, listen and reason, what additional approaches can you use when you minister to a child in a crisis situation?

1. Be flexible, and be able to shift gears as you work with children of different ages.
2. Don't be afraid of disqualifying yourself if you're not comfortable working with children. It is best to have children work with those who are most gifted and skilled with them.
3. Do not force the logic of an adult upon a child.

4. Communicate to a child how he or she is communicating to you.

5. Children are walking question marks. They ask questions for information; they also ask questions as a roundabout way of letting you know something is bothering them. An innocent question such as, "Do your children ever fall down and get bruises?" or "Did your mother ever drink?" may be informational, or it may be an indicator that the child has been abused or lives in a home with alcohol problems. Some questions can be a cry for help or a test to see if you think their question is dumb. Giving them simple answers with an occasional, "That's a question a lot of children ask" or "Lots of children want to know about that" may help to keep the questions and information flowing.

6. Do not ask questions that can be answered with a yes or no. They will be of little value to you and may not bring a direct answer. Asking for comparisons can be helpful, however, such as asking a child to describe two different events or two different people.

7. If you don't understand what a child is saying or what a child means, don't be afraid to let him or her know. You might say, "John, I think I understand what you are wanting to tell me, but I am not sure. Could you tell me that again with some different words?" Reflect on how the child looks as he or she is talking. This lets the child know you are receiving part of the message: "John, you looked a bit puzzled and hurt when you were telling me that. Tell me that story again, and I would like to know how you feel about it" or "Could you draw me a picture about that?"

8. If a parent or Sunday School teacher has asked you to talk with a child, be sure to let the child know your intentions. This can be a fearful time, for the child may be thinking he or she is going to be punished rather than helped; therefore, the child may hold back.

9. Don't force your behavioral expectations upon children. Most adults sit still, and most children do not. Especially under

duress, children may wiggle and fidget in the chair. Let them. Other children stand up and walk around. This may enable them to talk with you more easily.

Van Ornum and Mordock suggest some practical summary guidelines when talking with a child in crisis. Your role as a helper or counselor differs from that of an authority figure; therefore, be sure to avoid

- sounding didactic and professional;
- overwhelming the child with authority and wisdom;
- joining forces with the child in criticizing other authority figures in his or her life;
- ending statements with, "Isn't that so?"; "Get what I mean?"; or "That's right." Also avoid nodding or shaking your head in response or producing an inflection in the tone of your voice at the end of a sentence. These cues set up children's responses—they'll say what they think you expect from them;
- leaving the door open or talking within earshot of others (this limits privacy);
- approaching the child with misconceptions gleaned from others or from file records;
- defending feelings, ideas or friends that are attacked or denied by the child;
- becoming so confused during the interview that you can only ask, "What else is on your mind?"; and
- feeling inferior in the presence of a gifted child or superior in the presence of an average child.[10]

CHILDREN'S USE OF DEFENSE MECHANISMS

Children often need to hang on to their defenses while they are in a crisis situation. Helping to change a child's personality by interpreting what a child is doing and clarifying his or her hidden motivations is appropriate for the child who is *not* in a crisis. Taking this approach while a child is *in* crisis creates too much anxiety for the child. If you point out to a child the defenses that he or she is using to cope with the crisis, his or her anxiety level will be raised. Why? Because children in crisis handle their problems by increasing their defenses. This is what works for them. The following are some defense mechanisms children, adolescents and adults use:

- fantasy—daydreaming about solutions to a problem;
- hypochondriasis—using illness as an excuse not to deal with a problem;
- projection—blaming other people and things for their problems;
- displacement—taking out their feelings on someone or something other than the original source;
- repression—unconsciously blocking out strong feelings;
- suppression—consciously holding back feelings; and
- sublimation—substituting one set of feelings for another set of more socially acceptable feelings.

How do you support a child's use of defenses? By going along with what the child is doing at the time as long as it is not hurting himself or herself or someone else. A child may need to use fantasy, rationalization or displacement. For example, a minister was talking to a child about the child's dog, which had been run over and killed. The child had been talking about the dog and all of a sudden stopped talking. The following dialogue is an example of encouraging the child at the time the child needs his or her defenses:

Child: I don't want to talk about this anymore.
Minister: You feel upset about talking about your dog now.
Child: Yes, I don't want to.
Minister: Not talking about him helps you not feel so upset. Is there anything else you could do to not feel so upset?
Child: Oh, I don't know . . .
Minister: Well, do you ever use a memory or a fantasy to feel less upset? What might you think about?

Child (Pauses and smiles.): I thought about playing a game now.
Minister: Good. That might help.

The following is another way of helping children in crisis, which encourages positive feelings that have a calming effect:

Child: I was upset at the club meeting today.
Minister: You sound like you were upset. Do you feel upset now?
Child: Not too much, but a little—
Minister: When did you start to feel less?
Child: Hmm . . . oh, when I left.
Minister: What did you do?
Child: I thought about playing with my brother.

You can also calm a child by encouraging him or her to use his or her positive feelings for another person:

Minister: That sounds pretty good. Maybe you could do that the next time you're at the meeting if you start to feel upset. Are there times when you feel less nervous?
Child: Yeah. When I get to see my father.
Minister: Tell me what that feels like.
Child: I feel good, like I'm safe and don't have to be afraid.
Minister: You feel good, like you're safe and don't have to be afraid.
Child: Yeah, but when he isn't around, I don't feel very good.
Minister: Well, maybe when you don't feel good, you could think about being with your father—think about what you do with him and what it's like.

These are simple but effective techniques that work well with upset children.

CONCLUSION

Crisis counseling with children is supportive counseling. It is used when the child is about to be overwhelmed—to help the child recognize his or her problems and put them in perspective. As a child develops trust in you, this too will help him or her gain strength. Remember that when a child becomes distressed in a crisis, his or her thinking capability begins to deteriorate. Therefore, the child's unreasonable beliefs need to be replaced by reasonable ones. The child's self-defeating behavior needs to be explained, and he or she needs to be encouraged to develop problem-solving behaviors with your assistance.[11] You can be the encourager in his or her life.

CHAPTER 17

CHILDREN'S CRISES

Let's consider some of the most common types of crises children experience.

DEPRESSION

Perhaps it seems odd to discuss depression in children as a problem, but depression is no respecter of persons. It often goes undetected by parents and professionals alike. Children may be the most hidden age group of all in terms of incidence of depression. Parents often deny that their child is chronically unhappy. They fail to recognize, accept and respond appropriately to the child's depression. After all, who wants to admit their child is depressed? How do you recognize depression in a child?

Characteristics of Depressed Children

The following is a composite picture of how a child would appear *if every characteristic* of depression were present.

Appearance. First of all, a child may appear sad, depressed or unhappy. The child doesn't complain of this, and he or she might not even be aware of it. It is the child's behavioral responses that give the impression.

Withdrawal. Another characteristic is withdrawal and inhibition. Interest in activities is very limited. The child appears listless, and the parent thinks the child is bored or sick. Often the parent begins looking for some symptoms of a hidden physical illness, and indeed there may be some physical symptoms that further blur the fact of depression. These symptoms include headaches, stomachaches and sleeping or eating disturbances.

Discontent. A common mood is discontent. The child gives the impression of being dissatisfied and derives little pleasure from what he or she does. Often people wonder if someone else is responsible for the way the child feels.

Rejection. The child may feel rejected or unloved. The child may tend to withdraw from anything that might be a disappointment. As with other age groups, a negative self-concept and even feelings of worthlessness are present.

Irritability. Irritability and low frustration tolerance may be seen. Often the child is unaware of why he or she is bothered.

Provocative. Some depressed children, however, act just the opposite. Clowning around and provoking others are their attempts to deal with their depressive feelings. They may act this way at a time of achievement because they find it difficult to handle something positive. This provocative behavior makes other people feel angry.

Expressive. Children do not always experience and express their depression in the same way as adults. Because of their limited experience and physiology, they tend to express their depression as rebellion, negativity, anger or resentment. The depression expressed when parents divorce, for example, may be manifested by bed-wetting, attacking friends or siblings, clinging to parents, failing in school or exaggerating stories.[1]

Additionally, don't overlook the fact that even younger children commit suicide. It is difficult to comprehend that a child would want to take his or her life, but it's the tenth leading cause of death in children aged 1 to 14 years old. For each one who succeeds, at least 50 others make an attempt.[2]

Signs and Symptoms of Depression

The signs and symptoms of depression vary with the child's age. An infant who is depressed may simply not thrive. A parent's depression also may affect a small child. For example, a mother who is depressed may withdraw from her child who in turn becomes depressed. The child may not be able to overcome the depression until the mother overcomes her depression.

Depression is caused by any of the following:

- a physical defect or illness;
- malfunction of the endocrine glands;
- lack of affection, which can create insecurity in the child;
- lack of positive feedback and encouragement for accomplishments;
- death of a parent;
- divorce, separation or desertion by a parent;
- parental favor toward one sibling;
- poor relationship between stepparent and stepchild;
- economic problems in the home;
- moving to a new home or school; and
- punishment by others.[3]

Coping Mechanisms for Depression

Parents can handle a child's many depressive experiences without taking the child for counseling. But if the depression is severe and the child does not respond, he or she should have professional help.

Look for any type of loss that may have occurred in the child's life. This could be a divorce, loss of a pet or friend, or a severe rejection experience. Try to see the loss from the child's point of view. It is easy to misinterpret a child's perspective, especially if you have not been around children much.

Accept depression in the child as a normal reaction to the cause. If the child is grieving over a loss, allow the child a period of time to adjust to the loss. Let the child know that everyone experiences sadness and depression at one time or another. Be sure to put your explanation into terminology the child can handle. Explain that feelings like this are normal and that in time they will pass and the child will feel better. Let the child know that God understands his or her down times as well as happy times.

> ## Let the child know that God understands his or her down times as well as happy times.

Grief That Results in Depression

As a child goes through any sort of grief process, remember the characteristics of the magic and the middle years of the child (see chapter 16). For example, a child's thoughts and feelings over the loss of a parent through divorce may be similar to those experienced when there is a loss through death. In both age groups, the children need to

1. accept the pain of the loss;
2. remember and review the relationship with the loved person;
3. become familiar with all of the different feelings that are a part of grief, anger, sadness and despair;
4. express their sorrow, anger and sense of loss to others;
5. find an acceptable formulation for a future relationship with the deceased;
6. verbalize feelings of guilt; and
7. find a network of caretakers. They need many people to support them at this time.[4]

Most important, encourage children to tell God about their feelings. Assure them that their down feelings are not permanent and will go away.

A child needs to be helped to experience the depression from the grief as fully as possible. Resisting the depression does not help. It merely prolongs the experience. Encourage the child to be as honest as possible in admitting that he or she is depressed or sad. You need to allow the child to grieve naturally. If the grief is over divorce, do not expect the child to get over the grief quickly. This type can last longer and can recur from time to time.

The following are four ways to help the child recover from depressed feelings:

1. Help the child find some type of activity to engage in. A new game, a hobby, a sight-seeing trip or anything of interest is helpful.
2. Find a way for the child to experience success. Discover what the child does well or fairly well and help him or her use that special ability. The child's self-esteem can be elevated and rediscovered by small successes.
3. Help the child break out of his or her routine. Even simple things, such as serving new food at a meal or taking the child to a special restaurant, may help. Taking a day off from school for an outing may be helpful unless he or she enjoys school more than the outing.
4. Listen to the child without being judgmental or critical. The child needs your support.

Abuse

Although we have seen a great deal of media exposure recently about child abuse, it is nothing new. For centuries—in all cultures and social strata—children have been abused. Parents in your community and churches abuse their children physically and sexually. In most cases it is well hidden. Whether you want to or not, you will be confronted with these cases. A mother may come in and tell you that her child has just told her about being sexually molested by her uncle, her father or a man in the neighborhood. Or a father may come in and confess to you what he has been doing with his own child. It is important, as expressed earlier, that you become knowledgeable of the laws of your state in regard to reporting such cases.

Characteristics of Abused Children
The abuse of a child may involve being neglected or abused physically,

emotionally or sexually. Each type of abuse carries its own distinct characteristics, which help you to identify an abused child. Below are some of the characteristics that are common to all abused children regardless of the type of abuse:

- A child may appear to be different from other children in emotional or physical makeup. In some cases, parents of this child may describe him or her as being "different" or even "bad."
- A child may seem overly fearful of his or her own parents. The child may be hesitant to go to the parent and expresses his or her fear through the hesitancy.
- A child has extremes in behavior such as crying too easily or being overly sensitive. Or the child may block his or her emotions and appear not to care.
- A neglected child will show evidence of poor overall care. Clothes may be dirty, torn or not fit well. In the winter, the child may not be wearing proper clothing.
- A child may be cautious or wary of physical contact, especially when interacting with an adult. There also may be the other extreme, where an abused child appears starved for adult affection, but his or her methods of getting it are inappropriate.
- Some children show a radical change in their general overall behavior.[5]

Symptoms of Abused Children

Have you ever considered how an abused child feels? Most children want love from their parents. The home offers the greatest amount of love to children; therefore, children want to be in their home.

Take the Blame. Many abused children feel they are the cause for the abuse. They come to believe the many statements made to them that they are bad. They experience parents who yell and cuss at them and threaten to abandon them or make them leave home. Many grow up feeling unwanted. They learn to suffer silently from inconsiderate and inappropriate punishment, for they never know when they will be punished. They do not have to disobey flagrantly or violate a major rule to be beaten—there seems to be no reason except for the parent's rage.

Further, the abused child grows up feeling he or she never does anything right and never meets his or her parents' unrealistic expectations. Whatever problems occur within the family, the child is blamed.

Feel Anger and Rage. Abused children feel anger and rage, but at home they cannot express those feelings. They learn both to deny and to repress fear, anger, bitterness and hatred. Any expression of their feelings leads to further repercussion that they want at all costs to avoid.

The abused child grows up with a classic love-hate tension. The child needs his or her parents and wants to love them, but when the child tries to draw close, the abuse pushes him or her away. This tension begins to eat away at the child. If the child cannot get his or her feelings out, he or she becomes defiant and hostile with others as a means of release.[6]

Are Untrusting. An abused child has difficulty trusting other people. Treating such a child usually involves play therapy in a safe environment in which the child can express his or her feelings and learn to cope with the reality of abuse. Most of the cases you become aware of should be treated by a professional who specializes in working with abused children. Develop a network of professional counselors whom you can call on when you become aware of this unfortunate crisis that is all too prevalent in our society.

DIVORCE

One of the most frequent distressful situations that will occur with children in your congregation will be the divorce of their parents. Divorce can be one of the most traumatic experiences a child—as well as an adult—can face.

Newsweek magazine has estimated that 45 percent of all children will live with only one parent at some time before they are 18. Twelve million children under the age of 18 now have parents who are divorced.

What *is* divorce like for a child? The author of *The Unexpected Legacy of Divorce: A 25-Year Landmark Study* describes it:

> Divorce is a life-transforming experience. After divorce, childhood is different. Adolescence is different. Adulthood—with the

decision to marry or not and have children or not—is different.[7]

The author also states:

From the viewpoint of the children, and counter to what happens to their parents, divorce is a cumulative experience. Its impact increases over time and rises to a crescendo in adulthood. In adulthood it affects personality, the ability to trust, expectations about relationships, and ability to cope with change.

The first upheaval occurs at the breakup. Children are frightened and angry, terrified of being abandoned by both parents, and they feel responsible for the divorce. Most children are taken by surprise; few are relieved.

As the postdivorce family took shape, their world increasingly resembled what they feared most. Home was a lonely place. The household was in disarray for years. Many children were forced to move, leaving behind familiar schools, close friends and other supports.

As the children told us, adolescence begins early in divorced homes and, compared with that of youngsters raised in intact families, is more likely to include more early sexual experiences

> **We're moving to a family structure where the majority of children experience divorce. And for many it's not just once.**

for girls and higher alcohol and drug use for girls and boys. Adolescence is more prolonged in divorced families and extends well into the years of early adulthood.

But it's in adulthood that children of divorce suffer the most. The impact of divorce hits them most cruelly as they go in search of love, sexual intimacy and commitment.[8]

By the year 2010, the traditional family in our country will be the stepfamily. We're moving to a family structure where the majority of children experience divorce. And for many it's not just once.[9]

Losses for Children of Divorce

In divorce, children experience many types of losses. Have you ever wondered what it would be like to learn, as a child, that your parents were divorcing, and then in this panic begin to tell your friends? Fear becomes a daily companion.

> Children experiencing the crisis of divorce frequently must deal with ongoing or repeated experiences of loss coupled with feelings of rejection. In many cases, the decision to divorce is preceded by one or more parental separations involving the departure of one parent from the existing family. The child faces the additional complexity of knowing that the parental decision to separate and divorce was made by choice, which at some level is experienced by the youngster as a rejection. Typically, the youngster is also expected to develop relationships with subsequent parent substitutes and newly acquired siblings.[10]

When there is the loss of a parent, the child also may lose hope for the future. An uncertainty occurs and the child can feel out of control. The stable parents upon whom the child depended are no longer that solid rock. This may occur in a practical area like finances. For example, if a divorced father has promised to take care of the family through his monthly payments, what must a child feel when payments become irregular and eventually cease?

Characteristics of Children of Divorce by Age

Divorce affects children in different ways depending upon the age of the child.

3- to 6-Year-Olds. Young children aged 3 to 6 experience fear. The routine separations of life become traumatic. A parent going shopping or the child's leaving for school is a stressful experience. Children tend to regress to earlier behavior and become more passive and dependent. More and more they ask "What's that?" questions, which is their effort to overcome the disorganization of crisis.

These young children also have a great need for affection. They may refuse to feed themselves, and some even revert to a need for diapers. The children can create wild and imaginative fantasies in their minds because they are puzzled by what is happening to them. They are bewildered. Play does not have the same sense of fun anymore. A common thought is, *Did I cause my parents' divorce? Am I responsible for not having a family anymore?* In addition, these preschoolers may become aggressive with other children.

When you are counseling a 3- to 6-year-old child whose parents are divorcing, help the child verbalize his or her hurt and idea of why his or her parents are divorcing. Remember that at this age, the child may feel as though his or her behavior or thoughts actually caused the divorce. It is not easy to convince the child otherwise. Help the child see other possibilities. Let the child know his or her feelings are the same as other children's feelings. Comments such as the following help children open up and talk about their inner thoughts and feelings:

- You've made a mess at the table before—did your father leave then? Did your older sister ever make a mess?
- Perhaps you are afraid you'll never see your daddy again. Lots of children feel that way.[11]

6- to 8-Year-Olds. The 6- to 8-year-old child has his or her own set of reactions. Sadness is there, but the child's sense of responsibility for the parents' breakup becomes stronger. The child has deep feelings of loss. He or she is afraid of being abandoned and sometimes even of starving. The child yearns for the parent who left.

Frequently these children are angry with the parent who cares for them all the time. They have conflicting loyalties. They want to love both parents but struggle with the feeling that loving one is being disloyal to the other. Thus they feel torn and confused. Symptoms can include nail biting, bed-wetting, losing sleep and retreating into fantasy to solve family problems. Children of both this age group and the 3- to 6-year old age group become possessive.

9- to 12-Year-Olds. Preadolescent children aged 9 to 12 usually experience anger as their main emotional response. Their anger is directed toward the parent they feel is responsible for the family breakup—this could be the custodial parent. But anger, instead of coming out directly at the parent, may be directed at peers. They may alienate friends at the time when they most need them. Their self-image is shaken. Sometimes they throw themselves into what they are doing with great intensity, which is their way of handling the disruption in their lives.

This is a time of conscience development, and the divorce may have a shattering effect upon that process. Psychosomatic illnesses are not unusual at this stage.

All Ages. Children's reactions at any age will vary and often are dependent upon the behavior and reaction of the two parents. When there are hateful responses between the parents, such as child custody battles, visitation battles and using the child to get back at the other parent, you can expect emotional turmoil in the child. Children do not have the resources necessary to cope with this amount of stress. In some cases, parents actually use bribery in an effort to win the allegiance of a child. Unfortunately, some children learn to manipulate both parents and use one against the other. The more emotional turmoil involved in a divorce, the more potential for harm to a child.

In all the turmoil, children seem to have two major concerns:

1. *They dream of their parents' reconciling.* If reconciliation occurred between their parents, they think that this would alleviate all of their problems. They believe—in spite of previous problems—that the family was better off when their parents were together. The children may have seen the conflict when their parents were together, but they are usually willing to live with the conflict in order to have an intact family. After all, this is the only family they know.

2. *They are concerned about what will happen to them.* They are afraid that the parent they are living with will abandon them. One

parent already did abandon them. Why shouldn't the other? Or if one parent was forced to leave, as many are, the children's fears center on being thrown out like their mother or father was. Another fear concerns being replaced in their parents' affection by someone else. As the custodial parent begins to date, children wonder if this new person is going to become important to their parents. And if so, the children fear they may lose the time and attention they now receive.

Emotional Stages of Children of Divorce

In order to help the child or his or her parents, it is important to understand what a child of divorce experiences. Remember that the feelings experienced by a child from the divorce of his or her parents will change in time. There are fairly clear emotional stages through which the child passes as he or she struggles to understand and deal with the divorce. These stages are normal. They cannot be avoided or bypassed, and they have nothing to do with the spirituality of the child. Your goal as you counsel the child or parents is to help the child pass through these stages in order to produce positive growth and minimize the negative effects.

Whether a child's home is quiet and peaceful or filled with conflict, the child rarely expects a divorce to occur. The child usually does not like the conflict and hopes it will settle down eventually. Discovering that a separation or divorce is going to occur is a great shock to a child. Following are some of the emotional stages a child will pass through as he or she copes with the divorce:

Fear and Anxiety. These feelings occur because a child is now faced with an unknown future. A home and family with two parents is the child's source of stability. It is now about to be shattered.

Various indications of fear and anxiety may manifest themselves in restlessness, nightmares, sleeplessness, stomach problems, sweating and aches and pains. These are normal problems. Parents at this time need to give reassurance and discuss their future plans in detail. It is important to give facts, because a child's imagination may run wild. Knowing is better than wondering. A child may tend to think up worse problems than actually exist.

Abandonment and Rejection. After fear and anxiety come feelings of abandonment and rejection. The feelings of the initial stage recede and are replaced by this struggle. The child may know at one level that he or she will not be rejected or abandoned, but the child is still concerned that it might happen. A younger child has difficulty distinguishing between the parents' leaving one another and leaving him or her behind, and unfortunately, the child may focus upon the latter. This stage may be perpetuated by unkept promises on the part of a parent who leaves.

Aloneness and Sadness. These feelings eventually replace abandonment and rejection. As the family structure changes and settles down, the reality of what has occurred begins to settle in. A child feels this stage with a pain in the stomach and a tightness in the chest. This is a time for depression, and regular activities tend to be neglected. Many children do a lot of thinking, which is usually wishful daydreaming. And the fantasies follow the same theme—parents getting together again and everything being alright. Crying spells may become more frequent at this time.

Frustration and Anger. Then comes frustration and anger. Children whose parents divorce or separate are angry children. This is a natural response to the frustration they feel. In addition, they have seen angry and upset parents, and this modeling of anger is emulated by the children. Anger may continue to be the pattern for many years and may carry over into their other relationships.

For some children, anger may not show itself directly. It is an inward basic feeling that may be suppressed or masked. It may come out through negativity and moodiness. Whether expressed or not, anger is damaging. If it is present, it is far better for it to be admitted and handled rather than buried and waiting for an eventual explosion.

A child's anger is present for several reasons:

- It serves as a protection and a warning signal, just like depression.
- It is alerting the people the child interacts with to a problem and is often a reaction to hurt, fear or frustration.
- It is an involuntary response. Parents and counselors alike should not be threatened by the anger or attempt to deny its presence in the child.

- If it is not allowed as a direct expression, it will be expressed in a passive and indirect manner, which is far more dangerous.
- The child's anger may be expressed through a negative perspective on life, irritability, withdrawal, self-isolation and resistance to school, chores or whatever the child wants to resist.

The feeling of anger should never be denied. Rather, help the child learn to express and drain it. According to the child's ability, help him or her understand the reason for his or her anger and its purpose.

In order to resolve his or her anger, a child needs time alone with his or her parents each week. This can be difficult if there are several children in the family, but it is needed. Urge the parents to be good listeners and to help their child express his or her feelings.

Additionally, be on the lookout for signs of indirect expression. Sarcasm and resistance are fairly easy to spot, but the manifestations may occur in physical complaints such as asthma, vomiting, insomnia and stomachaches. Accept the normalcy of the child's anger. Encourage the child to talk it out but not act it out.

Rejection and Resentment. Eventually the child's anger moves into rejection and resentment. The child is not over his or her angry feelings but is now attempting to create some emotional distance between himself or herself and his or her parents. This is a protective device. Pouting can be one of the forms of rejection, as is the silent treatment. The child won't respond to suggestions or commands and often "forgets" to follow through with what he or she is supposed to do. The child becomes hypercritical.[12] This behavior is actually a reaction formation. As a child pushes a parent away, he or she really wants to be close to the parent. The child says hateful statements and yet wants to be loving. The child is just trying to protect himself or herself from rejection, so the child rejects others first.

Reestablishment of Trust. The final stage in the process of dealing with divorce is the reestablishment of trust. It is difficult to say how long this will take, as it varies with each situation and child and ranges from months to years.

Advice for Divorced Parents

What advice can you give to the parent or parents who are concerned about the effect of their divorce upon their children? Provide them with some of the basic principles of helping people in crisis discussed in this book. Listening, encouragement, reassurance and being available are very helpful to children. As a youth pastor for almost seven years, I was amazed at how these gave support to the adolescents with whom I worked. And in talking with others who worked with children, I found they used the same principles.

Suggest to the parents that they do the following:

1. Do not be overconcerned with your own feelings to the neglect of the children's feelings. Each day give them some time to discuss what they are experiencing and feeling.
2. Give the children time to process their feelings. There are no quick solutions or cures.
3. A stable environment is beneficial to the children. If possible, live in the same home and neighborhood. Keep everything the same as much as possible. The greater the change, the greater the stress and discomfort to the children.
4. Give positive feedback to the children and build their sense of self-confidence.
5. Reassure them that they are not the cause of the divorce or separation. Both parents need to give consistent and equal amounts of love.
6. According to the children's level of understanding, help them know in advance the different types of feelings they will be experiencing. Keep the children informed at all times of any expected changes, so they can prepare in advance.

FINAL THOUGHTS

Children need the assurance that even though their mother and father will be working through their own struggles, they will still be taken care of by their parents. Parents, friends and other relatives need to repeat this to the child so that the child begins to realize that more than one person is supporting him or her with this belief. Assist the child in selecting some task that he or she can accomplish to help overcome the feeling of helplessness.

Teach the parents of your congregation how to minister to their own children during a crisis time. This can be an opportunity to equip children to handle the crises of life.

RECOMMENDED RESOURCES

Resources to Use with Children in Grief

The Dougy Center. *Waving Good-bye*. An activities manual for children in grief.

The Dougy Center. *35 Ways to Help a Grieving Child*. You will find an extensive list of age-related resources on pages 45-48.

The mission of The Dougy Center is to provide loving support in a safe place where children, teens and their families who are grieving a death can share their experience as they move through the healing process. Through the National Center for Grieving Children and Families, support and local training—both nationally and internationally—are provided to individuals and organizations seeking to assist children and teens in grief.

The Dougy Center serves children and teens ages 3-19 who have experienced the death of a parent, sibling or friend to accident, illness, suicide or murder. The support groups are coordinated by professional staff and trained volunteers. In addition, the parents (or caregivers) of the youth participate in support groups to address their needs and the issues of raising children following a traumatic loss.

The Dougy Center
3909 SE 52nd Avenue
P.O. Box 86852
Portland, OR 97286
Phone: (503) 775-5683
Website: http://www.dougy.org

Wright, Norman H., and Gary Oliver. *Fears, Doubts, Blues, and Pouts: Stories About Handling Fear, Worry, Sadness, and Anger.* Colorado Springs, CO: Chariot Victor Publishing, 1999. Use this book for the 3- to 9-year-old child. This book covers the emotions of fear, worry, sadness and anger in story form with extensive discussion questions based upon each child's learning style. Available through Christian Marriage Enrichment at (800) 875-7560.

Choosing Wisely videocassette series (formerly called *Before You Divorce).* One of the best ways to help a child with divorce is to use an aggressive ministry that conducts a positive intervention with parents who are considering divorce. Church after church have shared stories of how couples who were in the midst of divorce proceedings viewed this series, stopped the divorce process and restored their marriages. You might consider showing this series to your adult couple's classes as a preventative measure. Available through Christian Marriage Enrichment at (800) 875-7560.

CHAPTER 18

GUIDELINES TO HELP CHILDREN IN GRIEF

Children are the forgotten grievers in our country. Adults seem to receive the attention, and children are left out of the equation. Children not only grieve, but their grief is unique and they need to grieve.

The following are several unique features of a child's grief:

- It comes out in the middle of everyday life. It can't be predicted.
- They can put it aside easier. One question may be about their grandfather's death and the next response is about their doll.
- It comes out in brief but intense episodes.
- They express their grief in actions. They're limited in their verbal expression.
- They often postpone their grief or part of it.

- Childhood grief often lasts throughout childhood and pieces of it last into adulthood.
- Children grieve differently from adults. Instead of experiencing ongoing intense distress, many children are likely at first to deny death and then grieve intermittently for many years.

This is why it's so critical to communicate with a child. Information is crucial. It solves many issues such as the following:

- It tames fears. By talking with children about death and grief you can recreate a secure place so that the children can learn to trust the world again.
- Information gives children a sense of control. They feel confused and besieged by new emotions. They need to be anchored by adults.
- Information gives children permission to express feelings they want to communicate. Children don't grieve on command. They need the freedom to come to adults at any time.
- Information helps them prepare for future losses. Most adults have never been prepared for this. Sheltered children can't cope as well as those who understand the truth of life.
- If you don't talk to them, they'll talk to themselves and fill in the blanks! Imagination and other children are not good resources.[1]

It also is important for us to identify what may inhibit a child's abilities to grieve the losses he or she experiences. The following factors most often contribute to this problem:

- The parents have difficulty grieving past or current losses.
- The parents are unable to handle and accept their children's expressions of painful experiences. They don't know how to respond.
- The children are worried about how the parents are handling the loss and attempt to protect them.

- The children are overly concerned with maintaining control and feeling secure and may feel frightened or threatened by the grief.
- The parent does not caringly prod, stimulate and encourage the children to grieve.
- The children don't have the security of a loving, caring environment.
- In the case of a loved one's death, children may question their role in making it happen. Their misplaced guilt is further enhanced if they have ambivalent feelings toward the loved one.
- The family fails to acknowledge and discuss the reality of death or loss.[2]

Regardless of the type of loss children experience, the following seven steps are important in the grieving process:

1. Children need to accept the loss, experience the pain and express their sorrow.
2. Children require assistance to identify and express the wide range of feelings they're experiencing.
3. Children need to know why others are sad and why they themselves are sad. Acknowledging these feelings lets a child know that it's *okay* to be sad. Tell them, "This is how we feel when someone dies."
4. Children must be told that it is the death that has made people sad. Without an explanation, they may think others' sadness is caused by something they did or didn't do. Start by saying, "This is a very, very sad time"; "A very, very sad thing has happened"; "Mommy and Daddy are sad because . . . "; and "People at church are sad because . . . ."
5. In the case of death, children need encouragement to remember and review their relationship with the loved one.
6. Children need help in learning to relinquish and say good-bye to what they lost.
7. Children respond differently to loss depending on their age and level of emotional maturity.

GRIEVING OCCURS IN
CHILDREN OF ALL AGES

Grieving is not just for adults or just for adolescents. Children of all ages experience grief.

Infants

Grieving occurs even in very young infants. Young children between four months and two years of age express distress when responding to a loss. At this stage, separation from the mother is a significant loss. If the separation is sudden, the child will express shock and protest. Prolonged separation creates despair and sadness. The child loses interest in objects and activities that are usually pleasurable. Unless a caring individual steps into the vacated role, the infant will become detached from everyone.

Keep in mind, too, that no matter how young children are when someone close dies, they are still impacted by the loss throughout their life. They may have no memories of the deceased, but they have experienced the loss of someone with whom they shared a significant bond. As members of a family, they are also impacted by the grief of other family members.

Toddlers to Preschoolers

Children between two and five years old may show their grief in a number of ways. Because they don't understand the significance of the loss, they may ask seemingly useless questions again and again. They may ask, "Hasn't he been dead long enough?" Concepts take time, and the concept of death hasn't been fully formed yet in the children's minds. They may appear bewildered and tend to regress in their behavior, becoming demanding and clinging. If what was lost is not returned, expressions of anger increase. An adult may need to assist the children toward acknowledging and expressing feelings of loss. Many adults, unfortunately, make the mistake of removing children from familiar surroundings following a family death or trauma. This further undermines the children's sense of security and raises their anxiety.

In the case of death, children at this age are obsessed with thoughts of the lost loved one and overwhelmed by an intense sadness. They tend to idealize this person, dwelling on reviewing and remembering their lost relationship.

Remember from chapter 16 that children between the ages of three and six years old engage in what is known as magical thinking. They believe that their own thoughts can influence people and events. For instance, a child who is upset about a parent taking a trip may wish that the car would get a flat tire so that the parent doesn't leave. Then when the parent is killed in a car crash caused by a blowout, the child feels responsible.

Additionally, this is an age when fears increase. Children become aware of threatening events in the world around them. They're curious about bodily functions. When they experience the death of a loved one, children may ask questions like: "Can he still eat?"; "Can she go potty?"; "Does he cry?"; "Will she get out of the box and hug me again?" and "Will he be a ghost?".

At this age, children don't understand the permanency of death. For them, it's reversible. E.T. came back from the dead. So did Jesus and Lazarus. And so does the coyote in the *Road Runner* cartoons. They may think that if you wish hard enough, a person will come back to life. When a pet dies, young children may act as if it is still alive by calling it, asking to feed it or looking under a bed for it. These kids see people and animals as cartoon characters—able to survive anything. To them death is merely a deep and temporary sleep. Parents often reinforce this misconception by telling them that the dead person is "resting" or "just didn't wake up." Even some of the terminology used by funeral homes reinforces the denial of the permanency of death, for example, the "slumber room."[3]

Children in this age group often focus their attention on one detail of an experience and ignore everything else. They have difficulty seeing the whole picture clearly. They don't comprehend the significance of loss.

If Grandpa dies, they may ask or think:

- *Does this mean someone else is going to die?*
- *Grandpa died from a headache; Mommy says she has a headache too . . .*
- *Old people die; Daddy is very old; Daddy may die too . . .*

Also be prepared for indirect questions aimed at finding out if someone else might die, such as, "How old are you?" or "How old is Daddy?"

Like the following indirect questions, you must explain the difference between

- very, very sick and just sick
- very, very old and over 20
- very old and very sick and very old and not sick[4]

As children get older, usually between the ages of 5 to 8, they develop the ability to understand loss and even death. They're especially vulnerable because they can grasp the significance of their losses but have limited skills to cope with those losses.

If there is a death, they often look on it as a "taker"—something that comes and gets you. The question, "Who killed him?" is common. They may accept death as a reality but not the fact that everyone is going to die. One of the worst prayers that has been taught to children over the years (including me) was:

Now I lay me down to sleep, I pray the Lord my soul to keep; if I should die before I wake, I pray the Lord my soul to take. Amen.

What damage does this do to young children?

When faced with loss, children may use denial as a coping mechanism. It's easier to act as if nothing has happened. Children also hide their feelings at this age because they don't want to look like a baby. Afraid of becoming out of control, children may vent their feelings only when alone. To others they may appear insensitive, uncaring and unaffected by the loss, which leaves the parent unaware of the extent of their grief. At this age, children need to be encouraged again and again to vent their feelings. Allowing children to see their parents grieve and talking about their own feelings can help them work though their grief.

VARYING REACTIONS TO A LOSS ARE NORMAL FOR CHILDREN

The death of a loved one is an extremely difficult loss for all of us to handle. But for children, it is even more difficult because they lack the resources to handle such a serious loss. Let's consider the reactions of children to a serious loss such as death.

Fear

Children who experience the death of a loved one can experience a number of fears including the following:

- Fear of losing the other parent, siblings or grandparents—they tend to see the remaining people as candidates for death;
- Fear of their own death—this is especially true if the child is younger than the sibling who died or is approaching the age at which the sibling died;
- Fear of going to sleep because they equate sleep with death—even the prayer, "If I should die before I wake . . . " reinforces this misconception. Dreams and nightmares intensify the fear; and
- Fear of separation because of the perceived insecurity of the home and family—they no longer feel safe and protected. They're hesitant to talk about their feelings because it may upset the other family members. One young girl told me, "When Daddy died, I wanted to talk to my mother about it. But I was afraid to because it made her cry, and I didn't want the others yelling at me 'cause I did that."

Guilt

The second feeling associated with grief is guilt. It is difficult to identify all of the sources of guilt, but there seem to be three main reasons children experience guilt when loved ones die:

1. "They died because I did something wrong. I misbehaved!" Children have a knack for remembering things they've done

that they think are wrong. They may have made a mistake, broken something or forgotten to say or do something. Just like adults, children can end up with an incredible list of "if only" thoughts, or regrets.

2. "I wanted them dead. I thought it, and it happened." It is important to remember that young children believe they can actually make things happen by thinking them. It's easy for kids to think their anger or aggression killed the loved one. Because they take on this responsibility, they live in fear of being found out and punished.

3. "I didn't love them enough." It is common for children to believe that if you love someone enough, it will keep them from dying. They long for a second chance to make things right.

Anger

Another common grief response is anger. A number of beliefs trigger children's anger. They often feel abandoned and left to face life on their own. They're angry because their future has been dramatically changed—they won't be with that special person anymore. They feel victimized by events that are out of their control.

Children may be angry at their parents for

- not telling them that the person who died was so sick;
- spending so much time with the sick person. They feel neglected and isolated; and
- just needing someone to be angry with.[5]

Kids express their anger in different ways. It may be targeted like a well-aimed bullet or sprayed in all directions like a shotgun pellet. It may be directed at family members, friends, teachers, pets or even at God. It may be expressed in tantrums, fights, silent hostility or verbal blasts. As difficult as it may be to experience these demonstrative expressions of anger, it is a healthy sign. The alternative response—bottling up the anger—can result in digestive problems and depression.

Confusion

Worth mentioning here is the sense of confusion that can accompany the loss of a loved one. Just imagine that you are a six-year-old child who has been raised in a Christian home and your mother dies. You probably wonder, *Where is God? Why didn't He keep my mother alive? Why didn't He make her well? My uncle told me Mom went to be with God. Why'd He do that?* Not only are children confused about God, but they are dealing with a mixture of feelings about the person who died.

> **Kids express their anger in different ways. It may be targeted like a well-aimed bullet or sprayed in all directions like a shotgun pellet.**

They're trying to sort through mixed messages and advice they receive from grown-ups. The expectations of adults often create confusion. One adult may be implying, *Oh, you poor little child. You must feel so sad and alone.* At the same time, someone else may be giving the message, *Now you're the man in the family. You'll have to be strong.* The child will be confused by these conflicting messages that say to be strong, sad, in control, a help to others and so on.

The child's memories of the deceased also can cause confusion. The survivors are talking about the person in a way that conflicts with the child's memories. They are praising and lauding the person's perfect qualities in a way the child cannot understand. The child may wonder, *Was Mom really as perfect as they say? I didn't know that. Sometimes I didn't even like her, and I thought she was bad when she yelled and went on and on. Maybe I was wrong. I hope no one finds out what I think.* You can see how this would create confusion as well as guilt for the child.

The fluctuating moods of others also generate confusion. Individuals around the child may be cheerful one moment and moody and quiet the next. While this is a normal response, the child is seeking stability and assurance from these people, but their changing moods cause the child to question his or her own responses. The child may ask himself or herself,

Is it me? Did I do something wrong? Do they want me around or not?[6]

CASE STUDY: WHEN A PARENT DIES

The following are points to remember when counseling children because of the death of a parent:

- The emotional responses and behaviors of children vary around the time of loss. They are strongly influenced by the reactions of the surviving parent as well as other adults.
- When a parent is in a terminal condition, the least likely to know are the younger children.
- Recapturing memories of the funeral and being able to talk about it increase over time for most children.
- Children who are prepared for the funeral are better able to handle it than those who weren't given any prior information.
- Including children in the planning of the funeral has a positive effect. It helps them to feel important and useful at a time when many are feeling overwhelmed.
- Children who are involved want the funeral to reflect the life of the parent more than focus on the loss itself or the afterlife.
- Children should be given a choice as to attending the wake, funeral or burial. These need to be informed choices by children who are prepared for what they will see and experience.
- Visiting the grave helps children remain connected with the dead parent. There's a huge vacancy in their life. This is a time when they are working through what place the deceased parent has in their current life.[7]

Prepare Children

Children should be told what is going to happen and what they are going to experience. Should they be brought to the funeral home, service or both? Definitely—if they are well prepared in advance. Tell them what will happen, and then give them the choice of going or not. Fit the following explanation around your family's plans and special traditions:

_____ will be taken from _____, where he died, to the funeral home. At the funeral home, _____ will be dressed in clothes that he (she) liked and put into a casket. A casket is a box we use so that when _____ is buried, no dirt will get on him (her). Because _____'s body isn't working any more, it won't move or do any of the things it used to do. But it will look like _____ always did.

People will come and visit us and say how sorry they are that _____ died. After _____ days the casket will be closed and taken to the church, where people will say prayers for the family. Then we will go to the cemetery where _____ will be buried in a place that _____ picked out.

If you like, you can come to the funeral home and visit for a while—and even go to the cemetery. You could bring something to leave with _____ if you want; that would be nice.

We have to go to the funeral home to make plans, and we'll let you know all about them when we come back. We will be gone for _____ hours.

For a cremation, use this additional information:

After we leave the funeral home, _____ will be taken to a crematory, a place where his (her) body will be turned into ashes. Then we will take those ashes and _____ (scatter them; keep them in an urn). Since _____'s body doesn't work and doesn't feel anything, being cremated doesn't hurt.

In addition, if the dead person has changed because of illness or accident, it is important to describe some of this change (i.e., it's still Grandpa, but you know he was sick and lost a lot of weight—so he will look thinner).[8]

Keep Children Connected
Children who remain connected after the loss are better able to talk about the dead parent. They can talk to family members as well as others.

They are likely to try to please the dead parent with their behavior.

It is important to have a relationship with the dead parent. This is part of the continuing process called constructing. The constructing process involves discovering the meaning of this loss rather than just letting go of their parent; this discovering continues to be a part of the child's life experience.[9]

Describe the Event

The following are six examples of how to describe to young children how and why a death occurred:

1. Old Age
   "When a person gets very, very, very old, his body wears out and stops working."
2. Terminal Illness
   "Because the disease couldn't be stopped, the person got very, very sick, his body wore out and stopped working."
3. Accident
   "A terrible thing happened (car crash and so on). His body was badly hurt and couldn't be fixed. It stopped working."
4. Miscarriage
   "Sometimes when a baby is just starting to grow, something happens that makes it stop. We don't know what it was; it wasn't anything anyone did."
5. Stillborn
   "Sometimes something makes the baby die before it is born. We're not sure why, but it's nothing anybody did or didn't do."
6. Sudden Infant Death Syndrome (SIDS)
   "Sometimes with little babies something makes their bodies stop working. It's nothing anybody did or forgot to do. Doctors are not sure why it happens."[10]

How can we help our children learn to handle the losses of life? Start early. Overprotection and denial rob our children of the opportunity to develop the skills they'll need throughout their lives.

Top 11 Points for Adults to Use with Grieving Children

1. Give Your Children Permission to Grieve and Encourage Them to Talk and Ask Questions

Whether the loss is the death of a family member, a major move or the loss of a pet, your children need permission to mourn. For certain kids, permission may not be enough. Some kids need an invitation to share their feelings, but they also need to be taught how to express sorrow. A few sensitive, well-directed questions can draw them out. If your children still do not talk, don't force it. Just let them know that you're available and ready to listen when they want to talk. You may wish to look for other ways for them to express what they're feeling.

> **Children whose questions are answered and who are given a forum for discussion have less need to fantasize and are much easier to help than nonexpressive children.**

Once children begin to talk about their feelings, it may seem like you've untapped a gusher. They are—in their limited capacity—attempting to make sense of what has happened and regain their security. Children whose questions are answered and who are given a forum for discussion have less need to fantasize and are much easier to help than nonexpressive children. If your children don't share their feelings, watch for indirect questions or statements of concern and try to put their feelings into words for them.[11]

2. Be Available When a Child Is Ready to Grieve

Being available may be the most important element in helping children grieve. Children need affection and a sense of security. Touching them and making eye contact will provide comfort and reassurance. Let the children know that it is normal to have ups and downs. They are not going crazy. Help them break the mourning into manageable pieces so that they don't get overwhelmed. Using illustrations and word pictures can help them identify and talk about their feelings.

Some helpers are surprised to find that children will have the same range of emotions as they do. These emotions include anger, panic, numbness, sadness and guilt. But the children are only starting to identify their emotions and learning what to do about them. Children need others to help them identify their feelings and the sources of those feelings, and express them in constructive ways.

The author of *The Grieving Child* suggests the following ways that helpers and parents can help children express themselves emotionally:

> For the most part, children deal with feelings through some kind of acting out, sometimes in a disruptive manner, yet there are simple ways that you can help your child identify and express feelings.
>
> Look around your child's room, note the materials she is comfortable with, and then see if these can be used as tools in teaching her about feelings. These materials might include paper, crayons, markers, clay, paper bags, puppets, dolls, old magazines, scrapbooks, balloons, a diary, a tape recorder, books or music. The key is that she be familiar with them and comfortable in using them. With some suggestions from you she can turn these materials into drawings, writings, collages, sculptures, plays, scrapbooks or tapes: all centered on her feelings about the death of a loved one, helping her to express those feelings and to cope appropriately with them. In the course of these exercises she will learn lessons that she will carry into adulthood and possibly pass on to her own children.[12]

3. How to Handle a Child Asking the Same Question Repeatedly or a Child Answering You with Why to Every Answer You Give Them

Remember their age. Children can't grasp what we can, and if we respond with an adult answer to a child's question, the answer is over their head and ability. And if they're in a state of shock or crisis, their thinking ability is lessened even more.

It's important that children ask questions and receive simple, concrete answers to what they've asked.

4. Give Them Opportunities for Creative Expression

Children who have difficulty verbalizing their feelings may find it easier to express them on paper. Drawing is an effective way for kids to gain control over their emotional pain and eventually eliminate it. When the loss is a death, drawing is especially important because it allows kids to actually see what their feelings look like. This action helps give them a sense of understanding and control.

Writing or journaling also is beneficial for children whose writing skills are developed. It is easier for kids to express on paper the reality of what's happened and their fantasies about it. Writing a letter to the deceased person or even to God can be helpful. Encourage your children to read aloud and discuss what they've written, but remember to respect their privacy. The choice whether or not to share needs to be theirs.

5. Create Opportunities for Playtime

Periodically, the child needs to be encouraged to take a break from their grief and to play with friends. Play is an important type of expression for children, especially for younger children whose verbal skills are limited. In the safety of play, a child can vent various feelings. Play helps them regain a feeling of safety and security. It gives them a feeling of power over the effects of loss and allows them to separate themselves from what has happened.[13] Watch what they do and say during their play.

They may feel like they're betraying the deceased if they have fun or allow themselves some enjoyment. But play is a normal and beneficial part of their lives and gives them time to recuperate. It also helps them realize that life goes on. Encourage playtime with peers and adults.

6. Watch Your Expectations

Everyone needs to be careful not to overprotect a child. Lecturing or making decisions for them is not helpful while they're coping with a loss. When possible, it is better if they learn to make their own choices and are allowed to grow through the experiences of their lives. You may have to give parents guidance about this.

The flip side of this issue, though, is that adults often have expectations that are inappropriate for their children's age level. I've overheard parents or other adults say to a child, "You're going to have to take over now and be the man of the family (or be the strong one)." This is an unrealistic expectation and places too much of a burden on the child. These kinds of messages will short-circuit the child's grieving process. They need to be given age-appropriate responsibilities.

7. Dismiss Their Myths

It is important to discover if the child has been practicing magical thinking. Younger children are particularly vulnerable to this (see chapter 16 for a more detailed explanation).

Kids will often be impatient with themselves because they feel sad longer than they think they should. They also feel that no one has ever felt the way they do, so they may be uncomfortable with their friends. They need to be told not to expect too much of themselves or others at this time; they need encouragement to talk with their friends—especially those who have experienced similar losses. Communicating with children of all ages normalizes what they're experiencing.

8. Make Honesty a Policy

While grieving, children look to adults for hope and encouragement. When children ask adults questions, adults need to avoid giving them platitudes and, instead, let them know it is alright to ask why when bad things happen. Adults need to admit that they don't have all the answers, but that they'll get through it together. One mother told her six-year-old son, "I know it is a sad time for you. We are all sad and wish things were different. There are many changes happening right now, but in time things will settle down. Someday the pain will go away. It may go away gradually and keep returning again and again, but as we help and love one another, it is going to go away."[14]

When there's been a death, discuss whether or not this is the child's first experience with death. If it is, the child will need help to understand the loss and sort out his or her feelings about it. Be especially sensitive to the child's reactions and anticipate the unexpected. Use words and phrases the child can easily understand. It may help to rehearse what you plan to say with someone else first.

> **When children ask adults questions, adults need to admit that they don't have all the answers, but that they'll get through it together.**

Parents, teachers, pastors and counselors will be confronted with difficult questions from children. How would you answer a five-year-old child who asks, "What does 'dead' mean?" How would you answer that question at their level? Always be clear and as factual as possible, telling the truth about the death and what caused it. When kids ask questions, give them accurate information such as, "Your brother's heart stopped beating and that is why he died." It is better to use proper death language such as, "Grandpa died," rather than, "Grandpa passed away." However, be sensitive about how many details you give. If you have no answer to their question, then say so. Let them know that when you do, you will share it with them.

The authors of *How Do We Tell the Children?* offer an example of this type of questioning and how to respond:

- "Will Grandpa ever move again?" (No, his body has stopped working.)
- "Why can't they fix him?" (Once the body stops working, it can't start again.)
- "Why is he cold?" (The body only stays warm when it's working.)
- "Why isn't he moving?" (He can't move because his body isn't working anymore.)
- "When will he come back?" (He won't. People who die don't come back.)

- "Is he sleeping?" (No. When we sleep, our body is still working, just resting.)
- "Can he hear me?" (No. He could only hear you if his body was working.)
- "Can he eat after he is buried?" (No, a person eats only when his body is working.)[15]

9. Allow Children to Respond in Their Own Way

Don't expect children to respond as adults. Initially, they may not seem upset or sad. Young children even may have difficulty remembering the deceased. They may need help to remember their relationship with the deceased before they can resolve their grief. Photos and videos are helpful. Reminiscing about times spent together and reviewing certain qualities of the person also may be helpful. Part of your ministry will be helping parents know how to respond.

Children often regress because they don't know how to grieve.[16] The important thing is to allow children to progress at their own rates. Adults need to be available to observe their reactions. If they begin to express strong feelings, encourage them—don't block them. Allow them to cry or express anger or even bitterness. In time, they will probably begin to ask questions. Answer them simply and honestly, even though you may struggle with them yourself, whether you're a parent, pastor or counselor.

10. Watch for Signs of Fear

Children need reassurance that their family still exists and that they are important parts of it. Children will tend to ask the same questions over and over again. Their questioning may become intense as they attempt to assimilate what has happened and how it will affect their lives. Parents and counselors may need an abundance of patience to answer them again and again in a loving way.[17]

Children will most likely become aware of their vulnerability to losing other important people or things as they evaluate how this loss will affect their lives. Anything of importance to them could become the object of fear. It may be their home, school, friends, church, pets, a daily routine, an activity or another loved one. They will require constant and consistent reassurance. It is important to discuss with children in advance if there are any planned changes in the future.

11. Encourage Children to Continue Normal Routines

It helps if children continue certain family routines. Routines provide security and let them know there are certain constants in their lives—things they can rely on to stay the same.

One of the most practical things to do is to encourage children to take good care of themselves—to get plenty of rest and exercise, and to eat balanced meals.

FINAL THOUGHT

Loss is a natural and inevitable part of life. A key element in a child's emotional development is learning to deal with the feelings associated with loss and growing through the experience. Parents, teachers and counselors who guide their kids through the troubled waters of the grieving process will equip them to handle the losses of their adult lives better.

CHAPTER 19

THE CRISES OF
ADOLESCENCE

You have a full day planned at your office. The church secretary has been informed that you do not want to be interrupted. You are settling in to work on your sermon. But there is an interruption. A teenage girl whom you recognize from the youth group barges in, visibly upset, and says, "Your secretary said you were busy, but I have to talk to someone. This can't wait. Please, could you talk to me for a few minutes?" You stop what you're doing and ask her to sit down. The story unfolds:

> I didn't know who to talk to about this. I've been dating this boy in the youth group—you know who he is. He's the president of the high school youth group. We've . . . well . . . I just found out I'm pregnant. I don't want to be pregnant [she starts to cry]! But I am. What can I do? He wants me to have an abortion. What should I do?

The next morning you sit down once again to begin preparing your sermon. Another interruption. This time it is John, a 14-year-old, who is in his first year of high school. You chat with him for a minute and then he says:

> I'm not sure what's wrong. I didn't bother going to school today. It's not much use, since I just can't seem to learn anything anymore. I try to, I really do, but I read the stuff and it doesn't register. And I'm tired all the time. I get enough sleep, but I am just tired. And I think there must be something wrong with me, too. I get all these aches and pains I never had before. I didn't want to talk to my parents about this, but I've got to tell someone. You spoke to our class three weeks ago and said if we ever wanted to talk to you, to come see you. So, I'm here. What's wrong with me?

That afternoon you receive a frantic call from a parent who tells you she will be there in 15 minutes with her 16-year-old son. When she arrives, her son follows her in looking sullen. "You've got to talk to him and find out what he's been up to!" she says. "He won't tell me, and I found these pills and other things in his room. I don't know what they are, but I'm sure they're drugs and maybe marijuana. I think he's been using these. Can you talk to him?"

The next morning you are called by one of your members who is a physician. He tells you he has just admitted a young girl to the hospital who has attended the youth group occasionally. He asks if you would call on her in the hospital. You agree and later that day you make the call. As you walk into the room, you are taken aback by what you see— a 15-year-old girl who is sitting up in bed, but she looks more like a skeleton. Her parents are there looking very concerned. She is suffering from anorexia nervosa. They are all looking to you for help.

Every case I have just described is a crisis situation.

WHO ARE ADOLESCENTS?

For some young people, adolescence is a time of continual crisis with a few respites in between. For others, their development is a bit smoother. But overall, adolescence is one of the most difficult transitions of life.

It is a roller-coaster experience—a time of stress and storm. This can be the time when self-doubt and feelings of inferiority are intensified and when social pressures are at their peak. The adolescent's self-worth is

> # The adolescent's self-worth is dependent upon one of the most unstable pillars in existence—peer acceptance.

dependent upon one of the most unstable pillars in existence—peer acceptance. Dr. Urie Bronfenbrenner, an eminent authority on child development at Cornell University, says the junior high years are probably the most critical to the development of a child's mental health.

Identity

The young person from 13 to 19 is becoming independent from his parents and at the same time experiencing a radical identity crisis. Many are able to establish their identity at this time, while others postpone it until adulthood.[1]

The adolescent search for identity has numerous sources. Family relations have a significant impact on identity formation. Creating an identity within a family can come from other acceptable or unacceptable responses. Out-of-the-ordinary events, such as a disabled or drug-involved sibling, family death or job loss, will have an influence.

Status symbols are another way to proclaim who they are. Friends, shoes, clothes, hairstyles, cars and so on add to whom a teen is. But to be authentic, behavior has to match the status symbol, which can lead to a reputation.

Grown-up behavior is a part of the identity package, and many of these are behaviors that they're too young to experience—smoking, drugs, sex and drinking.

Rebellion fits into the equation as well. It's their way of attempting to resolve incongruent ideas and find authentic identity. Often this creates inner conflict for many teens.

Other people's opinions also are essential. Teens need their self-image validated by others. Often their identity is shaped by how others see them.

Idols contribute to their identity, but often they overidentify and seem to lose their own individuality. Idols give them an opportunity to test new behaviors and attitudes before incorporating them into their identity.

Cliquish exclusion and the lack of tolerance for other people's differences also are part of the identity formation and perhaps even a defense against identity confusion.[2]

WHAT DO ADOLESCENTS FACE TODAY?

Today's generation of young people face a unique set of pressures. Young people experience instant information and media bombardment that usually transmits values antithetical to the Christian faith and beliefs. It is important to remember that children and youth are being

> **Children and youth are being raised in a promiscuous, violent, non-Christian society. And being a Christian can create additional stress that produces inner conflict.**

raised in a promiscuous, violent, non-Christian society. And being a Christian can create additional stress that produces inner conflict.

Morals

Moral choices are being made at a younger age today. These choices include sex, drugs, friends and drinking. The latest research indicates that one out of five junior high students has already had sexual intercourse.

The Last Generation

This present generation also lives under the potential of being the last generation. Young people face the possibility of having no future. Wars have always been a part of life, but never before have we had a generation that lives under the threat of being destroyed instantaneously. What do they hear from the media? The threat of war, the nuclear bomb, pollution, Social Security payments being exhausted and other frightening prospects. Thus, many young people seek to avoid these possibilities by finding pleasure wherever they can.

Divorce

More and more teens are coming from unstable homes. Divorce is commonplace, and the role models of stable marriages and stable family lives are lacking.

Commitment

This is also a generation unsure about and unable to understand and follow through with commitment. Perhaps that is partly because this generation has been given much more than the previous generation. Today's teens have not had to struggle as much as previous generations. It is difficult for them to delay rewards. They don't know how to handle discouragement and disillusionment very well, and thus, they are prone to experience crisis more readily. They look for instant solutions. Many of them use drugs as their escape, and in some cases, when nothing else works, they opt for suicide.[3]

HOW DO ADOLESCENTS REACT TO CRISES?

This is a disparaging picture, but unfortunately, many teenagers fit into this scenario. Although many others are committed, well-adjusted future adults, they, too, will experience crisis situations.

Some have asked the question, "Is it adolescence, or is it grief?" Adolescence itself is a life phase characterized by turbulence. Parents and youth workers alike wonder about teens' actions and attitudes. Adolescence is a life stage filled with an abundance of changes. This is a time between childhood and adulthood. It's a major transition of life, filled with loss. There are physical, mental and emotional changes—loss even on a daily basis. It's like a low fever of grief accompanies each adolescent through life. And if there's a major loss such as a death, there's compounded grief. Let's look closer at this sort of crisis.

The Crisis of Death

Teens react to a major loss or death like adults, or their grief may resemble that of a child. With a family death, teens may separate even more from other family members and become enmeshed in other activities or with other people. Development may come to a halt for awhile. A teen either will have difficulty resolving the loss, which blocks their continuing development, or they will develop greater maturity and growth.[4]

> **Adolescents need intimacy. If the one who died loved them unconditionally, there's a major hole in their life.**

What do adolescents need at a time of major loss? Security. Safety and security are major needs. Remember that what teens know is probably going to be different than what they feel. If a parent or the main adult in their life dies, they may feel abandoned. Teens appear much more mature than they are. They need to know someone is there for them physically, emotionally and spiritually. They need to know that other family members are available.

They also need intimacy. If the one who died—whether it be a parent, sibling or close friend—loved them unconditionally, there's a major hole in their life.

They also need connection to the one who died. One set of authors said:

It may be critical to his emotional well-being that he remain attached until he can move away on his own. If he is in the process of separating, he may hold on to the memory of the dead parent so that he can break away from him and continue the development process. The parent may die, but his anchor remains.[5]

The act of separation needs to be done in a healthy way. The sharing of feelings is necessary. And if at all possible, start a teen support group.

Teens also need to find some relief from the emotional pain. Their secure world has crumbled. Many teens who abuse alcohol or drugs or act out aggressively are actually trying to relieve the pain from some loss. And whenever possible, it's important for an adolescent to get back on track developmentally. They'll have to do it without some of the resources they had before, but they can learn to cope.[6]

Teenagers need to accomplish three important psychological tasks as well. Dr. Keith Olson describes them in this manner:

1. To develop a sense of personal identity that consistently establishes who he or she is as an integrated individual throughout each life role, separate and different from every other person.
2. To begin the process of establishing relationships that are characterized by commitment and intimacy.
3. To begin making decisions leading toward training and entry into a particular occupation.[7]

What happens in adulthood is really based upon the successful completion of these tasks. Part of the crisis of adolescence will be tied in to these developmental issues.

HOW ARE ADOLESCENTS SUCCESSFUL IN CREATING THEIR OWN IDENTITY?

To be successful as an adult, adolescents need to move away from the childhood dependence upon their parents. But this move toward independence often creates a crisis for the adolescent's parents because they are not in control of how this movement occurs. If the parents resist the breaking away, stress occurs for both parties. We'll look at the following 11 normal breaking-away behaviors:

1. Adolescents need quality time alone and with their peer group. They usually are neither eager for family get-togethers

nor as interested in them as they used to be.

2. They may withdraw from involvements, including church attendance. They tend to be secretive around their parents and do not confide in them like they used to as children. Parents who use their children for their own identity needs and self-esteem have difficulty handling this lack of confiding and wish for a return to the "good old days."

3. Teenagers are reluctant to accept advice or criticism from their parents. They are overly sensitive to suggestions because their insecurities seem to arise when they are given advice or criticism. Their lack of properly formed identity and low self-esteem tend to make them more sensitive at this time. They resent criticism. Discipline, criticism and advice are interpreted as domination, and they feel out of control. They need to be in control.

4. Rebellion is a very common reaction. But the more secure the teenager, the less rebellion there is. The more insecure, the more radical the rebellion.[8]

5. During the late teenage years, allegiance and commitment are shifted more to individual peers of both the opposite and same sex.

6. Increased involvement with peers often creates anxiety for parents. Evenings spent talking on the telephone and constant demands to be with friends are the norm. Changes in manners of dress, speech, musical tastes, enjoyable activities and general behavior are usually related to the peer group.[9]

7. Adolescents often are absorbed with their own world and are limited by self-centeredness. They react in a subjective manner. If they are self-critical, they tend to assume others are also critical of them. They think of themselves as unique and special. They are satisfied with old friendships that sustain them rather than wanting to build new friendships. Moving to a new location at this time of life can be traumatic.

8. Social fears are high on their list. They do not like feeling rejected, disapproved of or ignored, nor do they want to look

foolish or be out of control. Authority figures are among those to be feared.

9. The thinking process of adolescents is different from that of children. They recognize possibilities as well as actualities. They tend to overidealize and think conceptually in abstract and universal terms. In addition to a search for personal identity, their strong sense of idealism creates anger and frustration. They know the way things should be and are intolerant when things are not that way. Their views on life's issues and values can fluctuate daily.

10. They are overly dependent on feedback from their peers and may behave differently in different groups.

11. When faced with an unexpected crisis, they may lose the ability to see value in things. They become disillusioned, and when this occurs, they tend to become cynical and even degrade others. This all leads to a resistance to change that makes counseling more difficult.[10]

WHAT ARE THE CAUSES OF DEPRESSION IN ADOLESCENCE?

The causes of adolescent depression are very much the same as adult depression, with the transitional struggles thrown in as well.

Keep in mind that the concept of loss in the life of the adolescent and your involvement in his or her life have important implications. As you express both respect and interest in the teen as a person, this may provide a relationship that helps to make up for some of the teen's loss and will aid in lifting his or her depression. As a result, you will be able to direct the young person's efforts usefully toward coming to grips with what is creating his or her depression and finding some solutions.

Many of a teen's actions stem from loss, which again must be seen from the adolescent's perspective. Rejection by another, losing an athletic event, having to wear braces at 16 and the like are real losses to an adolescent. So are fantasized losses.

Real Versus Fantasized Loss

A fantasized loss is an unconscious or unrealistic concern that causes the person to feel deprived in the absence of any objective evidence to justify this overconcern.[11]

A very important difference between a real and a fantasized loss is this: A real loss tends to bring on a reactive depression in which the depression characteristics are readily observable. A fantasized loss tends to be the type of depression in which the manifestations are not apparent to the young person or to an untrained helper.

Death

There are other more serious losses. Grief is a part of loss, and the type of grief will differ with the type of loss. When adolescents lose a parent in death, they often deny it in order to protect themselves from this threatening experience and the ensuing feelings. If the relationship was close, there will be intense pain and anger at being left alone.

When an adolescent loses a parent in death, he or she is often cut adrift. Van Ornum and Mordock describe the process in this way:

> Adolescence is a time of separation from parents. When this happens abruptly, the gradual process required for healthy identification with a parent cannot take place. Adolescents first develop their own ideas by resisting the ideas of others. Through rebellion they discover who they are. When a parent dies, the process of resisting, developing independent ideas, and then rediscovering the parent's viewpoint has not been allowed to come full circle. Death of a parent can throw an adolescent into a tailspin.[12]

The teen becomes preoccupied with himself or herself, and this may create worries. For example, if a parent died because of an illness, a young person may develop intense fears of sickness, pain or disfigurement.

Encourage the adolescent to express his or her anger. The teen does not need to judge the anger or experience the judgment of others against his or her anger.

Other adults need to be available to fill in the gap that the death of a parent creates; this will help the young person continue to develop.

The death of a brother or sister also brings a sense of loss, but there are disruptive feelings because of the mixture of both positive and negative feelings that siblings have for one another.

If an adolescent loses a friend in death, there is strong anxiety. Teenagers are aware that adults die, but the death of a peer is shocking and unnerving. They have to face their own mortality at an age when they are not prepared to do so.

Divorce

Another loss that many adolescents face is the divorce of their parents. When this occurs, there is a loss of security and confidence in the future. Anger at the parent who left usually is stronger and lasts longer than if the person had died. In death, the parent did not make a choice to leave. In divorce, the person does have a choice. So why did he or she leave?

The guilt the young person feels over the part he or she thinks he or she played in the divorce is strong and difficult to resolve. The teen does not blame himself or herself for the divorce as much as younger children do; however, the teen may spend more and more time away from home because home is no longer as safe and secure as it once was. The teen may experience too much freedom and temptation that he or she is not yet equipped to handle. The young adult may fear losing his or her friends now. If the person already has a tendency toward depression and withdrawal, it will be accentuated at this time.

The divorce of parents hampers the normal development of the adolescent for a period of time. The adolescent feels abandoned, and his or her need for strength from the family is disrupted. What occurs is the adolescent's acceleration of autonomy—he or she has to grow up too soon. Parents' divorcing can have a lasting effect upon both attitudes and values. The young person becomes disillusioned about commitments and relationships: *If my own parents divorce, who can I depend on? How do I know that if I marry, it will last?*

Symptoms of difficulty with handling parents' divorce include emptiness, fear, concentration problems and fatigue. These teenagers become critical about their parents and their behavior. They feel betrayed and are afraid of talking about their pain and embarrassment for fear of having others see them as a failure. How do they defend against this? Through anger and rage.[13]

Other teens feel relief over the divorce because there is no more fighting. Yet it is difficult to express this. The grief process is involved in both the death of a parent and the divorce of the parents. But in death there is a finality to the grief process, whereas in divorce there is no closure. The hurt and wounds can continue for years.

Illness

Another loss teens face is when a parent, sibling or friend has a chronic, debilitating illness. This creates fear about his or her own vulnerability. The teen's fear may cause him or her to withdraw, which then creates guilt, because the teen is not responding as he or she should.

Friends

Even a friend's moving away brings a sense of loss. The pain suffered is as severe as rejection. The same sense of loss can occur when the person has to change schools or make any other type of move.[14]

Developmental Process

Another factor to consider is that the normal developmental process presents teenagers with a number of real losses and threats to their self-esteem. During this time they are expected to loosen their dependence upon their parents, which they may do. But some are tied closer to their parents than others and are hesitant, whereas others break away as fast as they can. Now they are expected to receive emotional fulfillment from their peer group, which is a far less secure and stable group than their parents. They also are expected to take responsibility for their future and eventually the running of their lives. They are learning to live without some of the previous sources of gratification, which can be another underlying factor for depression.

Remember that the better a teenager is prepared to meet the transitional challenges of adolescence, to give up his or her earlier attachments and to cope with real and fantasized losses, the more likely the teen will avoid depressive episodes during this age. When you are confronted with the depressed teenager, these are some of the issues to consider and deal with in your treatment plan.

HOW DOES DEPRESSION AFFECT DIFFERENT AGED ADOLESCENTS?

It is essential to be able to identify some specifics that are unique to the depressed teenager in a crisis state. Because teenagers are in transition between childhood and adulthood, their depression shares the characteristics of the depression of both these periods of life. Some of their depressions are related to their developmental struggles.

Because they are separating from their parents and endeavoring to establish their own identities, they will frequently experience the feeling of loss. And as we have seen before, loss is at the basis of much depression. Probably the most common loss of the adolescent is that of self-esteem.

Depression is actually more normal for this developmental stage than for some other stages. Unfortunately, some of the depression of adolescence goes undiagnosed because the person is considered to be going through the normal adolescent throes of adjustment.

Young Adolescents

There is a difference in the depression of adolescents aged 13 to 17 as compared with older adolescents. Teenagers at the younger end of the scale have strong needs to deny self-critical attitudes. They avoid admitting personal concerns to others. Because of this, they do not exhibit or even experience the hopelessness, gloom and self-depreciation seen in adult depression. They are also at a developmental stage in which, like children, they are oriented less to thinking about something than to doing something. They are more likely to express their depression through overt behavior than through the introspective preoccupations that characterize adults.

As you observe the behaviors of younger adolescents, you will note three manifestations of depression: (1) some of them are reflective of the inner state of being depressed; (2) some represent efforts to get rid of or to avoid the depression; and (3) others are an appeal for help. Let's look at the symptoms of early adolescent depression from these three manifestations.

Depression reflecting the inner state of being depressed usually is evidenced by three major symptoms:

1. The teenager experiences an excessive amount of fatigue. If he or she complains of fatigue even after adequate rest, it could be that the teen is suffering from depression that he or she can neither resolve nor express.
2. Hypochondriasis is another symptom. Young adolescents are concerned about the ongoing changes that are normal for their age group, but when there is an excessive preoccupation with their bodily changes, it could reflect depression concerns about their own inadequacy. The young person has difficulty admitting this to himself or herself and expressing it to others.
3. Inability to concentrate is possibly the most common complaint that leads the person to seek help. It may be seen in school performance but may appear in other situations as well. The young adolescent often denies being apathetic or having anything on his or her mind that is bothersome. You may hear the teen say that his or her schoolwork is going downhill. No matter how hard the teen studies, he or she cannot grasp the material or retain it. When you hear this, look for depression.

Depression characterized by attempts to defend against the depression reflects three very common symptoms:

1. *Boredom or restlessness.* One way to avoid feeling depressed is to keep busy so that you can keep your mind off things. Because the young teenager wants so much to avoid the feeling of depression, his or her activity level may become excessive. The teen seems to be driven and is very restless and bored. He or she alternates between a high level of interest in new activities

and becoming quickly disenchanted with them. Notice those teens who have difficulty handling the routines of life and are constantly searching for new and exciting activities. This may be a defense against depression.

2. *Fight or flight.* These adolescents frequently dread being alone and look for constant companionship. They move from person to person searching for those who can give them time and attention. They want people for company who are not preoccupied with their own activity. Unfortunately, this frantic search leaves them with little time for their necessary functions. Sleep, chores, obligations and schoolwork receive the leftovers. On the other hand, some teenagers prefer to be alone because being around others increases their fear of being rejected or abandoned. If the teenager takes this avenue of avoidance, he or she will pursue his or her own private activities with a tremendous intensity. The teen may have a higher interest in hobbies, pets or anything that does not hold the potential for the rejection he or she so greatly fears.

3. The third manifestation of depression is represented by some type of an *appeal for help.* This is usually evidenced by behavior that may include temper tantrums, running away, stealing and a variety of other rebellious and antisocial acts. Acting out in an attempt to deal with depression has definite purposes for the teenager. When the teen is engaged in some act, if it is exciting and new, it helps him or her avoid coming to grips with what is bothersome. If the new behavior is getting positive feedback from the teen peer group, his or her self-image is bolstered. The behavior may also be manifested by a person who does not have much impulse control, and this in itself is a cry for help. It is a message to others that the teen is in pain and cannot handle his or her own life. The teen's misbehavior is rarely carried on secretly. The actions are usually public in some way and conducted in such a manner that he or she is going to get caught.[15]

Older Adolescents

Older adolescents tend to manifest their depression in ways similar to those of adults. Yet they may still express depression indirectly through maladaptive behavior. What are these manifestations?

Drug use is one means of expression. Yes, there are a multitude of reasons for drug use, but some of it is related to depression. It can serve several purposes: (1) it can help the young person defend himself or herself against being depressed; (2) the secrecy of obtaining illegal drugs can add a sense of excitement to the person's life; and (3) sharing the drug experience offers peer relationships.

Sexual promiscuity also is used as a defense against depression—more frequently by girls than boys. The attention and the feeling of being needed and wanted can overcome the feelings of sadness and being alone and unloved.

Suicidal behavior is another manifestation. A significant rise in suicidal behavior and actual suicide with both early and later adolescents is occurring. It may be a manifestation of depression, or it may be tied in with other causes.

WHAT CAUSES TEEN SUICIDE?

Over the years many researchers and doctors have tried to determine what motivates a person to take their life. Several have attempted to classify the various types of adolescent suicide. Based upon research, five types of adolescent suicide have been suggested:

1. Some adolescents take their life because of psychosis or personality disintegration. You have probably heard of the teen who experienced auditory hallucinations ordering him or her to die.

2. Other teens kill themselves because of intense rage at another person, which cannot be expressed. As the rage churns around inside the adolescent, it's turned back against the person. It could be said that self-murder could represent the murder of someone else.

3. Some use suicide as retaliation for actual or imagined abandonment. The teen hopes his or her suicide will accomplish
two things: (1) help the teen stay two steps ahead of the other
person (You can't do anything to me. I'm outta here. I'm leaving); or (2) demonstrate power as a reaction to feeling helpless.

4. I've seen some use suicide as blackmail or even manipula-
tion—"If you don't do what I say, I'll kill myself." Threats such
as this are used as a source of power. Sometimes a teen threatens and then makes an attempt not really intending to take
his or her life, but something goes amiss. Sometimes a teen
takes his or her life in order to be reunited with someone they
love who has died. This could be another teen, a boyfriend or
girlfriend or even a family member. This occurs when the teen
is unable to move through the grieving process.

5. The most common and most successfully treated is suicide as
a cry for help. The teen has a problem and would like some
other way of dealing with it. They are at a place where nothing
has worked. They feel blocked, so the only resource is suicide.[16]

Indicators

Among the greatest tragedies in the world today are child and adolescent
suicide, which have numerous indications. One symptom by itself may
not be overly alarming, but the more of these you see, the greater the risk.
If you see some of these indications, look carefully for any of the others
and then intervene. If you feel the risk is high, don't leave the child or
adolescent alone. Consider the following indications (remember, some of
these may be couched in their terminology or vocabulary). These are
applicable for both children and adolescents:

- Look for previous suicide attempts. The risk is higher if they
were recent.
- Some express their intent by talking, writing, reading or drawing about themes of death or depression.
- Verbal suicide threats or comments of futility, such as, "No one

will miss me"; "They'll be better off if I weren't here" or "I wish I was dead," are messages.

- Look for any talk about self-anger or hopelessness.
- Self-destructive acts can include cutting or even scratching the body.
- Look for recent family or friendship losses. It could be death, divorce or even a breakup.
- Behavior changes such as withdrawal, moodiness or aggression.
- Frequent residence moves or instability at home.
- Physical symptoms involving sleeping or eating.
- Increasing isolation from family or friends.
- Additional losses which were traumatic.
- Friends or family members who in the past attempted or committed suicide.
- Mood swings ranging from gloom and depression to jubilance or euphoria. Sometimes the decision to take one's life is the cause for this change.
- Valued possessions are given away. This could be a form of saying good-bye or a cry for help.
- The expression of extreme anger or disappointment. It could be toward others, themselves or the world in general.[17]

There are some additional factors which lend themselves to an adolescent suicide profile. The following are additional ways of viewing which teens are most likely to take their life:

- 84 percent have a stepparent;
- 72 percent have at least one parent absent;
- 20 percent who complete suicide are alcoholics;
- 70 percent are firstborn;
- 16 percent have an alcoholic parent;
- 22 percent have suicidal mothers;
- 42 percent have witnessed physical abuse between family members;

- 30 percent have school problems;
- 52 percent of events leading to an attempt are related to marital problems of parents;
- A high percentage of suicidal adolescents have tragic deaths among their close relatives; and
- A high percentage of suicidal adolescents are more likely to be above their grade level academically.[18]

Behavior

Child and adolescent suicide also can be detected through behavioral changes.

Loneliness. Loneliness—with its accompanying depression—is a key factor for those who actually complete suicide. These teens tend to be isolated rather than simply withdrawn. William Blackburn gives a simple explanation of how a faltering support system can lead to suicidal behavior:

The sources of support become shaken foundations. When the foundations become shaky, some young people turn to alcohol and other drugs for solace. The agents, when mixed with a teenager's romantic notions of death, a society that glorifies violence, and easy access to suicide, combine into a powerfully lethal mixture that spells death for more and more adolescents. Finally, suicide becomes suicide. Suicide attempted or completed plants the idea of self-generated death in the minds of others. Also, suicide in the family especially pulls other family members closer to that option.[19]

Often an adolescent responds with behavior that has a hidden message. For example, self-mutilating teens—through their deliberate and radical behavior—express their independence. This behavior can also be their way of trying to control their fear of sexual thoughts, as well as their violent and aggressive impulses. In talking to a young person, you may hear him or her say, "It's my body, and I will do with it what I want, and nobody can stop me. Just try. It won't work." Any efforts to control their outward behavior without dealing with their feelings will be ineffective.[20]

Suicide. Schools today are concerned about student suicide. Many have developed programs of intervention and education following a suicide. The same approach could be used by churches.

A recent study showed that with adolescent suicide there *is* a tendency for suicide contagion to occur unless discussions and psychological debriefings take place with the other students.[21]

Alienation and Personality Restriction. Older, depressed adolescents feel apathetic and out of touch with themselves and others. They do have some social contact with others that gives the pretense of intimacy and belonging; however, the group often reinforces depression because of the membership. This alienation and personality restriction is characterized by inaction. The young person avoids anything that might lead to a failure and any aspiration that could bring disappointment. The teen will not expose himself or herself to any heartache. The teen is not a risk taker.

CHAPTER 20

HELPING THE ADOLESCENT

How do you proceed to help the transitional adolescent? As you work with an adolescent through an actual loss, help him or her through your discussion of the event to take a different perspective such as seeing it as less tragic and permanent, if that is possible. If the loss is a fantasized loss, your task will be more difficult. You may need to use a more speculative interpretation of what has occurred to help the teen discover what has previously been unknown to him or her.[1]

Some adolescents who experience stress and crisis respond by running away. This is a logical solution for them. They not only run away from stress, but they also run toward something. They usually run toward less-alienated feelings and additional control of their lives. When youth are disillusioned by a crisis, they need to reestablish commitment bonds, increase their self-esteem and find purpose in life. Teens want these things to fall into place immediately, but they fail to realize that they need to work through the shock state of the crisis that is blocking their efforts to end the stress. It takes time and patience on your part to see results.

Remember that insight, in and of itself, is not sufficient. Teens need to do something about the symptoms and the direction of their life. You may become frustrated in counseling adolescents, because you may be putting adult expectations for change on people who are not yet adults. Because of some teenagers' depressive helplessness, they may expect too much from you, including an instant, magical cure.

> **It is common for an adolescent to say, "I just don't know what to do. You tell me what to do."**

It is common for an adolescent to say, "I just don't know what to do. You tell me what to do." As you know, this can be a deadly trap if you respond as the teen wishes. If you do respond affirmatively, then the counselee is directing the counseling session, but you are supposed to be in charge of what occurs. However, if you don't give the young adult the answer or help as he or she perceives it, you'll receive the brunt of the teen's anger in one way or another. This is just part of the risk of counseling.

LEARNING TO COUNSEL TEENS

When adolescents come in to see you, either on their own or because someone made them, you will see a range of reactions. Some will hesitate to converse with you. You may have to use indirect procedures, such as reflecting their silence or responding to their nonverbal communication. Those who are reluctant to talk are usually afraid. They fear their own vulnerability and not being able to find the words to tell you what they are feeling. They also fear your domination in the session and the possibility of your telling others what they will say. Other teens may get angry at you, however, and your resolution should be to let them and just accept it. Let them know that you may get angry, too, if you were in their place.[2]

Referral

Not all of us can work effectively with teens, and we need to face that possibility. Referral is not a sign of weakness on our part, but it is a positive step in order to give the counselee in crisis a greater amount of help, whether it be a child, adolescent or adult.

> **Referral is not a sign of weakness on our part, but it is a positive step in order to give the counselee in crisis a greater amount of help.**

Dr. Keith Olson suggests some characteristics of those who work effectively with depressed adolescents. Evaluate yourself on the basis of the following list:

1. They have a very strong capacity for developing immediate, warm and empathetic contacts with depressed youth.
2. They are dependable and consistent in their responses.
3. They control themselves and the counseling setting through an intelligent use of their authority that in no way demeans or devalues the adolescent counselee.
4. Their presentation of themselves offers a positive picture for the formation of an ego ideal for the counselee.
5. They tolerate being mistrusted without feeling angrily defensive or self-doubt.
6. They develop relationships comfortably with their teenage counselees that are marked by narcissistic self-absorption on the part of their counselees.
7. They are very encouraging and supportive of their counselees' movements toward independence.
8. They tolerate their counselees' hostile, angry attacks without reacting with anger, defensiveness or self-doubt.
9. They should be counselors who because of their appearance,

personality, counseling style and overall presentation are generally accepted and well received by teenagers.[3]

Confidentiality

Adolescents may not be overly impressed with seeing a minister for a crisis situation unless a relationship already has been established. To help the counseling process, you need to inform the person about any limits to confidentiality. The adolescent is concerned that you may inform his or her parents. The teen needs to know that what he or she says will be held in confidence. However, you may want to tell the teen that if he or she is involved in some kind of destructive behavior, and if the teen cannot stop it after working with you, you may have to resort to letting others know what he or she tells you for his or her own protection, even though the teen may not want you to do so.[4] Above all, know the laws of your state and county.

Positive and Hopeful

Because of the adolescent's tendency to focus on the negative and on unpleasant experiences, you will need to bring out the positive as well as attempt to reflect hopeful feelings. The teen will feel more capable as you help him or her develop strengths. The teen has solved problems before; therefore, help him or her to remember how he or she accomplished prior success. There are times to relate what has worked for you, but be sure it doesn't appear to be advice or moralizing.

Communication

In working with adolescents, you need to encourage them to write out their feelings, since many teens have difficulty expressing themselves face-to-face. Writing is private and helps them uncover avoided or denied feelings. By writing, they focus on their situation and feelings and become involved in looking at the feelings without embarrassment.

T. J. Tuzil, in working with adolescents, has suggested the use of a daily writing log. As a young person works through a crisis experience, this kind of writing helps the teen clarify feelings and raises his or her level of objectivity.

The daily log is organized into two different categories: "situations" and "myself." Using the "situation" column, the adolescent writes accounts of at least two situations that happened but that he or she did not initiate. The teen then writes his or her reactions to what occurred and how he or she feels about the reactions. This is important since so many crises happen to the person from an outside source.

In the "myself" column, the young person writes actions or behaviors that he or she chose to initiate by providing reasons, reactions and feelings. After completing this log for several days or weeks, the person becomes more aware of his or her feelings and why he or she behaves in a certain way.[5]

Sometimes writing letters, which are not sent, helps an adolescent work through his or her crisis feelings. For example, the teen might write to a parent or sibling who is no longer there because of divorce or separation.

Support System

If an adolescent is disillusioned by crisis, help him or her develop a support system, build his or her self-esteem and discover meaning and purpose. How? By following the steps necessary to help any person in crisis (see chapters 7-9), but especially through empathy, listening and problem solving. A young person receives support when you listen and understand his or her feelings. The teen wants his or her point of view to be heard and respected. As you listen to the young adult, he or she in turn will listen to you as you offer your suggestions.

HELPING IN A TIME OF TRAUMA

I received a phone call one morning. My friend Mike said, "Norm, I hope you don't mind, but I gave your name to the principal of the middle school my daughter attends. You probably heard about that family in Irvine where the stepfather killed his wife and stepson. Well, his stepson was my daughter's friend and sat next to her. Her whole class is traumatized and needs help." What would you have done to help those students if you had been asked to come in and help? These situations are happening more and more.

It could happen not only in your area schools but also in your church. The shootings at Columbine High School and Wedgewood Baptist Church in Texas are not isolated incidents.

When the twin towers in New York were destroyed, it was witnessed by students in Lower Manhattan's Stuyvesant High School. The school was evacuated and used for awhile as a ground zero personnel center. Hundreds of these students gathered in Greenwich Village the Sunday after 9/11 and painted two giant commemorative murals to be mounted on their campus. They also created a commemorative issue of the student newspaper, *The Spectator*. The contributions to this paper actually were collective narratives of the kind found to be a healing element when a tragedy occurs. The following are some examples:

> A reporting of the traumatic event and the witnesses' part in it: "So what did you learn in school today?" On September 11, I gave a horribly truthful answer to this familiar question: "I learned that it is easy to tell a falling body from a falling piece of debris because bodies fall much faster." We stood in the ninth floor chemistry lab for almost an hour, shocked by the sight of men and women in expensive clothes glancing back into what was once their office before throwing themselves toward the chaotic sidewalk hundreds of feet below. Some appeared to have had a running start while others stood at the edge until the flames licked their skin and pushed them off into the endless cloud of smoke. Some held hands, while others preferred to dive alone into whatever fate followed that smoke . . . teachers' authority disappeared as each burst into hysterical tears. By ten o'clock, there were six teachers lined up next to the four of us, crying on each others' shoulders just like we were.[6]
>
> Thoughts/feelings about the traumatic event and worldview: "It was shocking. It made you realize how vulnerable we are as a country, how unprepared. It was so easy to do what they did. The scariest part of it, for me, is that we're fighting an unconventional war . . . there's no military base to bomb, no country to target . . . I'm very doubtful of our ability to eliminate terrorism."[7]

In another traumatic event, in El Cajon, California, a high school student opened fire with a shotgun on students and faculty, wounding four:

The principal used the public address system to announce the emergency and evacuate students. When school reopened, the faculty and staff noticed that students were responding with high anxiety whenever the principal would use the P.A. system. The principal began to make a daily practice of getting on the P.A. and wishing the students a good day. She would reassure them that all was well, and then she would proceed to the day's announcements. She noticed that this practice served to desensitize students to the sound of her voice on the P.A. and helped reduce their trauma-related anxiety.[8]

What are the results of trauma impacting an adolescent? They're likely to engage in the following:

- They act out their distress through isolation, drug and alcohol abuse, sexual activity, violence, delinquency, running away and suicidal expressions.
- They experience low self-esteem and are quick to blame themselves for the way they responded to the trauma.
- They seem to grow too old too fast. Some develop lifestyles years ahead of where they should be.
- Their anger is often displaced toward those at school since they're safer than others.
- Their concern is with themselves. They will interpret an event on the basis of how it affects them.[9]

When adolescents experience a crisis or trauma, they often regress, which is why a knowledge of child-counseling procedures is important. It may be helpful to refer back to chapters 16 through 19 to review what children and adolescents have said was helpful and what wasn't.

The author of *Trauma in the Lives of Children* suggests that any type of help for an adolescent requires three elements.

The first is *reliving*. The young person needs to face whatever the trauma was and relive it by revisiting the memories with as much detail as possible. Questions to help bring out the emotions that are part of this experience are as follows:

- What do you remember seeing?
- What were some of the sounds?
- Were there any tastes that occurred?
- Do you recall any touch that may have occurred?
- What were your reactions or feelings at the time?

Do you see what details you are helping them remember? Visual, auditory, olfactory, tactile and kinesthetic.

Another question to help round out the picture is, What was occurring or what happened just prior to this event? It's important to complete the picture by describing events leading up to the incident.

You also need to discover the meaning this event has in the life of the adolescent. If you are approachable and trust is established, children and adolescents will open up to tell you what happened.

Using direct-prompt statements can be beneficial. Some direct-prompt statements are as follows:

- Experiencing something like that can knock a person off their feet.
- When something like that happens, it's hard not to be afraid.
- I guess I'd be kind of angry if that happened.

The second element is the *releasing* of feelings. Many feelings can be bound up and jumbled together in memories and interpretations. Memories of trauma hurt. Many don't want to remember, and a number of children, adolescents and adults repress the memories. Additionally, some people may not want to revisit the memories. Feelings sometimes come out all at once like a flood, or they seep out slowly or in spurts. Remember, many teens are hesitant to share feelings that may poorly reflect upon them. They don't want to look bad in anyone's eyes, and they are hesitant to open up since their feelings can be frightening.

The third element is *reorganizing.* Simply put, it means helping teens sort through their thoughts, feelings and emotional responses about what happened, discovering their own responsibility and personal control over events and identifying former and present attitudes toward people, places and events in their life. Since the security of the past has been disrupted, you are helping the adolescent "reconstruct the present based upon changed perceptions regarding the past."[10]

CHOOSING APPROPRIATE COUNSELING STYLES

Adolescents struggle with their feelings. They need specific suggestions and guidelines. What would you suggest to the teen who is sitting there and states that he or she is full of guilt over the loss of a person in his or her life? How would you help the teen? After you've created a safe environment and talked about his or her guilt, what guidelines would you offer? The following are a few adapted from *The Grieving Teen:*

1. Help them distinguish between feelings of guilt and regret.
2. Ask them to list what they feel guilt about as well as the reasons for it.
3. Ask them to make a list of reasons of their regrets.
4. Which of these regrets are the worst? Prioritize them.
5. Identify what they could do now about each item.
6. Write everything they feel bad about on a balloon and let it go in the air.
7. Help them accept that they will have unanswered questions.
8. If they're a Christian, talk with them about how they get rid of guilt and apply forgiveness.
9. Encourage them to write a letter to the person they lost and express what they wish they had expressed before. Take it to the gravesite or the person's room and read it aloud. They could then ask for forgiveness.

10. Suggest that they use a journal to retain thoughts and feelings as well as to note improvement.
11. Identify what they could do to help others at this time.
12. What have they learned from this experience?
13. What were the positive things they did in their relationship with the person they lost?
14. Teach teens how to forgive themselves.
15. Talk with them about what they will do differently in their relationship with others now.[11]

Styles Adolescents Prefer

Adolescents themselves have identified what they need as well as what they don't need in a trauma or crisis. The following is what works:

My mom or dad . . .

- allowed me to talk;
- showed warmth and acceptance;
- listened well;
- respected my privacy;
- showed patience;
- came through in the past;
- showed understanding;
- made helpful suggestions; and
- was there when I needed them.

Styles to Avoid

Teens also identified three types of adult responses that actually hurt them.

Withholding. One style is *withholding*, in which parents focus upon their own needs rather than the child's. They also deny the seriousness of the child's or adolescent's experiences and discount their feelings.

Incompetence. The second style is *incompetence*. It is when parents glibly give false reassurance, discourage discussion about the problem and have difficulty themselves handling what happened or fulfilling their role as parents.

Reactive. The third type is the *reactive* or *escapist* parent who makes false assumptions about the child's role in the incident, which usually leads to blaming the child. Then they shut down talking about it.

These three styles—if reflected during a child's crisis—lead to adolescent problems.[12]

When helping a child or adolescent (individually or in a group), the following are some types of interaction that need to be avoided after a crisis.

Too Emotional. Whoever is helping needs to avoid *falling apart*. When this happens, it tells a child or adolescent that you can't really be trusted with what he or she has shared with you. It is essential for you to stay in emotional control. If you know it's a difficult day or you're beginning to get shaky, hand off your responsibilities to someone else. Remember, you are to take care of the child, not vice versa. Empathy must be in balance.

Too Wordy. Do not share what you're not sure of or what isn't true. Just say, "I'm not sure, but I'll find out for you." It's a matter of trust. Don't say, "Everything will be alright," unless you are 100 percent sure you know what that means and that it will be alright. *False promises* cripple your credibility.

Too Judgmental. Avoid any kind of *judgments* at this point, whether verbal or nonverbal. Your focus is on the needs of the child rather than what we think ought to be or should have been.

Too Inquisitive. You are not an *inquisitor*. Constant questioning can overwhelm and push a child or adolescent into silence. When questioning, you need to be gentle and give the teen time to think and reflect about what you've asked.

Too Reserved. If you don't know what to do or say, don't withdraw. Children and adolescents need helpers around to support, normalize and affirm them.[13]

Styles to Use When Relating to School

Because school is a major part of the adolescent's life, issues related to school need to be addressed. If there's been a loss or trauma in the adolescent's life and it's time for the teen to rebuild his or her routine and reenter school, what are some of the concerns? The teen may wonder who knows what happened and who doesn't know. The young adult may dread seeing classmates for the first time, because he or she is wondering what they're thinking or will say.

They may be wondering if they'll be embarrassed or treated differently because of what happened. Will their friends want to hang around with them or come over knowing there's a difference and a loss in their life? How much should be shared with others? What if they start crying in class? Should they get back into sports or cheerleading or go to the prom?

You as a counselor should bring up all of these issues and ask if they've been wondering about them. This will not only normalize what they're feeling and wondering, but it will help the teens receive some guidelines and answers. Some of the suggestions you could make to the teens are as follows:

1. Let your friends know what happened. Write a letter indicating what happened and give it out as well as sending e-mails or asking the school counselors to assist in getting the word out.
2. Before resuming classes, you should visit school to pick up assignments and see your school counselor.
3. Be sure you know how to contact parents during your first day back.
4. Contact each teacher to let them know that you're back and how your life is going.
5. Let teachers know if it is difficult to concentrate or complete homework.
6. Write down assignments on a regular pad and enlist your friends to help remind you.
7. You may need to alter your study habits in terms of length and time.
8. Don't be hard on yourself. It will take weeks to get back into a new groove.
9. Ask for assistance from teachers to help you prioritize missed assignments.

10. Most important, don't try to go it alone. Friends are there to help at a time like this. Let friends know what you need from them. When they offer help, accept it and show your gratitude. If they say dumb statements, be patient. Most adults don't know what to say. If a friend sees something in you or something you're doing, listen to them. You may not be objective.[14]

RECOMMENDED RESOURCES

Resources to Use with Adolescents in Grief

Fitzgerald, Helen. *The Grieving Child*. New York: Simon and Schuster, 2000. Be sure to read this in advance, as many of the suggestions for the teen you can use in counseling them.

Pernu, C., ed. *Help for the Hard Times: Getting Through Loss*. Center City, MN: Hazelden Information Education, 1995.

USING SCRIPTURE AND PRAYER AND MAKING REFERRALS

As you minister to people in all types of crisis situations, you will find this is a tremendous opportunity to lead people to Christ, to help believers become aware of the strengthening power and comfort of the Word of God and to assist them in the practical application of the Scriptures in their lives. The Word of God can be used in a healthy way to give insight and strength. Or it can be merely tacked on to the person's problem or used to increase guilt and distress.

SCRIPTURE

It is vital that you be sensitive to the leading of the Holy Spirit concerning when to bring in Scripture and which Scripture to discuss. Be sure you do not shortcut the person's expression of feelings or grief by bringing in a verse too soon. Sometimes because of our own anxiety or lack of knowing what to say to someone's angry questions, we rattle off verses indicating

> **It is vital that you be sensitive to the leading of the Holy Spirit concerning when to bring in Scripture and which Scripture to discuss.**

that God is in charge, everything will work out according to His will or there is a purpose in your suffering.

The following are two questions to ask the counselee:

1. What passages of Scripture have been of help to you during this time?
2. Which passage do you feel would help you right now?

As you discuss a passage with your counselee, you might ask, "How do you feel this passage can assist you at this time? Let's talk about what it means to you and how you see it as being useful."

Questions They'll Ask

One of the questions you might hear during a time of crisis is, "Where is God in all of this?" That is an excellent question. Where is He? He is present just as He was before the problem occurred. If you are asked that question, respond with a question of your own: "Where is God for you right now? I hear you questioning where He is and that is an honest question. We feel abandoned. In fact, you may feel that if God were around, this wouldn't have happened." Some counselees may really mean what they say in their question, whereas others are just venting their anger. Let them express their questioning; do not be threatened by it. You may have asked the same question at times. At the proper time you can respond to the question.

Discoveries They'll Make

These types of questions raise an important issue surrounding God's omnipresence. This concept is important for you as the counselor to understand as well as for the counselee. You need to realize that during the most painful and difficult counseling sessions, God is there with you. And as the counselee is guided and directed to discover and define his or her difficulty, God is present, working in the person's life.

A person discovers God's omnipresence not by envisioning that God is everywhere but by recognizing that He already *is* there. This can be dealt with through two means: (1) the counseling session and (2) the assignments between sessions. The Scriptures dealing with the concept of God's omnipresence are Joshua 1:9; Psalms 16:11; 23:4; 73:28; 121:1-8; Matthew 28:20 and Hebrews 13:5.

The following list contains specific ways to help a counselee understand the meaning of God's omnipresence in his or her life. The Scriptures can be interchanged in some of the methods. A few of these assignments accomplish the same aim but in a different way, so you need to select the way of dealing with the concept that will be most comfortable for the counselee:

1. Memorize the last part of Joshua 1:9: "For the LORD your God will be with you wherever you go." Then concentrate on being more conscious of God's presence by selecting something you always have with you. For example, it could be a watch, ring, tiepin or neck chain. Each time you are conscious of that item, say the verse and know that God is there with you.

2a. Read Joshua 1:9; Psalms 16:11; 23:4; 73:28; 121:1-8; Matthew 28:20 and Hebrews 13:5. Then identify the characteristic of God that these verses describe.

b. Select one passage and memorize it.

c. Write a paragraph describing what your life would be like during the next week if you were to be more aware of this attribute of God.

3a. Choose a second passage and follow the instructions for 2b and 2c.

b. Choose a third passage and follow the instructions for 2b and 2c.

c. Write one of these verses on a card and put it in a prominent place where you spend a lot of time (i.e., the kitchen sink, bulletin board, desk, refrigerator and so on).

4a. Read Psalm 139:7-12 and rephrase it.

  b. List at least 15 different places where you will be this week and write a paragraph explaining how this passage will apply to your life in those situations.

5. Describe your life tomorrow if you were to be consciously aware of God's presence every hour of the day.[1]

Scripture They'll Consult

The following Scriptures are organized by category. When you are struggling with loneliness, go to the comfort section and look up all or one of the Scriptures provided in that category. This is a great tool to use and resembles that of a concordance.

Comfort
Numbers 14:9
Deuteronomy 31:6
Psalm 27:10
Psalm 46:7
Psalm 73:23
Psalm 94:14
Psalm 103:17
Isaiah 41:17
Matthew 28:20
John 6:37-39
Romans 8:38-39

Peace
Exodus 33:14
Numbers 6:24-26
Psalm 85:8
Psalm 119:165
Isaiah 26:3
Isaiah 32:17
Isaiah 57:2

Matthew 11:29-30
John 14:27
Romans 5:1-2
Ephesians 2:14
Colossians 3:15

Fear
Deuteronomy 1:17
Deuteronomy 7:21
1 Chronicles 16:25-26
Nehemiah 4:14
Psalm 4:8
Psalm 28:7
Psalm 56:3
Proverbs 16:6
Isaiah 35:4
Isaiah 41:10
Jeremiah 15:20
Joel 3:16
2 Corinthians 1:10
Philippians 4:9

Hebrews 13:6

Anxiety
Genesis 28:15
Job 34:12
Psalm 20:7
Psalm 50:15
Psalm 55:22
Psalm 68:19
Psalm 86:7
Proverbs 3:5-6
Isaiah 40:11
Isaiah 41:13
Matthew 11:28
John 16:33

For Those Who Feel Weak
1 Chronicles 16:11
Psalm 37:10-11
Psalm 55:18

Psalm 62:11

Psalm 72:13

Psalm 142:3

Psalm 147:6

Isaiah 57:15

Jeremiah 10:6

Habakkuk 3:19

2 Corinthians 12:9

Ephesians 3:16

Despair

Psalm 46:1

Psalm 100:5

Psalm 119:116

Isaiah 40:29

Isaiah 51:6

Jeremiah 32:17

Ezekiel 34:16

Daniel 2:23

Haggai 2:4

Ephesians 1:18

2 Thessalonians 3:3

Hebrews 10:35

James 1:12

Grief

Psalm 34:7

Psalm 71:20-21

Psalm 116:15

Psalm 119:28

Psalm 119:50

Psalm 121:5-8

Isaiah 43:2

2 Corinthians 1:3-4

Times of Trouble

Psalm 9:12

Psalm 34:7

Psalm 37:39-40

Psalm 46:1

Psalm 50:15

Psalm 121:5-8

Psalm 138:7

John 16:33

Feeling Desperate and Depressed

Psalm 30:5

Psalm 34:18

Psalm 40:1-2

Psalm 42:11

Psalm 126:5

Zephaniah 3:17

John 10:10

PRAYER

Prayer is a very important part of counseling. There will be times when you pray during the session and times when you pray during the week for the counselee. Sometime during the counseling, it might be helpful to discover the person's pattern of prayer and what he or she usually

> **Sometime during the counseling, it might be helpful to discover the person's pattern of prayer and what he or she usually prays about.**

prays about. Many Christians have not been taught the meaning and purpose of prayer. Teach your congregation the importance of prayer, and help them experience a meaningful and consistent prayer life. It will be a tremendous resource during the crises of life.

How to Encourage Through Prayer

Ask the counselee, "How can I pray for you at this time?" and "How can I pray for you during this week?" Be sure you let the people know at the next session that you were praying for them. Many counselees have told me that the only thing that kept them functioning and even alive was the knowledge that they knew one person was praying for them.

Sometimes I ask them exactly what they would like me to pray about and allow them to direct me. On other occasions I say, "This is how I'm going to pray for you this week." There will be times when this is what keeps your counselee going. Before you give this request to others or put it on a prayer chain, you need to find out if this is alright with the other person. It is a way of also asking, "Who do you want to know about this?"

How to Determine Appropriate Times for Prayer

Do not feel you should open every counseling session with prayer. The needs of the person you are helping should determine your prayer ministry. Ask yourself and God the question, *Is prayer a resource that is applicable at this time with this person?* Praying for or leading people into prayer when they are reluctant is not helpful.

Additionally, be careful in asking your counselees to pray. They may be angry at God or just not have the words at this time:

> Grief has a way of plundering our prayer life, leaving us feeling immobile and empty.[2]

What People Think of Prayer

Some people feel prayer is a form of magic. They feel that by praying they will influence God to lift the problem and reverse the process. As one person said, "I don't know about prayer and God. When I was sick the last time, I prayed and got better, but this time I prayed and I'm not any better. Where is God?" This is a limited view of prayer and God. Prayer is not just a way to reverse difficulty but a means of giving meaning to what is occurring in our lives.

Some in their prayers will raise the question, "Why, God? Why?" This is not so much a question as it is a protest. It is a normal part of working toward acceptance and greater faith in the midst of adversity. Telling a person he or she should not question at this time, or directing them to another person who never expressed such questions and who had an "outstanding faith and trust in God," creates guilt and is damaging. Each of us progresses through the Christian life at a different rate. Faith is easier for some than for others. Protesting to God and raising questions of Him is one form of prayer. Unfortunately, we may not have included that in our definition of prayer. It is helpful to let the person know that his or her protest is prayer.

You also may find some people who do not want to pray because they say they are bitter and angry toward God. Ask them to imagine God sitting in another chair in the room and telling Him how they feel. As the person does this, you can tell him or her that what was expressed is prayer. God does want us to discuss all of our feelings with Him.

How to Pray for the Counselee

How then do you pray for the counselee? Don't be intrusive with prayer. Ask the counselee if he or she would like you to pray with him or her or for him or her. And don't pray long! Keep it brief but sensitive. If you have the opportunity to pray for someone in the midst of deep difficulty, it is a privilege. I have seen some who pray because they either don't know what to say or are uncomfortable with silence. However, you be the one to pray in order to bring the counselee before God and to His resources.

During this time of stress and crisis, you will be able to discover the person's concept of God. Often his or her prayer pattern prior to or during this time will give you this information. The use of prayer can raise many questions about God. Who is this God that we call on in prayer? What is God's responsibility during life's problems and distresses? What kind of power does God have to relieve a person of distress? Some people find help in accepting their troubles as the will of God. Others refuse to accept this perspective. The book of Job raises many questions regarding the trials and crises of life that people still ask today. God is involved in every crisis and stress situation. He does care.

As you pray for the person, be careful what you ask God to do. It is important that we ask God for His comfort, His strength, His support and His insight. We also need to thank Him for what is going to occur in the future, even though we do not know what is going to happen.

I like what Lloyd Ogilvie says in his book *God's Will in Your Life:*

When we are in a tight spot, not knowing what to do, we need to praise God for the very thing which is causing our tension or pressure. . . . Consistent praise over a period of time conditions us to receive what the Lord has been waiting patiently to reveal to us or release for us.

Prayer is not overcoming God's reluctance to guide us; it puts our wills in a condition to receive what He wills for us. It changes our moods and gives us keen desires.[3]

Reaching this attitude and belief is a process, and it can't be forced upon the person to whom you minister. Through the process of counseling, you can look into the Word and pray, which will help the counselee progress. Consider your own beliefs and practice of prayer. Many helpful and practical books aid us and others in this process.

As you pray, be sure to rely upon the Holy Spirit for instruction in how to pray. Allow the Holy Spirit *to bring to mind through your imagination* the direction needed in prayer. Too often we quickly pray with our own words, which come from our intellect. Our prayer lacks freshness because it reflects our own direction and not that of the Holy Spirit. It is as though we are uncomfortable with silence and feel that we must offer the right sounding prayer. Too often our quick words block out the words the Holy Spirit wants to say to us.

The following are examples of prayers to share:

Prayer When Troubled

O God, You are the Ruler of the universe; to You we commit our lives and trust in You for all our needs.

We don't understand the reason for the problems that we've experienced, nor do we need to. Our intent is to trust fully and to accept fully the gifts you give as necessary and beneficial for us. Teach us to be thankful, even when our immediate reaction is fear and distrust. Help us to be strong in our faith, to seek You, and in every circumstance to give thanks, as this is Your will for our lives.

Finally, Father God, bring us at last into Your presence, where all will be known to us as it has been known to You from before the beginning of time.

Amen.

Prayer at a Time of Divorce

Lord, we feel so alone and abandoned. I know You are still beside us, but help us to be more aware of Your presence and what You might be trying to teach us through this crisis.

Protect us and protect our children. Help us to forgive and to learn to be content—even in times of trial and tribulation.

I know that You desire good for us. Please guide and direct our paths.

Amen.[4]

Prayer When Grieving

O Lord, we have experienced a great tragedy and wrong. We are suffering and grieving over our pain and loss. Please help us. Please come and comfort us in our heartache and grief. Give us wisdom to know how to help one another through this crisis. Give us strength to do the practical things that are necessary. Give us discernment to help each other in our personal and corporate

suffering. Give us renewed faith to trust in You. And give us hope
that we may be vessels of Your goodness and mercy as we wait
upon you.

Amen.[5]

The following prayer I found years ago, which gives clear guidelines
on how to pray at a time of bereavement:

> In his prayer at the home, as well as at the funeral, the pastor
> should identify the feelings of the people and then relate those
> feelings to the God of all grace.
>
> Father, we come today as confused and broken-
> hearted children. We don't understand, but we do trust
> You and know that You are still in control. We cannot
> change the past, but we do need strength for today and
> hope for the future. We know You see our sorrow, and we
> remember that Jesus wept. We're thankful that He is
> here with us to heal the brokenhearted. You know the
> feeling of shock that we have experienced, and You have
> promised to meet our needs.
>
> The pastor has accomplished several things in this prayer so
> far: (1) he has verbalized how people feel and has shown that he
> understands; (2) he has made it clear that God expects us to
> grieve—tears are normal; (3) he has affirmed the presence of the
> Lord; and (4) he has opened the way for God to graciously meet
> their needs. He will express those needs as he continues to pray.[6]

In the book *Praying Our Goodbyes*, the following is an example of a
prayer of a person experiencing an adult transition:

> O Lord of revelation, once again I find myself opening up to
> another life process, full of pain, full of mystery and a certain
> aching wonder. I hear you calling me to face new beginnings, to
> leave the old behind, to discover new and deeper parts of my
> total being. O Lord God, help me to realize that I can be free,

that I am being freed at this present moment. Let me look beyond my own small world and smile on the mysterious way that you allow each one of us to grow into the best of our own uniqueness. I want to live and to love the mystery. I remember the wonder and newness of discovering myself as a person. I recall how I began to respect and love the secret of who I am, of how I began to sense the greater and fuller dimensions of becoming "me." I thank you for all the tastes you have given to me of myself through the crises of my life.[7]

The following prayers are taken from the book *Finding God's Peace in Perilous Times*. This devotional resource was published in response to the tragedy of 9/11.

Dear Lord,
When disaster strikes, we so easily become lost. We have no idea what to do. So we turn to you. Thank you that you are in your holy temple; thank you that you are on your throne in heaven. We know that you are in control; we acknowledge our dependence on you. Thank you for your strength, for your presence within us. Thank you that no matter what happens; we can lean on you, resting in your arms and relying on your steadfastness. Thank you for your unconditional love for us. Amen.[8]

Dear Lord,
When we are "pressed on every side by troubles," help us to recognize your presence. Remind us that you are a sovereign God who sees the whole picture, while we see just our present situation. Thank you for your reassuring promise of joys to come that will last forever. Amen.[9]

Dear Lord,
What comfort it gives us to know that you are mindful of everything—everything—that concerns us. You are intimately involved with even the smallest details that affect our souls. May we trust

in this, Lord, even when our world seems to crumble around us. Let us not forget that you still hold us in the palm of your hand. Amen.[10]

Dear Lord,

You know that when we experience great loss, it feels like a light has gone out inside of us and nothing can ever turn it back on again. We know that only you can fill that empty place in the canyon of sorrow that has been left in our hearts. Even when life as we knew it is forever destroyed, you are the one constant in our lives that can never be lost to us. All else is temporary and changing.

Our loss has brought us such pain that we wonder if we can survive it. We wonder if we will hurt forever, if we will ever feel normal again. Yet when we walk with you through our times of sorrow, we trust that you will soothe our pain, comfort our souls, heal our wounds, and fill the empty place in our hearts. We want to reach up and take your steadying hand, Lord. Please draw us close to you and lead us through this river of grief to the other side.

We know that you are a good God and that your love for us is endless. Help us to cast our whole burden of grief on you and let you carry it. Sustain us, and enable us to get beyond it. We realize that life must go on, and we ask you to help us take the next step we need to take today. We know that with you all things are possible and that your healing power can restore any-thing—even our broken hearts. Walk with us, Lord. We trust you to take our hands and lead us until we can feel your light on our faces and your joy in our hearts. Amen.[11]

What to Pray Together

What's the best way to pray with your friends? Let me share what Dr. Gordon MacDonald suggested at a trauma conference sponsored by the American Association of Christian Counselors in New York, one month after 9/11, on how to pray for those in difficulty.

The following are five kinds of prayers that your friends need as an intervention during their time of difficulty.

Prayer of Encouragement. "Encourage" means to press courage into a person. "Discourage" means to suck courage out of a person. Your hope, your courage, your belief in them and the future can be transferred to your friends. Ask God to encourage your friends, to give them strength and courage. You might share with them how precious they are in God's sight. Read Scripture to the person, such as Ephesians 4:4-6 (*NLT*):

> We are all one body, we have the same Spirit, and we have all been called to the same glorious future. There is only one Lord, one faith, one baptism, and there is only one God and Father, who is over us all and in us all and living through us all.

A prayer reflecting this Scripture might be, "O God, my friend means so much to me and to You. I believe as You do that she has the ability and the strength to carry on in the midst of this difficulty. Give her a clear mind, a peaceful mind and Your guidance."

When your friends question whether God cares for them or not, share portions of this song, an adaptation of Psalm 54:2-4 and Zephaniah 3:14-17:

> And the Father will dance over you in joy!
> He will take delight in whom He loves.
> Is that a choir I hear singing the praises of God?
> No, the Lord God Himself is exulting over you in song!
> And He will joy over you in song!
> My soul will make its boast in God,
> For He has answered all my cries.
> His faithfulness to me is as sure as the dawn of a new day.
> Awake my soul, and sing!
> Let my spirit rejoice in God!
> Sing, O daughter of Zion, with all of your heart!
> Cast away fear for you have been restored!

Put on the garment of praise as on a festival day.
Join with the Father in glorious, jubilant song.
God rejoices over you in song![12]

The following is another prayer you could share:

Dear God,
Thank You for Your act of choosing, adopting and making my
friend Your heir. Thank You that she is never out of Your mind.
Thank You for the never-ending joy You have over her. May she
experience all of this at this moment in time.

Prayer of Restoration. This is for the people who have failed or
think they've failed. They have nothing left and are exhausted. Grief has
overwhelmed them. They need someone to pray and restore a sense of
grace in their life. And they need this often. Their tanks are empty and
need to be filled. Perhaps it's as simple as praying, "Lord, just fill my
friend with hope for today and tomorrow. May she be secure in Your
arms" or "Lord, help my friend to know she is loved."

At the American Association of Christian Counselors in New York,
Gordon MacDonald prayed for a friend in this way:

O Lord God, here's my friend whom I've come to love. You know
how much he's hurting today, Lord. I know that he's fearful.
I know that he's in physical pain. Lord, he needs something from
You that no human being can give him. He needs new power in
his life. He needs new courage in his life. He needs to know that
tomorrow can be brighter than anything that's been in the past.
Lord, he needs the kind of strength that only heaven can give.
So, Lord, would You take my friend today? I put my hands on
him so You know who he is. Would You take my friend today
and bring healing to his broken life?

Prayer of Affirmation. This is the prayer in which you recognize
something in your friends that they cannot see themselves:

Lord, I thank You for the way my friend is making such good decisions in this past week and the way she continues to. We see what You are doing in her life.

When you pray a prayer of affirmation for your friends, when you pray before the Lord on behalf of your friends, you are building value and confidence that God wants them to have. In doing this, you're a "balcony person" in your prayers. You're leaning out of the balcony and saying, "Yes, you can do it. You're capable. See what you've already done. Wow!"

Continue to be affirming in your comments and your prayers.

Prayer of Blessing. This prayer is when you pronounce upon other people what you know is God's purpose and will for them. It is also an act of one person verbally invoking God's gracious power in another's life. You find this within the Scriptures again and again:

The LORD bless you and keep you; the LORD make his face shine upon you and be gracious to you; the LORD turn his face toward you and give you peace (Num. 6:24-26).

What could you say in response to this?

- Blessed be the God and Father of our Lord Jesus Christ. May He bless you with . . .
- May the Lord bless you and keep you strong in . . .
- May the Lord give you hope that will neither despair nor disappoint . . .

Prayer of Intercession. This prayer is used when your friends are so weak and needy that you need to stand between them and God and pray on their behalf. In John 17, Jesus intercedes for His disciples. We are called to pray on our friends' behalf. You will know what is needed as you listen to what your friends say to you.

You could pray the following:

Lord Jesus, I pray the very words and thoughts of God for the protection of my friend. Please honor my prayers and surround my friend with Your protection. Protect my friend from all evil. In the name of Jesus.

Father, sometimes events intrude into our lives that bring distress and discouragement. Use Your word and the work of Your Holy Spirit to lift this from my friend and bring comfort. I thank You in advance for doing this. In Jesus' name I pray.

Dear God, my friend needs the Holy Spirit as the great comforter at this moment to overcome pain and distress.

Be simple in your prayers. Be brief. Be sincere. And if you promise to pray, write it down so that you are faithful. Let your friend know that you've been praying.

You will never understand the power of prayer in your hurting friend's life.

Referrals

Many of those who come to you will benefit from your counsel. But some will need to be referred to another professional with more expertise because of the severity of their difficulties. Some of the best counsel you can give is to make a referral. It is a sign of inner strength and security to be able to refer without condemning yourself for your lack of knowledge. Some in ministry feel very possessive and have an inflated estimate of their capability. Knowledge and acceptance of your ability and spiritual gifts is essential. Paul said:

Do nothing from factional motives [through contentiousness, strife, selfishness, or for unworthy ends] or prompted by conceit and empty arrogance. Instead, in the true spirit of humility (lowliness of mind) let each regard the others as better than and superior to himself [thinking more highly of one another than you do of yourselves]. Let each of you esteem and look upon and be concerned for not [merely] his own interests, but also each for the interests of others (Phil. 2:3-4, *AMP*).

I make referrals to other professional counselors, ministers, lawyers, medical specialists, financial specialists or whoever has the necessary expertise. It is unreasonable to expect every counselor to be able to help in every situation. Our training, experience and personalities are all variables that affect what happens in counseling.

How Do You Know When to Refer?

One of the most common reasons to refer is when the person in crisis needs specialized assistance that a minister is not able to give. This does not necessarily mean the counselee's need or problem is severe or radical, but it is one that you are not able to handle. Do not convey to the person that his or her problem is very serious, for this can increase the stress and crisis. Instead, let the counselee know a different specialization is needed.

> **Whenever the counselee's well-being is at stake, ask yourself the question, *Do I have the time and capability to assist this person?***

Another reason for referral is when there may be indications of a potentially serious risk that is beyond your training or expertise. Whenever the counselee's well-being is at stake, ask yourself the question, *Do I have the time and capability to assist this person?* This may be a case in which referring to a professional therapist, such as a psychologist, psychiatrist or marriage and family therapist, is necessary.

Another reason to refer is when a counselee prefers a different approach from the one you have to offer. However, this does not happen often with immediate crisis counseling.

Additionally, if the crisis situation that prompted the person to seek counsel begins to lessen, but there is indication that longer-term counseling for the problem is needed, referral may be necessary. Most ministers have not been trained for long-term treatment, nor do they have the time for all those who come in with a crisis.

How Do You Find a Referral?

You can get personal recommendations from other ministers and from Christian doctors and lawyers. Local seminaries, Christian colleges and private Christian schools also are able to provide referrals. Many communities have Christian business and professional directories that list only therapists who profess to be Christians.

Referrals to Christian therapists also may be obtained from

- Focus on the Family, 8605 Explorer Drive, Colorado Springs, CO 80995
- American Association of Christian Counselors, 1639 Rustic Village, Forest, VA 24551, (800) 526-8673.

It is perfectly alright to call a therapist or meet the therapist for purposes of gaining more information concerning his or her approach and beliefs.

What Are the Steps Involved in Actually Making the Referral?

Do Your Homework. First of all, be sure you have done your homework by gathering all of the information the counselee will need: location, hours, type of counseling, services offered and financial policies.

The way you broach the subject and handle this discussion will be very important for the referral to be successful. It is easy for the person in counseling to feel either that his or her problem is so severe and radical that you must refer, or that you do not like or want to help the counselee, which makes him or her feel rejected. Your care and sensitivity need to be evident here. A casual, relaxed approach is much better than leaning forward with a serious expression of deep concern. A statement such as, "I appreciate all that you have shared with me, since it helps me know how much I'll be able to assist you, and I want to help you the best way possible. I think I can help you the most at this time by putting you in contact with a professional counselor who works with these issues and situations far more than I do and has more training and expertise than I do. How do you feel about this possibility?"

The person may accept this very readily or may seem hesitant and puzzled. The counselee may say, "You don't want to help me" or "You don't want to see me anymore."

"No," you reply, "I *do* want to help you and may continue to see you from time to time. But I want you to have the finest help available, and that is why I'm making this recommendation."

The counselee may reply by saying, "But I've shared so much with you, and it's difficult for me to share, and now you want me to talk with a stranger."

"I realize that it's a bit scary to begin this process again," you assure the person, "but it took courage for you to come see me and share as openly as you have. I feel you still have this courage and capability to begin with someone who is better equipped than I am. What could I do to make this transfer easier for you?"

Help the Counselee Make a Personal Choice. After you have offered your recommendation, the counselee then has the choice of accepting or rejecting your suggestion of referral. The person needs to make his or her own decision. If the person has a serious difficulty—deep depression, physical difficulty, is suicidal or was abused—an immediate referral is needed. You may have to insist gently by asking the counselee to go along with your decision and trust your judgment. In a nonemergency situation, ask the person to consider your suggestion and let you know. Be sure you let the counselee know that he or she does not have to accept the referral of the person(s) you are suggesting just to please you. You may want to suggest two or three names if possible.

Always remember to see or call the counselee following his or her first visit with the new source of help. Let the counselee know that you will continue to pray for him or her and that you are interested in his or her continued growth.

RESOURCES FOR THE BEREAVED

AIDS Related Programs

The Living Legacy Program II

Boston Pediatric and Family AIDS Project

Dimock Community Health Center

55 Dimock Street

Roxbury, MA 02119

Telephone: (617) 442-8800, ext. 1331

TAG: Teen Age Grief, Inc.

P.O. Box 220034

Newhall, CA 91322-0034

Telephone: (805) 253-1932

Website: http://www.smartlink.net/~tag

Provides training and resources for helping grieving teens.

Tragedy Assistance Program for Survivors (TAPS)

2001 S Street, NW, #300

Washington, DC 20009

Telephone: (800) 959-TAPS
Fax: (202) 639-5312
Website: http://www.taps.org
Provides support for survivors of military deaths.

Curricula
Family Program for Bereaved Siblings. Manual
B. Kempler or G. Koocher
Department of Psychiatry
Children's Hospital Medical Center
300 Longwood Avenue
Boston, MA 02115
Telephone: (617) 355-6000

Growing Seasons—Helping Children Heal from Divorce and Other Losses.
Jean Brunson.
Turning Point
P.O. Box 22127
Chattanooga, TN 37422-2127

*Growing Through Grief: A K-12 Curriculum to Help Young People Through All Kinds of
Losses.*
Compassion Books
477 Hannah Branch Road
Burnsville, NC 28714
Telephone: (628) 675-5909
Fax: (628) 675-9687
E-mail: Heal2grow@aol.com
Website: http://www.compassionbooks.com

Hospice Expressive Arts Loss Support Program (HEALS) Training Manual
The Center for Creative Healing
P.O. Box 1576
Battleboro, VT 05302
Telephone/Fax: (802) 257-1600

Learning About Loss: Bringing Death into the Life Cycle.
A K-2 Curriculum.
Available from J. Katz
Lexington Educational Foundation
1557 Massachusetts Avenue
Lexington, MA 02420

Mutual Help Organizations
American Self-Help Clearinghouse
St. Claire's Hospital
25 Pocono Road
Denville, NJ 07834-2995
Telephone: (973) 625-6000
Website: http://www.mentalhelp.net/selfhelp

Bereaved Families of Ontario
562 Eglinston Avenue, E., Suite 401
Toronto, Ontario, Canada M4P 1P1
Telephone: (416) 440-0290
Fax: (416) 440-0304
E-mail: BFO@inforamp.net
Website: http://www.inforamp.net/~BFO

Candlelighters Childhood Cancer Foundation
7910 Woodmont Avenue, Suite 460
Bethesda, MD 20814-3015
Telephone: (800) 366-2223 or (301) 657-8401
E-mail: info@candlelighters.org
Website: http://candlelighters.org

Compassionate Friends
P.O. Box 3696
Oak Brook, IL 60522-3696
Telephone: (630) 990-0010
Fax: (630) 990-0246

E-mail: TCF_national@prodigy.com
Website: http://compassionatefriends.org

Cystic Fibrosis Foundation
6931 Arlington Road
Bethesda, MD 20814-5200
Telephone: (800) 344-4823
E-mail: info@cff.org
Website: http://www.cff.org

Grieving Widows and Widowers
Telephone: (888) 999-5838

Mothers Against Drunk Driving (MADD)
511 E. John Carpenter Freeway, Suite 700
Irving, TX 75062
Telephone: (214) 744-6233
Victim hot line: (800) GET-MADD
Fax: (972) 529-5300
Website: http://www.madd.org

Muscular Dystrophy Association
3300 E. Sunrise Drive
Tucson, AZ 85718-3208
Telephone: (520) 529-2000
Fax: (520) 529-5300
E-mail: MDA@mdausa.org
Website: http://www.mdausa.org

Parents of Murdered Children
100 E. 8th Street, B-41
Cincinnati, OH 45202
Telephone: (513) 721-5683
Toll free: (888) 818-POMC
E-mail: NatlPOMC@aol.com
Website: http://www.pomc.com

Sudden Infant Death Syndrome (SIDS) Alliance
1314 Bedford Avenue, Suite 210
Baltimore, MD 21208
Telephone: (410) 653-8226 or (800) 221-7437
Fax: (410) 653-8709
Website: http://www.sidsalliance.org

Suicide Prevention Programs
American Association of Suicidology
4201 Connecticut Avenue, NW, Suite 408
Washington, DC 20008
Telephone: (202) 237-2280
Fax: (202) 237-2282
Website: http://www.suicidology.org

Violence Prevention Programs
Kids Alive and Loved (KAL)
Institute for Minority Health Research
Rollins School of Public Health of Emory University
1518 Clifton Road
Atlanta, GA 30322
Telephone: (404) 727-4437 or (800) 401-7050
Fax: (404) 727-1369

Living After Murder Program (LAMP)
Roxbury Comprehensive Community Health Center
Behavioral Health Collaborative
330 Martin Luther King Boulevard
Roxbury, MA 02119
Telephone: (617) 541-3790
Fax: (617) 541-3797
E-mail: vovu@gis.net

Louis D. Brown Peace Curriculum
5 Louis D. Brown Way

Dorchester, MA 02124-1011
Telephone: (617) 825-1917
Fax: (617) 265-2278
Website: http://www.institute4peace.org

National Organization for Victim Assistance
1757 Park Road, NW
Washington, DC 20010
Telephone: (202) 232-6683
Fax: (202) 462-2255
E-mail: nova@digex.net
Website: http://try-nova.org

Violence Prevention Program
Harvard School of Public Health
718 Huntington Avenue, 1st Floor
Boston, MA 02115
Telephone: (617) 432-0814
Fax: (617) 432-0068

ENDNOTES

Chapter 1

1. Gary Collins, *How to Be a People Helper* (Ventura, CA: Vision House/Regal Books, 1976), p. 37.
2. William Crane, *Where God Comes In: The Divine Plus in Counseling* (Dallas, TX: Word Publishing, 1970), p. 28.

Chapter 2

1. Peter Buntman and Eleanor Sais, *How to Live with Your Teenager* (Pasadena, CA: Birch Tree Press, 1979), n.p.
2. Paul F. Wilczak, "Listening as Ministry," *Marriage and Family Living* 3, no. 122 (March 1980), p. 4.
3. Harold Ivan Smith, *When You Don't Know What to Say* (Kansas City, MO: Beacon Hill Press, 2002), p. 87.
4. Legal exceptions to confidences will be discussed later. Regarding the examples cited in this book, the people involved have given me permission to use them, and sufficient information has been changed to ensure privacy.
5. Judith K. Acosta and Richard L. Levenson, Jr., "Observations from Groud Zero at the World Trade Center in New York City, Part II: Theoretical and Clinical Considerations," *International Journal of Emergency Mental Health* 4, no. 2 (Spring 2002), p. 124.
6. Frederick Buechner, *Peculiar Treasures: A Biblical Who's Who* (New York: Harper and Row, 1979), p. 65.
7. Kenneth S. West, *Word Studies in the Greek New Testament* (Grand Rapids, MI: Eerdman's Publishing, 1966), p. 239.
8. Frederick C. Thorne, "Principles of Personality Counseling," *Journal of Clinical Counseling* (1950), n.p., quoted in G. Keith Olson, *Counseling Teenagers* (Loveland, CO: Group Books, 1984), p. 187.

Chapter 3

1. Girard Egan, *The Skilled Helper* (Monterey, CA: Brooks and Cole, 1975), p. 76.
2. Dr. Timothy Clinton and Dr. George Ohlschlager, executive eds., *Competent Christian Counseling* (Colorado Springs, CO: Water Brook Press, 2002), p. 207.
3. D. Crydon Hammond, Dean H. Hepworth, and Vern G. Smith, *Improving Therapeutic Communication* (San Francisco, CA: Jossey-Bass, 1977), pp. 114-115.
4. This is just a brief introduction to the concept of speaking another's language. If this is new to you or you've not read much on this, please read H. Norman Wright, *Communication: Key to Marriage* (Ventura, CA: Regal Books, 2000).
5. William Crane, *Where God Comes In: The Divine Plus in Counseling* (Dallas, TX: Word Publishing, 1970), p. 57.
6. Egan, *The Skilled Helper,* p. 158.

7. Crane, *Where God Comes In: The Divine Plus in Counseling,* p. 60.
8. Egan, *The Skilled Helper,* p. 158.
9. Ibid., p. 190.

Chapter 4

1. Suzane C. Thompsen, "Blockades to Finding Meaning and Control," in *Perspectives on Loss—A Sourcebook,* ed. John H. Harvey (Philadelphia: Bruner-Mazel, 1998), p. 21.
2. Kim Kluger-Bell, *Unspeakable Losses* (New York: Quill, 1998), p. 22.
3. Dr. Ronald W. Ramsay and Rene Noorbergen, *Living with Loss* (New York: William Morrow and Company, 1981), pp. 47-48.
4. U.S. Bureau of the Census, "Pregnancies Number and Outcome: 1967-92," *Statistical Abstract of the United States 1996* 116, no. 109 (Washington, DC), p. 83.
5. Kluger-Bell, *Unspeakable Losses,* p. 20.
6. R. Scott Sullender, *Losses in Later Life* (New York: Paulist Press, 1989), p. 3.
7. Ibid., p. 79.
8. Ibid., pp. 16-18.
9. Deirdre Feldoton, M.A., Seminar presentation at The American Academy of Bereavement.
10. Sullender, *Losses in Later Life,* p. 3.
11. Ibid., p. 45.
12. Pauline Bass, *Ambiguous Loss* (London, England: Harvard University Press, 1999), pp. 5-9.
13. Kenneth Doka, ed., *Disenfranchised Grief: Recognizing Hidden Sorrow* (Lanham, MD: Lexington Books, 1989), p. 4.
14. Kenneth Doka, *Disenfranchised Grief: Recognizing Hidden Sorrow* quoted in James Fogarty, *The Magical Thoughts of Grieving Children* (Amityville, NY: Baywood Publishing Company, 2000), adapted, pp. 78-80.
15. Suzane C. Thompsen, "Blockades to Finding Meaning and Control," *Perspectives on Loss—A Sourcebook,* pp. xi, xii.

Chapter 5

1. Therese A. Rando, *Grieving: How to Go on Living When Someone You Love Dies* (Lexington, MA: Lexington Books, 1988), pp. 11-12.
2. Susan J. Zonnebelt-Smeenge and Robert C. DeVries, *Getting to the Other Side of Grief* (Grand Rapids, MI: Baker Book House, 1999), p. 47.
3. Source unknown.
4. Harold Ivan Smith, *When Your People Are Grieving* (Kansas City, MO: Beacon Hill Press, 2001), p. 38.
5. Rando, *Grieving,* pp. 18-19.
6. Al Martinez, "A Shadow on the Moon," *Los Angeles Times.*
7. Roy W. Fairchild, *Finding Hope Again: A Pastor's Guide to Counseling Depressed Persons* (San Francisco: HarperCollins, 1980), pp. 113-114.
8. Ibid., p. 117.
9. Bob Deits, *Life After Loss* (Tucson, AZ: Fisher Books, 1988), p. 41.
10. Smith, *When Your People Are Grieving,* p. 31.
11. Deits, *Life After Loss,* p. 27.

12. For losses of any kind, encourage the person to read my book *Recovering from the Losses of Life* (Revell, 2000). If the person lost a spouse, encourage him or her to read Susan J. Zonnebelt-Smeenge and Robert C. DeVries, *Getting to the Other Side of Grief* (Baker Book House, 1999). If the person had a relationship breakup, suggest my book *Let's Just Be Friends* (Revell, 2002).

13. Rando, *Grieving,* pp. 231-234.

14. John James and Frank Cherry, *The Grief Recovery Handbook* (New York: Harper and Row, 1988), pp. 109-121.

15. Rando, *Grieving,* p. 251.

16. Ibid., p. 19.

17. Prior to working with anyone suffering a loss, take the time to search out the various grief support and recovery groups in your area. Talk with those in charge of each group and find out content, resources, spiritual orientation and so on. Encourage anyone with a significant loss to become involved with a group. Even the smallest communities and churches can create this ministry now by using *GriefShare*, a series of 13 sessions that establishes a 13-week grief-recovery seminar/ support group. A church is equipped with a video session for each meeting, a leader's guide, leader-equipping video and workbooks for group participants. *GriefShare* groups are designed to be lay led (i.e., a church doesn't need a professional; qualified laypeople can lead the program). *GriefShare* videos feature interviews with 30 leading authors, speakers, counselors and pastors with broad expertise in grief recovery from a biblical Christ-centered perspective. This material is available from Christian Marriage Enrichment, P.O. Box 2468, Orange, CA 92859, (800) 875-7560, or go to http://www.hnormanwright.com.

18. Deits, *Life After Loss,* p. 89.

19. If you're not familiar with Programmed Cry, it's described in my book *Recovering from the Losses of Life* (Grand Rapids, MI: Revell, 2000), p. 50; and in Bob Deits, *Life After Loss* (New York: Fisher Books, 1999), pp. 144-146.

20. R. Scott Sullender, *Grief and Growth* (New York: Paulist Press, 1985), p. 56.

21. You'll find this chart in my book *Recovering from the Losses of Life* (Grand Rapids, MI: Revell, 2000), p. 59.

22. If you need additional information, see the DSM IV or Albert J. Bernstein, Ph.D., *Emotional Vampires* (McGraw Hill, 2000).

23. J. William Worden, *Grief Counseling and Grief Therapy,* comp. Rev. Terry L. Irish (New York: Springer Publishing Company, 1991), pp. 31-34.

24. You may reproduce this letter to hand out to individuals, or see my book *Recovering from the Losses of Life* (Revell, 2000), pp. 60-61.

25. Deits, *Life After Loss,* pp. 150-151.

26. The Communicating with Your Grief exercise is taken from Bob Deits, *Life After Loss* (Tucson, AZ: Fisher Books, 1988), pp. 93-94, 146-147.

27. Ibid.

28. Rando, *Grieving,* pp. 18-19.

Chapter 6

1. You may duplicate copies of the ball of grief image to give to your counselees.

2. Dennis and Matthew Linn, *Healing Life's Hurts* (New York: Paulist Press, 1978), pp. 102-103.

3. Used by permission of Dave Nair, who created and compiled these suggestions.

4. Ann Kaiser Stearns, *Coming Back* (New York: Ballantine, 1988), pp. 104-105.

5. Ibid., pp. 110-112.

6. Prayer by Nan Kenton, 1991, Glendale, Arizona, adapted by Rev. Terry L. Irish, Sunnyvale Church of the Nazarene, Crescent City, California.

7. Harold Ivan Smith, *When Your People Are Grieving* (Kansas City, MO: Beacon Hill Press, 2001), p. 22.

Chapter 7

1. *Webster's New World College Dictionary*, s.v. "crisis."

2. J. Callahan, *Defining Crisis and Emergency Crisis* 15, no. 4 (1994), pp. 164-171.

3. Lisa Barnes Lampman, ed., *Helping a Neighbor in Crisis* (Wheaton, IL: Tyndale House, 1997), p. 9.

4. Julian Whetsell Mitchell, *The Dynamics of Crisis Intervention* (Springfield, IL: Charles C. Thomas, 1999), p. 4.

5. Morton Bard and Dawn Sangrey, *The Crime Victim's Book* (New York: Basic Book House: 1979), quoted in Lisa Barnes Lampman, ed. *Helping a Neighbor in Crisis* (Wheaton, IL: Tyndale House, 1997), p. 9.

6. Ibid., p. 10.

7. J. Callahan, *Defining Crisis and Emergency Crisis*, p. 167.

8. Naomi Golan, *Passing Through Transitions* (New York: The Free Press, 1981), p. 12.

9. Charles M. Sell, *Transitions Through Adult Life* (Grand Rapids, MI: Zondervan Publishing House, 1991), p. 22.

10. David C. Morley, *Halfway up the Mountain* (Old Tappan, NJ: Revell, 1979), p. 26.

11. Aaron Lazare et al., "The Walk-In Patient as a 'Customer': A Key Dimension in Evaluation and Treatment," *American Journal of Orthopsychiatry* 42 (1979), pp. 872-883, quoted in Dr. G. Keith Olson, *Counseling Teenagers* (Loveland, CO: Group Books, 1984), pp. 283-284.

12. Lewis B. Smedes, *How Can It Be All Right When Everything Is All Wrong?* (New York: Harper and Row, 1982), pp. 16-17.

13. Charles R. Swindoll, *Growing Strong in the Seasons of Life* (Portland, OR: Multnomah, 1983), pp. 274-275.

14. Aleksandr Isaevich Solzhenitsyn, *The Gulag Archipelago* (New York: Harper Perennial, 2002), quoted in Philip Yancey, *Where Is God When It Hurts?* (Grand Rapids, MI: Zondervan Publishing House, 1977), p. 51.

15. Swindoll, *Growing Strong in the Seasons of Life*, pp. 274-275.

Chapter 8

1. Howard J. Parad and Libbie G. Parad, *Crisis Intervention*, vol. 2 (Milwaukee, WI: Family Service America, 1990), p. 8.

2. Jane Crisp, "Crisis Intervention," *Helping a Neighbor in Crisis* (Wheaton, IL: Tyndale House, 1997), p. 12.

3. Judith K. Acosta and Richard L. Levenson, Jr., "Observations from Ground Zero at

the World Trade Center in New York City, Part II: Theoretical and Clinical Considerations," *International Journal of Emergency Mental Health* 4, no. 2 (Spring 2002), p. 124.

4. Judith Acosta and Judith Sumon Prager, *The Worst Is Over: What to Say When Every Moment Counts* (San Diego, CA: Jodere Group, 2002), p. 9.

5. Ibid., p. 58.

6. Dutch Sheets, *Tell Your Heart to Beat Again* (Ventura, CA: Regal Books, 2002), p. 78.

7. Adapted from numerous resources.

8. K. A. Slaikeu, *Crisis Intervention: A Handbook for Practice and Research,* 2nd ed. (Boston: Allyn and Bacon, 1990), p. 164.

9. William Pruitt, *Run from the Pale Pony* (Grand Rapids, MI: Baker Books, 1976), pp. 9-10.

Chapter 9

1. Lydia Rapoport, "Crisis Intervention As a Mode of Brief Treatment," quoted in R. W. Roberts and R. H. Nee, eds., *Theories of Social Casework* (Chicago: University of Chicago, 1970), p. 277.

2. Naomi Golan, *Treatment in Crisis Situations* (New York: The Free Press, 1978), pp. 98-99.

3. Karl A. Slaikeu, *Crisis Intervention: A Handbook for Practice and Research* (Boston: Allyn and Bacon, 1984), pp. 89-90.

4. Ibid., pp. 90-91.

5. Golan, *Treatment in Crisis Situations,* pp. 98-101.

6. Douglas Puryear, *Helping People in Crisis* (San Francisco, CA: Jossey-Bass, 1980), p. 62.

7. Ibid., p. 49.

Chapter 10

1. Robert Hicks, *Failure to Scream* (Nashville, TN: Thomas Nelson, 1993), p. 15.

2. Donald Meichenbaum, *A Clinical Handbook/Practiced: Therapist Manual for Assessing and Treating Adults with Post-Traumatic Stress Disorder (PTSD)* (Waterloo, Ontario: Institute Press, 1994), p. 23.

3. Aphrodite Matsakis, *I Can't Get Over It! A Handbook for Trauma Survivors* (Oakland, CA: New Harbinger Publishers, 1992), p. 23.

4. Elie Wiesel, "We Choose Honor," *Parade Magazine* (October 28, 2001), pp. 4-5.

5. Sandra L. Brown, *Counseling Victims of Violence* (Alexandria, VA: American Association for Counseling and Development, 1991), p. 9.

6. Judith K. Acosta and Richard L. Levenson, Jr., "Observations from Ground Zero at the World Trade Center in New York City, Part II: Theoretical and Clinical Considerations," *International Journal of Emergency Mental Health* 4, no. 2 (Spring 2002), pp. 120-121.

7. Judith Herman, M.D., *Trauma and Recovery* (Grand Rapids, MI: Baker Books, 1992), p. 175.

8. Jerry Mungadze, presentation at American Association of Christian Counselors World Conference, August 2001.

9. Katy Butler, "The Biology of Fears," *Networker Magazine* (July/August 1996), pp. 40-46.

10. Francine Shapiro and Margot Forest, *EMDR* (New York: Basic Book House, 1997), p. 49.

11. Source unknown.

12. Herman, *Trauma and Recovery*, p. 47.

13. Babette Rothschild, *The Body Remembers: The Psychophysiology of Trauma and Trauma Treatment* (New York: WM Norton and Company, 2000), p. 65.

14. Herman, *Trauma and Recovery*, p. 47.

15. Diane Langberg, "Coping with Traumatic Memory." Paper presented at The Soul Care Trauma Response and Intervention Project (TRIP) conference, New York, October 2001.

16. Paula Smith, "Secondary Survivors," unpublished paper.

17. Ibid.

18. Rothschild, *The Body Remembers: The Psychophysiology of Trauma and Trauma Treatment*, p. 66; Judy Foreman, "Roots of Violence May Lie in Damaged Brain Cells," *Los Angeles Times* (April 29, 2002), n.p.

19. Meichenbaum, *A Clinical Handbook/Practiced: Therapist Manual for Assessing and Treating Adults with Post-Traumatic Stress Disorder (PTSD)*, pp. 510-511.

20. Matsakis, *I Can't Get Over It!*, pp. 6-7.

21. Ibid., pp. 23-24.

22. Ibid., pp. 10-13.

23. Langberg, "Coping with Traumatic Memory."

24. Hicks, *Failure to Scream*, p. 21.

25. C. S. Lewis, *A Grief Observed* (London: Fober and Fober, 1961), p. 9.

26. Herman, *Trauma and Recovery*, p. 37.

27. Brown, *Counseling Victims of Violence*, pp. 22-24.

28. C. S. Lewis, "Relapse," *Poems,* ed. Walter Hooper (New York: Harcourt Brace Jovanovich, 1964), pp. 103-104.

29. Hicks, *Failure to Scream*, p. 46.

30. Herman, *Trauma and Recovery*, pp. 42-43.

31. Ibid.

32. Matsakis, *I Can't Get Over It!*, pp. 18-22.

33. Raymond B. Flammery, Jr., *Post-Traumatic Stress Disorder* (New York: Crossroad, 1992), pp. 36-37.

34. Terence Monmaney, "For Most Trauma Victims Life Is More Meaningful," *Los Angeles Times* (October 7, 2001), p. 9; citing research from Richard Tedeschi, University of North Carolina; Dr. Robert Ursano, Uniformed Services University of the Health Sciences in Bethesda, MD; Dr. Sandra Bloom.

Chapter 11

1. Wendy Zubenko and Joseph Capozzoli, eds., *Children and Disasters* (New York: Oxford University Press, 2002), pp. 38-39.

2. For information on training opportunities, contact Bob Vandepol at Crisis Care at (888) 736-0911 or the American Association of Christian Counselors at (800) 526-8673.

3. George S. Everly and Jeffrey T. Mitchell, *Critical Incident Stress Management* (Ellicott City, MD: Chevron Publishing Corporation, 1999), pp. 86-87.

4. The best resource with guidelines and hundreds of insightful questions is Dr. Donald Meichenbaum, Ph.D., *A Clinical Handbook/Practiced: Therapist Manual for*

Assessing and Treating Adults with Post-Traumatic Stress Disorder (PTSD) (Institute Press, 1994).

5. Dr. Donald Meichenbaum, "Treating the Effects of Severe Trauma in Adults and Children," workshop syllabus, pp. 35-40.

6. Source unknown.

7. An excellent resource to help in the recovery process is Dena Rosenbloom and Mary Beth Williams, with Barbara E. Watkins, *Life After Trauma: A Workbook for Healing* (New York: Guilford Press, 1999). It gives multiple exercises on developing a sense of safety, trust, regaining control, closeness, stress and so on.

8. Babette Rothschild, *The Body Remembers: The Psychophysiology of Trauma and Trauma Treatment* (New York: W. W. Norton, 2000), p. 87.

9. Matsakis, *I Can't Get Over It! A Handbook for Trauma Survivors,* pp. 114-115.

10. One of the best examples I've seen of positive self-talk's helping in trauma recovery is found in Aphrodite Matsakis, *I Can't Get Over It!*, pp. 127-130. This book is a must for those of us involved in helping others.

11. Contact EMDR Institute for Seminars and Resources, P.O. Box 51010, Pacific Grove, CA 93950; (831) 372-3900; http://www.emdr.com.

12. Rothschild, *The Body Remembers,* n.p.

13. Ibid., p. 90.

14. Ibid., p. 79.

15. Matsakis, *I Can't Get Over It!,* p. 134.

16. Ibid., pp. 15, 153.

17. Ibid., p. 159.

18. Ibid., pp. 160-163.

19. Judith Herman, *Trauma and Recovery* (New York: Basic Book House, 1992), p. 207.

20. Ibid., chapters 8-10.

21. Matsakis, *I Can't Get Over It!,* p. 236.

22. *The NIV Worship Bible* (Dana Point, CA: The Corinthian Group, 2000), p. 773.

Chapter 12

1. Cyris L. Sulzberger, *My Brother Death.*

2. William Worden, *Grief Counseling and Grief Therapy* (New York: Springer Publishing, 1991), pp. 136-137.

3. Mary Ann Emswiler, M.A., M.P.S., and James P. Emswiler, M.A., M.Ed., *Guiding Your Child Through Grief* (New York: Bantam Books, 2000), p. 61.

4. Source unkown.

5. Juliann W. Mitchell, *The Dynamics of Crisis Intervention* (Springfield, IL: Charles C. Thomas Publishers, 1999), n.p.

6. Susan J. Zonnebelt-Smeenge and Robert C. DeVries, *Getting to the Other Side of Grief* (Grand Rapids, MI: Baker Book House, 1999), p. 29.

7. Carol Staudacher, *Beyond Grief* (Oakland, CA: New Harbinger, 1987), pp. 56-60.

8. Ibid., pp. 64-66.

9. Naomi Golan, *Passing Through Transitions* (New York: The Free Press, 1981), pp. 171, 175-182.

10. Joe Bayley, *The Last Thing We Talk About* (Elgin, IL: David C. Cook, 1973), pp. 40-41.

11. H. Norman Wright, *Recovering from the Losses of Life* (Grand Rapids, MI: Baker Books, 1991), pp. 182-183.
12. Joyce Landorf, *Mourning Song* (Tarrytown, NY: Fleming H. Revell, 1974), p. 145.
13. For additional insight, I encourage you to read the book I authored entitled *Recovering from the Losses of Life* (Baker Books, 1991).
14. Therese A. Rando, *Grieving: How to Go On Living When Someone You Love Dies* (Lexington, MA: Lexington Books, 1988), pp. 227-250.
15. Zonnebelt-Smeenge and DeVries, *Getting to the Other Side of Grief*, p. 68.
16. Bayley, *The Last Thing We Talk About*, n.p.
17. Judith Acosta and Judith Simon-Prager, *The Worst Is Over: What to Say When Every Moment Counts* (San Diego, CA: Jodene Group, 2002), p. 261.
18. Rando, *Grieving*, pp. 106-116.
19. Ibid., pp. 115-116.
20. Richard Schult, *The Psychology of Death, Dying and Bereavement* (Reading, MA: Addison-Wesley, 1978), pp. 140-141.
21. John Powell, dedication to *The Secret of Staying in Love* (Allen, TX: Argus Communications, 1974).

Chapter 13

1. Carol Staudacher, *Beyond Grief* (Oakland, CA: New Harbinger, 1987), p. 82.
2. Ibid., p. 73.
3. Ibid., p. 94.
4. Fiona Marshall, *Losing a Parent* (Cambridge, MA: Fisher Books, 2000), p. 45.
5. Dennis Klass, Phyllis R. Silverman, and Steven L. Nickman, *Continuing Bonds: New Understandings of Grief* (Philadelphia: Taylor and Francis, 1996), pp. 76-81.
6. Therese A. Rando, *Grieving: How to Go On Living When Someone You Love Dies* (Lexington, MA: Lexington Books, 1988), pp. 135-151.
7. Marshall, *Losing a Parent*, pp. 19-21.
8. Staudacher, *Beyond Grief*, p. 90.
9. Marion Sandmaier, *Original Kin* (New York: E. P. Dutton, 1994), pp. 207, 214.
10. Rando, *Grieving*, pp. 154-158.
11. Sandmaier, *Original Kin*, p. 224.
12. Harold Ivan Smith, *Friendgrief* (Amityville, NY: Baywood Publishing, 2002), p. 2.
13. Ibid., p. 9.
14. Kenneth Doka, ed., *Disenfranchised Grief: Recognizing Hidden Sorrow* (Lanham, MD: Lexington Books, 1989), pp. 82-86.
15. Ibid., p. 83.
16. F. Sklar and S. F. Hartley, "Close Friends As Survivors: Bereavement Patterns in a 'Hidden' Population," *Omega* 21, no. 2, p. 104.
17. Smith, *Friendgrief*, pp. 60-61; W. V. Hocker, *Unrecognized and Unsanctioned Grief: The Nature and Counseling of Unacknowledged Loss* (Springfield, IL: Charles C. Thomas Publishers, 1990), pp. 104-121.
18. Smith, *Friendgrief*, p. 61.
19. Ibid.
20. Ibid., p. 60.

21. K. R. Hanson, *The Journal of Pastoral Care* 60, no. 3, pp. 249-256, quoted in Harold Ivan Smith, *Friendgrief* (Amityville, NY: Baywood Publishing, 2002), p. 226.

22. Smith, *Friendgrief*, p. 70.

23. Ibid., p. 222.

24. G. S. Silverman, "A Year of Mourning," *Forum* 26, no. 4 (July/August 2000), pp. 6-8.

25. P. R. Silverman, *Never Too Young to Know: Death in Children's Lives* (New York: Oxford University Press, 1999), p. 185.

26. Smith, *Friendgrief*, p. 225.

27. Ibid., p. 226.

28. Cheri Barton Ross and Jane Baron-Sorenson, *Pet Loss and Human Emotion* (Philadelphia: Accelerated Development, 1998), pp. 21, 27.

29. Ibid., p. 15.

30. Ibid., p. 4.

31. Ibid., p. 83; T. H. Pettit, *Hospital Administration for Hospital Staff* (Goleta, CA: American Veterinary Publications, 1994), p. 64.

32. Barbara D. Rosof, *The Worst Loss* (New York: Henry Holt and Company, 1994), pp. 175-176.

33. NFO Research, Inc., "When a Child Dies," *Survey of Bereaved Parents,* (Oak Brook, IL: The Compassionate Friends, June 1999).

34. Ronald Knapp, *Beyond Endurance: When a Child Dies* (New York: Schocken, 1986), p. 41.

35. Klass, Silverman, and Nickman, *Continuing Bonds: New Understandings of Grief*, p. 197.

36. Therese A. Rando, *Parental Loss of a Child* (Champaign, IL: Research Press, 1986), pp. 22-24.

37. Staudacher, *Beyond Grief*, pp. 100-101.

38. Rando, *Parental Loss of a Child*, pp. 164-165.

39. Ibid., p. 105.

40. Staudacher, *Beyond Grief*, p. 109.

41. Knapp, *Beyond Endurance: When a Child Dies*, p. 184.

42. Ibid., p. 4.

Chapter 14

1. National Center for Health Statistics at Centers for Disease Control and Prevention, (Washington, DC, Summer 2000).

2. Jan Fawcett, *Before It's Too Late* (West Point, PA: Merck, Sharp and Dohme, 1979), p. 2.

3. Keith Olson, *Counseling Teenagers* (Loveland, CO: Group Publishing, 1984), p. 370.

4. Brent Q. Haden and Brenda Peterson, *The Crisis Intervention Handbook* (Englewood Cliffs, NJ: Prentice Hall, 1982), p. 122.

5. Edwin S. Schneidman, *The Suicidal Mind* (New York: Oxford University Press, 1996), p. 13.

6. Ibid., p. 25.

7. Ibid., pp. 59-61.

8. Fredrick F. Flach and Suzanne C. Draghi, eds., *The Nature and Treatment of Depression* (New York: Wiley, 1975), p. 230.

9. Ibid., p. 231.

10. Haden and Peterson, *The Crisis Intervention Handbook,* p. 125.
11. Rita Robinson, *Survivors of Suicide* (Franklin Lakes, NJ: New Page Books, 2001), pp. 80-81.
12. Ibid., p. 86.
13. "Suicide: Retired Professor Chooses Death," *Los Angeles Times,* 1989, pp. 1, 10.

Chapter 15

1. Keith Olson, *Counseling Teenagers* (Loveland, CO: Group Publishing, 1984), p. 382.
2. Source unknown.
3. Fredrick F. Falch and Suzanne C. Draghi, eds., *The Nature and Treatment of Depression* (New York: Wiley, 1975), p. 241.
4. Paul Pretzel, *Understanding and Counseling the Suicidal Person* (Nashville, TN: Abingdon, 1972), pp. 93-95.
5. For additional information, see Rita Robinson, *Survivor of Suicide* (Franklin Lakes, NJ: New Page Books, 2001).
6. Iris Bolton, *The National Newsletter for the Compassionate Friends* (Winter 1981).
7. Eric Marcus, *Why Suicide?* (San Francisco: Harper and Row, 1996), p. 164.
8. Ibid., p. 145.
9. Ibid., p. 146.
10. *The National Newsletter for the Compassionate Friends* (Winter 1981).
11. Marcus, *Why Suicide?* p. 134.
12. Ibid., p. 137.
13. Ibid., p. 139.
14. Earl A. Grollman and Max Malikow, introduction to *Living When a Young Friend Commits Suicide* (Boston: Beacon Press, 1999).

Chapter 16

1. John W. James and Russell Friedman, *When Children Grieve* (New York: HarperCollins, 2001), p. 5.
2. Jonathan Sandoval, ed., *Handbook of Counseling: Intervention and Prevention in the Schools* (Mahwah, NJ: Lawrence Erlbaum Associates Publishers, 2002), pp. 13-15.
3. William Van Ornum and John B. Mordock, *Crisis Counseling with Children and Adolescents: A Guide for Nonprofessional Counselors* (New York: Continuum, 1983), p. 15.
4. Wendy Zubenko and Joseph Capozzoli, eds., *Children and Disasters* (New York: Oxford University Press, 2002), p. 43.
5. Kendall Johnson, *Trauma in the Lives of Children* (Alameda, CA: Hunter House Publishers, 1988), p. 63.
6. Zubenko and Capazzoli, *Children and Disasters,* pp. 96-97.
7. Ibid., p. 99.
8. Carl Rogers, *A Way of Being* (Boston: Houghton-Mifflin, 1980), n.p.
9. Van Ornum and Mordock, *Crisis Counseling with Children and Adolescents,* pp. 21-39.
10. Ibid., pp. 37-38.
11. Ibid., pp. 62-67.

Chapter 17

1. Archibald Hart, *Children and Divorce: What to Expect and How to Help* (Dallas, TX: Word, Inc., 1982), pp. 124-125.
2. C. G. Workman and M. Prior, "Depression and Suicide in Young Children," *Issues in Comprehensive Pediatric Nursing* 20, no. 2 (April-June 1997), pp. 125-132.
3. Brent Q. Hafen and Brenda Peterson, *The Crisis Intervention Handbook* (Englewood Cliffs, NJ: Prentice-Hall, 1982), pp. 110-111.
4. E. Lindemann, "Symptomatology and Management of Acute Grief," *American Journal of Psychiatry* 139 (1982), pp. 141-148.
5. Hafen and Peterson, *The Crisis Intervention Handbook*, p. 83.
6. William Van Ornum and John B. Mordock, *Crisis Counseling with Children and Adolescents: A Guide for Nonprofessional Counselors* (New York: Continuum, 1983), pp. 146-147.
7. Judith S. Wallerstein, Julia M. Lewis, and Sandra Blakeslee, *The Unexpected Legacy of Divorce: A 25-Year Landmark Study* (New York: Hyperion, 2000), p. xxvii.
8. Ibid., pp. 298-299.
9. L. L. Townsend, *Pastoral Care with Stepfamilies: Mapping the Wilderness* (St. Louis, MO: Chalice Press, 2000), n.p.
10. Jonathan Sandoval, ed., *Handbook of Counseling: Intervention and Prevention in the Schools* (Mahwah, NJ: Lawrence Erlbaum Associates Publishers, 2002), p. 91.
11. Van Ornum and Mordock, *Crisis Counseling with Children and Adolescents*, pp. 94-95.
12. Hart, *Children and Divorce: What to Expect and How to Help*, pp. 66-74.

Chapter 18

1. Mary Ann Emswiler, M.A., M.P.S., and James P. Emswiler, M.A., M.Ed., *Guiding Your Child Through Grief* (New York: Bantam Books, 2000), pp. 100-106.
2. Carol Staudacher, *Beyond Grief* (Oakland, CA: New Harbinger, 1987), pp. 129-130.
3. William Van Ornum and John B. Mordock, *Crisis Counseling with Children and Adolescents: A Guide for Nonprofessional Counselors* (New York: Continuum, 1983), pp. 21-33.
4. Dan Schaefer and Christine Lyons, *How Do We Tell the Children?* (New York: New Market Press, 1986), p. 122.
5. Ibid., p. 129.
6. Staudacher, *Beyond Grief*, pp. 131-138.
7. J. William Worden, *Children and Grief: When a Parent Dies* (New York: Guildford Press, 1996), pp. 33-34.
8. Schaefer and Lyons, *How Do We Tell the Children?* pp. 33-34.
9. Worden, *Children and Grief: When a Parent Dies*, pp. 33-34.
10. Schaefer and Lyons, *How Do We Tell the Children?* pp. 124-125.
11. Staudacher, *Beyond Grief*, pp. 146-147.
12. Helen Fitzgerald, *The Grieving Child* (New York: Simon and Schuster, 1992), p. 106.
13. Staudacher, *Beyond Grief*, p. 151.
14. Therese A. Rando, *Grieving: How to Go On Living When Someone You Love Dies* (Lexington, MA: Lexington Books, 1988), p. 218.
15. Schaefer and Lyons, *How Do We Tell the Children?* p. 142.
16. Rando, *Grieving*, p. 218.

17. Staudacher, *Beyond Grief,* pp. 138-139.

Chapter 19

1. Jay Kesler, *Parents and Teenagers* (Wheaton, IL: Victor, 1984), p. 17.
2. Dr. Les Parrott III, *Helping the Struggling Adolescent* (Grand Rapids, MI: Zondervan Publishing House, 2000), pp. 18-21.
3. Kesler, *Parents and Teenagers,* pp. 151-155.
4. Mary Ann Emswiler, M.A., M.P.S., and James P. Emswiler, M.A., M.Ed., *Guiding Your Child Through Grief* (New York: Bantam Books, 2000), p. 155.
5. Ibid., p. 159.
6. Ibid., pp. 157-162.
7. Keith Olson, *Counseling Teenagers* (Loveland, CO: Group Books, 1984), pp. 27-28.
8. Ibid., pp. 55-56.
9. Ibid., p. 57.
10. William Van Ornum and John B. Mordock, *Crisis Counseling with Children and Adolescents: A Guide for Nonprofessional Counselors* (New York: Continuum, 1983), pp. 41-43.
11. Frederic Flach and Suzanne C. Draghi, *The Nature and Treatment of Depression* (New York: Wiley), pp. 104-107.
12. Van Ornum and Mordock, *Crisis Counseling with Children and Adolescents,* p. 76.
13. J. S. Wallerstein and J. B. Kelly, "The Effects of Parental Divorce: The Adolescent Experience," quoted in E. J. Anthony and C. Koupernik, eds., *The Child in His Family: Children at Psychiatric Risk* (New York: Wiley, 1974), n.p.
14. Olson, *Counseling Teenagers,* pp. 495-496.
15. Flach and Draghi, *The Nature and Treatment of Depression,* pp. 104-106.
16. Governor's Office for Children, "Focus on Teen Suicide" 1, no. 3 (December 1988). This material presented by Teresa McIntier at the Bereavement Facilitator Certificate Award Program Conference, San Diego, CA, November 18-22, 1996.
17. Max Suafford, M.Ed., *Children in Crisis—A Parent's Guide* (Ingrove, TX: Westwind Publications, 1998), pp. 35-36.
18. Governor's Office for Children, "Focus on Teen Suicide" 1, no. 3 (December 1988). This material presented by Teresa McIntier at the Bereavement Facilitator Certificate Award Program Conference, San Diego, CA, November 18-22, 1996.
19. William Blackburn, *What You Should Know About Suicide* (Waco, TX: Word Books, 1982), p. 31.
20. R. R. Ross and B. McKay, *Self-Mutilation* (Lexington, MA: Lexington Books, 1979), n.p.
21. Soili Poijula, M.A., Karl-Erik Wahlberg, Ph.D., and Atle Dyregron, Ph.D., "Adolescent Suicide and Suicide Contagion in Three Secondary Schools," *International Journal of Emergency Mental Health* 3, no. 3 (2001), pp. 163-168.

Chapter 20

1. Frederic Flach and Suzanne C. Draghi, *The Nature and Treatment of Depression* (New York: Wiley, 1984), pp. 106-111.
2. William Van Ornum and John B. Mordock, *Crisis Counseling with Children and Adolescents: A Guide for Nonprofessional Counselors* (New York: Continuum, 1983), p. 50.

3. Keith Olson, *Counseling Teenagers* (Loveland, CO: Group Publishing, 1984), pp. 360-361.

4. R. A. Garner, *Psychotherapeutic Approaches to the Resistant Child* (New York: Jason Aronson, 1975), p. 62.

5. T. J. Tuzil, "Writing: A Problem-Solving Process," *Social Work* 23 (1978), pp. 63-70.

6. Dylan Tatz, *The Spectator,* p. 19, quoted in Joanne Tortorici Luna, Ph.D., "Collaborations Assessment and Healing in Schools After Large-Scale Terrorist Attacks," *International Journal of Emergency Mental Health* 4, no. 3 (Summer 2002), p. 205.

7. Robert Sandler, social studies teacher, *The Spectator,* p. 16, quoted in Joanne Tortorici Luna, Ph.D., "Collaborations Assessment and Healing in Schools After Large-Scale Terrorist Attacks," *International Journal of Emergency Mental Health* 4, no. 3 (Summer 2002), p. 205.

8. G. Torres, personal communication, March 30, 2001, quoted in Joanne Tortorici Luna, Ph.D., "Collaborations Assessment and Healing in Schools After Large-Scale Terrorist Attacks," *International Journal of Emergency Mental Health* 4, no. 3 (Summer 2002), pp. 205-206.

9. Kendall Johnson, *Trauma in the Lives of Children* (Alameda, CA: Hunter House Publishers, 1988), pp. 72-73.

10. Ibid., pp. 154-155.

11. Helen Fitzgerald, *The Grieving Teen* (New York: Simon and Schuster, 2000), pp. 100-102.

12. Johnson, *Trauma in the Lives of Children,* p. 99.

13. Ibid., pp. 99-100.

14. Fitzgerald, *The Grieving Teen,* pp. 112-120.

Conclusion

1. Adapted from a paper by Betty Chase, graduate student, Talbot Theological Seminary.

2. J. Rupp, *Praying Our Goodbyes* (Notre Dame, IN: Ave Maria Press, 1988), p. 79.

3. Lloyd Ogilvie, *Discovering God's Will in Your Life* (Eugene, OR: Harvest House, 1982), pp. 136, 164.

4. Lisa Barnes Lampman, ed., *Helping a Neighbor in Crisis* (Wheaton, IL: Tyndale House, 1997), p. 40.

5. Ibid., p. 68.

6. Source unknown.

7. Joyce Rupp, OSM, *Praying Our Goodbyes* (New York: Ivy Books, 1988), pp. 137-138.

8. Tammy Faxel, ed., *Finding God's Peace in Perilous Times* (Wheaton, IL: Tyndale House, 2001), p. 94.

9. Ibid., p. 116.

10. Ibid., p. 141.

11. Ibid., pp. 175-176.

12. Mark Hayes, "And the Father Will Dance," by Hinshaw Music, Chapel Hill, NC. All rights reserved. Used by permission.

INDEX

Also by Norm Wright

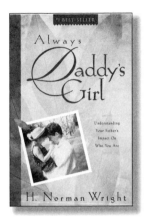

Always Daddy's Girl
Understanding Your Father's
Impact on Who You Are
Paperback • ISBN 08307.27620

Communication @ Work
How to Get Along with
Anyone at Home, at Work
and at Church
Paperback • ISBN 08307.27779

Communication:
Key to Your Marriage
A Practical Guide to Creating a
Happy, Fulfilling Relationship
Paperback • ISBN 08307.25334
Video • UPC 607135.004639

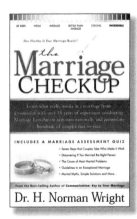

Discover Your Personality
Type and How to Get
Along with Others
Based on the Myers-Briggs
Type Indicator
Video • UPC 85116.01090

How to Counsel a Couple
in Six Sessions or Less
A Tool for Marriage Counseling to
Use in Tandem with *The Marriage
Checkup Questionnaire*
Paperback • ISBN 08307.30680

The Marriage Checkup
How Healthy Is Your
Marriage Really?
Paperback • ISBN 08307.30699